DATE DUE

| | |
|---|---|
| | |
| | |
| | |
| | |
| | |
| | |
| | |
| | |
| | |
| | |
| | |
| | |
| | |
| | |
| | |
| | |

AGQ 4444
nDLC/HB

DATE DUE

| | |
|---|---|
| | |
| | |
| | |
| | |
| | |
| | |
| | |
| | |
| | |
| | |
| | |
| | |
| | |
| | |
| | |
| | |

DEMCO, INC. 38-2931

# World Survey of Economic Freedom 1995-1996

## A Freedom House Study

**Richard E. Messick**
Editor and Coordinator

**Kaku Kimura**
Research Coordinator

**Freedom House**

**Transaction Publishers**
New Brunswick (U.S.A.) and London (U.K.)

This book is printed on acid-free paper that meets the American National Standard for Permanence of Paper for Printed Library Materials.

ISBN: 1-56000-929-2
Printed in the United States of America.

# Contents

## World Survey of Economic Freedom Board of Advisors



## Freedom House



## Freedom House Publications



The following helped make this survey possible, either by coordinating its production or by compiling and writing the essays on individual countries: Suzanne Boughner, Charles Graybow, Thomas R. Lansner, Arch Puddington, and George Zarycky.

# Introduction

Michael Novak

Nearly fifteen years ago, in 1981, I cited the Freedom House annual survey of political rights and civil liberties during a debate at the United Nations Commission on Human Rights in Geneva. I have never forgotten the retort of the Representative of the Soviet Union, Vladimir Zorin (once nicknamed the "Butcher of Prague"), who asked the Commission dismissively, "why does it matter to anyone what a private group says?" In his mind, only states mattered. No one else had any real rights, power, or weight.

Listening to the Soviets talk at the Commission, conversationally, was a revelation to me. I had learned from books what their official ideology held. But to hear real persons speak only in its terms gave my soul a jolt. The horror of what Zorin said and his unself-conscious certitude were unforgettable.

For a long time, in any case, I have been a fan of the Freedom House survey on political rights and civil liberties around the world. Seeing liberty in a worldwide context and yet with attention to the particular detail of individual countries has long helped lift my mind from parochial problems. The great story of our time, as Pope John Paul II recently said at the fiftieth-anniversary session of the United Nations, is the story of liberty. On the political side, the annual reports of Freedom House have for over twenty years supplied, as it were, a record of liberty's good health and ill, nation by nation, and thus a diagnosis of the state of the world in each year.

What I particularly liked about the Freedom House surveys over the years was their emphasis upon the *institutions* of liberty. I have always loved the line of James Madison about the rights and liberties of Americans—that they are protected, not by parchment barriers, but by the habits and institutions of the American people, including our private associations. Unlike Ambassador Zorin, I have always thought that our self-governing associations—and through them, our civil society—are more important than and prior to the state. Moreover, much as I admire organizations that report on *individuals* whose rights are being abused, I judge that the health of the *institutions* on which Freedom House reports is the more basic systemic issue.

In praising these reports to James Finn, then publications director at Freedom House, I mentioned some years ago that they would be even better if they also measured economic liberties. The studies I did in preparing *The Spirit of Democratic Capitalism* (1982) led me to think of *economic* liberty as a leading indicator of the arrival of *political* liberty. Peter Berger was later to formulate a sociological hypothesis: That a free economy is a necessary but not sufficient condition for democracy. This hypothesis has not been falsified in the experience of any nation in this century, but has been confirmed in that of many nations.

To be sure, there have been many capitalist nations that have not been democratic. In that sense, capitalism (by which Berger meant a relatively free economy) is not a sufficient condition for democracy. But there seem to be no cases of genuine democracy—that is, marked by the rule of law, limited government, separated powers, the protection of the rights of individuals and minorities—that do not have free economies.

Not long before the twentieth century began, as Joshua Muravchik has pointed out, there were only four democracies on this planet. Indeed, when the United Nations Charter was first signed, there were only forty-nine independent signatories. Today, there are nearly 200 independent nations in the world. We have seen a great many experiments in political economy come (and sometimes go) during our lifetime. Never in history has the world had so large a trove of empirical evidence to survey, in order to reach the sort of hypotheses that Peter Berger has formulated (See his *The Capitalist Revolution*, 1986).

As Berger notes, moreover, there seems to be a tendency for nations that become capitalist—that leave more and more room to individual economic initiative—to move toward democratic institutions as well. The world has seen this happen in Greece, Portugal, Spain, Chile, South Korea, and other places. The reasons for this seem to be twofold. First, capitalism depends on the rule of law; as Montesquieu noted, nations committed to commerce tend to become pacific, lawlike, and committed to the prudence that measures small losses and small gains rather than to high-risk, high-cost and heroic feats of glory. As regimes go, capitalism tends to rank among the less romantic—much to the disgust of artists. The capitalist preference for law and due process leads naturally enough to the aforementioned basic institutions of democracy: The rule of law, limited government, separated powers, and the protection of the rights of individuals and minorities.

This last point is important. Entrepreneurs often derive from minority ethnic groups. In the nature of the case, they often constitute in themselves a highly exposed minority. They make their investments long before these bear fruit; they are dependent on many others to meet commitments made and fulfill contracts entered into; their work is fraught with risk. In most cultures, they do not share in the esteem paid to hereditary aristocrats, the clergy, the military, artists, and others. Indeed, in most world literatures and religions, entrepreneurs and people of commerce are treated with considerable disesteem.

Second, once a critical mass of successful business people has been reached, they recognize that they are at least as smart and able as their social "betters," whether aristocrats or commissars or generals. Accordingly, they begin demanding representative government.

Furthermore, for purposes of longterm stability (a factor of much importance to visionary business people), one-man rule is, for two reasons, much less adequate than democracy under the rule of law. Not only are dictators temperamental and given to making decisions without consulting those most immediately affected. The one-man regime has also proved incapable of solving the problem of succession. Seldom is the appointed heir as acceptable as his benign and wise predecessor may have been; indeed, rarely does the predecessor think so, either. Few dictators have been observed to step down early, to hand things over to their appointed heir before the bell tolls their own hour of death.

There are several reasons, in short, why the institutions of the free economy foreshadow the coming of democracy.

Looking at this question from the other direction, there are also many reasons why the health of democracy is dependent on the institutions of the free economy. For one thing—one can see this visibly in Eastern Europe today—people cannot be satisfied with democracy if all it brings them is the chance to vote every two or four years. For most people, it is crucial that their daily economic conditions improve. They may have learned in the twentieth century not to expect paradise, but they do insist on seeing tangible economic improvement from year to year in their own immediate circumstances.

There are two senses, especially, in which people rightly expect economic improvement. First, they expect real incomes to rise incrementally, slowly perhaps but steadily, so that they can reasonably expect—on the basis of experience—that tomorrow will be better than today. Jefferson's phrase in the Declaration of Independence, the right to "the pursuit of happiness," has here a more profound meaning than we usually give to it. The greatest threat to republican self-government is envy. When people see no hope in their own future, they begin to compare their lot with their neighbors', indeed to envy their neighbors, and to try to tear their neighbors down. Closed horizons breed dissension and destruction.

On the contrary, when people see attractive possibilities in their own future, they do not compare themselves with their neighbors. Rather, they compare where they are today with where they plan to be tomorrow. They compare themselves with themselves, and do not really mind what their neighbors—even their own brothers and sisters—are doing, as long as they themselves are happy in what they are pursuing. To each his own dreams. To each his own talents and ambitions. In this way, a whole republic can thrive without envy or dissension, and in a spirit of amity. For such opportunities, economic growth throughout the nation is indispensable.

The second sense in which people expect economic improvement is related to the first, but with emphasis on the pursuit of individual talent and inclination. People want and need an open economy, so that they can find in it the niches they want individually to fill. For work is not merely an impersonal, machine-like act. It is the act of a human subject, who seeks in work some measure of personal growth and fulfillment. People put institutions, habits, and relations between economics and politics and culture that can account for these vivid differences.

Freedom House is surely right in its intuition that the institutions of economic liberty, carefully distinguished from one another and subject to a degree of measurement, represent a crucial key. That is why this new annual survey, sharpened and improved as it will be over the years, may well become as important a tool in awakening the world's peoples as were the annual surveys of political rights and civil liberties that preceded them. Peoples and governments will now be able to inspect in brief compass how they are doing, relative to other parts of the human race.

For who can doubt that the most profound secret to human life is human liberty? "The God who gave us life gave us liberty at the same time," Thomas Jefferson wrote. For both Judaism and Christianity, the fundamental human story is what happens in the recesses of the human will. In these religions, all individuals are to be as provident over their own destiny as their Creator is over the universe as a whole. When it is said that each person is made in the image of his Creator, then, it is this aspect—liberty—that is intended. To evaluate economic systems by how well they measure up to the demands of human liberty, and thus suit the dignity of the human person, is no unfair test. On the contrary, it is the key to everything else.

I would like to close by expressing my esteem for the team at Freedom House that devised this first cut at a usable tool of intercultural institutional analysis. Freedom House will welcome criticism, suggestions for revision and improvement, and the correction of inadvertent errors of fact or of judgment. The editors will be grateful for communications regarding either individual countries or the general analytic scheme. They have accomplished the creative act of getting a process of interactive analysis going, in a field in which the relevant data are not yet adequately kept. If democracies are to survive in the twenty-first century, it is crucial that the health of institutions of economic liberty be closely attended to. It is a privilege to have been allowed to contribute to this project.

*Michael Novak is George Frederick Jewett Chair in Religion and Public Policy at the American Enterprise Institute.*

# World Survey of Economic Freedom, 1995-1996

Richard E. Messick

Each year, Freedom House conducts a survey of the worldwide state of political rights and civil liberties. The findings are published in a report, *Freedom in the World*, which is now accepted as an authoritative assessment of the state of global democracy. Two years ago, Freedom House expanded its investigation into the state of world freedom by initiating a survey of press freedom around the world. Freedom House has extended the scope of its evaluation of the condition of freedom by inaugurating a new study, an annual *World Survey of Economic Freedom*.

The *World Survey of Economic Freedom* is divided into two sections. The first consists of essays on each of eighty-two nations surveyed during 1995. This section describes the state of economic freedom at year's end and reviews significant developments that resulted in either an expansion or a loss of economic freedom during the year. In the second section, Freedom House rates each country as either economically "free," "partly free," "mostly not free," or "not free." The designations are based on whether the state circumscribes its citizens' rights to own property, earn a living, operate a business, invest their earnings, or trade internationally either through direct limitations or by failing to provide a legal framework within which these rights can be exercised.

As is the case with its other surveys, the purpose of Freedom House's economic survey is to advance the cause of freedom around the world. By spotlighting those counties where citizens are denied the freedom to buy, sell, trade and otherwise pursue economic opportunities, Freedom House seeks to add economic freedom to the agenda of freedom, both within the United States and abroad. Once the relevance of economic freedom is recognized, the obstacles to its fulfillment will surely begin to fall, for the logic of freedom is so powerful that no honest discussion can fail to further its cause.

## Part I: How Freedom House Measures Economic Freedom

Economic freedom is frequently equated with a government that refrains from dictating wages, controlling prices, erecting trade barriers, or otherwise hindering private economic endeavors. It is of course elementary that an individual cannot be free if the state infringes his or her rights to exchange goods and services or join together to pursue economic ends. But for its citizens to be able to fully exercise their economic freedoms, the state must do more than simply stand aside and let the market work. As one contemporary champion of economic freedom has explained, government must also act as the arbiter and interpreter of the rules governing the economic game.[1] Contracts must be enforced, property rights defined, and the other institutional prerequisites required for the conduct of economic affairs set in place.

### A. The Two Dimensions of Economic Freedom

Freedom House's method of measuring economic freedom captures both these dimensions.

It first considers to what extent government hinders or prevents its citizens from exercising their right to:

- own property,
- earn a living,
- operate a business,
- invest one's earnings,
- trade internationally, and
- participate equally in all aspects of the market economy.

In measuring the freedom to earn a living, for example, such factors as whether wage rates are controlled by the government or freely determined by market forces and whether there are laws denying individuals the right to join together to bargain with their employer are examined. Likewise, in gauging the freedom to operate a business Freedom House looks at whether there are controls on prices or rules restricting entry into certain lines of commerce.

Of course, every nation interferes with economic activity in ways inconsistent with economic freedom, and if the ideal state were the standard, no country would earn the designation of "free." Crucial to the Freedom House ratings is the degree of state intrusion. If the amount of interference is not great, a country can still qualify as "free." Thus, even though the United States and West European nations control the price and supply of many agricultural commodities and Japan restrains foreign trade in a number of ways, these factors alone did not bar these countries from being rated "free" in the 1995 *Survey*.

The second criterion a nation must satisfy to be economically free is a legal and institutional framework within which market transactions can occur.[2] In evaluating the freedom to own property, Freedom House thus asks whether laws have been enacted to protect the right to property, and if so, whether they are enforced. Particular attention is paid to intellectual property rights, and in poorer nations, where land is the majority's most important asset, whether there is a well-managed land registry that assures both ownership rights and transaction security.[3] Because no nation is free unless all its citizens are free, Freedom House takes into consideration whether women or members of minority groups are free to enter the professions, open businesses, own and transfer property, and otherwise fully participate in the market economy.

Requiring an adequate legal and institutional framework for economic participation penalizes counties where a government's intentions have not been matched by effective action. In Bolivia, Peru, and Senegal, for example, the right to property is protected by law, but the judicial systems of all three do not effectively enforce this right. Each has made significant progress in liberalizing its economy, but so long as the institutions necessary for a market economy to function remain weak, none can be judged to have achieved genuine economic freedom.

Although the criteria for a "free" rating may appear difficult for many countries to meet, the *Survey* results show that they are not biased against any particular culture or region. With the exception of the Middle East, one or more countries from every region examined earned a rating of "free," and nations as diverse culturally as Chile and Estonia, South Africa and Poland, and Argentina and Japan all were rated economically free.

## B. The Method for Scoring Countries

Table One identifies the factors selected to evaluate the degree of freedom present for each indicator surveyed. The freedom to own property, earn a living, operate a business, and invest were graded on a scale of zero to three with three being the most free and zero signifying little or no freedom. Because of problems with the comparability of data involving different nations, two of the indicators—freedom to trade and freedom to participate in the market economy—were scored on a scale of zero to two, again with two indicating the greatest degree of freedom and zero little or no freedom. The procedures followed in scoring each indicator are described in the appendix.

The highest score a nation therefore can attain is sixteen and the lowest zero. Countries scoring thirteen or better are rated "free," and those with a six or less are rated "not free." With thir-

# Table 1 Freedom House Indicators of Economic Freedom

| | |
|---|---|
| **Freedom to Hold Property** | Is the right to property recognized by law? Is the right to intellectual property protected? Does the legal system give effect to the right to property? Are there restrictions on selling, exchanging, or devising property? Can individuals structure their property holdings among themselves as they choose? |
| **Freedom to Earn a Living** | Can individuals form voluntary associations to bargain over wages? Are unions state-controlled? Are wages controlled or freely set? Can individuals change jobs freely? Are there any vestiges of indentured servitude, debt peonage, or slavery? |
| **Freedom to Operate a Business** | Can individuals freely join together to pursue mutual economic interests? Are the rules governing the formation of business enterprises so complex that large sectors of the population are foreclosed from forming businesses? Is entry into certain lines of commerce restricted? Are government contracts competitively let? Are raw materials, finished goods, services or other prices controlled? |
| **Freedom to Invest One's Earnings** | Are interest rates regulated? Is credit allocated by the market or by government fiat? Are rates of return on investments controlled? Can individuals invest abroad? Can they hold foreign currency and securities? Is there an independent central bank or other institutional mechanism to protect citizens' savings loss through inflation? |
| **Freedom to Trade Internationally** | Are there restrictive tariffs, quotas, or other barriers to importing goods from abroad? Are there export taxes or other impediments on the right to sell to foreigners? Are there limits on the right to enter or leave the country? Is foreign investment regulated? Are there exchange controls? |
| **Freedom to Participate in the Market Economy** | Are racial or ethnic minorities or women foreclosed from certain occupations or from running certain types of businesses? Are there limits on minorities' or women's rights to hold or transfer property? Are the laws necessary for a market economy to function enforced? Is corruption so widespread as to interfere with normal market forces? |

teen as the breakpoint, a country could score one less than the maximum on three of the six indicators and still be rated "free." At the other end of the scale, a country had to merit at least a two on one of the six indicators to escape a "not free" rating. Countries scoring between thirteen and six were divided into two groups. Those at the higher end, with scores of twelve, eleven, or ten are classified as "partly free," while those with ratings of nine, eight, or seven are termed "mostly not free."

### C. Criteria Used to Select the Indicators

The six indicators of economic freedom and the factors selected to evaluate each were chosen with four objectives in mind. First, because the purpose of the *Survey* is to inject the issue of economic freedom into the public dialogue, Freedom House constructed a study that would reach a broad audience both within the United States and overseas. Accordingly, technical or econometric variables were avoided. Whereas economists have constructed indices such as taxes on international trade as a percentage of exports plus imports to measure the freedom to trade internationally,[4] Freedom House focuses on the presence of legal barriers to importing or exporting or controls on foreign exchange.

Second, Freedom House chose criteria that could be readily adjusted by a government that adopted the expansion of economic freedom as a priority. One indicator selected is whether citizens are free to invest their earnings, and a key factor in gauging the level of this freedom is the stability of the monetary system. When the rate of inflation is so great that the national currency no longer serves as a store of value, investment choices are severely limited and the citizenry's economic freedom is consequently diminished. Whereas a nation's annual rate of inflation might serve as a direct measure of the degree of economic loss inflation produces, Freedom House chose to measure whether the central bank or other monetary authority was independent of the political authorities. While a government committed to the control of inflation may find the task extremely challenging, the creation of an independent monetary authority, or the strengthening of an existing institution, can readily be accomplished by a government devoted to a free economy.

In developing the Freedom House criteria, our third objective was to select indicators on which there was a consensus among those who believe in the paramount importance of human liberty. While a commitment to individual liberty is at the core of the liberal tradition, within this tradition there is a divergence of views on the proper role of government in economic affairs.[5] How far should government go to rectify the failures or perceived failures of the marketplace? At what point does the rate of taxation reduce individual economic freedom?

These are important debates. But they are carried on within a community committed to the expansion of freedom and which values the primacy of individual freedom above all else. The purpose of the *Survey of Economic Freedom* is not to cause friction within this community, but to enlarge it by publicizing those ways in which less free nations deny their citizens freedoms commonly found in freer ones.

A fourth objective of the *Survey* is to broaden the constituency for economic freedom. The critics of the market economy often depict economic freedom as of benefit only for large corporations or the foreign investor, and indeed, some of the indicators Freedom House has chosen, such as the protection of intellectual property rights, may seem of greater practical import to the business community. However, a government unwilling or unable to protect property rights in patents or copyrights is more likely to trespass on more basic rights.

A more direct way to demonstrate why economic freedom is important for society as a whole is to draw attention to restraints that harm those not usually considered a part of the business community. Thus the *Survey* asks whether the rules for forming businesses are so complex that microentrepreneurs are deprived of the opportunity to legally register their enterprises,[6] whether women or minorities are foreclosed from certain occupations or businesses, and whether there are limits on the rights of women or minorities to own or transfer property. Inclusion of such indicators underlines how economic freedom or its absence affects everyone in a society.[7] It also ensures that the *Survey* accurately ranks those countries that, although they maintain a favorable business climate, deny their citizens a full measure of economic freedom.

These objectives set the *Survey* apart from other efforts to compare the level of economic freedom in different nations. The Fraser Institute in Vancouver, British Columbia, has sponsored a major study of economic freedom, but its aim was to explore the correlation between economic freedom and political freedom and between economic freedom and growth and prosperity.[8] The Washington, D.C.-based Heritage Foundation also has begun compiling an annual index of economic freedom, but the primary purpose of its work is to provide evidence of the futility of development assistance.[9]

As important as these goals may be, Freedom House has initiated its *Survey of Economic Freedom* for the very different reasons described above. It should not be surprising, then, that its indicators of economic freedom differ in several respects from those used in other studies. Nor should it be surprising when, as will be noted below, its conclusions about the level of freedom in certain nations do not always agree with those of either the Fraser Institute or the Heritage Foundation.

## Part II: The 1995 Freedom House Ratings of Economic Freedom

Eighty-two countries were reviewed for this first *Survey of Economic Freedom*, a group that includes nations at every level of economic development and with differing political, cultural, and religious traditions. Moreover, while, as Table Two shows, the eighty-two surveyed countries represent fewer than half the independent countries in the world, together they contain 90 percent of the world's population and account for over 99 percent of the total global output of goods and services.

### A. Principal Findings

Although the work that launched the discipline of economics demonstrated that freedom is the cause of the wealth of nations, Adam Smith's followers have shown little interest in exploring his powerful insight into the relationship between freedom and economic development. The 1995 *Survey*'s most important finding is that modern economists have ignored a crucial variable in their search for the answer to why some societies are prosperous and some chronically poor. As Table Two reveals, whereas only twenty-seven of those nations sampled, with just 17 percent of the world's population, merited a "free" rating, these twenty-seven nations produced 81 percent of total world output. By contrast, the twenty nations rated "not free" contain more than a third of the world's people yet produce only 5 percent of total output. The *Survey* thus joins a handful of recent studies in showing that economic freedom is the surest path to growth and development.[10]

Table Two also discloses the most discouraging finding in this year's *Survey*: despite the worldwide trend toward economic liberalization in recent years, some 3.6 billion people, or just under two-thirds of the world's population, continue to live in countries that are either "not free" or "mostly not free." Indeed, at the close of 1995 only 942 million people, or 17 percent of the world's population, resided in "free" nations with another 395 million, or 7 percent of the total population, living in "partly free" ones.

### B. Developments in Eastern Europe and the former Soviet Union

One of the most encouraging findings to emerge from this year's *Survey* is the relative speed with which governments committed to economic freedom can achieve that objective. Table Three lists by region the eighty-two countries surveyed and provides their economic freedom rating. While, as one would expect, the developed nations of Western Europe, along with the United States, Canada, Japan, Australia, and New Zealand constitute the bulk of the "free" nations, the list also includes four countries—the former Communist states of Poland and the Czech Republic, and the former Soviet republics of Estonia and Latvia—that not long ago would have ranked at or near the bottom of any index of economic freedom.

In these four countries, Communist-era wage and price controls were lifted, independent cen-

## Table 2 Summary of Findings of 1995 Survey

| | Number of Countries | Population (in millions) | Gross Domestic Product (trillions of U.S. dollars) |
|---|---|---|---|
| Free | 27 | 942 (17%) | 18.8 (81%) |
| Partly Free | 22 | 395 (7%) | 1.1 (5%) |
| Mostly Not Free | 13 | 1,645 (30%) | 1.9 (8%) |
| Not Free | 20 | 1,974 (36%) | 1.1 (5%) |
| Not surveyed | 109 | 546 (10%) | .2 (1%) |
| Total world | 191 | 5,502 | 23.1 |

tral banks were created, laws recognizing the right to own private property were enacted, and labor unions were freed from government control. A World Bank survey of Polish entrepreneurs found business start-up licenses and permits could be obtained "painlessly and easily," and in the Czech Republic land has been returned to its pre-Communist owners and a land registry established. After the fall of the Soviet Union, Estonia quickly jettisoned Soviet-era trading restrictions, adopting in their stead trade policies that rank among the world's most liberal. In Latvia, moreover, the Soviet system of collective farming has been replaced by one based on private ownership.

Nor are these four the only recently unfree states to undergo a rapid transition. Table Four reports each nation's total score on the *Survey*'s index as well at its score on each of the six indicators. The figures reveal that the former Communist nation of Hungary, and the former Soviet Kyrgyz Republic and Lithuania also have made rapid progress toward economic freedom as well, all three falling short of a "free" rating by a single point. In the case of Hungary, one reason for the failure to attain a "free" rating was the slow and cumbersome process of registering new enterprises. Hungary was further penalized because competition for government contracts is still not entirely free and open. The Kyrgyz Republic and Lithuania both missed a "free" rating because certain Communist-era economic controls have yet to be jettisoned. Nonetheless, in Hungary, Kyrgyz Republic, and Lithuania remarkable progress is being made in enlarging citizens' economic freedom.

While the former Soviet republics of Estonia, Latvia, Lithuania, and Kyrgyz Republic have all made enormous strides in freeing their economies from statist controls, the same cannot be said for the other states that made up the old Soviet empire. As Table Four shows, two of the eleven former Soviet republics surveyed—Russia and Ukraine—barely escaped being rated "not free," and five—Azerbaijan, Belarus, Kazakhstan, Turkmenistan and Uzbekistan—all scored "not free."

The performance of Russia is particularly disappointing. Though the country has received a great deal of technical and material aid from countries and international financial institutions that support economic reform, the *Survey* shows that little progress has been made. The rules for opening a business pose serious obstacles to small entrepreneurs, the central bank is not independent, less than 5 percent of farmers own their land, and only a few collective farms have been privatized. Further, the current political situation in Russia suggests the situation is unlikely to improve during 1996.

### C. The Relationship Between Economic and Political Freedom

A comparison of the results of Freedom House's 1995 survey of political rights and civil liberties with the economic freedom survey lends support to a claim long advanced by freedom's proponents—that democracy is the best guarantor of individual liberty.[11] With few exceptions, countries the *Survey* rated economically "free" during 1995 also earned a "free" rating on political rights and civil liberties. Similarly, those that were "not free" economically were, in most cases, "not free" on political rights and civil liberties as well. The economic freedom survey divides countries falling between "free" and "not free" into two categories whereas the political freedom survey uses a single category of "partly free." If, for comparison's sake, the categories between "free" and "not free" in the two surveys were considered equivalent, 79 percent, or sixty-five, of the eighty-two nations covered in this year's *Survey of Economic Freedom* merited the same ranking on both surveys.

Table Five lists the nations that recorded an economic freedom ranking that differed from their ranking on the survey of political rights and civil liberties. Each country's rating on the economic freedom survey is shown along the side of the table, while its political rights and civil liberties rating runs across the top. Thus, for example, the countries shown in the box at the upper left beginning with Uruguay rated "free" on the survey of political rights and civil liberties but only "partly free" economically.

As the table shows, only seventeen ranked differently on the two surveys, and upon review many of these differences turn out to be quite small. As the asterisks indicate, for eight of the seventeen the difference between the economic freedom rating and the political freedom rating was a single point. In the

## Table 3

# Country Rankings by Region

| | Americas | Western Europe | Central and Eastern Europe & NIS | Asia | Middle East | Africa |
|---|---|---|---|---|---|---|
| **FREE** | Argentina<br>Canada<br>Chile<br>United States | Austria<br>Belgium<br>Denmark<br>Finland<br>France<br>Germany<br>Ireland<br>Italy<br>Netherlands<br>Norway<br>Portugal<br>Spain<br>Sweden<br>Switzerland<br>United Kingdom | Czech Republic<br>Estonia<br>Latvia<br>Poland | Australia<br>Japan<br>New Zealand | | South Africa |
| **PARTLY FREE** | Bolivia<br>Colombia<br>Costa Rica<br>El Salvador<br>Peru<br>Uruguay | Greece<br>Turkey | Bulgaria<br>Hungary<br>Kyrgyz Republic<br>Lithuania<br>Slovakia | Malaysia<br>Philippines<br>Singapore<br>Taiwan<br>Thailand | Israel<br>Jordan | Ghana<br>Senegal |
| **MOSTLY NOT FREE** | Brazil<br>Mexico<br>Venezuela | | Romania<br>Russia<br>Ukraine | Cambodia<br>India<br>Korea, South<br>Pakistan | Egypt | Cote d'Ivoire<br>Kenya |
| **NOT FREE** | Cuba<br>Haiti | | Azerbaijan<br>Belarus<br>Kazakhstan<br>Turkmenistan<br>Uzbekistan | Bangladesh<br>Burma (Myanmar)<br>China<br>Indonesia<br>Korea, North<br>Vietnam | Iran<br>Iraq<br>Saudi Arabia<br>Syria | Mozambique<br>Nigeria<br>Zaire |

# Table 4 Economic Freedom Indicators

| | Freedom to Own Property (0-3) | Freedom to Earn a Living (0-3) | Freedom to Operate a Business (0-3) | Freedom to Invest One's Earnings (0-3) | Freedom to Trade Interna-tionally (0-2) | Freedom to Participate in a Market Economy (0-2) | Freedom Ranking |
|---|---|---|---|---|---|---|---|
| **Free** | | | | | | | |
| Denmark | 3 | 3 | 3 | 3 | 2 | 2 | 16 |
| Netherlands | 3 | 3 | 3 | 3 | 2 | 2 | 16 |
| New Zealand | 3 | 3 | 3 | 3 | 2 | 2 | 16 |
| Sweden | 3 | 3 | 3 | 3 | 2 | 2 | 16 |
| United Kingdom | 3 | 3 | 3 | 3 | 2 | 2 | 16 |
| United States | 3 | 3 | 3 | 3 | 2 | 2 | 16 |
| Austria | 3 | 3 | 2 | 3 | 2 | 2 | 15 |
| Belgium | 3 | 3 | 2 | 3 | 2 | 2 | 15 |
| Canada | 3 | 3 | 3 | 3 | 1 | 2 | 15 |
| Czech Republic | 3 | 3 | 3 | 3 | 2 | 1 | 15 |
| France | 3 | 3 | 2 | 3 | 2 | 2 | 15 |
| Germany | 3 | 3 | 2 | 3 | 2 | 2 | 15 |
| Ireland | 3 | 3 | 3 | 3 | 1 | 2 | 15 |
| Norway | 3 | 3 | 3 | 3 | 1 | 2 | 15 |
| Spain | 3 | 3 | 3 | 3 | 2 | 1 | 15 |
| Argentina | 2 | 3 | 3 | 3 | 2 | 1 | 14 |
| Australia | 3 | 3 | 2 | 3 | 1 | 2 | 14 |
| Finland | 3 | 3 | 2 | 3 | 1 | 2 | 14 |
| Poland | 1 | 3 | 3 | 3 | 2 | 2 | 14 |
| Portugal | 3 | 3 | 2 | 2 | 2 | 2 | 14 |
| Switzerland | 3 | 3 | 2 | 3 | 1 | 2 | 14 |
| Chile | 2 | 2 | 3 | 3 | 1 | 2 | 13 |
| Estonia | 2 | 3 | 2 | 2 | 2 | 2 | 13 |
| Italy | 2 | 3 | 2 | 3 | 2 | 1 | 13 |
| Japan | 3 | 3 | 2 | 2 | 1 | 2 | 13 |
| Latvia | 2 | 3 | 3 | 2 | 2 | 1 | 13 |
| South Africa | 3 | 3 | 2 | 2 | 1 | 2 | 13 |
| **Partly Free** | | | | | | | |
| Bolivia | 1 | 2 | 3 | 3 | 2 | 1 | 12 |
| Colombia | 2 | 1 | 3 | 2 | 2 | 2 | 12 |
| Ghana | 2 | 2 | 2 | 2 | 2 | 2 | 12 |
| Greece | 3 | 3 | 2 | 2 | 1 | 1 | 12 |

# Table 4 cont'd. Economic Freedom Indicators

| | Freedom to Own Property (0-3) | Freedom to Earn a Living (0-3) | Freedom to Operate a Business (0-3) | Freedom to Invest One's Earnings (0-3) | Freedom to Trade Interna-tionally (0-2) | Freedom to Participate in a Market Economy (0-2) | Freedom Ranking |
|---|---|---|---|---|---|---|---|
| **Partly Free** | | | | | | | |
| Hungary | 2 | 3 | 2 | 2 | 1 | 2 | 12 |
| Israel | 2 | 3 | 2 | 2 | 1 | 2 | 12 |
| Lithuania | 2 | 2 | 3 | 3 | 1 | 1 | 12 |
| Malaysia | 3 | 2 | 2 | 3 | 1 | 1 | 12 |
| Peru | 2 | 2 | 2 | 3 | 2 | 1 | 12 |
| Senegal | 2 | 3 | 2 | 2 | 2 | 1 | 12 |
| Singapore | 3 | 1 | 2 | 3 | 2 | 1 | 12 |
| Thailand | 2 | 2 | 3 | 3 | 1 | 1 | 12 |
| Bulgaria | 2 | 2 | 3 | 2 | 1 | 1 | 11 |
| Taiwan | 2 | 2 | 2 | 2 | 2 | 1 | 11 |
| Turkey | 2 | 2 | 2 | 2 | 2 | 1 | 11 |
| Costa Rica | 2 | 2 | 2 | 2 | 1 | 1 | 10 |
| El Salvador | 2 | 1 | 2 | 3 | 1 | 1 | 10 |
| Jordan | 2 | 2 | 2 | 1 | 1 | 2 | 10 |
| Kyrgyz Republic | 1 | 1 | 2 | 3 | 2 | 1 | 10 |
| Philippines | 2 | 3 | 1 | 2 | 1 | 1 | 10 |
| Slovakia | 2 | 2 | 2 | 2 | 1 | 1 | 10 |
| Uruguay | 1 | 3 | 2 | 1 | 1 | 2 | 10 |
| **Mostly Not Free** | | | | | | | |
| Côte d'Ivoire | 1 | 2 | 2 | 1 | 1 | 1 | 8 |
| India | 2 | 1 | 1 | 2 | 1 | 1 | 8 |
| Kenya | 2 | 1 | 2 | 1 | 1 | 1 | 8 |
| Mexico | 2 | 1 | 2 | 1 | 1 | 1 | 8 |
| Romania | 1 | 2 | 2 | 0 | 2 | 1 | 8 |
| Ukraine | 1 | 2 | 2 | 1 | 1 | 1 | 8 |
| Brazil | 1 | 2 | 1 | 1 | 1 | 1 | 7 |
| Cambodia | 0 | 2 | 2 | 1 | 2 | 0 | 7 |
| Egypt | 2 | 1 | 1 | 1 | 1 | 1 | 7 |
| Korea, South | 2 | 1 | 1 | 1 | 1 | 1 | 7 |
| Pakistan | 1 | 1 | 2 | 1 | 1 | 1 | 7 |
| Russia | 1 | 1 | 2 | 1 | 1 | 1 | 7 |
| Venezuela | 1 | 3 | 1 | 0 | 1 | 1 | 7 |

# Table 4 cont'd. Economic Freedom Indicators

| | Freedom to Own Property (0-3) | Freedom to Earn a Living (0-3) | Freedom to Operate a Business (0-3) | Freedom to Invest One's Earnings (0-3) | Freedom to Trade Interna-tionally (0-2) | Freedom to Participate in a Market Economy (0-2) | Freedom Ranking |
|---|---|---|---|---|---|---|---|
| **Not Free** | | | | | | | |
| Bangladesh | 1 | 1 | 1 | 1 | 1 | 1 | 6 |
| Haiti | 1 | 1 | 1 | 1 | 1 | 1 | 6 |
| Indonesia | 1 | 1 | 1 | 2 | 1 | 0 | 6 |
| Mozambique | 0 | 3 | 1 | 0 | 1 | 1 | 6 |
| Saudi Arabia | 1 | 0 | 1 | 2 | 1 | 0 | 5 |
| Turkmenistan | 1 | 0 | 1 | 1 | 1 | 1 | 5 |
| Vietnam | 1 | 1 | 1 | 1 | 0 | 1 | 5 |
| Belarus | 1 | 1 | 0 | 0 | 1 | 1 | 4 |
| Iran | 1 | 1 | 1 | 1 | 0 | 0 | 4 |
| Nigeria | 1 | 1 | 1 | 0 | 0 | 1 | 4 |
| Uzbekistan | 0 | 0 | 2 | 1 | 1 | 0 | 4 |
| Syria | 1 | 0 | 1 | 0 | 0 | 1 | 3 |
| Zaire | 0 | 1 | 1 | 1 | 0 | 0 | 3 |
| China | 1 | 0 | 0 | 0 | 1 | 0 | 2 |
| Kazakhstan | 0 | 0 | 1 | 0 | 1 | 0 | 2 |
| Azerbaijan | 0 | 0 | 1 | 0 | 0 | 0 | 1 |
| Cuba | 0 | 0 | 0 | 0 | 0 | 1 | 1 |
| Burma (Myanmar) | 0 | 0 | 0 | 0 | 0 | 0 | 0 |
| Iraq | 0 | 0 | 0 | 0 | 0 | 0 | 0 |
| Korea, North | 0 | 0 | 0 | 0 | 0 | 0 | 0 |

box at the upper right, four countries—Greece, Hungary, Lithuania and Israel—scored 12 on the economic freedom survey, one point short of a "free" ranking. And with one exception, the other countries came within just two points of receiving the same rating for economic freedom as they received for political rights and civil liberties.

The exception is South Korea. Although Freedom House recently changed its political freedom rating from "partly free" to "free," thanks to the election of the country's first civilian president in three decades, and the improvements in the state of civil liberties the new government has initiated, South Koreans still are not economically free. The country scored only a seven on this year's economic freedom survey, or just enough to avoid a "not free" rating. As the essay in this volume explains, South Korea's low rating is principally attributable to the government's policy of encouraging the growth of a few large conglomerates at the expense of the freedom of wage earners and would-be entrepreneurs.

The authoritarian governments that preceded Kim's rule believed such favoritism would foster economic development, and at least for now their gamble appears to have paid off. Over the past decade South Korea has had one of the highest economic growth rates in the world. Yet whether South Koreans will remain in the anomalous position of enjoying a considerable degree of political freedom accompanied by little economic freedom remains to be seen. The evidence suggests that over the long run an unfree economy is un-

# Table 5

## Nations whose Rankings on the Economic and Political Surveys Differ

| Economic Freedom Survey Rank | Political Rights and Civil Liberties Survey Rank: | Free | Partly Free | Not Free |
|---|---|---|---|---|
| | **Free** | | | |
| | **Partly Free** | Uruguay, Costa Rica, Greece*, Hungary*, Bulgaria, Slovakia, Lithuania*, Israel* | | |
| | **Mostly Not Free** | South Korea | | Cambodia*, Egypt*, Kenya, Côte d'Ivoire |
| | **Not Free** | | Haiti*, Belarus, Bangladesh*, Mozambique | |

*Indicates that the score on the economic freedom survey fell one point short of yielding a ranking equal to that on the political rights and civil liberties survey.

likely to continue performing well. Furthermore, South Koreans may begin exercising their newly won democratic freedoms to insist on greater economic freedom as well.

### D. Differences with Fraser Institute and Heritage Foundation Rankings

Despite the fact that Freedom House chose different indicators of economic freedom than either the Fraser Institute or the Heritage Foundation, there is a striking degree of similarity between the Freedom House ratings and those of these two organizations. There are some notable exceptions, however. While the Heritage Foundation ranked Singapore the second freest nation among the 140 it surveyed during 1995 and Fraser Institute analysts also scored it quite high,[12] the Freedom House *Survey* rated Singapore only "partly free," and within the "partly free" category below such countries as Peru, Ghana, Malaysia, and Uruguay.

Singapore's high rating on these other scales is explained by its low tax rate, the small share of gross domestic product consumed by government, and its foreign investment laws. Singapore's less impressive showing on the Freedom House *Survey* is the result of three factors: trade unions are under the de facto control of the ruling party; private firms find it difficult to compete against government-linked companies in several areas; and Singaporean authorities treat earning a living or operating a business as a privilege rather than a right, something that can be suspended or curtailed if a citizen opposes government policy. Thus, while Singapore maintains a highly favorable climate for foreign businesses, its own citizens do not enjoy full economic freedom.[13]

Another nation where ratings diverged was South Africa. In its 1995 study, the Heritage Foundation rated South Africa as "mostly not free," whereas on the Freedom House scale it earned a "free" rating. The difference would again appear attributable to the fact that the Heritage survey evaluated both the level of taxation and government consumption of economic output in its study, two areas where South Africa scored particularly low. By contrast, the Freedom House indicators reflect the opportunities for individual economic advancement within society. While there had been concerns that the new majority government in South Africa would curtail individual economic freedom in favor of some collective approach to economic development, the *Survey* shows that, as of the end of 1995, these fears are unfounded. Indeed, removing apartheid-era barriers to full participation in the economy has enhanced economic freedom.

Although the Freedom House rankings—as opposed to the Fraser and Heritage surveys—did not employ as a criterion the share of the gross domestic product consumed by government, this issue was not ignored in compiling the 1995 ratings, since it is obvious that under certain circumstances government economic domination will curtail the economic freedom of the individual.[14] Freedom House had initially tried to measure government dominance of the economy by examining the number and size of state-owned enterprises and direct government participation in the economy, but this approach had to be abandoned due to a lack of data. The information that was found, however, is reviewed in the country essays, and in looking at those countries that fell on the borderline between "mostly not free" and "not free" Freedom House considered whether government dominance of the economy was so great that a "mostly not free" rating ought to be lowered to a "not free." On the basis of the information available, however, none of the six borderline countries—Brazil, Egypt, Pakistan, Russia, Ukraine, and Venezuela—warranted such a downward adjustment.

### E. Significant Changes in Economic Freedom during 1995

By conducting surveys of political and press freedoms on an annual basis, Freedom House is able to make comparisons of changes in the level of these freedoms within a country over the years. While such comparisons will be incorporated into next year's *Survey of Economic Freedom*, there were some significant changes in the level of economic freedom that occurred during 1995 that bear mention.

Syria has finally begun to move away from the *dirigiste* economic philosophy of Baath Socialism. A new law governing foreign investment has been enacted, the commercial code has been updated, and private firms are beginning to form. A significant expansion in economic freedom is also taking place in Peru thanks to the government's recent commitment to issue legally valid land titles to the nation's property owners. Already a modest demonstration program has had spectacular results in reducing transaction costs and increasing access to credit. In Japan a series of deregulation proposals has been advanced that, if adopted, will enhance economic freedom. The proposed changes are small given what could have been offered, but the proposals are nonetheless significant because they represent an acknowledgment by Japan's powerful bureaucracy that change is needed.

In two of the countries surveyed, Venezuela and Zaire, there unfortunately was a significant deterioration in the level of economic freedom during 1995. Venezuela continued a pattern set in 1993 when it began restricting its citizens' economic freedom in the name of economic stability. This past year, despite evidence suggesting that the loss of freedom has increased the level of instability, economic freedom was further curtailed through a decree imposing controls on foreign exchange and strengthening state control of private banks. In Zaire the judiciary and the other institutions required for a market economy have atrophied so substantially in the face of the political upheaval that economic freedom has virtually disappeared.

## Conclusion

The most promising finding to emerge from this first *Survey of Economic Freedom* is that there are no limits to the spread of economic freedom. Countries with cultures and histories as different as Chile, Estonia, Italy, Japan, South Africa and the U.S. can all reach a level where their citizens are free to work at jobs they choose, own businesses, trade, invest and realize their full economic potential. The most disappointing finding is that despite the lessons of recent history many nations refuse to extend their citizens these fundamental rights.

*Richard E. Messick is the coordinator of the* World Survey of Economic Freedom, 1995-1996.

## Notes

1. Milton Friedman, *Capitalism and Freedom* (Chicago: University of Chicago Press, 1962), pp. 14-15, 25-27.
2. Economists' current thinking on this subject is summarized in Malcolm Rutherford, *Institutions in Economics: The Old and New Institutionalism* (Cambridge: Cambridge University Press, 1994).
3. On the importance of the institutions securing rights to land, see Hernando de Soto, "The Missing Ingredient," *The Economist*, September 11, 1993, pp. 8-12.
4. James Gwartney, Walter Block and Robert Lawson, "Rating the Economic Freedom of 100 Countries: 1975-1990," prepared for the conference Rating Economic Freedom IV, held November 18-21, 1993.
5. See, for example, the discussion in John Gray, *Liberalism*, 2d ed. (Minneapolis: University of Minnesota Press, 1995), pp. 70-77.
6. See Hernando de Soto, *The Other Path: The Invisible Revolution in the Third World* (New York: Harper & Row, 1989), pp. 59-92 & 133-34.
7. The U.S. Agency for International Development took a tentative step in this direction in the late 1980s, constructing an economic opportunity index that it then used to demonstrate that countries that provided their citizens with greater economic opportunities grew faster. U.S. Agency for International Development, *Development and the National Interest: U.S. Economic Assistance into the 21st Century* (Washington, D.C.: U.S. Government Printing Office, 1989), p. 52.
8. James Gwartney, Robert Lawson, and Walter Block, *Economic Freedom of the World: 1975-1995*, (Vancouver: The Fraser Institute, 1996). See also Walter Block, ed., *Economic Freedom: Toward a Theory of Measurement* (Vancouver: The Fraser Institute, 1991), and Stephen T. Easton and Michael A. Walker, eds., *Rating Global Economic Freedom* (Vancouver: The Fraser Institute, 1992).
9. Bryan T. Johnson and Thomas P. Sheehy, *1996 Index of Economic Freedom* (Washington, D.C.: The Heritage Foundation, 1996), p. v.
10. Besides those surveys sponsored by the Fraser Institute and the Heritage Foundation, see Surjit S. Bhalla, "Freedom and Economic Growth: A Virtuous Cycle?" in Axel Hadenius, ed., *Democracy, Victory and Crisis: Nobel Symposium 1994* (Cambridge: Cambridge University Press, 1996).
11. See Raymond Aron, *An Essay on Freedom*, trans. Helen Weaver (Cleveland: The New American Library, 1970), pp. 86-98.
12 The Heritage Foundation, *1996 Index of Economic Freedom*, p. xxvi, and Gwartney, Lawson and Block, *Economic Freedom of the World*, pp. 196-97.
13. A recent survey of ten leading economists also revealed differences of opinion over the level of economic freedom in Singapore, with some rating it reasonably free and others scoring it quite low. See "Economic Freedom: Of Liberty and Prosperity," *The Economist*, January 13-19, 1996, p. 23.
14. See Alan Peacock, "Economic Freedom," *The Invisible Hand*, eds. John Eatwell, Murray Milgate, and Peter Newman (New York: W.W. Norton, 1989), pp. 88-93.

# Appendix

## Rules for Scoring the Degree of Freedom in Each Area of Economic Activity

**1. Freedom to Hold Property**. No right to own property or no legal framework governing property-holding merits a zero. Significant deficiencies in the framework, (e.g., certain groups cannot own land) or rampant non-enforcement of land or intellectual property rights yields a one. The existence of a basic legal framework but with ineffective enforcement, typically either failure to enforce patent, copyright and trademark laws, or weal land registries, or restrictions on transferability, for example foreigners not allowed to own land, yields a two.

**2. Freedom to Earn a Living.** A country that either formally prohibits workers from organizing, rigidly controls all unions, or imposes controls on wages scores a zero. Those states with some state control of unions, significant limits on those industries that can organize, or where enforcement of laws banning indentured servitude, bonded labor, or child labor are extremely poor receive a one. Ineffective enforcement of laws banning child labor and the like or some state harassment (e.g., Turkey sends government officials to all meetings to record them) or interference (e.g., cumbersome registration requirements) regarding unions yields a two.

**3. Freedom to Operate a Business**. A country rates a zero if individuals are not free to open a business or if price controls are pervasive. Complex rules for opening a business or substantial price controls (that is, outside of gas, water and other utilities plus agriculture) yields a one. A two indicates an absence of substantial price controls and the freedom to form a business (many countries, under de Soto's influence, have adopted simplified registration laws that at least look good in print) but subject to a) some price controls; b) government procurement not open to all; c) restrictions on entry into more than a few key industries (like national defense and electric power); or d) the existence of some red tape in opening a business despite simplified registration laws.

**4. Freedom to Invest One's Earnings.** The two key variables are interest rate regulation and central bank independence or the equivalent (e.g. Estonia's currency board). Interest rate regulation along with little or no central bank autonomy results in a zero. Interest rate regulation alone, absence of central bank autonomy or credit allocation by the government earns a country a one, some regulation of capital flows a two.

**5. Freedom to Trade Internationally**. With the above four indicators the conceptual distinction between a one and a two is clear and in most cases the data exists to make the distinction. Not so with this indicator. The extremes are easy to identify, but distinguishing between a one and a two is not possible given the divergence in the quality and amount of data and therefore this indicator has been scored on a scale of zero to two. Zero is for those countries where there are either significant restraints on the export of people or on the import or export of goods and services. These are Burma, Cuba, Iran, Iraq, North Korea, Zaire, and Syria.

All countries have some restraints on trade, of course, with agriculture being the most commonly controlled sector. As long as the restraints are not significant, the country rates a two. Those with more significant restraints score a one.

**6. Freedom to Participate in the Market Economy**. Like the trade indicator, with the data at hand meaningful distinctions among those in the middle category are not possible. Countries with any significant legal barrier to entry into the private sector or to holding or transferring property rate a zero. Those countries, such as Nigeria and Zaire, where corruption is so pervasive that the rule of law cannot be said to exist in any formal or practical sense, also score a zero. A two rating indicates that there are no significant formal or practical barriers to participation and that an adequate legal structure exists that is effectively enforced. All others scored a one.

# Introduction to Country Essays

What follows are essays on each of the 82 nations Freedom House surveyed for its *World Survey of Economic Freedom, 1995-1996*. The essays contain separate sections describing citizens' freedom to hold property, earn a living, operate a business, invest their earnings, trade internationally, and participate without discrimination in all aspects of the market economy. How a country rated on each indicator is shown at the beginning of each section. A 1/3, for example, means the country scored one out of a possible three on the indicator. A section entitled "Freedom from Unreasonable Government Interference" is also included. This section discusses such issues as the number of government owned enterprises, policies on privatization, and other matters bearing on the extent and character of government involvement in the economy.

The front of each essay lists the ranking for all three Freedom House *Surveys*—economic, political rights and civil liberties, and the press. Population and Purchasing Power Parity (PPP) figures are also listed. PPP adjusts national gross domestic product figures to account for real buying power. PPP figures were obtained from the United Nations Development Program.

**Political Freedom v. Economic Freedom for the Americas**

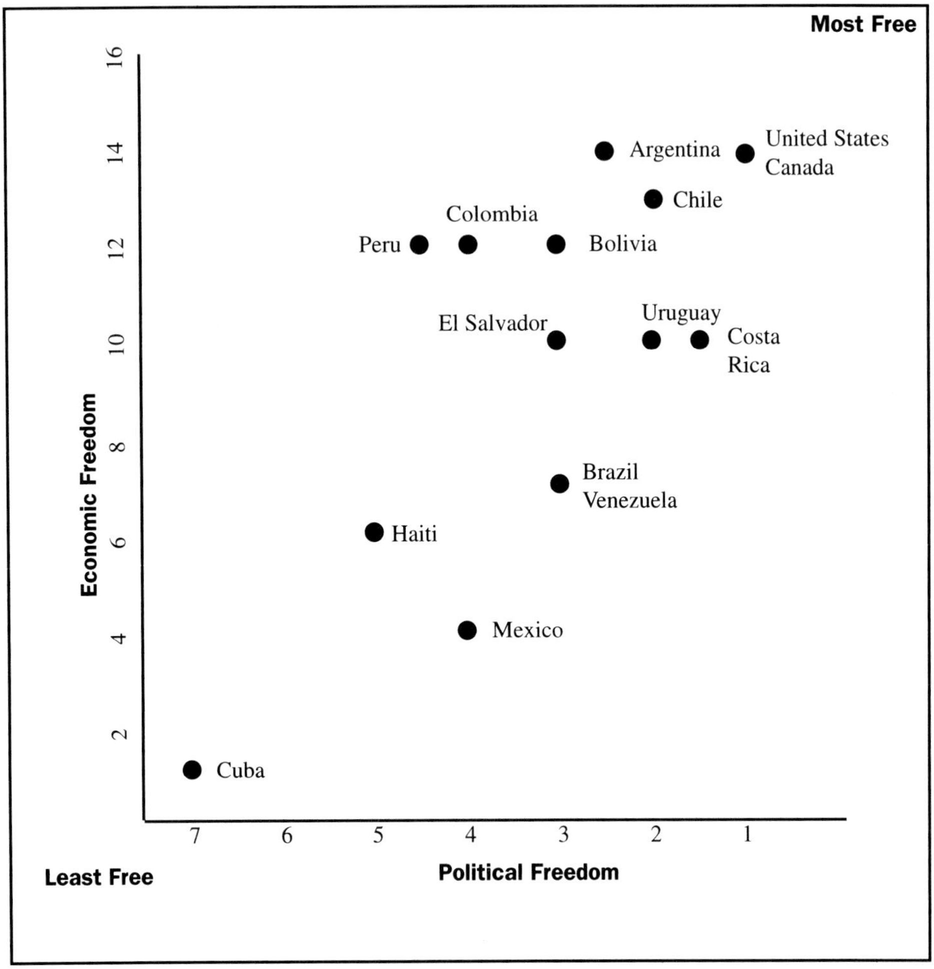


## POLITICAL FREEDOM VERSUS ECONOMIC FREEDOM

The graph above shows the relationship between the level of political freedom and economic freedom for countries in the Americas. The ratings for political freedom were derived by averaging Freedom House's political rights and civil liberties ratings from the *Freedom in the World: The Annual Survey of Political Rights and Civil Liberties, 1995-1996*. A score of "1" represents the most free and "7" the least free.

Economic freedom is graphed on the vertical scale with "0" representing "Not Free" and "16" representing "Free."

# THE AMERICAS

## Argentina

ECONOMIC FREEDOM STATUS: **FREE**
POLITICAL RIGHTS AND CIVIL LIBERTIES STATUS: **FREE**
PRESS FREEDOM STATUS: **FREE**
POPULATION: **34,587,000**
PPP: **$8,860**

### Background

After a long period of political and economic turmoil, political stability and economic freedom appear to be taking hold in Argentina. The country has been continuously ruled by civilian presidents since 1983, and within the last decade the nation's traditional statist and inflationary economic policies have been abandoned. Citizens are now free to earn a living, open a business, trade internationally, and invest their earnings without fear they will be ravaged by inflation. However, enforcement of intellectual property rights remains somewhat problematic—a symptom of the broader problems the country is experiencing in institutionalizing the rule of law.

### Freedom to Hold Property 2/3

The constitution guarantees the right to hold property, and the legal system gives effect to this right. There are no restrictions on selling or exchanging property and individuals can structure their holdings as they choose.

Argentina adheres to most international treaties and agreements on intellectual property, but enforcement can be weak and patent protection for pharmaceuticals remains a problem. Under U.S. pressure, the executive branch decreed a law in October 1995 that was far stronger in protecting patents than one passed by the legislature. Lawmakers threatened to contest the executive decree in the courts.

### Freedom to Earn a Living 3/3

There are no government controls on wages. Workers are able to form unions and bargain collectively. The government has proposed a national mediation service to promote more effective collective bargaining. Labor is well organized and dominated by federations identified with the ruling Peronist party. Union influence has diminished, however, because of corruption scandals and sharp internal divisions over the government's economic restructuring program. Individuals can freely change jobs, a right somewhat limited by the leap in unemployment in 1995 to almost 19 percent.

Forced labor is prohibited and there have been no reports of the practice. There have been reports of abuses of immigrant workers from neighboring Peru and Paraguay.

**Freedom to Operate a Business** **3/3**

Foreign and domestic private entities may form and run businesses. By Latin American standards, the formation of a corporation is not overly cumbersome. Few sectors of the economy are closed to private investment. Government procurement is competitive although political favoritism is evident in the process.

Prices for raw materials, finished goods and services are determined by supply and demand.

**Freedom to Invest One's Earnings** **3/3**

The autonomous central bank is prohibited from printing pesos not backed by hard currency in a reserve account. As the peso is pegged exactly to the dollar, the central bank in effect operates as a currency board. Inflation has remained at around 4 percent.

The government has eliminated most of the policies that once directed finance to favored sectors, and interest rates have been freed from government controls. In recent years, the private sector has had access to a growing number of credit alternatives. However, the banking crisis in 1995 tightened markets.

Individuals can hold foreign currency, collect interest in foreign currency and sell property against payment in foreign currency. Rates of return on investments are not controlled and Argentines can invest abroad.

**Freedom to Trade Internationally** **2/2**

The government has eliminated virtually all non-tariff barriers and most duties on imports.

There are no prohibited imports and licenses are required only for automobiles, one of the few sectors still protected by quotas and higher duties. Import customs procedures remain inefficient and time-consuming. There are no export controls.

There are no limits on leaving or entering the country. Foreign investors are welcome in virtually every economic sector, and can count on national treatment, a free foreign exchange regime and no price controls.

The peso has been pegged at par to the dollar by law since 1991.

**Freedom from Unreasonable Government Interference in the Economy**

The national government has largely completed the privatization of large public-sector enterprises. Provincial governments have hardly begun the process.

Although the government has striven to implement free-market reforms, it still has the impulse to take protectionist measures, as it did with some tariff hikes during 1995. Nearly all subsidies to public enterprises were cut back in 1994.

Because the judicial system is overpoliticized and manipulated by the executive branch, and because of generalized corruption, the law is frequently wielded as an instrument of favoritism and punishment in commercial matters.

**Freedom to Participate in the Market Economy** **1/2**

There are no legal restrictions against women or minorities entering any occupation they choose or starting a business. There are no restrictions on women holding property. There have been several disputes involving developers who infringe on the land rights of indigenous groups.

The transparency of legal, regulatory and accounting systems remains inadequate compared with the situation in more developed capital markets. The government has worked to enhance transparency through an independent body to regulate these otherwise self-regulated markets.

Corruption is endemic, permeating all branches of government. In August 1995 the finance minister himself charged that market reforms were being sabotaged by "mafias" operating in league with government officials. Scandals that reach up to the presidency are frequent, and corrupt practices, including the bribing of foreign investors, continued in 1995 with impunity. The judiciary is riddled with corruption and manipulated by the executive branch, and the rule of law exists more on paper than in practice.

# Bolivia

ECONOMIC FREEDOM STATUS: **PARTLY FREE**
POLITICAL RIGHTS AND CIVIL LIBERTIES STATUS: **PARTLY FREE**
PRESS FREEDOM STATUS: **FREE**
POPULATION: **7,428,000**
PPP: **$2,410**

## Background

Economic freedom in Bolivia has been on the rise since 1985 when the government introduced a series of measures to end hyperinflation and liberalize the economy. Under the current administration of Gonzalo Sanchez de Lozada these reforms have continued, and the president has introduced his own innovative privatization program. Thanks to successive governments' commitment to reform and liberalization, the economy is now growing at the rate of 4 percent per year.

Despite the marked increase in economic freedom Bolivians have experienced in the past decade, a legal and institutional framework protecting the right to property remains absent, and the government continues to use force, including states of siege, against independent organizations. Property rights are recognized by law, but the legal system does not ensure that the right to different kinds of property will be protected. The system for registering title to land, for example, is so weak that ownership of much of the nation's land is in doubt. Adding to the problem is an ineffective judicial system.

## Freedom to Hold Property 1/3

Property rights are recognized by law, but legislation is inadequate. Land registration is poor and because of a corrupt and overburdened judicial system, enforcement of property rights in general is very weak.

Intellectual property rights laws regarding film and copyrights were passed in 1992, but enforcement is lax. The congress has ratified four treaties in order to join the World Intellectual Property Organization and the Bern, Rome and Paris Conventions. Patent protection remains inadequate, although there is recognition that the ninety-year-old law needs revision.

There are no restrictions on selling, exchanging, or devising property and individuals can structure their holdings as they choose.

## Freedom to Earn a Living 2/3

The government does not control wages. Workers can form and join independent unions and there are no restrictions on changing jobs. However, the labor code requires government authorization to establish a union, permits only one per enterprise, and allows the government to dissolve unions. Civil servants are prohibited from organizing. Collective bargaining is allowed, but the process has recently broken down. In April 1995, a six-month state of siege was imposed in response to labor strikes and protests.

Forced labor is outlawed, but mineworkers endure conditions that approach indentured servitude. Child labor is prohibited, though apprenticeships for children as young as twelve are permitted. The labor ministry does not adequately monitor or enforce child-labor laws.

### Freedom to Operate a Business 3/3

Individuals are legally free to form businesses in any sector of the economy. The rules governing business formation have been streamlined significantly in recent years. Access to those sectors dominated by the state remains difficult but the opening for private competition should increase as the privatization program continues.

Government contracts are awarded competitively, but the process is tainted by corruption, and the judiciary is unreliable when it comes to contract enforcement. The central government controls fuel prices and municipal governments control bread prices. All other prices are determined by market forces.

### Freedom to Invest One's Earnings 3/3

The government does not regulate interest rates. Bolivia has an autonomous central bank and inflation has dropped to around 7.5 percent. Commercial banks are allowed to set their own interest rates and credit is market-allocated. Rates of return on investments are not controlled. Individuals can invest abroad and can hold foreign currencies and securities.

### Freedom to Trade Internationally 2/2

All quantitative import restrictions have been eliminated. Tariffs have been reduced from 16 percent to 10 percent; tariffs on capital goods are now 5 percent.

Export taxes were eliminated in 1993 with the Export Bill and export procedures were simplified with the establishment of a one-stop registration office. There are no limits on the right to enter or leave the country.

The investment law guarantees remission of profits, freedom to set prices, convertibility of currency, national treatment and authorization of international arbitration. The exchange rate is set daily by the government exchange house, under the supervision of the central bank. Rates reflect market forces because currency exchanges in hotels, banks and on street corners are legal and active. The parallel exchange rates normally display a less than one percent difference from official rates.

### Freedom from Unreasonable Government Interference in the Economy

In 1990, the latest year for which information is available, state-owned enterprises accounted for 14 percent of GDP. In 1994, again the latest year for which data if available, government expenditures represented 40 percent of GDP.

In 1992 the congress approved a privatization law that allows the government to sell state assets. The recently initiated "capitalization" program is slated to sell off the six largest state monopolies—oil, electricity, telecommunications, railroad, airline and smelting—which combined account for more than half the nation's economic activity. However, public-sector dominance and the existing institutional framework have restricted private-sector expansion into the mining, hydrocarbons, telecommunications and electricity sectors.

In return for half-ownership and management control, foreign investors are asked to make investments in companies amounting to 50 percent of the assessed value. The remaining shares are to be divided among the 3.2 million adult Bolivians, to be held in retirement accounts in a new pension system.

There are implicit subsidies in electricity and other utilities and indirect subsidies on exports as the still government-run railroad charges lower shipping rates on exported commodities than on imported goods. Enforcement of commercial codes and regulations is generally equitable.

**Freedom to Participate in the Market Economy** **1/2**

There are no legal barriers to women and minorities owning and operating businesses, and there are no legal barriers to property ownership by women. But women and Indians—who make up about 70 percent of the population—suffer discrimination in their efforts to gain access to land and especially credit.

Commercial laws are generally liberal. But enforcement remains a major problem because of weak administrative capability and the judicial system, which despite some recent reforms remains riddled with corruption, overpoliticized and subject to the compromising power of traffickers in the multi-billion-dollar drug trade. The huge flows of drug money interfere with normal market forces, although it is difficult to gauge to what extent.

Corruption in Bolivia is not as bad as in some other Latin American countries, but it remains entrenched in most of the country's institutions. Corrupt practices are curbed to a limited extent by the existence of a relatively free press.

# Brazil

ECONOMIC FREEDOM STATUS: **MOSTLY NOT FREE**
POLITICAL RIGHTS AND CIVIL LIBERTIES STATUS: **PARTLY FREE**
PRESS FREEDOM STATUS: **FREE**
POPULATION: **157,800,000**
PPP: **$5,240**

**Background**

Brazil has been cursed by a series of governments built on cronyism and corruption that have stymied its potential to be one of the economic giants of the Hemisphere. The distribution of income is also one of the most unequal in the world, and the country remains mired in poverty and underdevelopment.

Brazil lacks the legal and institutional infrastructure necessary for citizens to exercise any significant degree of economic freedom. Thus, while the right to property is theoretically recognized by law, without political connections it means little. Opening a small business is such a complex undertaking that one must hire a professional skilled in the ways of the bureaucracy to obtain the needed permits and licenses. And the economic rights of the poor and indigenous peoples are virtually nonexistent.

**Freedom to Hold Property** **1/3**

The right to hold property is recognized by law. However, wealth and political influence provide the only real guarantees of ownership given the arbitrary and corrupt nature of the legal system and police. In September, President Fernando Henrique Cardoso signed fourteen decrees expropriating 40,343 hectares of land in eleven states to settle 1,500 families.

Land holdings are the most unequal in the world and there are an estimated 2 million families in search of land. The current government has taken some steps toward land reform, but little has changed and enforcement of even limited reforms is poor. The institutions assuring security of ownership are very weak. By the end of 1995, only 280,000 families had formal title to their land. In the last ten years, there have been some 5,700 conflicts in the countryside over land rights involving more than 5.5 million people. Since 1990, Brazil has been committed to strengthening intellectual property laws. But progress has been slow and enforcement of existing laws lax. Foreign investors are prohibited from owning border area property.

### Freedom to Earn a Living **2/3**

The rights to organize unions, bargain collectively and strike are enshrined in the 1988 constitution. In practice, however, respect for worker rights is at best uneven, and egregious violations occur in rural areas on a wide scale. Industrial unions are independent of the government, but are often connected to political parties and prone to corruption.

Agricultural workers confront systematic abuse and violent intimidation in Brazil's vast rural and Amazon areas. Brazil's landowners control nearly 60 percent of arable land, while the poorest 30 percent of the population share less than 2 percent. In rural areas tens of thousands of workers are held in virtual slavery by large landowners through debt bondage and coercion. Every year dozens, sometimes hundreds, of activists, lay Catholic church workers and rural unionists are killed by paramilitary groups and hired killers in the pay of landowners.

The government does not control wage rates. Forced labor is prohibited by law, but the judicial response to widespread violations is generally indifferent and abuses continue with impunity. Child labor, also illegal, is prevalent, as is debt bondage of child workers. About 3 million children between the ages of ten and fourteen are reported to be working in rural areas.

### Freedom to Operate a Business **1/3**

Citizens are free to form businesses, but confront a maze of often contradictory laws and red tape, a labyrinthian, corrupt bureaucracy and a chaotic tax system. The Portuguese word, *jeito*, which roughly translates as "wrangle," describes the ways Brazilians try to get around the myriad institutional obstacles to doing business. *Despachantes*, or expeditors, are professionals, with their own union and entrance examinations, who are hired by individuals, companies and even government agencies to deal with Brazil's vast federal, state and local bureaucracies. An estimated 37 percent of GDP is produced in the informal sector.

The legal system is a battleground in which those with enough money or influence attack their competitors. As the Brazilian expression goes, "For friends, everything; for strangers, nothing; for enemies, the law."

The 1988 constitution restricts domestic and foreign investment in certain sectors of the economy. The current government has begun a privatization program targeting major industries like petroleum, telecommunications and electricity, but the going has been slow as powerful special interests have balked at many of the necessary constitutional reforms.

The constitution gives preferential treatment to national capital in the procurement of goods and services by the government, and foreign companies can be excluded from certain bids and competition.

In its attempt to establish macroeconomic order, the government has manipulated price indices. Although price controls have been lifted, companies suspected of having marked up prices "excessively" must justify their markup to both the Ministry of Finance and the Price Supply Agency (SUNAB). SUNAB uses cost-profit expense formulas to set profit margins for reporting companies' operations.

### Freedom to Invest One's Earnings **1/3**

Interest rates are controlled by the Ministry of Finance and credit is restricted by the government. The central bank executes the monetary and credit policies formulated by the National Monetary Council. The annual inflation rate is around 20 percent. The Real Plan, based on a new currency, has significantly lowered what had been chronic high inflation. A broad de-indexation of financial markets, taxes and contracts was begun in mid-1995.

Individuals and firms can purchase stock on Mercosur (Argentina, Uruguay and Paraguay) exchanges subject to various controls and limitations. Firms can pay up to $1 million for services abroad but must notify the central bank. Upon closing activities abroad, firms must repatriate their capital.

Individuals can hold foreign currency but all foreign investment, including securities, must be registered with the central bank.

## Freedom to Trade Internationally 1/2

On top of increases in 1994, further Brazil raised tariffs on some 100 imports to 70 percent following Mexico's financial crisis. The government claims these were only emergency measures, rather than a reversal of trade liberalization. Tariffs on autos were raised to 70 percent in March and the total number of cars that could be imported restricted to 300,000.

Export taxes remain, but exporters have been given numerous incentives, including tax and tariff exemptions on imported goods and equipment needed to enhance exports. There are no limits on entering or leaving the country.

Foreign investment is constitutionally prohibited in many key economic sectors. The current government's attempts to reform the constitution and initiate privatization are proceeding very slowly.

Theoretically the exchange rate has floated since 1992. But in effect there are three exchange rates: a commercial rate adjusted daily by the central bank based on inflation estimates, a tourist rate and a parallel rate, which fluctuate, although the central bank will intervene in the tourist rate.

Since 1990 Brazil has been committed to strengthening intellectual property laws. But progress has been slow and enforcement of existing laws lax. Foreign investors are prohibited from owning border-area property.

## Freedom from Unreasonable Government Interference in the Economy

The current government focuses on reducing the state's role in the economy, and Brazil has moved away from price controls and import substitution. But powerful interests and constitutional mandates remain in the way, and the statist economic culture is so institutionalized that it is difficult for officials to effect reforms. State-owned enterprises accounted for 12 percent of GDP in 1994.

The regulatory regime is so complex and contradictory that the application of legal requirements is discretionary and often applied only if one is unfortunate enough not to have a professional expeditor or to have angered someone with the authority to enforce regulations.

In rural areas local police tend to side with large landowners against peasants and workers during land and wage disputes. In urban areas, vigilante groups in the pay of merchants and often made up of off-duty police carry out "social cleansing," including executions, of the indigent and those at the lowest rung of the informal economy.

## Freedom to Participate in the Market Economy 1/2

Theoretically there are no restrictions on racial or ethnic minorities entering any occupation they choose or operating a business. However, deep-seated societal discrimination against blacks and Indians is a major obstacle to the pursuit of economic opportunity. The lack of land reform, and the lack of enforcement of land rights, as in the case of legally demarcated Indian lands, also remain an impediment.

To implement economic liberalization the last two governments have often resorted to decrees to bypass a recalcitrant congress. These measures are usually challenged in the courts and a number have been declared unconstitutional. The regulatory instability makes conducting business extremely difficult. Moreover, the large size of the informal sector is testament to the lack of a legal framework in which a market economy can operate.

Government and judicial corruption at the federal, state and local levels profoundly undermines the functioning of Brazil's economy.

# Canada

ECONOMIC FREEDOM STATUS: **FREE**
POLITICAL RIGHTS AND CIVIL LIBERTIES STATUS: **FREE**
PRESS FREEDOM STATUS: **FREE**
POPULATION: **29,600,000**
PPP: **$20,520**

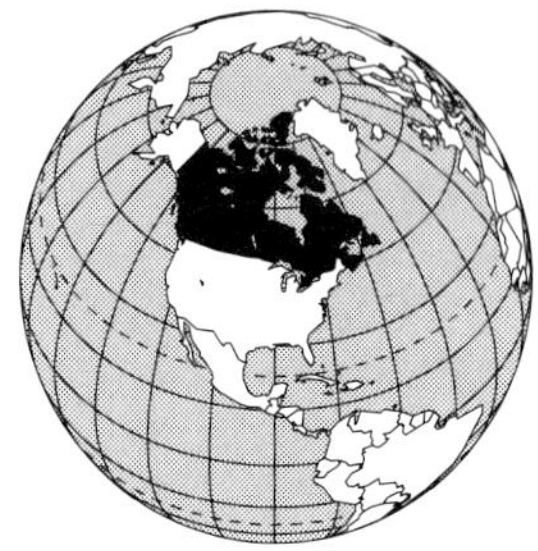

## Background

With the exception of some restrictions on international trade Canadians enjoy a full measure of economic freedom. But Canada's economic policies continue to be vigorously debated.

In Ontario there was a sudden and unexpected shift from a Socialist to a conservative government, attributed by many to anger over high taxes, unemployment and the former New Democratic Party government's reluctance to cut spending from the generous social safety net the party had helped to create. However, Ontario's new premier, Michael Harris, has been confronted with boisterous protests from citizens feeling the effects of sharp budgetary cuts. In September, roughly 5,000 protesters rushed the provincial parliament and were met with pepper spray and police billyclubs. Quebec's sovereignty referendum in October left Canada uneasy but intact by a margin of under one percent of the vote. Elsewhere in the country, several territorial disputes led to armed standoffs between police and Indians occupying private land they claimed had never been ceded to Canada.

## Freedom to Hold Property 3/3

The right to property is recognized and protected by law. Intellectual property rights are also fully protected.

Indigenous groups no longer face official discrimination in owning property but several tribes have filed claims to regain traditional land holdings. Court rulings since the 1970s have confirmed that the indigenous tribes still hold title to their traditional territory, and tribal claims have been slowly working their way through the court system. Many tribes, however, are becoming frustrated with the slowness of the process and complain that federal and provincial authorities are deliberately dragging their feet.

## Freedom to Earn a Living 3/3

With the exception of members of the armed forces, workers are able to form and join unions. Public and private-sector employees, with the exception of police, can bargain collectively. All trade unions are independent of the government. Outside of a minimum wage, set by the central government for industries under federal jurisdiction and by the provinces for all other industries, there are no controls on wages.

Forced labor is illegal and is not practiced.

### Freedom to Operate a Business 3/3

Canada's rules of business formation are transparent and virtually identical to those of the United States. The government does not restrict entry into any line of commerce, although provincial monopolies over electric energy generation and distribution exist in every province except Alberta and Nova Scotia. However, exceptions have been made for some private energy production. In addition, Canada's public health system makes it virtually impossible to open a private hospital.

Contradictory regulations among the provinces sometimes hinder business efficiency. Currently Ottawa is pushing to harmonize the federal goods and services tax with provincial sales taxes in order to improve public-sector efficiency and simplify regulations for businesses. In addition, the province of Quebec has language requirements designed to preserve the French-Canadian identity, which can be a minor barrier to business operations.

While the North American Free Trade Agreement will introduce more competition into the government procurement process, currently companies with links to parties in power are more likely to win government contracts.

Canada has no general system of price controls but does set prices on some agricultural products and health services.

### Freedom to Invest One's Earnings 3/3

Canada has an open market for credit and financial services. There are no restrictions on investing abroad. The independent central bank has kept inflation at 2.9 percent, one of the lowest among industrialized countries.

### Freedom to Trade Internationally 1/2

Canada maintains a relatively open trading system although some significant barriers still exist. The average tariff rate is 4.9 percent and Canada maintains trade barriers against dairy products, liquor, poultry, and wheat. There are no significant export taxes.

Canada limits or prohibits foreign investment in several sectors, and special investment rules apply to cultural industries and financial services. The Canadian dollar is fully convertible and there are no exchange controls.

### Freedom from Unreasonable Government Interference in the Economy

Although government policy generally promotes competition, government-owned industries have traditionally played a significant role in the economy. The government has privatized forty Crown corporations (public enterprises) and government holdings since the mid-1980s. The ten provinces of Canada continue to have wide jurisdiction over most aspects of health, education and social welfare.

The government offers incentives in financial services, pharmaceuticals, and information technology industries.

### Freedom to Participate in the Market Economy 2/2

Canada does not maintain any significant restrictions against women or minorities. Historically, however, indigenous tribes have been the victims of official discrimination. Laws enacted since the 1970s have tried to remedy this discrimination. For example, the 1994 Employment Equity Act, passed in Ontario, requires employers to remove barriers against women, aboriginals, and minorities. Corruption is not a significant problem.

# Chile

ECONOMIC FREEDOM STATUS: **FREE**
POLITICAL RIGHTS AND CIVIL LIBERTIES STATUS: **FREE**
PRESS FREEDOM STATUS: **FREE**
POPULATION: **14,251,000**
PPP: **$8,410**

## Background

The Republic of Chile was founded in 1818 and has enjoyed democratic government for most of its history. A plebiscite in 1988 and elections for a civilian government in 1989 ended seventeen years of repressive military rule.

During the 1970s, General Augusto Pinochet implemented a program of free-market liberalism designed by Western-trained economists. The Christian Democratic government that took office in 1990 inherited an economy based on private property and the rule of law, a system it not only continued but built on. As a result, Chileans enjoy a high degree of economic freedom. Chile is poised to join Canada, Mexico, and the United States as a party to the North American Free Trade Agreement.

## Freedom to Hold Property 2/3

The right to property is recognized by law, and the legal system gives effect to property rights. In 1981 Chile enacted a law creating property rights to surface and groundwater that has become a model for nations seeking a method for allocating water efficiently.

The law does give the government broad powers to expropriate property, though it has not exercised these powers in recent years. There are no restrictions on selling or exchanging property, and individuals can structure their property holdings as they choose.

Chile's Industrial Property Law is compatible with international norms, but intellectual property rights protection remains deficient. Chile has been on the United States Trade Representative's "Special 301" watch list since 1989.

## Freedom to Earn a Living 2/3

Workers are able to form and join unions and to strike. Only the police and military cannot form unions. However, despite reforms, the labor code inherited from the former military dictatorship effectively prevents many sectors from organizing. Collective bargaining provisions remain weak and rules governing labor contract negotiations favor businesses. New legislation was proposed in July 1995 that would strengthen collective bargaining rights and the ability of the labor ministry to oversee business compliance with labor law. Unions are independent of the government, but union leaders are usually elected from lists based on political party affiliation and maintain ties to their parties.

There are no restrictions on changing jobs, and wages are not controlled. Forced labor is prohibited and there is little evidence that it occurs.

## Freedom to Operate a Business 3/3

Individuals are able to form businesses. The process is neither expensive nor time-consuming. Participation in certain sectors reserved for the state, such as oil, is restricted.

Government procurement contracts are competitively let, although in certain cases negotiation is permitted.

Prices are freely set except in regulated utilities.

## Freedom to Invest One's Earnings 3/3

Interest rates are not controlled by the government. The central bank monetary policy targets real interest rates, though in mid-1995 the bank stopped setting ninety-day rates and began concentrating on the one-day rate.

Credit is allocated by the market but the central bank reserves the right to restrict access to the interbank credit market, at which firms would have access to the informal market, whose rate is usually within 2 percent of the interbank rate. Rates of return on investments are not controlled.

Individuals can invest abroad and hold foreign currency and securities. The central bank is independent and mid-year projections for inflation in 1995 were around 9 percent.

## Freedom to Trade Internationally 1/2

Tariffs are generally low and there are few import barriers. Chile is a member of GATT and has free trade agreements providing for duty-free trade in most products with Mexico, Venezuela, Colombia, Ecuador and the Mercosur countries. The most significant non-tariff barrier is the import price band system for certain agricultural goods (in 1995 wheat, vegetable oils and sugar), which are subject to duties designed to maintain a minimum domestic price. There are no export taxes or other impediments to selling to foreigners. There are no limits on leaving or entering the country.

To control short-term capital inflows, foreign firms are made to wait one year after investing before they can repatriate profits. Otherwise, foreign investment regulation is nondiscriminatory, entails relatively simple procedures, and allows access to most sectors and markets.

The central bank pegs the peso to a basket of currencies composed of the dollar, the mark and the yen. The bank makes adjustments to reflect inflation differentials between Chile and major trading partners. Exporters must remit most of their foreign exchange earnings through the interbank market. A legal parallel market operates, with rates typically within one percent of the interbank rate.

## Freedom from Unreasonable Government Interference in the Economy

Businesses are predominantly owned and controlled by private interests. The public-sector budget is approximately 25 percent of GDP. The government retains holdings in several industries, primarily mining, shipping and electricity, accounting for about 13 percent of GDP. The state-owned CODELCO is the world's largest copper company. In 1995 the government was planning to divest from the electricity and shipping sectors.

There is an anti-monopoly law designed to prevent abuse of a dominant position, but enforcement is uneven and several industries are characterized by high concentration and oligopolistic behavior.

## Freedom to Participate in the Market Economy 2/2

There are no legal barriers against women or minorities choosing their occupations or forming businesses. Women's right to own property is protected. A recently enacted law creates conjugal property as an option in marriage, though a prior law gives women the right to half their husbands' assets but gives a husband no right to his wife's.

The laws necessary for a market economy to function are generally enforced. The judicial system deals relatively well with commercial matters. Corruption is somewhat of an impediment to normal market forces, and money-laundering is a problem. However, corruption is less of a factor than in other Latin American countries because in Chile, unlike in most Latin countries, rule is based for the most part on respect for law rather than the raw exercise of power.

# Colombia

ECONOMIC FREEDOM STATUS: **PARTLY FREE**
POLITICAL RIGHTS AND CIVIL LIBERTIES STATUS: **PARTLY FREE**
PRESS FREEDOM STATUS: **PARTLY FREE**
POPULATION: **37,707,000**
PPP: **$5,480**

## Background

The Republic of Colombia was established in 1886, and politics has since been dominated by the Liberal and Conservative parties. Liberal President Cesar Gaviria (1990-94) introduced a series of economic reforms that were continued by Ernesto Samper, the former economic development minister who succeeded him.

Although Colombians now enjoy a higher level of economic freedom there is very little freedom to earn a living. Workers' rights to associate freely are severely restricted, and when they do form a union, it is subject to a great deal of government harassment and control. A weak judiciary, restrictions on the rate of return on certain investments and problems in the enforcement of intellectual property rights are also concerns.

## Freedom to Hold Property 2/3

The 1991 constitution explicitly protects individual rights against actions of the state and upholds the right to private property. The state, however, reserves the right to expropriate in cases of public necessity, and can seize land that is connected with criminal activities. The judicial system is uneven in giving effect to the right to property; most problems exist in rural areas and involve land disputes. There are no restrictions on selling or exchanging property, and individuals can structure their property holdings as they choose.

There are substantial deficiencies in patent and copyright protection, and enforcement of intellectual property laws is weak at the police and judicial levels.

## Freedom to Earn a Living 1/3

Workers' rights to unionize and to bargain collectively are severely restricted both in law and in practice. The law allows supervision of internal union management by the government and the presence of government officials at union meetings. Temporary employment has been institutionalized to the point where it is impossible in practice for workers to belong to unions and conclude collective agreements.

Colombia is the most dangerous place in the world for trade unionists. In 1994, 178 unionists were killed in Colombia, either by state security forces, paramilitary groups that often collaborate with them, killers hired by drug traffickers and landowners, or left-wing guerrilla groups. Killings of unionists are carried out with impunity. According to a report by the office of the Colombian Public Prosecutor, unionists are also subject to systematic, arbitrary arrest by security forces who consider them to be the "enemy from within."

Workers are free to change jobs, and outside of a government-set minimum wage, the government does not try to control wages. Slavery, other forms of compulsory labor, and child labor are outlawed. Child labor, however, is prevalent, with the country's first lady admitting in 1995 that about 1.8 million children toil in agriculture and mining and in the informal economy.

**Freedom to Operate a Business 3/3**

Citizens are free to form businesses, although the procedures for doing so legally remain onerous, thus accounting in part for the sizable informal sector. Practically all lines of commerce that were once the domain of the state have been opened up to private companies—even the provision of health care to the poor, once an exclusive preserve of the state.

A recent law was designed to make bidding for government contracts competitive and transparent, but its impact is as yet unclear.

The prices of a few pharmaceutical products, petroleum derivatives, gas, certain petrochemicals, a number of consumer goods, school books and tuition, residential rents, and public utility services are controlled. Wholesale prices for major agricultural products are set by the Ministry of Agriculture.

**Freedom to Invest One's Earnings 2/3**

The 1991 constitution provides for an autonomous central bank. In late 1995, President Samper attempted to exert pressure on it by calling for a "reform of the bank," but the bank was able to preserve its independence. The bank has the authority to set maximum limits on interest rates. There are still some restrictions imposed by the bank on rates of return on investments, but the trend has been toward a relaxation of capital flows. The incidence of forced investment has been reduced in favor of market-determined credit flows.

Colombians can hold foreign currencies and securities, and can invest abroad. However, many capital flow restrictions exist as part of a near-futile effort to combat narco-business and money-laundering.

**Freedom to Trade Internationally 2/2**

Almost all import licenses have been eliminated and import procedures have been simplified. Still effectively barred are used vehicles, used tires, used clothing and textiles, dairy products, meat, and items the government says are related to national security. There are no export taxes or other impediments to selling to foreigners. There are no restrictions on entering or leaving the country.

Foreign investment has been liberalized, with few restrictions if any on profit remittance and granting of national treatment. One hundred percent foreign ownership is permitted in virtually all economic sectors.

There are no exchange controls.

**Freedom from Unreasonable Government Interference in the Economy**

The port system, banking and telecommunications industries have been privatized as part of an ongoing program begun in 1991. However, Colombia suffers from relatively high industrial concentration in a few large conglomerates. There is weak enforcement of anti-trust laws. Political influence, bribery and favoritism continue to affect the regulatory landscape.

Bureaucratic requirements for conducting business remain onerous, though less so than in the past.

Some export subsidies still exist, but in general, unfair subsidies have been eliminated.

**Freedom to Participate in the Market Economy 2/2**

Racial and ethnic minorities are not legally foreclosed from any occupation or running any type of business, and there are few limits on the ability of minorities or women to hold or transfer property. However, longstanding racial discrimination remains an obstacle for blacks and Indians, which is one reason why they tend to remain outside the formal economy.

The 1991 constitution provides the judiciary with greater financial and administrative independence from the executive branch. The government now rarely interferes in commercial matters. Still, the judicial system remains clogged and cumbersome. The commercial code was updated in 1994 and bankruptcy provisions were added. Although the judiciary remains vulnerable to influence by powerful drug traffickers, private business is less affected by the corruption that taints the judicial system.

The huge flows of drug money interfere with normal market forces, especially in the real estate and construction industries, and in the prices of imported goods.

# Costa Rica

ECONOMIC FREEDOM STATUS: **PARTLY FREE**
POLITICAL RIGHTS AND CIVIL LIBERTIES STATUS: **FREE**
PRESS FREEDOM STATUS: **FREE**
POPULATION: **3,347,000**
PPP: **$5,480**

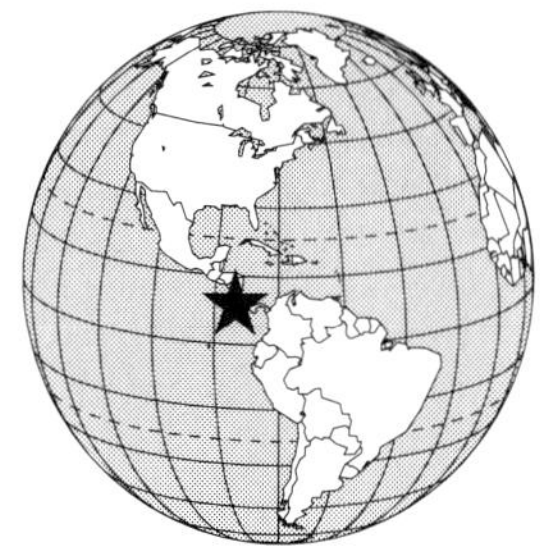

## Background

Costa Rica became independent in 1821 and became a republic in 1848. Democratic government was instituted in 1899 and briefly interrupted in 1917 and 1948. The 1949 constitution, which bans the formation of a national army, provides the framework for democratic governance.

Despite increased economic liberalization, Costa Rican's economic freedom remains hampered by a combination of several factors. Customs procedures are cumbersome and rife with corruption, interfering with the freedom to import and export. Obtaining compensation for property the government expropriates can be time-consuming and costly. The government steers credit to certain enterprises through state-owned banks, and registering new businesses takes time and effort. Furthermore, entry into many occupations is rigidly controlled.

## Freedom to Hold Property 2/3

The right to hold property is recognized by law. The government has expropriated large tracts of land for national parks, biological and indigenous reserves and squatters without providing prompt, adequate and effective compensation. Obtaining compensation through the courts is time-consuming and costly. Land tenure laws tend to favor squatters. There are no restrictions on the selling and transferring of property.

Protection for intellectual property rights is poor. The government said in fall 1995 it would seek to provide greater protection of patents and brand names.

## Freedom to Earn a Living 2/3

Workers are able to change jobs and to form labor unions. Unions are independent of government control. Minimum wages are set by the National Wage Board, composed of representatives from the government, businesses, and labor unions. The private sector uses Solidarity, an employer-employee organization, as an instrument to prevent independent unions from organizing.

The constitution prohibits forced or compulsory labor. There have been no reported instances of either.

## Freedom to Operate a Business 2/3

Individuals can form and operate businesses, except in four major sectors that despite reform proposals in 1995 remained dominated by the state—telecommunications, energy, insurance and banking. New businesses encounter cumbersome bureaucratic procedures when seeking to register. Many service industries and professions, including doctors, lawyers, CPAs and engineers, are tightly controlled through mandatory guild memberships and residency and other requirements.

There is open public bidding for government procurement contracts, but the process is overly complicated, lengthy and costly. Although prices of a few agricultural goods are controlled, all others are freely set.

## Freedom to Hold Property 2/3

The central bank is independent but has nonetheless experienced difficulties in keeping inflation below 15 percent as the economy has been growing at a healthy 6.1 percent per year. Interest rates are not controlled and reached 40 percent in 1995. There are no controls on rates of return. There are no restrictions on investing abroad and citizens can hold foreign currency and securities.

The private sector has access to a variety of credit instruments. Credit is allocated on market terms, but state-owned banks are obligated to finance high-risk or unprofitable activities deemed by the government to be in the public interest.

## Freedom to Trade Internationally 1/2

There is a relatively open international trade and investment regime, except in the four state monopolies. Tariffs have been reduced as Costa Rica has joined a number of regional trade agreements. Import permits are required for many agricultural goods, but not for most other products. All exports must be registered with the central bank and there are export controls on a number of raw materials and basic commodities. Costa Rican customs procedures are onerous, inefficient, costly and riddled with corruption. There are no restrictions on leaving or entering the country.

Equity in Costa Rican companies can be owned by both domestic and foreign companies. Foreigners can own real estate. Investment laws, however, are administered by a cumbersome bureaucracy. There are no restrictions on repatriating capital. There are no foreign exchange restrictions.

## Freedom from Unreasonable Government Interference in the Economy

The government's share of GDP is 26 percent. Efforts to privatize or otherwise end the state monopolies on telecommunications, energy, insurance and banking have been hamstrung by a lack of political backing in the legislature and strong statist traditions. In fall 1995 the government said it might permit private-sector co-generation of energy and more private-sector involvement in public works such as road construction. The government continues to provide subsidies to public enterprises.

Government policy and the legal system occasionally retard competition and opportunity. For example, in 1995 a U.S. company was forced to cease cellular phone operations when the Supreme Court ruled in favor of the monopoly granted to a state telecommunications company.

## Freedom to Participate in the Market Economy 1/2

Racial and ethnic minorities and women are not foreclosed from any occupation or from running any type of business. There are no restrictions on minorities or women holding or transferring property.

Costa Rican laws and regulations generally foster competition. The civil and commercial codes provide for arbitration of commercial disputes, but the cost of litigating is so costly and time-consuming that it makes the process almost unworkable.

Government corruption, especially in the customs system, is a growing problem, as is the increase in money-laundering connected to the hemispheric drug trade.

# Cuba

ECONOMIC FREEDOM STATUS: **NOT FREE**
POLITICAL RIGHTS AND CIVIL LIBERTIES STATUS: **NOT FREE**
PRESS FREEDOM STATUS: **NOT FREE**
POPULATION: **11,168,000**
PPP: **$3,412**

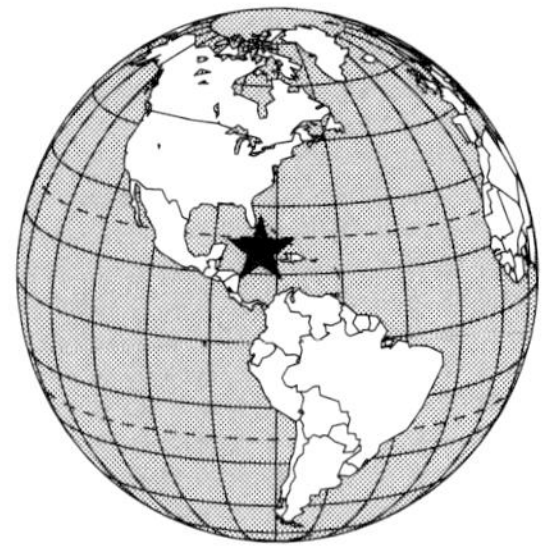

## Background

Fidel Castro has dominated the Cuban political system since 1959, transforming it into a one-party Communist state. As president of the Council of Ministers, chairman of the Council of State, commander-in-chief of the Revolutionary Armed Forces and first secretary of the Cuban Communist Party (PCC), Castro controls every lever of power in Cuba. The PCC is the only authorized political party and it controls all governmental entities from the national to the municipal level.

The collapse of the Soviet Union undermined the Cuban economy, forcing Castro to impose a "special period" of severe rationing and blackouts. A mass exodus of refugees from Cuba symbolized the desperate state of the economy. Castro has reluctantly introduced economic reforms along the lines of China's market socialism. During 1994-95, foreign investment has been allowed, dollars have been legalized, and basic self-employment and production have been permitted.

However, the economic changes cannot be viewed as reforms. Rather, they are stop-gap measures utilized reluctantly by a government with few options. The Cuban government is unlikely to relinquish its tight control over the economy, and economic reforms have often been accompanied by increased social and political repression. Although technically within the law, informal entrepreneurs face police crackdowns and much of the informal economy remains secretive. As a result, Cuba's economy is among the world's least free.

## Freedom to Hold Property 0/3

Citizens do not have private property rights.

Agricultural cooperatives have limited independence from state oversight, but the state owns the land and all decisions must fall within parameters determined by the state.

Private farms represent about 10 percent of agricultural production. Small land parcels are leased on a longterm basis to families who must fulfill a quota to the state before selling their excess in farm markets.

## Freedom to Earn a Living 0/3

The sole legal labor organization, the Confederation of Cuban Workers (CTC), is an instrument of the state controlled by the PCC. The handful of workers who have attempted to organize independently are subject to persecution—blacklisting, arbitrary arrest and attacks by government-organized mobs.

The right to bargain collectively is not recognized. The CTC does not promote or protect worker rights. Its responsibility is to ensure that government production goals are met and to carry out worker layoffs as part of the current downsizing of state payrolls.

All wages are set by the government. In fall 1995 professionals earned the equivalent of less than $9 per month; average workers earned about half that. Even with subsidized health care and education, most Cuban workers are unable to support their families adequately. In foreign ventures, workers are provided by the government, which collects a fee in hard currency for each worker from the company and then pays the worker a fraction of that amount.

Workers who refuse extra "voluntary" work assigned by the state risk job discrimination and dismissal. Citizens cannot change jobs or residence without government permission.

## Freedom to Operate a Business 0/3

Limited self-employment was legalized in 1993 and licenses are now issued for 200-plus trades like shoe repair, hair cutting, flower arranging and piñata-making. The self-employed must pay a license fee and taxes. They cannot hire employees and must purchase all materials from the state. Approximately 170,000 licenses had been issued by summer 1995. Self-employment is authorized for professionals—but not in their specialties and not during normal working hours. However, the government has banned self-employed traders from selling their wares near hotels, schools, hospitals and on main commercial streets in Havana. Policemen can be seen rounding up those believed to be engaged in unauthorized business activity. Private restaurants were legalized in mid-1995. Proprietors must pay a fee of $400 per month, purchase all food and drink at government stores, and employ only family members.

In fall 1994 farmer and artisan markets were opened. State farms and cooperatives and the country's few smallholders can sell their excess goods there after fulfilling their quota to the state. The state oversees the markets and takes a cut of all sales. There is evidence that the state keeps the prices artificially high in many of the markets.

The dollar was legalized in 1993. The state controls prices in the network of "dollar" stores it has opened, selling basic goods at prices comparable to those in U.S. stores. Cubans without dollars can purchase goods listed in their ration books at low prices in pesos-only stores, but all basic goods have been scarce in these stores since 1990.

Pricing and production controls remain in place for most state enterprises.

## Freedom to Invest One's Earnings 0/3

Given the nature of the economic system, opportunities for investment are severely restricted. There is no stock exchange and commercial lending is not permitted. The National Bank of Cuba is under the direct control of the government, though the government recently announced plans to modernize its banking system and create an autonomous central bank. Cubans can deposit pesos in state-controlled savings banks, which for the first time have begun to advertise dollar accounts paying close to market interest rates in a move perceived to allow ordinary Cubans an opportunity to accumulate capital in hard currency.

A handful of foreign banks with representative offices in Cuba lend to state enterprises but are off-limits to private citizens who hold hard currency.

## Freedom to Trade Internationally 0/2

All international trade is negotiated and carried out directly by the government. Direct participation by citizens in any foreign venture is prohibited. Attempting to leave the country for any reason without permission is a punishable offense.

According to the new foreign investment law of September 1995, foreign investors may own up to 100 percent of businesses in Cuba and enjoy free repatriation of profits. They can buy buildings, but not land. All deals are subject to approval by Cuba's Council of Ministers headed by Fidel Castro, in a process that can take up to a year. The government forswears expropriation, except in cases of national interest, in which case investors are to be compensated. Cuban exiles seeking to invest in Cuba have the same rights as other investors.

However, foreign investors still must contract employees through a state employment agency that charges companies in dollars, but pays employees in pesos at the official rate of one-to-one. With the black-market exchange rate at 25-30 pesos to the dollar in fall 1995, the state continued to pocket most of the workers' salaries.

**Freedom from Unreasonable Government Interference in the Economy**

Practically every aspect of the economy is controlled directly by the government. The farm and artisan markets are tightly monitored and there is evidence that the government manipulates the price of goods to keep them high. Limited self-employment is tightly controlled. There is also evidence that the government has penetrated the thriving black market in order to artificially enhance the value of the peso.

Massive, across-the-board subsidies to state enterprises are slowly being cut as the government attempts to narrow a huge budget deficit. The result has been mounting unemployment and a surge in black-market activities. Those with suspect political loyalties are the first to be fired.

**Freedom to Participate in the Market Economy** **1/2**

While the government woos foreign investors and tries to impose what in effect is a classic International Monetary Fund restructuring program, it continues to maintain one of the most tightly controlled societies in the world.

Cubans without dollars endure a brutish existence with no opportunity to better their lot other than by stealing from the state. Those with dollars can traffic in the black market, about the only arena for advancement in the country for most Cubans, or they can buy goods in the state-run dollar stores that are designed to suck hard currency out of the population at extortionate prices and into state coffers.

However, although racial and sexual discrimination exists, the status of women and minorities in the Cuban economy is generally comparable to that of the general population. The constitution forbids discrimination and the government has striven to ensure equal access to education and employment.

The depth and breadth of the black market indicate that corruption is now pervasive, as most Cubans, fueled by desperation and imbued with cynicism, are willing to risk arrest in order to survive.

# El Salvador

ECONOMIC FREEDOM STATUS: **PARTLY FREE**
POLITICAL RIGHTS AND CIVIL LIBERTIES STATUS: **PARTLY FREE**
PRESS FREEDOM STATUS: **PARTLY FREE**
POPULATION: **5,870,000**
PPP: **$2,250**

**Background**

After over a decade of civil war, El Salvador is trying to rebuild both its political system and its economy. A major step on the political front was the multiparty elections held in 1994. The National Republican Alliance (ARENA), a right-wing party that enjoys significant support from the business community, won a plurality in the legislature and its candidate, Armando Calderon Sol, was elected president.

Progress is also being made on the economic front. Salvadorans now enjoy a modest level of economic freedom, raised by the economic reforms of the Alfredo Cristiani administration between 1989 and 1994. What remains is the construction of a viable institutional and legal structure. Land rights for both urban and rural dwellers are still not completely protected, and the judiciary is not independent. In addition, ARENA's leaders still have a tendency to confuse policies that favor some businesses with those that promote economic freedom.

### Freedom to Hold Property 2/3

Property rights are guaranteed in the constitution but definitions and enforcement remain problematic. As part of the peace accords that ended the twelve-year civil war in 1992, the government guaranteed former army soldiers, guerrilla fighters and their peasant backers plots of land for farming. However, distribution has been slow, hindered by claims of large landowners, many with ties to the ruling party, and the destruction or loss of formal titles and other records during the war. In fall 1995 there were numerous instances of land occupations, with peasants and former fighters claiming the government had failed to meet its commitments.

Theoretically, there are no restrictions on selling or exchanging property and individuals can structure their property holdings as they choose. In general, however, property rights are inadequately protected in law and in practice. Registering land ownership and transfers is expensive and time-consuming and thus many transactions are not recorded. The result is that the land registry does not accurately reflect who owns what.

Intellectual property rights protection is inadequate and enforcement is weak, despite the government's stated commitment to improve protections.

### Freedom to Earn a Living 1/3

Although public-sector workers are unable to form unions and bargain collectively, private-sector workers can. But the current labor law makes organizing very difficult. Many companies are imposing the Solidarity system, essentially a company-union scheme imported from Costa Rica, on workers in order to undermine independent organizing.

In the fast-growing export-processing zones, foreign firms, especially Asian companies, systematically intimidate and fire workers who protest or attempt to exercise their legal right to form unions. The companies do so with impunity because the current government is anti-union and the judicial system, despite reforms, remains politicized and riddled with corruption.

Individuals can change jobs freely but for most people there are few prospects beyond the burgeoning informal economy. Wages are market-determined. Laws against compulsory labor are generally complied with. Child labor is not evident in the industrial sector, but more than a quarter million children work up to twelve hours a day in the informal sector.

### Freedom to Operate a Business 2/3

Citizens are free to establish businesses in any sector of the economy except the utility sectors. Registering is complex, although the government has tried to streamline the process. There is a sizable informal sector in El Salvador. Government procurement policies require open competition, but there remain questions about the small number of bidders and political influence. Although controls on more than 200 consumer products have been eliminated, some price controls on consumer goods still remain.

### Freedom to Invest One's Earnings 3/3

Interest rates were deregulated in 1994 and credit flows are now determined by the market.

Individuals are free to invest abroad and can hold foreign currency and securities. Rates of return on investments are not controlled.

The central bank is autonomous. At present the rate of inflation is 13 percent.

## Freedom to Trade Internationally 1/2

Import licenses are generally not required except for vegetables, animals and firearms. Tariffs on imports have been lowered to between 5 and 35 percent, and quotas and prior deposit requirements eliminated. Customs procedures are overly complicated and slow, and there is a problem with low-level corruption. There are no export taxes but exporters need to register with a government export-monitoring agency. There are no restrictions on leaving or entering the country.

Exchange controls were lifted a number of years ago and foreign exchange houses made legal.

Foreign investors enjoy unrestricted remittance of net profits, a fixed tax rate for resident corporations and duty-free import of raw materials for investors in export-processing zones However, while less cumbersome than in other Central American countries, foreign investor registration procedures are lengthy and marked by bureaucratic inefficiency and the occasional need for bribery to grease the wheels.

## Freedom from Unreasonable Government Interference in the Economy

The government share of GDP was 14 percent in 1994. In late 1995 the government encountered broad popular and union opposition to its effort to further reduce the role of the state.

Government laws and practices tend to promote competition, except in the public-utilities sector which remains in state hands. The government and government-sponsored monopolies in the export of coffee and sugar have been broken up, and the state-run grain board has been closed. However, large private agricultural enterprises still receive favorable treatment due to owners' close ties with the ruling party.

Moreover, wealthy elites are still able to act above the law because they are able to manipulate the corrupt judiciary and buy political influence at the local and national levels. Small entrepreneurs are frequently victimized by the arbitrary application of commercial laws and corruption in the judiciary.

## Freedom to Participate in the Market Economy 1/2

The small indigenous minority and women are not legally foreclosed from running any type of business or choosing any occupation. In practice, however, discrimination remains pervasive. Women do not have equal access to credit and more than two-thirds of working women toil in the informal sector.

Women also do not have equal rights regarding land ownership. Few Indians possess land titles and are unlikely to acquire them, just as they are unlikely to gain access to bank loans or other forms of credit.

The government has been working to make the changes necessary to establish a legal framework for a market economy. However, many laws are still lacking, and enforcement of existing laws remains weak because of inefficiency and corruption in the legal system. Honest and objective contract arbitration is practically impossible.

Corruption is pervasive in government and, despite an ongoing reform program, in the judiciary. Wealth and political influence invariably supersede the law. Money-laundering associated with the hemispheric drug trade is a mounting problem.

# Haiti

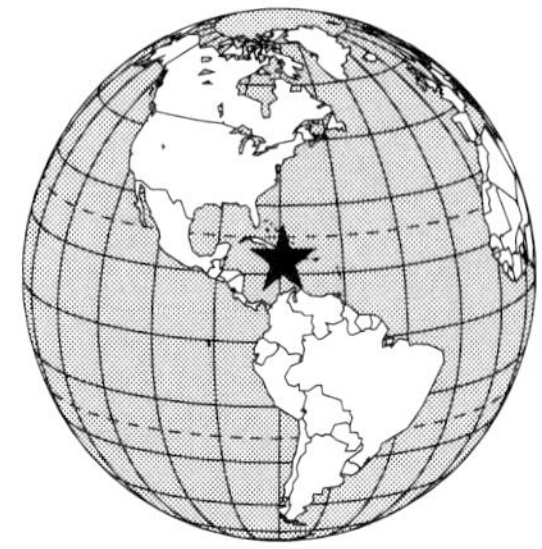

ECONOMIC FREEDOM STATUS: **NOT FREE**
POLITICAL RIGHTS AND CIVIL LIBERTIES STATUS: **PARTLY FREE**
PRESS FREEDOM STATUS: **PARTLY FREE**
POPULATION: **7,180,000**
PPP: **$1,046**

## Background

Despite significant material and technical assistance from the United States and other Western Hemisphere nations, most Haitians are no closer to economic freedom today than they were before the U.S. intervention. The Haitian government is unable to provide mechanisms to enforce contracts, secure property rights, or otherwise facilitate voluntary exchanges among its citizens. Where the government has asserted itself, as in the control of the money supply, the results have been a disaster. Those Haitians who hold their savings in the local currency, the gourde, have watched as inflation has destroyed their purchasing power.

The Haitian economy has long been dominated by an extremely wealthy and corrupt elite that has benefited from monopolies. President Jean Bertrand Aristide delayed the privatization of Haiti's nine state enterprises, which was to have prohibited the elite from participating for at least five years in an effort to finally reduce the tremendously unequal distribution of wealth in the small island country. Rene Preval, who won the December 1995 presidential election, faces popular opposition in implementing what is widely perceived to be a U.S. economic liberalization and privatization program.

## Freedom to Hold Property 1/3

The right to hold property is recognized by law, but the legal system is inefficient, lacking in basic resources, and riddled with corruption. Moreover, the land titling system is anarchic, so that property guarantees are based on power and force rather than law. In 1995 a spate of squatter takeovers of public and private land threatened to turn violent and the government seemed to be in a quandary as to how to address the issue.

Intellectual property rights protection is inadequate in Haiti.

## Freedom to Earn a Living 1/3

Workers have the constitutional right to form unions. However, the labor code is weak on protection of organizational and collective bargaining rights, and in practice labor rights are violated with impunity, particularly in the private sector.

The ranks of Haiti's unions were decimated under military rule, but some organizational structures were preserved underground. Since the return of civilian rule, unions have been regrouping, although with great difficulty because of a dearth of resources and a continuing national unemployment rate of 70-80 percent. Public-sector workers are better organized. Seventy-five percent of the private sector is controlled by mostly mulatto elites who continue to use intimidation and force with impunity to keep workers from organizing.

Wages are not controlled, but those few Haitians with steady jobs receive the lowest wages in the Western Hemisphere. Individuals are free to change jobs but there are no options.

Many peasants, who constitute a majority of Haitian workers, remain under the thumb of middlemen who dominate small agriculture and rural credit allocation. Continuing a tradition, these speculators use force to control commodity prices and hold many peasants in virtual debt peonage.

Tens and possibly hundreds of thousands of children work in rural areas and in the informal sector. Thousands of the poorest children, homeless or unable to be cared for by their families, endure a form of domestic bondage, living and working in the homes of families that are less poor.

## Freedom to Operate a Business 1/3

Haitians are free to form businesses, but because the government bureaucracy remains inefficient and corrupt, the process of legal formation remains for most Haitians unfathomable and too costly. That is why most small and medium entrepreneurs operate informally. The formal economy, much of which is nominally in the hands of the state, is dominated by a small group of mostly mulatto elites who have amassed fortunes under a string of corrupt dictatorships. This handful of families does not pay taxes and through bribery of government officials continues to control Haiti's supply of petroleum, phones, electricity, cement, sugar, flour, plastic, soap, cooking oil, steel and iron. These lawless private-public monopolies are referred to in Haiti as "The Mix." The Mix, whose tentacles reach down through Haitian society, determines the markets and sets the prices for most goods and services. Government contracts are still often controlled through the corrupt interplay between officials and the elites who dominate the economy.

## Freedom to Invest One's Earnings 1/3

In early 1995 the government began decontrolling interest rates to allow these to be determined by the market. The few foreign banks operating in Haiti extend credit on the basis of business and economic factors. Rates of return on investments are not controlled. Individuals can invest abroad and much of the wealthy's assets are invested abroad.

The central bank is not autonomous and inflation reached nearly 60 percent in 1994.

## Freedom to Trade Internationally 1/2

Under a new law passed in February 1995, import tariffs were reduced from a 50 percent maximum to 0-15 percent, with the higher rates on agricultural products. This was done to attract foreign investors, particularly in the small manufacture-for-export assembly sector. Few of Haiti's economic elites bother to pay import tariffs or taxes of any kind. Under military rule, they built a new marine terminal where customs inspectors were banned. There are no restrictions on entering or leaving the country.

There are no equity restrictions on foreign ownership except in a number of "strategic" sectors. Haiti offers tax holidays to investors and customs duties and income tax incentives to manufacturers of products for both domestic consumption and export. Investors are allowed full repatriation of profits and dividends.

The foreign currency market is deregulated and the decline of the gourde leveled off in 1995 to around fifteen to the dollar.

## Freedom from Unreasonable Government Interference in the Economy

Nominally, thirty-three enterprises are in the hands of the state, a large chunk of the economy that includes electricity, telecommunications, ports, airports, domestic banks, cement, flour and agribusiness. But many of these monopolies are dominated through corruption by a handful of elite families. Government expenditure is estimated at 14.5 percent of GDP.

Foreign donor countries have made continued aid dependent on a major privatization program that the government originally agreed to. However, in fall 1995 the government backed away from its initial commitment to sell off nine major enterprises. The government had been pressured by its own left-wing supporters, who opposed the sell-off on ideological grounds and because state enterprises remain a source of political patronage. It also was pressured by powerful elite families that did not want to give up their ability to dominate the economy.

The powerful elites are also able through power and money to co-opt the legal system in order to undermine upstart competitors, while remaining above the law themselves.

### Freedom to Participate in the Market Economy 1/2

Most Haitians are poor and black. They have been and continue to be denigrated, especially women, by powerful, mostly mulatto economic elites who prey on the state and the economy as a whole with impunity. The current government has committed itself to establishing a rule of law, but little progress had been made.

The government has verbally committed itself to a market economy and has taken a number of steps in that direction. But new laws are irrelevant to most Haitians, and until a functioning judiciary and a semblance of a rule of law are established, the corruption that permeates government and the conduct of the economy will prohibit the play of normal market forces.

## Mexico

ECONOMIC FREEDOM STATUS: **MOSTLY NOT FREE**
POLITICAL RIGHTS AND CIVIL LIBERTIES STATUS: **PARTLY FREE**
PRESS FREEDOM STATUS: **PARTLY FREE**
POPULATION: **91,840,000**
PPP: **$7,170**

### Background

Mexico gained its independence in 1810 and became a republic in 1822. The current constitution dates to 1917. Since 1929, the Institutional Revolutionary Party (PRI) has dominated the state through a top-down, corporatist, authoritarian structure maintained through cooptation, patronage, corruption and repression. Although it is too soon to draw hard conclusions, under the current administration of President Ernesto Zedillo, Mexico gives signs of moving toward a more open system.

President Carlos Salinas (1988-94) introduced a series of economic reforms and in 1993-94 joined the North American Free Trade Agreement (NAFTA) with the United States and Canada. In December 1994, a sharp devaluation of the peso weeks after the inauguration of President Ernesto Zedillo and the government's subsequent fiscal austerity program plunged Mexico into a serious recession in 1995. Inflation jumped from under 10 percent in 1994 to 52 percent in 1995. Intervention by the United States and other international donors helped to ease the crisis.

There has been a substantial liberalization of the economy in the last two years, particularly in the lowering of trade barriers. However, without political reforms, the corrupt collusion among the ruling PRI, the unions, and elite businesses and landowners remains a fundamental barrier to economic freedom. Progressive laws exist on the books yet are often not enforced in practice.

### Freedom to Hold Property 2/3

Private property rights are protected by law. In recent years, the government has undertaken a reform that has resulted in the breakup of the *ejidal* (common property) land system, but despite laws allowing this land to be privately owned, the land registry system is inefficient and record-keeping obsolete, making it difficult to realize the right in practice. Moreover, property rights protection is undermined by the lack of a rule of law.

Mexico has recently strengthened copyright and intellectual property rights laws. But again, enforcement remains weak, and piracy of intellectual property, particularly tapes and videos, is still a major problem.

## Freedom to Earn a Living 1/3

Wages and prices are controlled by the government. According to Mexican law, workers may form independent unions, bargain collectively and strike. However, in reality, the freedom to exercise these rights is circumscribed.

Organized labor in Mexico is in large measure dominated by the Confederation of Mexican Workers (CTM), which is an arm of the ruling Institutional Revolutionary Party (PRI). The government does not grant legal recognition to unions that attempt to form independently of its will. Independent unions, peasant organizations and activists are often subject to intimidation, firings, blacklisting and occasionally, violent repression. Dozens of independent labor and peasant activists have been killed with impunity in recent years, particularly in rural states with large indigenous populations.

The CTM, in turn, is a corrupt and authoritarian organization. It operates as a vote machine for the PRI during elections, as it did in the 1994 presidential elections. It inhibits strikes and has endorsed and helped enforce the government's low wage ceilings for the last decade, and it cooperates with foreign-owned companies against attempts at independent organizing in their enterprises.

Workers can change jobs, but with unemployment climbing over the last decade—steeply since the peso collapsed—the only alternative for most workers is the informal economy, which may now account for 30-40 percent of all economic activity.

Child labor is prohibited by law. However, there are numerous reports that teenage women are exploited in the *maquiladora* (manufacturing-for-export) sector. In agriculture, debt peonage is not uncommon, particularly in southern states with large Indian populations where local PRI bosses dominate local economies and the poverty rate is exceptionally high.

## Freedom to Operate a Business 2/3

Citizens are free to form and operate businesses, but the procedures can be time-consuming and costly. A 1995 study done in the state of Morelos, by the National Chamber of the Transformation of Industry, reports that to open a manufacturing business an individual must comply with twenty-six different administrative procedures and meet 107 federal, state, and municipal regulatory requirements. On average these procedures took 362 days and cost more than $5,200 per business created. Opening a retail store means complying with twenty-two administrative procedures and eighty-six regulatory requirements, which takes 294 days and costs $4,500. But as part of its Alliance for the Recovery of Economic Growth announced 29 October 1995 the government has agreed to streamline the procedures required for opening a new business.

Several sectors of the state have recently been opened to private investment—including railroads, ports, and even the petrochemical wing of Pemex, the state oil company. Pemex itself remains off-limits. Several sectors once reserved for Mexican nationals are now being opened to foreign investors, including telecommunications and banks.

Theoretically, government contracts are competitively let. However, influence-peddling and bribery are pervasive and bidding is frequently rigged. A recent scandal involving allegations of bribery on an IBM bid to sell the government aerial navigation equipment suggests that inherent corruption affects foreign players as well.

Since 1987 wages and prices have been controlled by the government through an annual tripartite pact with business and the PRI-controlled Confederation of Mexican Workers.

### Freedom to Invest One's Earnings 1/3

Interest rates are regulated. Bank privatization was completed in 1992. Directed and subsidized credit programs have been eliminated. Rates of return on investments are not controlled. Individuals are free to invest abroad and to hold foreign currency and securities.

Theoretically, the Bank of Mexico is autonomous. However, there is compelling evidence that it continues to bend to pressure from the executive branch of the government. Annual inflation reached 52 percent in 1995.

### Freedom to Trade Internationally 1/2

Import licenses have been removed under NAFTA for goods originating in the U.S. and Canada. But agricultural products and finished motor vehicles face tariff rate quotas. The 1993 foreign trade law eliminated most non-tariff restrictions and established procedures for remedying unfair trade practices such as export subsidies and dumping. There are few export controls. There are no limits on the right to enter and leave the country.

The state oil company, Pemex, is one of the few sectors of the economy that remain off-limits to foreign investment. Foreign investors cannot acquire title to residential real estate within 50 kilometers of the coasts and 100 kilometers of all borders.

Since the collapse of the peso in December 1994 the currency has been allowed to float. However, occasional intervention by the central bank in 1995 has made it a "dirty" float.

### Freedom from Unreasonable Government Interference in the Economy

Currently there are fewer than 200 state-owned enterprises. The government has privatized or shut down 900 such enterprises since 1986.

In 1993 the government passed laws to promote greater competition, limit monopolistic behavior and prohibit practices hindering trade. However, in June 1995 the Federal Commission on Competition approved the telecommunications alliance between the telephone monopoly Telmex and Televisa, the PRI-allied media conglomerate, suggesting that political power and influence continue to supersede the law.

Despite deregulation efforts, bribes, political influence and favoritism continue to define much of the regulatory landscape for domestic and foreign firms, particularly at the state and local levels. In general, despite some progress in recent years, the rule of law still exists more on paper than in reality in Mexico, and justice, whether involving contract disputes or other legal questions regarding business activity, is generally limited to those who can pay for it.

### Freedom to Participate in the Market Economy 1/2

Corruption exists in the systems of many industrialized countries, but it is a particularly severe problem in Mexico. Minimal reforms to the judiciary, which is still influenced by the executive branch, have done little to alter the situation. One bright spot is the appointment of a reform-minded attorney general from the conservative opposition party.

In lower courts and in law enforcement bribery is widespread. Direct bribes to higher-court judges are less common, but payoffs to court staff are usually necessary. Leasing and credit contract breaches can produce legal nightmares for collecting parties. Despite the presence of some honest officials in the judicial branch, legal procedures can take from two to seven years to complete. The costs put smaller business owners at a significant disadvantage relative to larger companies, which themselves must budget for the enormous legal costs of conducting business. For foreign firms it is mandatory to employ Mexican legal representation skilled in navigating a judicial-political labyrinth whose rules remain largely unwritten.

The exposure of government corruption rarely results in legal proceedings unless a political vendetta is involved. Favoritism is prevalent in the privatization process. The Federal Judicial Police are notoriously corrupt and occasionally carry out criminal actions against businesses with impunity. Abetted by Mexico's location next to the world's largest drug-consuming nation, drug-related corruption has permeated politics and penetrated certain sectors of the economy including tourism and real estate. Mexico is now one of the world's major money-laundering centers.

Racial and ethnic minorities are not legally foreclosed from any occupation or business. In reality, however, discrimination against indigenous peoples (approximately 15 percent of the population), particularly regarding land and property rights, access to credit, markets and legal recourse, is severe, especially in southern states. The result is entrenched and worsening inequities.

Women may own property in their own names and the labor code grants them the same rights as men. In practice, Mexican culture can make it difficult for women to get ahead in its male-dominated society, and women workers frequently endure discrimination and outright exploitation in both the formal and informal sectors of the economy.

# Peru

ECONOMIC FREEDOM STATUS: **PARTLY FREE**
POLITICAL RIGHTS AND CIVIL LIBERTIES STATUS: **PARTLY FREE**
PRESS FREEDOM STATUS: **PARTLY FREE**
POPULATION: **23,981,000**
PPP: **$3,300**

## Background

President Alberto Fujimori suspended the constitution and dissolved the Congress in 1992, but under pressure from critics both at home and abroad he restored electoral processes, and through a referendum realized the adoption of a new constitution, which for the first time in Peruvian history allowed a sitting president to seek reelection. In 1995, Fujimori was elected to a second term. During a visit two months before the election, Human Rights Watch noted certain practices that it believed threw into question the credibility of the electoral process. The National Democratic Institute, however, reported that national and international observer groups present during the campaign period and on election day endorsed the official election results and pronounced polling free from serious irregularities.

Since assuming office in 1990, Fujimori has pursued an economic liberalization program that has expanded Peruvians' economic freedom. Trade barriers have been reduced, a number of regulations smothering private sector initiative reformed or repealed, and a start made on constructing the legal and institutional framework necessary for a market economy to function.

For Peruvians to be truly free economically will require continued progress in removing government regulations that hinder economic freedom, the establishment of a judiciary that is independent and free of corruption, and the creation of institutions that protect the property rights of all citizens.

### Freedom to Hold Property 2/3

The 1993 constitution recognizes the right to private property. The government can expropriate private property if it deems it in the public interest, and if the legislature passes a specific law to that effect. No expropriations have been carried out by the current government.

The principal asset of most Peruvians is land, but some 60 percent of the real estate in the cities and almost 90 percent of rural parcels are not formally titled and registered because registration is expensive and time-consuming. As a result, the property rights of the majority of Peruvians are not legally secure. A new, less expensive method of titling land was used to title almost 200,000 urban and rural lots, and in November the government announced that it would undertake a program to title and register all of Peru.

There have been intellectual property rights reforms and the creation of a new semi-autonomous oversight body. Although there has been some improvement, legislation and enforcement still fall short of international standards in the areas of music video recordings and products requiring a lengthy development process.

There are a several mechanisms for resolving investment disputes, but enforcement of property and contractual rights is poor because the judicial system is slow and marked by endemic corruption. As 1995 drew to a close a major effort at reforming the judiciary was being debated.

### Freedom to Earn a Living 2/3

The 1993 constitution recognizes the right of public- and private-sector workers to organize independent unions, bargain collectively and strike. However, the new labor code restricts collective bargaining rights and does not prohibit anti-union discrimination.

Under the new code, firms can now change work schedules, work conditions and wages. Collective bargaining agreements can be suspended for up to ninety days. Workers need only be given fifteen days' notice.

Forced labor, including child labor, continues to exist in the gold-mining regions of Amazonia and the Andes.

### Freedom to Operate a Business 2/3

It is now somewhat easier for people to form businesses. New and simpler procedures for business and property registration have helped to bring many in the informal sector within the law. However, barriers to entering the formal economy remain substantial. There are still large backlogs in the registration process. Regulations and how they are applied still add significantly to the cost of doing business. For example, firms are unable to retire workers, even when they have reached retirement age.

Government contracts are let competitively, and prices are not controlled.

### Freedom to Invest One's Earnings 3/3

Rates of return on investments are not controlled and individuals can invest abroad. Credit flows are determined by the market. Foreign currency accounts are permitted for residents and nonresidents. Foreign investors are granted the same rights and responsibilities as domestic investors.

New laws and a new charter have increased central bank autonomy regarding monetary policy. Inflation has been significantly reduced through tight monetary and fiscal policies. It is the central bank's policy that interest rates for the financial sector be determined competitively, but within limits set by the bank. The large difference between the bank's ceilings and existing market rates is explained by the bank's position during the former period of hyperinflation, when immense profits could be made.

### Freedom to Trade Internationally 2/2

Import licenses have been abolished for practically all products and most non-tariff barriers eliminated. Most tariffs are now at 15 percent, but import surcharges on five basic agricultural products remain. Almost no exports require licenses. There are no limits on the right to enter and leave the country.

Peru has one of the most open foreign investment regimes in Latin America, with no restrictions on profits, dividends, royalties or capital. There are no exchange controls and rates are determined by supply and demand.

### Freedom from Unreasonable Government Interference in the Economy

The state's share of the economy was reduced from 35 percent in 1992 to 5 percent at the outset of 1995. The government's plan was to sell seventy-five state companies, of which forty-nine, accounting for about 40 percent of the state's initial stake in the economy, had already been sold by early 1995. Privatization of oil, water, steel, electricity, rails and mining was proceeding, if unevenly, in 1995.

However, the hierarchical relationships among firms have led to a structure of inefficiency and monopolistic stagnation. Business success is often determined less by competitiveness than by obtaining largesse through bribes and influence. Due to the arbitrary, though reduced, nature of the regulatory regime and an overly politicized judiciary, the potential for law enforcement favoring or punishing certain sectors or firms remains strong. State subsidies for certain sectors or firms have generally been eliminated.

### Freedom to Participate in the Market Economy 1/2

Women and the country's Indian majority are not legally foreclosed from participating in the market economy or holding property. However, deep-seated traditions of discrimination and male dominance, a weak rule of law, and widespread poverty affecting more than half the population make it very difficult for most to participate in the formal economy. The informal economy remains the principal mode of survival for a majority of Peruvians.

In the formal economy, the government has created laws to promote business competition. But enforcement of commercial law remains extremely weak, arbitrary and costly, and confidence in the judicial system is lacking. The judiciary, despite reforms in recent years, remains politicized and corruption is endemic. One businessman told a World Bank team, "we prefer paying bribes to going to court because it is cheaper."

# United States

ECONOMIC FREEDOM STATUS: **FREE**
POLITICAL RIGHTS AND CIVIL LIBERTIES STATUS: **FREE**
PRESS FREEDOM STATUS: **FREE**
POPULATION: **262,200,000**
PPP: **$23,760**

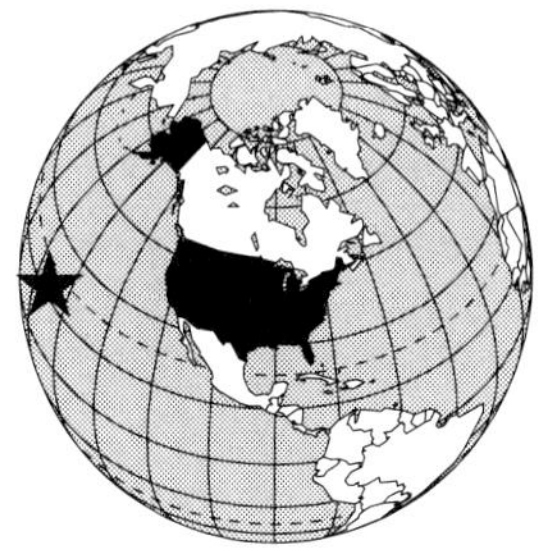

## Background

Since 1789 the United States has had elected civilian rule under a constitution providing for a president, bicameral legislature and independent judiciary headed by a Supreme Court. Although, as explained below, both the federal and the state governments infringe to some degree on individual economic freedom, by and large Americans enjoy one of the highest levels of economic freedom in the world. Compared to other industrialized nations, trade barriers are low, restrictions on private enterprise few, and direct government involvement in the production of goods and services minimal. Indeed, since the Sherman Antitrust Act of 1890 outlawed price fixing, cartels and other restrictive arrangements, free and open competition has been the official economic policy of the United States.

A strong rule of law tradition also furthers Americans' economic freedom. The common law system inherited from Great Britain continues to provide, to a large extent, a stable and predictable legal framework within which Americans can buy, sell and trade. Several provisions in the U.S. Constitution also promote economic freedom, such as those barring states from erecting barriers to trade across state boundaries and protecting private property from uncompensated government takings. In some fields, such as bankruptcy and securities, the common law has been supplanted by federal statutes that have further enhanced the citizen's ability to enter into voluntary exchanges. The Uniform Commercial Code, a codification of the common law of the merchant, has brought uniformity and certainty to a wide range of commercial transactions, again increasing the number and kind of transactions citizens can enter into, and state corporation laws make it simple and inexpensive to create new businesses.

## Freedom to Hold Property 3/3

The right to private property is enshrined in the country's Constitution, which provides that property may not be taken for public purposes "without just compensation." Property rights are also protected in many state constitutions and under federal and state laws. A major debate in the courts and Congress is now underway regarding the point at which government regulation of property becomes a "taking" under the Fifth Amendment, thus entitling the owner to compensation. The Private Property Rights Act passed by the House of Representatives in March 1995, for example, stipulates that "Private property owners are entitled to receive compensation for a 'measurable' reduction in the value of their property (defined as a decline of 10 percent or more in the property's value) resulting from government environmental restrictions on otherwise lawful use of it."

Intellectual property rights are protected under both federal and state laws. Federal statutes provide for civil and criminal penalties for the infringement of patents and copyrights, and state unfair competition laws afford trademark owners a variety of remedies against infringement.

### Freedom to Earn a Living 3/3

U.S. citizens are not restricted in choosing places of residence or employment. With the exception of setting a minimum wage, the government does not control wage rates.

Workers are free to join and form unions and bargain collectively to determine wages and working conditions. Unions are free of government control. The National Labor Relations Board regulates labor/management relations, but the extent to which its regulations favor one side or the other is the subject of an ongoing debate in the United States.

Forced labor is prohibited, and enforcement, by the federal Department of Labor and state agencies, is vigorous. Nonetheless, instances of illicit forced labor continue to occur. Migrant workers have been paid less than the federally set minimum wage, and their working conditions are often difficult. The government and labor organizations have uncovered cases of sweatshop labor in New York, San Francisco and elsewhere where immigrant laborers, both legal and illegal, are working in the garment industry for low or no wages in dangerous and coercive conditions.

### Freedom to Operate a Business 3/3

Individuals are free to form enterprises, and the formation process is straightforward and inexpensive. But depending on the type of business, federal, state, and local regulations can be an obstacle to new entrants. The public outcry over perceived regulatory excesses has led government at all levels to reassess and reduce the amount of regulation involved.

Occupational licensing of lawyers, barbers, beauticians, and other professions beyond what is necessary to protect the public health and welfare has in several instances reduced individuals' freedom to pursue careers of their choosing. Government restrictions on entry into certain businesses, such as taxi driving, also limit individual freedom. In agriculture, the peanut, sugar, and tobacco industries are essentially closed to any increase in entrants due to government regulations. With the exception of programs to assist minority-owned firms, now under intense scrutiny as the result of recent court decisions, government contracts are competitively let.

The prices of certain agricultural products and services provided by public utilities are controlled. All other prices are set by market forces.

### Freedom to Invest One's Earnings 3/3

There are few restrictions on the ability to invest, either domestically or abroad. The Federal Reserve Bank is independent of the government and is responsible for monetary policy. Americans have access to a wide range of financial options and invest heavily abroad. The government does not control the flow of credit.

### Freedom to Trade Internationally 2/2

There are few restrictions on the ability to import. However tariffs for certain goods are high and the government has imposed non-tariff barriers such as "voluntary" export restraints and import licensing. Recent U.S. actions threatening to invoke the "Super 301" provisions have contravened World Trade Organization rules. In addition, the import of many agricultural products is restricted or prohibited while other import restrictions have been put in place for exclusively political reasons. The U.S. government has actively worked to promote American exports abroad, though some licensing is required for sensitive technologies and exporting to embargoed countries. There are no exchange controls.

### Freedom from Unreasonable Government Interference in the Economy

There are very few state-owned enterprises in the United States. The notable examples are the passenger rail service Amtrak, the U.S. Enrichment Corporation, the Tennessee Valley

Authority, and certain state entities. The government heavily subsidizes the agriculture sector with price supports, quotas, and direct subsidies. Subsidies are also given to the shipping and high-tech, defense-related industries.

Although government contracts are competitively let, affirmative action programs designed to increase minority-owned business participation in contracting are under increasing attack as reverse discrimination. U.S. regulatory codes are generally applied evenly and fairly.

### Freedom to Participate in the Market Economy 2/2

There are no legal restrictions on women and minorities pursuing the occupation of their choosing or owning property, and federal and state civil rights laws ban any such discrimination. Several native American groups have cases pending against the federal government charging violation of treaty provisions relating to control over land and resources. Because minority group members and women are not represented in all occupation groups in proportion to their numbers in the population as a whole, it is argued that anti-discrimination laws have not been effective. These issues are vigorously debated in both the courts and federal and state legislatures.

The American judicial system functions well and corruption is not a serious impediment to the economy.

# Uruguay

ECONOMIC FREEDOM STATUS: **PARTLY FREE**
POLITICAL RIGHTS AND CIVIL LIBERTIES STATUS: **FREE**
PRESS FREEDOM STATUS: **FREE**
POPULATION: **3,186,000**
PPP: **$6,070**

### Background

After twelve years of military rule, democracy was restored in Uruguay in 1985. Although its current president, Julio Sanguinetti, has acknowledged the need to open up the Uruguayan economy, Uruguay has not been in the forefront of Latin American nations seeking to liberalize their economies.

The state continues to direct credit flows and maintain barriers to trading internationally. In addition, would-be entrepreneurs face a considerable amount of red tape when trying to open a new business, and there is a need for laws that spell out property-holders' rights.

### Freedom to Hold Property 1/3

Property rights are ill-defined, as reflected in cases where a firm has gone bankrupt but has not been permitted to shut down by the government. In such a case, the legal ownership of the firm and its assets is ambiguous, leaving shareholders, workers and creditors with no legal basis for securing their interests. A weak judiciary and a lack of adequate laws contribute to the uncertainty.

There are no restrictions on selling, exchanging or devising property. Individuals can structure their property holdings among themselves as they choose.

Intellectual property rights are not adequately protected in Uruguay. However, patent and trademark protection favors domestic rather than foreign firms. For example, local firms are free to use well-known international trademarks to market their own products.

### Freedom to Earn a Living 3/3

Employees are free to organize and join unions. Unions traditionally organize independently of the government and of political parties. The Workers Interunion Plenary-National Workers Convention (PIT-CNT), the country's leading labor federation, tends to be associated with the leftist Broad Front coalition.

Private-sector salaries are determined through collective bargaining. Salaries in the public sector are negotiated between the state and public-sector unions. By law, public-sector salaries cannot be raised during a presidential election year.

People may choose and change their place of employment without interference. The constitution forbids forced or compulsory labor and there is no evidence of its existence.

### Freedom to Operate a Business 2/3

Individuals can freely join together to form businesses. New enterprises do not need to be licensed except in some restricted sectors, such as passenger transport, where the number of licenses is limited. Except for micro-enterprises, direct entry costs are seldom an obstacle to entry. However, indirect costs entail waiting time and time spent complying with a plethora of bureaucratic requirements.

Private entities can participate in a number of state-run sectors. Government contracts are competitively let. However, in banking, cement, sugar, hotels, print and car repair shops, there are limits on private-sector entry due to the state's presence. Some prices are set by the state. Often its dominant position in the cement, sugar and oil industries allows it to set market prices. Sugar prices, for example, are more than double the world price, sustained by protectionist policies.

### Freedom to Invest One's Earnings 1/3

The autonomous central bank has not been able to bring inflation below 45 percent. Interest rates are not controlled though credit is rationed and subsidized by the large, intermediary role of state banks. The rates of return on investments are not controlled. Individuals are usually able to invest abroad, but there is an old legal provision requiring permission from monetary authorities to take capital out of the country. The economy is essentially dollarized, with some 70 percent of financial assets held in dollars.

### Freedom to Trade Internationally 1/2

Despite tariff reforms, two protectionist instruments are still utilized. Reference prices were introduced in 1981 to discourage under-invoicing of imports. Minimum prices were introduced in 1983 to respond to unfair trade practices. In practice, both have become instruments of protection. Since 1984 the export tax has been 5 percent. Duty drawback rates were reduced in 1991. There are no restrictions on entering or leaving the country.

Although there are a number of foreign investment regulations, they are not enforced. But because they remain on the books, investors are often confused about their applicability. There are no exchange controls.

### Freedom from Unreasonable Government Interference in the Economy

Government share of GDP in 1994 was 35 percent and public-sector participation in the labor force was 27 percent. The private sector dominates many areas including agriculture, manufacturing and services. However, the state controls vital sectors such as electricity, gas, cement, alcohol, water, petroleum refining, air transport, railroads, ports, telecommunications and many financial services.

The private sector is circumscribed by the state in numerous instances. Decision-making regarding the level and compositions of output and input, investment, savings, and sales and purchases in the domestic versus foreign markets is highly conditioned by the state. The state excessively monitors firms' exit from a sector and overly protects firms from bankruptcy through a series of legally mandated subsidies. Firms exiting a sector must endure an expensive and tedious four-to-five-year process that includes steep labor compensation costs.

Entry of new firms into several sectors is often prevented by a tight oligarchical structure. Anti-trust legislation is lacking. In many sectors, a single producer dominates the industry and protection barriers give them considerable market power. Cartel-like behavior and collusion among firms appear to be pervasive. There is a lack of impartial consumer information and protection groups. Regulations and laws at times are applied unequally because of procedural weaknesses in the judiciary.

### Freedom to Participate in the Market Economy 2/2

There are no restrictions against women or minorities participating in business. In general there are few limits on the right of women and minorities to hold and transfer property.

By Latin American standards, the judiciary is relatively free of corruption. However, it provides incomplete protection regarding contracts and transactions. Delays of up to five years in adjudicating cases are not uncommon. Judges are free to interpret the law without consideration of previous rulings, making it difficult to establish precedents. A new corporate law, while an improvement over the previous commercial code, is somewhat cumbersome.

## Venezuela

ECONOMIC FREEDOM STATUS: **MOSTLY NOT FREE**
POLITICAL RIGHTS AND CIVIL LIBERTIES STATUS: **PARTLY FREE**
PRESS FREEDOM STATUS: **PARTLY FREE**
POPULATION: **21,844,000**
PPP: **$8,520**

### Background

President Rafael Caldera took office in February 1994 in the midst of economic recession and in an attempt to spur the economy exacerbated the situation by curtailing Venezuelans' political and economic rights. Economic conditions continued to worsen, and Caldera responded with greater restrictions during 1995. No other country in the Hemisphere has suffered such a sharp contraction in economic freedom in recent times. As a result, Venezuela now has one of the least free economies in Latin America.

### Freedom to Hold Property 1/3

In June 1994 the government suspended civil liberties, including the right to private property, due process for the expropriation of property, freedom of movement, freedom of expression, freedom from arbitrary arrest and the right to participate in financial activity. These rights were restored in July 1995, but not until after the passage of four laws, including an exchange regime law that gave the executive branch enormous powers to curtail these rights unilaterally at its discretion, especially as they pertain to property and financial and economic activities. There is little recourse to the judicial system, which remains politicized, inefficient and riddled with corruption

Laws protecting intellectual property remain weak and enforcement lax, particularly as regards patents, trademark and copyright protection in pharmaceuticals, computer software and movies.

## Freedom to Earn a Living 3/3

Constitutional guarantees regarding the formation of unions are generally respected. Unions are well organized but highly politicized and prone to corruption. The 1991 labor code encourages collective bargaining and makes it illegal to dismiss employees without compensation, though the latter provision is often ignored. The suspension of many civil liberties, including freedoms of expression and movement, from June 1994 to July 1995 undermined the free exercise of labor rights.

Individuals can change jobs, but with more than half the population living in poverty and unemployment high (17-20 percent), the only option for many is toiling in the large informal sector. The informal economy provided 46.5 percent of the country's employment in 1995 according to official sources.

Although wages are not controlled, the Labor Code provides that wages may be increased by a government decree approved by the Congress. There is also a minimum wage.

Forced labor is outlawed. There have been a few reports of forced labor in isolated areas along the Brazilian border.

## Freedom to Operate a Business 1/3

Individuals can form businesses. But navigating through the bloated, corrupt bureaucracy is onerous and costly, especially for small entrepreneurs, which is why so many operate in the informal sector.

The government has been uneven and at times contradictory in promoting foreign and domestic investment in key export sectors. For the first time since 1975 it is opening its once-sacred petroleum sector to large-scale foreign investment. But it is failing to fulfill terms of recent foreign investment deals in telecommunications. Also, the ongoing fiscal crisis and strict price and exchange controls have made potential investors skittish, as have President Caldera's occasional allegations that foreign investors, the media and business are conspiring to bring his government down.

Strict price controls have been in effect on consumer goods, some services, and even films, since 1994. Gasoline is subsidized and the price set by the government, about 20 cents per gallon, is one of the lowest in the world.

## Freedom to Invest One's Earnings 0/3

Interest rates are controlled by the government. As a result of the 1994 banking collapse, more than half the nation's banks are administered by the government. The bank bailout cost the government about $7 billion. Bank solvency nonetheless remains questionable and credit remains tight.

Although the central bank is nominally independent, under the powers the executive has assumed to deal with the economic emergency its independence is dwindling. Thanks to laws passed in 1995 the executive has broad powers governing foreign exchange transactions, powers that supersede those of the bank.

Access to foreign currency is tightly controlled through the 1995 Exchange Regime Bill, which assigns jail sentences of up to five years for "misuse" of foreign currencies. Crimes include exporting foreign currency, using false data to obtain foreign currency, using foreign currency for a different purpose than the one stated upon applying for it, and not declaring foreign currency income. Penalties for currency crimes are now equal to or greater than those for drug trafficking and child molestation.

## Freedom to Trade Internationally 1/2

The government has imposed new taxes on imports as well as discretionary and arbitrary standards and specifications. As of October 1995, because of dwindling foreign reserves all applications for hard currency for imports are to be screened by a government committee. In the event of domestic shortages, the government can apply controls to exports. The right to leave the country is somewhat limited by the controlled access to hard currency.

All capital inflows must be registered with the authorities to ensure access to currency for repatriation. The registration process is multi-layered and cumbersome.

Foreign investment is limited in a number of sectors, for example, the press and media, medicine, consulting and "basic industries." The government controls the exchange rate. The rate was frozen in 1994 at 170 bolivars to the dollar, and finally devalued (from 170 to 290) in December 1995.

## Freedom from Unreasonable Government Interference in the Economy

The government owns and operates extensive portions of the economy—representing at least a quarter of GDP—and the economy overall is heavily subsidized. Moreover, the collapse of the banking sector in 1994 led to a de facto nationalization of the system. The government's tight price and exchange controls have severely hobbled the ability to conduct business both at home and externally. The official Institute for the Defense and Education of the Consumer, which some in the private sector call the "economic police," conducts raids on retailers and manufacturers accused of price-gouging and hoarding. President Caldera frequently refers to businesspersons in general as "traitors."

## Freedom to Participate in the Market Economy 1/2

The labor code prohibits discrimination against women with regard to wages and working conditions, and mandates pregnancy leave. Unions claim that most employers comply but women's groups say that some discrimination continues.

Women and minorities are not barred by law from owning or transferring property or from operating a business.

The judicial system is nominally independent. But as stated above, it is highly politicized and undermined by the chronic corruption that permeates the entire political system, notwithstanding President Caldera's anti-corruption rhetoric. Between the corruption and rigid government controls it is extremely difficult to do business in Venezuela. Normal market forces are further undermined by the vast flows of drug money that have made the country a major money-laundering center.

## Political Freedom v. Economic Freedom for Western Europe

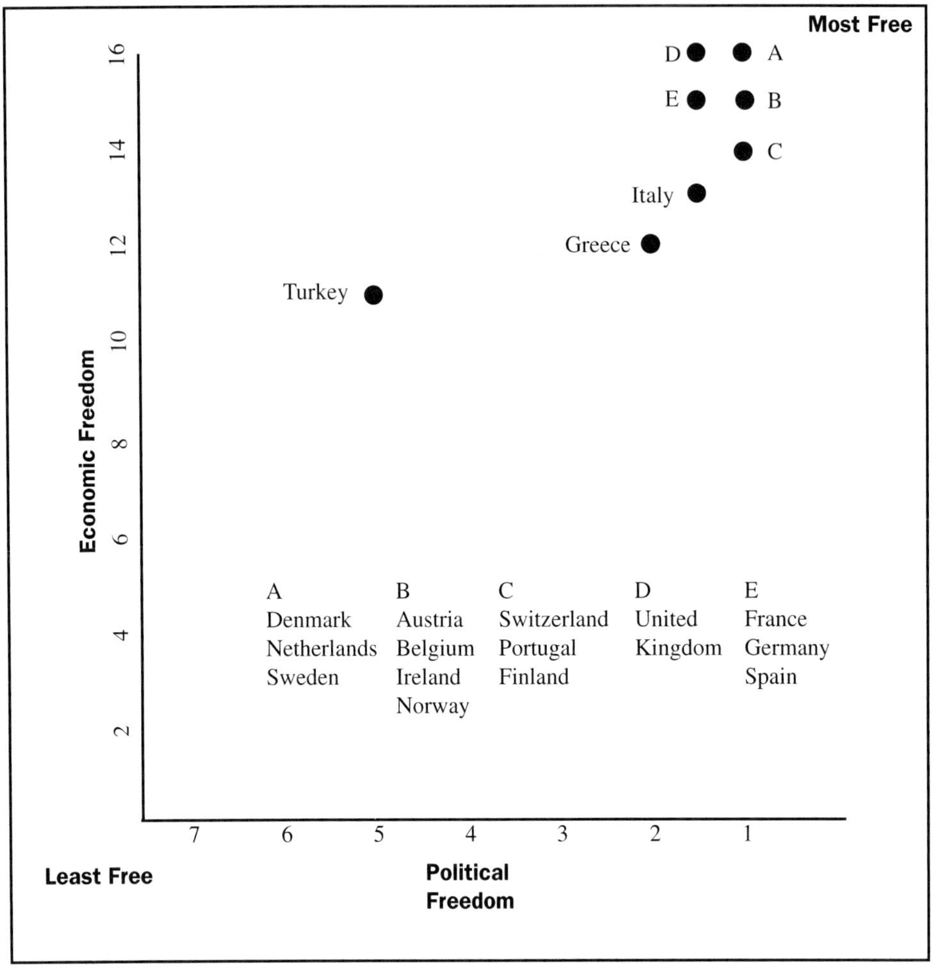


### POLITICAL FREEDOM VERSUS ECONOMIC FREEDOM

The graph above shows the relationship between the level of political freedom and economic freedom for countries in Western Europe. The ratings for political freedom were derived by averaging Freedom House's political rights and civil liberties ratings from the *Freedom in the World: The Annual Survey of Political Rights and Civil Liberties, 1995-1996*. A score of "1" represents the most free and "7" the least free.

Economic freedom is graphed on the vertical scale with "0" representing "Not Free" and "16" representing "Free."

# Western Europe

## Austria

ECONOMIC FREEDOM STATUS: **FREE**
POLITICAL RIGHTS AND CIVIL LIBERTIES STATUS: **FREE**
PRESS FREEDOM STATUS: **FREE**
POPULATION: **8,095,000**
PPP: **$18,710**

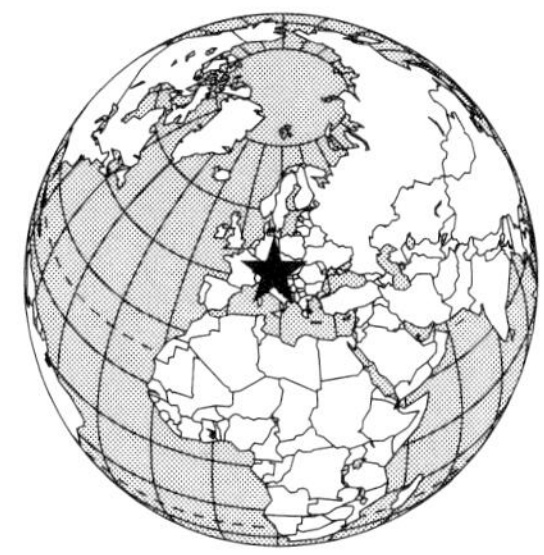

**Background**

The Republic of Austria was established in 1918 after the defeat of the Austro-Hungarian Empire and reborn in 1945 after seven years of annexation under Nazi Germany. The two leading parties, the Christian Democratic Austrian People's Party (OVP) and the Social Democratic Party (SPO), have governed the country for nine years. Austria joined the European Union (EU) on 1 January 1995, and as a result lowered a number of tariffs and further liberalized its economy. The government provides an extensive array of social services, Austrians face no significant restrictions on the rights to earn a living, invest their earnings, open a business, trade or otherwise participate in the market economy.

**Freedom to Hold Property 3/3**

The Austrian civil code provides that all citizens are free to hold property and the institutions to secure property rights are effective. Nationalization of property by the government has not been a problem in Austria. Austrian law contains a variety of provisions to protect intellectual property.

**Freedom to Earn a Living 3/3**

There are no significant restrictions that impede Austrians' right to earn a living. All workers are able to form and join unions. Although there is no legislated national minimum wage, nationwide collective bargaining agreements negotiated by the Austrian Trade Union Federation set minimums for each industry. Some factions of individual unions and the Austrian Trade Union Federation are closely allied with political parties, but there is no state control of unions and they remain a strong, independent force in Austria. Although there are no regulations that restrict individuals from changing jobs, Austrian law and tradition require that a person be certified to perform most jobs. Therefore, it can be difficult and costly for a person to make a change of occupation.

Labor is free and unforced.

**Freedom to Operate a Business 2/3**

Individuals are free to form, own, or operate a business in Austria. However, the state requires that individuals receive significant training and education before they are certified to perform certain operations. Therefore, some people may be effectively barred from certain lines of commerce that require certification in that field before being allowed to open a business. The Austrian government frequently provides subsidies to help small and medium-sized businesses.

As a member of the European Union (as of January 1995) and a subscriber to the GATT Public Procurement Procedures, Austria lets contracts competitively. Some major contracts are still negotiated by invitation, and provincial and municipal authorities are not obligated to follow GATT requirements. For security reasons, the Austrian military controls the letting of its contracts.

Price controls have been virtually eliminated in Austria. Therefore, while price controls are still legally allowed in many sectors of the Austrian economy, in practice they are no longer implemented. The Common Agricultural Policy of the EU will require Austria to guarantee minimum price levels for many agricultural goods. Pharmaceuticals is the only other major industry subject to government-mandated price controls.

### Freedom to Invest One's Earnings 3/3

Austrians have access to a full range of domestic and international financial services in which to invest their earnings. The government does not control interest rates. Credit is allocated by the market and rates of return on investments are not limited by the government. Austrian firms are free to invest abroad and capital movements are fully liberalized.

The independent Austrian National Bank maintains the schilling within the European Monetary System Exchange Rate Mechanism currency bands and has kept inflation at 2.7 percent. Despite its intention to participate in the European Monetary Union, the Bank has stated it will continue to peg the schilling to the German mark if the European Currency Unit is softer.

### Freedom to Trade Internationally 2/2

Membership in the EU will require Austria to lower any remaining import and export barriers between itself and other EU countries. All GATT signatories have been granted most-favored-nation status. Austria has lifted restrictions on imports of all industrial items with a few exceptions including weapons and pharmaceuticals. There are no significant export restrictions except on sensitive goods such as weapons.

There are no major barriers for foreigners wishing to invest in Austria, although competition in state-owned monopolies is restricted.

### Freedom from Unreasonable Government Interference in the Economy

Although membership in the EU will force Austria to privatize, the government still maintains a significant role in the economy. In 1994, one-third of Austria's workforce remained in the public sector, a percentage far above the EU average. The government continues to control broadcasting, railroads, telephone, postal services, and gas and electricity supply. Privatization attempts have been halting and limited. The government still defends its monopoly on radio and television and has frustrated any attempts to introduce private competition. Although the government had planned to sell its 70 percent stake in the country's second largest bank, Creditanstalt-Bankverein, the Finance Ministry recently announced the suspension of this sale.

Despite extensive state control, government policy generally supports competition. Monopolies and market dominance are not illegal but companies are not allowed to abuse a dominant position by price-fixing or controlling the market. With the exception of subsidies to the agricultural sector required under the Common Agricultural Policy, the majority of government subsidies are maintained to promote private industry. Most subsidies are granted to fund research and development and the creation of high-tech enterprises. As mentioned above, small- and medium-sized industries are also eligible for government support.

### Freedom to Participate in the Market Economy 2/2

There is little legislated economic discrimination against women or minorities. However, Austria still maintains a law that prohibits women from night work in most occupations. This ban is sometimes used as an excuse not to hire women and can limit the types of employment women can enter.

There are no significant cases of corruption in the Austrian economy.

# Belgium

ECONOMIC FREEDOM STATUS: **FREE**
POLITICAL RIGHTS AND CIVIL LIBERTIES STATUS: **FREE**
PRESS FREEDOM STATUS: **FREE**
POPULATION: **10,151,000**
PPP: **$18,630**

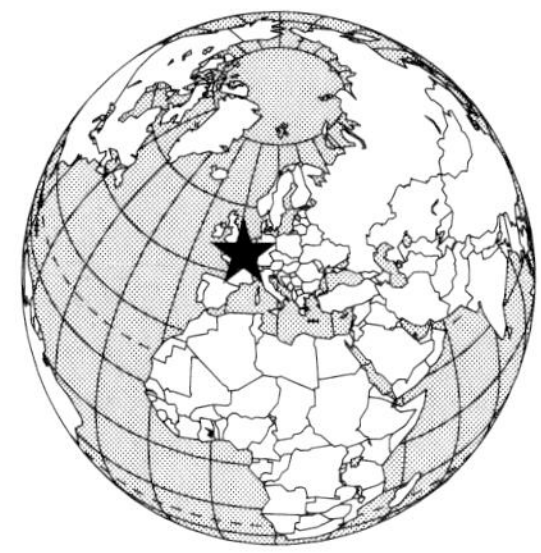

### Background

Belgium has a mature, market-based economy and its citizens enjoy the full range of economic freedoms. The country has become a major force in advocating greater European integration; however, its efforts to meet the requirements of monetary union have placed a strain on the economy. High unemployment and taxes coupled with one of the most generous social spending programs in Europe compound the burden.

An ethnically and linguistically diverse country, Belgium declared its independence from the Netherlands in 1830 and has been a constitutional monarchy since 1930. A series of constitutional amendments since 1970 has shifted power from the central government to regional councils.

Despite investigation of a national bribery scandal and predictions of significant gains for the right, general elections in May 1995 left the ruling coalition virtually unchanged. With elections out of the way, Christian Democratic Prime Minister Jean-Luc Dehaene and his center-left coalition focused once again on the country's huge national debt, nearly 14 percent unemployment, and the costly social security system.

### Freedom to Hold Property 3/3

Belgian law acknowledges the right to own and dispose of property, and the legal system protects this right. In addition, Belgium is a member of all major intellectual property agreements and effectively enforces intellectual property law.

### Freedom to Earn a Living 3/3

The government does not control wages. Belgians are not restricted in changing residence or places of work and are free to engage in most remunerative activities.

Belgians can join unions and bargain collectively. Minimum wages in the private sector are set by biennial nationwide collective bargaining. Public-sector minimum wages are determined in negotiations between the government and civil-service unions. Unions are not controlled by the government but many have informal links with political parties.

Forced labor is illegal and does not occur.

## Freedom to Operate a Business 2/3

Belgian laws governing the formation of businesses are relatively transparent and designed to encourage competition. Special permission from the government is required to open certain types of businesses including department stores, transportation, and the production and sale of some food items.

Although Belgium is subject to European Union (EU) public procurement guidelines, it has been slow to implement them. The government does not effectively advertise public procurement contracts and the process generally lacks transparency. These factors tend to favor local suppliers at the expense of foreign firms, and there are allegations of high-level bribery in the acquisition of lucrative government contracts.

In April 1993, the government revised its system of price controls, abolishing the obligation for many industries to give prior notification of price increases. Prices are still controlled, however, on homes for the elderly, residential real estate, certain breads, and compulsory insurance. Notification of price increases is still required from firms that provide public utility services such as gas, electricity, water distribution and certain types of motor vehicles. As a member of the EU, Belgium guarantees minimum prices on many agricultural goods.

## Freedom to Invest One's Earnings 3/3

Belgians have access to a full range of foreign and domestic financial services. There are no restrictions on investing abroad or holding foreign currency. Rates of return on investment are not controlled, nor does the government allocate credit. The National Bank of Belgium has linked Belgium's interest rates to Germany's, thus pursuing a strong anti-inflationary policy. Although the government owns 50 percent of the shares of the National Bank, the bank works independently of the government and inflation has stayed around 2 percent for 1995. However, since 1990, Belgium has bound its monetary policy to Germany's by indexing its currency to the German mark.

## Freedom to Trade Internationally 2/2

Belgium has implemented EU policy toward imports and exports. However, unclear divisions of responsibility among local, regional and federal authorities have led to some bureaucratic obstacles in importing certain items.

The Belgian government encourages foreign investment and there are no specific sectoral or geographic limitations on foreign investment. There are no exchange controls in Belgium.

## Freedom from Unreasonable Government Interference in the Economy

The government promotes a free-market philosophy, and state-owned enterprises constitute only a small percentage of industrial activity. State-owned industries are primarily public utilities and financial institutions, and there are very few monopolies.

Government spending is high (52.5 percent) and endangers Belgium's chances of participating in the European Monetary Union at the end of the decade. Currently Belgium's accumulated public debt equals 136 percent of its GDP, higher than the rate for the traditionally high-spending nations of Italy and Greece.

Law enforcement does not favor any particular sector or industry.

## Freedom to Participate in the Market Economy 2/2

The laws necessary for a market economy to function are effectively enforced. There are no significant restrictions on the economic participation of women and minorities.

Recently corruption charges involving the bribery of government officials in return for government contracts have surfaced, causing growing disillusionment among Belgians. It is unclear to what extent these cases of corruption have interfered with the free-market process.

# Denmark

ECONOMIC FREEDOM STATUS: **FREE**
POLITICAL RIGHTS AND CIVIL LIBERTIES STATUS: **FREE**
PRESS FREEDOM STATUS: **FREE**
POPULATION: **5,210,000**
PPP: **$19,080**

## Background

As the oldest monarchy in Europe, with a constitution dating from 1849 and a unicameral parliament established in 1953, Denmark has a long history as a model of political democracy. Queen Margrethe II has served as head of state since 1972.

In a 1992 referendum, Danish voters rejected the Maastricht Treaty, believing that increased European integration would result in a loss of Danish national identity. Despite the referendum results, Prime Minister Poul Nyrup Rasmussen's center-left governing coalition has pursued European Monetary Union-tailored economic policies since coming to power in 1994.

## Freedom to Hold Property 3/3

Denmark fully enforces the right to property. Public expropriation of private property is limited to public construction projects and there is proper compensation.

Denmark adequately protects intellectual property rights and is a member of several International Property Rights conventions and treaties.

## Freedom to Earn a Living 3/3

There are no restrictions on Danes' choice of residence or employment, and the government does not control wage rates.

Workers can join unions and bargain collectively. All workers except for civil servants and the military can strike. The unions are independent of the government and political parties. Although there is no legally mandated minimum wage, national labor agreements effectively set a minimum.

## Freedom to Operate a Business 3/3

Danes are free to establish, own or dispose of a business. Registration fees are nominal and procedures for setting up and registering a company are transparent. The government maintains a government monopoly over the Danish telecommunications network and restricts access to broadcasting. Danish business owners complain, however, that the labor market is too inflexible to meet their needs. High taxes, generous benefits, and centralized pay bargaining have made the cost of labor extremely high for small and medium-sized businesses.

Denmark is a member of the GATT Government Procurement Code and most procurement practices are transparent.

Although the government continues to have the legal authority to control prices on a wide variety of goods and services, Denmark has been steadily decreasing price controls to comply with European Union (EU) requirements. Under the Common Agricultural Policy, minimum prices on many agricultural goods are set.

## Freedom to Invest One's Earnings 3/3

The independent central bank maintains interest rates close to those of Germany and has kept inflation at 2.5 percent. Danish citizens are free to invest abroad and hold foreign currency and securities. The government does not control access to credit.

### Freedom to Trade Internationally 2/2

Denmark's trade policy is governed by the EU. Consequently, it maintains EU-mandated tariffs against non-EU countries. These tariffs generally range from 5 to 14 percent. There are no major impediments to selling to foreigners except on the export and re-export of strategic commodities. Although Denmark maintains reporting requirements on currency exchange, there are no restrictions.

Foreign investment is not subject to extensive restrictions or screening. Foreign ownership is restricted only in national security sectors.

### Freedom from Unreasonable Government Interference in the Economy

Government policy generally promotes competition and there is no tradition of strong involvement in the economy. The government currently holds stakes of at least 45 percent in fewer than fifty companies. Government expenditures equals 55.8 percent of GDP and at 50 percent of GDP, Denmark's tax burden is one of the highest in the world. The government offers minimal subsidies and is prohibited from giving subsidies to an individual firm. The Danish Competition Act of 1990 focuses on increased transparency and the control of anti-competitive practices. The government has been trying to decrease government spending and increase competition and efficiency.

### Freedom to Participate in the Market Economy 2/2

There are no legal restrictions on the participation of women or minorities in the economy. Like other Scandinavian countries, Denmark has a strong tradition of gender equality in the workplace. Approximately 70 percent of working-age women are in the labor market.

Corruption is not a problem.

# Finland

ECONOMIC FREEDOM STATUS: **FREE**
POLITICAL RIGHTS AND CIVIL LIBERTIES STATUS: **FREE**
PRESS FREEDOM STATUS: **FREE**
POPULATION: **5,084,000**
PPP: **$16,270**

### Background

The Social Democratic Party dominated the March 1995 general elections, ending the reign of prime minister Esko Aho's Center-Right coalition, which had set Finland on a course to economic recovery through strict austerity measures. Paavo Lipponen, Social Democratic party leader and the new prime minister, set out to build a broad-based and strong government by forming a coalition with the Conservatives, the Swedish People's Party, the Left Alliance and the Environmentalists.

This year's general elections produced results that were very close to projections. Former Prime Minister Aho of the rural-based Center Party had employed rather unpopular austerity measures to pull the nation out of its deepest recession this century. With the collapse of the Soviet Union in 1990, so went an enormous portion of Finland's export market. The first three years of the decade saw a 15 percent drop in GDP, a teetering banking system and unemployment as high as 20 percent. Aho's program assisted in producing an 18.5 percent increase in export volume in 1993, followed by 12.5 percent in 1994. Under his care, the deficit shrank rapidly and Finland took a step toward aligning itself to Western Europe by joining the European Union (EU).

Although the new ruling party won the election in part because of the center-right's unpopular spending cuts, prior to taking office the new coalition outlined further cuts in welfare and unemployment benefits, state transfers to local governments, and housing and agriculture subsidies. According to Prime Minister Lipponen, this government will focus on the nation's rising debt and unemployment as well as meeting the Maastricht Treaty requirements for economic and monetary union.

### Freedom to Hold Property 3/3

Private property rights are well protected in Finland and Finns are able to conduct transactions in property freely. Ownership on the Island of Aland is limited to Aland Island residents only. Intellectual property rights protection has been improved in the last five years and is now very strong.

### Freedom to Earn a Living 3/3

Workers are guaranteed the right to organize and bargain collectively. Unions are independent of the government and political parties. Finns face no restrictions in choosing and changing occupations. Forced labor is not a problem and wages are not controlled by the government.

### Freedom to Operate a Business 2/3

Although there are no restrictions against private enterprise, the level of entrepreneurship in Finland is low. There are many complex laws and bureaucratic procedures that effectively discourage the formation of small and medium-sized businesses. In addition, high taxes and inflexible labor laws make starting a business very expensive. However, there is no evidence that the regulations are arbitrarily applied or discriminatory.

With the exception of some national security contracts, government contracts are competitively let. Because of limited domestic industry, most government contracts are awarded to international firms. Procurement procedures are based on EU guidelines and apply to local as well as national agencies.

There are no restrictions to entering any line of commerce. Transportation is currently owned by the government but there are no barriers to private investment. Most prices are determined by the market but the prices of agricultural goods are kept artificially high by government subsidies. In order to be in line with EU Common Agricultural Policy levels Finland has reduced its level of government subsidies, which it is predicted will lead to a drop in agricultural prices of up to 40 percent.

### Freedom to Invest One's Earnings 3/3

Finns may invest their earnings as they wish. Credit flows are not controlled by the government. There are no restrictions on capital movement or interest rates. The independent Bank of Finland controls monetary policy and has kept inflation at just 1.5 percent despite economic expansion of around 5 percent in 1995.

### Freedom to Trade Internationally 1/2

Since joining the EU in January of 1995, Finland has discarded many of its highly projectionist policies, such as import licensing schemes and high tariffs protecting its farmers. However, non-EU producers have open market access only for items that are in short supply. Export licenses are required for certain high-technology goods including ships and scrap metal. There are no limits on international travel.

Most restrictions on foreign investment and ownership were removed in 1993. Distinctions between domestic- and foreign-owned companies were eliminated. However, the security, media, real estate, and road construction sectors are closed to foreign investment. Most foreign companies no longer need to apply for licenses but simply must register their status with the Ministry of Trade and Investment. There are no foreign exchange controls.

### Freedom from Unreasonable Government Interference in the Economy

The Finnish government controls a significant proportion of the economy. Government expenditures for 1992 were almost 43 percent of GDP, and in 1994 the state owned thirty-one major companies and many smaller enterprises operating primarily in transport, services, and special financial fields. Currently, four of the ten largest companies in Finland are government-owned. Eleven state companies in manufacturing and energy are now being listed for privatization, but there have been no efforts to privatize public companies in the transportation and communication sectors.

Although monopolies are not illegal, specific provisions of the 1992 Act on Restrictions on Competition restrict their abuse of power. This law brings Finland into line with EU competition policies, making it more difficult for companies to collude on prices and market share. Government subsidies to agriculture are high and subsidies to industry are increasing, though the government has made some efforts at rationalizing and reducing industrial subsidies. Government subsidies totaled 9.3 percent of GDP in 1993.

The links between government and industry are strong and personnel move between the two frequently. Political influence over state-owned enterprises is also strong and presents significant conflicts of interest.

### Freedom to Participate in the Market Economy 2/2

There are no legal barriers to women or minorities owning businesses or property in Finland. Corruption is not a problem and the judicial system functions well.

# France

ECONOMIC FREEDOM STATUS: **FREE**
POLITICAL RIGHTS AND CIVIL LIBERTIES STATUS: **FREE**
PRESS FREEDOM STATUS: **FREE**
POPULATION: **58,109,000**
PPP: **$19,510**

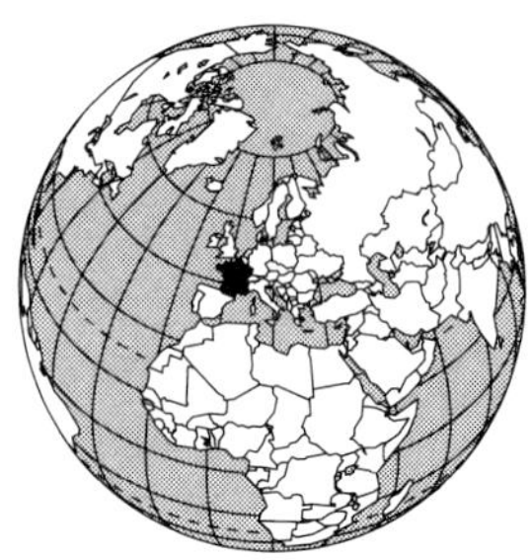

### Background

The rights to hold property, earn a living, open a business, and otherwise fully participate in the market economy are well established in France. But while these basic economic freedoms are no longer in dispute, the question of government's appropriate role in the economy is by no means settled.

Former premier Jacques Chirac of the conservative Rally for the Republic (RPR) became president in May and appointed Alain Juppe premier. Faced with 12 percent unemployment and sluggish economic growth, Juppe proposed cutting back on France's generous transfer and subsidy payments. Widespread strikes began in October as France's seven traditionally divided unions formed a common front, organizing millions of civil servants against Juppe's proposed pay freezes, job cuts and privatization. Paris was left with virtually no public services amid sporadic violence between demonstrators and police. Juppe relented after over three weeks without services, virtually abandoning his plans for pension reform and layoffs in the state railroad, France's most indebted and subsidized company.

### Freedom to Hold Property 3/3

The right to hold property is guaranteed and protected by French law. Among the European Community members, France has one of the best records in passing European Union (EU) legislation on property rights. Owners are largely free to structure their property holdings as they wish and the market for property is healthy.

Intellectual property rights are strongly defended and France has been a leader in expanding Intellectual Property Rights protection.

### Freedom to Earn a Living 3/3

There are few restrictions on choosing one's residence or occupation. Wages are determined by market forces and unions are independent of government control and very active in protecting worker's interests.

French workers may form and join unions of their choosing, and annual collective bargaining in both the private and public sectors is mandated by law. Although the International Labor Organization reported that French prisoners are sometimes made to work for private enterprises at less than minimum wage, there are no other cases of forced or child labor in France.

### Freedom to Operate a Business 2/3

The process of registering and formalizing a business involves navigating a labyrinth of red tape and licensing requirements. Both Prime Minister Alain Juppe and Finance Minister Alain Madelin have called for the cutting of bureaucratic requirements to aid small businesses. The *Centre des Formalitées des Entreprises* exists to help businesses with the registration process. However onerous the procedure may be, approval is generally transparent and automatic once the requirements and paperwork are met. Although some price controls and subsidies exist in agriculture and pharmaceuticals, most prices are market-determined. There are some unique restrictions designed to protect the identity of particular products deemed of cultural importance, such as wine and cheese.

General price controls were removed in 1987 with the Competition Law. However, prices are still controlled in the following sectors: pharmaceuticals, books, tobacco, agricultural products (in accordance with European Community's Common Agricultural Policy), coal, steel products, and those sectors with monopolies (public-sector services, telecommunications, public infrastructure, electricity, rail). The competition law bars discriminatory practices and seeks to increase transparency in government contracts, but monopolies are not forbidden. The Competition Council oversees regulations and in the last two years has gotten tougher in enforcing the law.

### Freedom to Invest One's Earnings 3/3

The independent central bank was granted statutory independence to set monetary policy in 1994 and has kept inflation down. The Bank of France has brought interest rates down to "normal levels" as promised and has kept the franc within European Rate Mechanism (ERM) bands. There are no restrictions or administrative controls on capital flows. Credit flows are determined by market forces.

**Freedom to Trade Internationally 2/2**

Import restrictions are largely in the form of tariffs determined by the Common External Tariff and the value added tax. There are no restrictions on the export of merchandise except for strategic and antique products.

Foreign investment procedures have been streamlined in recent years and most investments do not require prior notification or approval by authorities. Foreign exchange is readily available and the rate is market-determined within the ERM bands. Foreign travel is generally not restricted. However, with the recent spate of terrorist activity, foreigners from thirteen countries considered sensitive will have to obtain exit visas before leaving the country.

**Freedom from Unreasonable Government Interference in the Economy**

A venerated *dirigiste* tradition is difficult to eliminate, but over the last decade the French government has accepted that reducing its involvement in the economy is the best way to spur economic growth. Since 1993, the government has begun privatizing twenty-one state-owned enterprises, including such giants as Elf-Aquitaine. At the beginning of 1993, seventy SOEs accounted for 30 percent of French GDP, employing over a quarter of the salaried work force. The government still infuses capital into its enterprises.

**Freedom to Participate in the Market Economy 2/2**

By and large women and minorities are not legally barred from starting businesses or owning property and are protected by various laws from racial and gender discrimination. However, there are difficulties in terms of unequal pay and glass ceilings. There are increasing nationalist calls for greater controls of the immigrant community and preferential treatment for French citizens in employment, housing and benefits.

The French market is mature and sophisticated. In 1994-95 there were several high-profile cases of official corruption involving illegal funding of electoral campaigns by corporations. However, corruption is not encountered in most business functions.

# Germany

ECONOMIC FREEDOM STATUS: **FREE**
POLITICAL RIGHTS AND CIVIL LIBERTIES STATUS: **FREE**
PRESS FREEDOM STATUS: **FREE**
POPULATION: **81,704,000**
PPP: **$21,120**

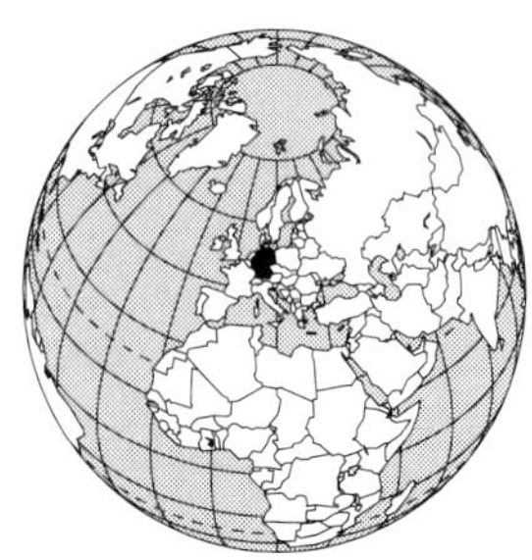

**Background**

Germany has the largest economy in Europe and the third largest in the world. Germans enjoy one of the highest living standards in the world. Five years after reunification, Germany continues to adjust. Growing social unification is apparent in the increasing numbers of former East Germans who now identify themselves simply as Germans. The economy grew by 2.6

percent in 1995, but unemployment is still rising. Entrenched vested interests have hindered deregulation, leading German businesses, especially the small and medium-sized *Mittelstand*, to move offshore as operating costs increase.

**Freedom to Hold Property 3/3**

Property rights and intellectual property rights in Germany are well defined and protected.

The merger with East Germany has led to difficulties in restitution for land seized by both the Nazis and the Communists. Over 1.1 million claims on more than 1.3 million property titles remain outstanding and have little hope of being resolved in the next ten years. The reunification treaty stipulated that former property owners whose land had been confiscated by the Nazis and the Communists would be entitled to full restitution or compensation. But this promise has been difficult to implement in practice. Lawyers have attributed difficulties to a combination of red tape, inefficiency, and above all a reluctance to return assets to their former owners.

**Freedom to Earn a Living 3/3**

Although there are no explicit controls over what occupations Germans may enter, certification and training requirements effectively serve as restraints in various occupations. German workers may freely organize and join unions of their choice and can strike and bargain collectively. German workers enjoy some of the highest benefits in the world thanks in large part to the powerful influence yielded by the *Deutscher Gewerkschaftsbund*, the Federation of German Unions.

**Freedom to Operate a Business 2/3**

The process of registering a business in Germany is not difficult, but some lines of commerce are restricted by extensive training and certification requirements. In addition, Germany's labor costs are some of the highest in the world, limiting the entry of small businesses and forcing the mainstay of Germany's economic strength, the Mittelstand, to shift their investments abroad. Recent efforts at deregulation, like the expansion of allowable shopping hours (the *Ladenschlussgesetz*), have fizzled in the face of opposition by trade union and small business interests. There are also other restrictions facing retailers. German law requires that anyone who wants to open a large store in a town needs to obtain the approval of existing competitors. The law also prohibits price-cutting prices or sales. Toys-R-Us, the ubiquitous American chain, faced difficulties obtaining permits and convincing local suppliers to deliver. However, foreign competition is slowly forcing the retailing environment to cater to consumer needs.

Prices are generally market-determined although some agricultural goods are controlled under the Common Agricultural Policy and there are caps on residential rent prices. Government procurement is competitive.

**Freedom to Invest One's Earnings 3/3**

There are very few restrictions on capital transfers and investment abroad. Germans enjoy strong banking and investment sectors with access to numerous, market-determined credit instruments. Interest rates are set by market forces, and the *Bundesbank* maintains independent control of the monetary supply.

**Freedom to Trade Internationally 2/2**

Germany has a relatively liberal trading regime, having eliminated most import and export license requirements and restrictions. As a member of the European Union (EU), Germany has a free trade agreement with other EU countries as well as with members of the European Free

Trade Association, Lome Convention, and numerous developing countries with which bilateral Guaranteed System of Preferences agreements have been signed. Imports can be restricted due to extremely high import standards.

There are no restrictions on traveling abroad and foreign exchange is easily accessible. Foreign investment is accorded national treatment and in general capital transfers are unhindered. The government does, however, have the right to restrict or prohibit foreign investment for security or policy concerns, though this power has yet to be exercised.

### Freedom from Unreasonable Government Interference in the Economy

Government consumption as percentage of GNP was 18.1 in 1994, while private consumption equaled 55.8 percent. German regulation of citizens' economic lives is extensive in social benefits and environmental protection.

Germany has been rapidly privatizing the large state-owned sector in East Germany. Since 1991, 25,000 small businesses and almost 15,000 larger firms have been privatized. In the former West Germany, privatization efforts at the federal level have reduced government holdings in companies from almost 1,000 in 1982 to 400 in 1994. Giants Deutsche Telecom and Lufthansa are slowly being privatized. However, divestment by state-level *Lander* and local governments has proceeded much more slowly. In both eastern and western Germany, the federal government has been subsidizing existing industries.

Germany has one of the world's most active anti-trust programs and few private monopolies exist.

### Freedom to Participate in the Market Economy 2/2

There are no barriers to women or minorities starting or owning businesses in Germany. Commercial laws are well defined and enforced. Although there have been some worries about small-scale corruption in Germany, most observers discount its impact.

## Greece

ECONOMIC FREEDOM STATUS: **PARTLY FREE**
POLITICAL RIGHTS AND CIVIL LIBERTIES STATUS: **FREE**
PRESS FREEDOM STATUS: **FREE**
POPULATION: **10,456,000**
PPP: **$8,310**

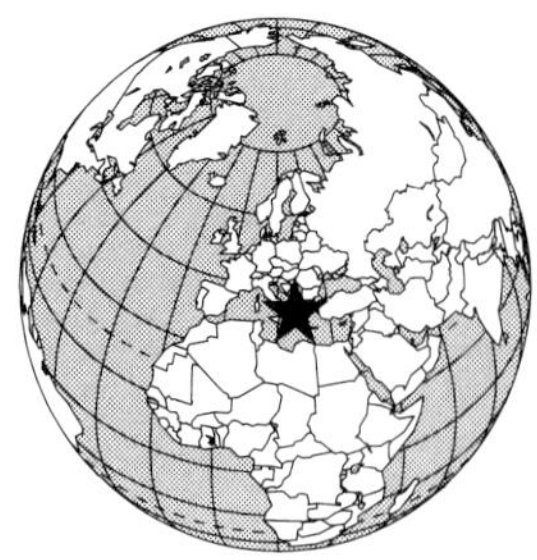

### Background

After a period of military rule, Greece returned to civilian rule under a parliamentary democracy in July 1974, and a year later the current constitution went into effect. Greece is currently governed by the Pan-Hellenic Socialist Movement (PASOK). In recent years the party has splintered into a pro-European faction seeking participation in European monetary union to combat economic and foreign-policy problems, and the more traditional, populist Socialists. In March, PASOK narrowly avoided the dissolution of parliament and an election by securing the election of popular conservative Costis Stefanopoulos to the presidency. PASOK's latest challenge has been maintaining party unity.

A member of the European Community, Greece has succeeded in reducing inflation to single digits, though still well above the desired European Union (EU) average. However, this success has been due in part to the temporary regulation of wholesale and industrial prices. High government and trade deficits and high real interest rates continue to slow economic growth.

Would-be entrepreneurs face a bewildering amount of red-tape when seeking to open a business, the government continues to allocate credit to favored enterprises, women are discriminated against in pursuing certain occupations, and corruption remains a significant problem.

### Freedom to Hold Property 3/3

Property rights are well defined and protected in Greece. There are no restrictions on property transactions and individuals may structure their property holdings as they choose. Although Greek intellectual property rights laws are in line with international standards, piracy of copyrighted goods remains a problem.

### Freedom to Earn a Living 3/3

The constitution protects the rights of workers to organize and join unions of their choice, and the right to bargain collectively is respected in practice. Unions are highly politicized and are affiliated with political parties, but unions are independent from direct government control. Wages are determined by the market and labor mobility is free.

### Freedom to Operate a Business 2/3

Greek citizens are free to establish any legal business except in the airline and public utility sectors, which are reserved as government monopolies. Government regulations can be very complex and frequently change without notification. As a result, entrepreneurs often ignore legal procedures and operate businesses illegally.

Competition for government contracts is peculiar and lacks transparency. Price controls were largely eliminated in 1992 though bread, pharmaceuticals, transport fares, insurance, and telephone service are still controlled. Rents for 60 percent of the rented residential market are also controlled. Some agricultural prices are regulated in keeping with EU regulations.

### Freedom to Invest One's Earnings 2/3

Although the Bank of Greece is technically independent, its governor is appointed by the government and it is traditional for the governor to step down with a change in government. The Bank of Greece has maintained high interest rates since 1992 to fight inflation. Credit flows are mostly determined by market forces, and a variety of credit instruments is available to the private sector. Public enterprises have traditionally had easier access to credit through the state-controlled banks, but as the system modernizes and adopts EU norms the state banking system is being forced to be more market-oriented.

Citizens are can invest abroad and hold foreign currency.

### Freedom to Trade Internationally 1/2

There are few barriers to trade in Greece other than those imposed by the EU. Greek citizens can travel abroad freely though there are limits to the amount of currency they can take with them. Most currency controls have been lifted in the past few years and medium- and long-term capital movements for both EU and non-EU countries have been fully liberalized. Short term controls were lifted in mid-1994. Despite the easing of controls, bureaucratic procedures continue to complicate and limit capital transfers.

Greece is open to foreign investment, and grants foreign investors national treatment and

100 percent ownership rights. However, many investors complain about the complexity of Greek regulations, the need to deal with many layers of bureaucracy, and the conflicting involvement of several agencies at once. Foreign investment is restricted in law, accounting, aviation, tourism and movie production. Non-EU investors face additional restrictions in land ownership and in the banking and mining sectors.

### Freedom from Unreasonable Government Interference in the Economy

The central government plays a large role in the economy, with government expenditure in 1994 at 31.2 percent of GDP. The state controls fifty-two public enterprises, social organization funds, and approximately 75 percent of the banking sector. The government was originally planning to privatize the telecommunications, electric power, and oil sectors but has opted to sell shares in the public utilities while maintaining state control over management. The state subsidizes the shipbuilding and motion picture industries.

Extensive government involvement in the economy has reduced the level of competition and hurt Greek industries. Labor laws restrict worker layoffs and Greek competition laws lack transparency.

### Freedom to Participate in the Market Economy 1/2

There are no legal barriers against women and minorities in terms of owning a business or holding property. Women have entered traditionally male-dominated occupations, though discrimination against women exists in hiring, wages and promotions.

Despite Greece's membership in the EU and apparent adoption of EU laws, many Greek bureaucratic procedures inhibit the full implementation of these laws. Corruption and government inefficiency remain significant barriers to economic activity.

# Ireland

ECONOMIC FREEDOM STATUS: **FREE**
POLITICAL RIGHTS AND CIVIL LIBERTIES STATUS: **FREE**
PRESS FREEDOM STATUS: **FREE**
POPULATION: **3,588,000**
PPP: **$12,830**

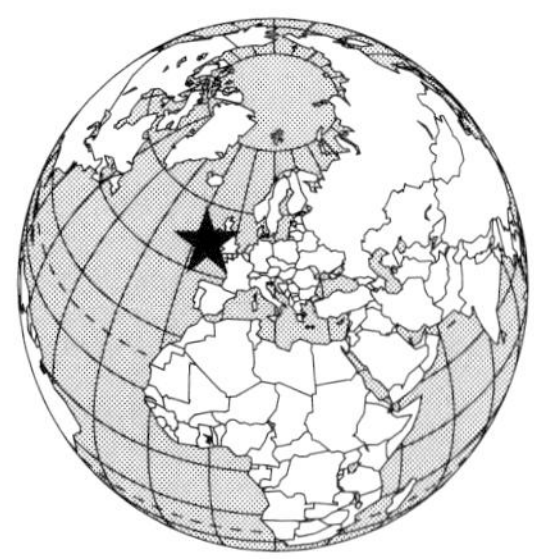

### Background

Ireland's economy is heavily dependent on trade, and the nation joined the European Union in 1973. Unemployment and government debt remain very high. The ruling conservative coalition of *Fine Gael* (Family of the Gaels) faces the challenge of reducing both, as Ireland prepares to join the initial group of European Monetary Union countries. The economy grew by 4 percent during 1995 while inflation has remained low. With the exception of some restraints on citizens' freedom to trade internationally, the Irish enjoy a full range of economic freedoms.

### Freedom to Hold Property 3/3

The right to own private property is protected by law. There are no restrictions on selling, transferring or structuring property holdings. Intellectual property rights are protected by laws that are consistent with international legal norms.

### Freedom to Earn a Living 3/3

There are no restrictions on choosing one's place of residence or employment. Wages are market-determined and workers are free to join or form unions and engage in collective bargaining. Unions are independent of the government and political parties.

### Freedom to Operate a Business 3/3

It is not difficult to start a business in Ireland and the right to establishment is protected by law. Since Ireland is a member of the European Union (EU), some agricultural prices are controlled. The government maintains monopoly control in some sectors but the economy is otherwise open to private investment. Ireland has an extensive social welfare system that has made labor costs excessively high.

### Freedom to Invest One's Earnings 3/3

There are few restrictions on investing earnings. The independent central bank has maintained a tight monetary policy to keep inflation down. Credit flows are determined by the market, and various credit instruments are available to Irish investors. There are no restrictions on capital investment abroad.

### Freedom to Trade Internationally 1/2

Ireland maintains among the strictest animal and plant health import restrictions in the EU. These restrictions, coupled with EU import duties, effectively prevent many meat-based foods, fresh vegetables and other agricultural products from being imported. Aside from this, Ireland does not have significant barriers to trade. Exchange controls have been liberalized in accordance with EU standards and exchange controls for foreign travel have been eliminated.

Foreign investment requires the approval of the Central Bank, as does the remittance of profits and the repatriation of capital. However, these regulations are routine and are for monitoring purposes only. Foreign investment is allowed in every sector except those deemed sensitive to national security. In addition, foreigners are not allowed to own agricultural land except for stud farms.

### Freedom from Unreasonable Government Interference in the Economy

The state seldom interferes with business but it does control industries in the airline, energy, communications, steel and forestry sectors. The government has been slowly reducing its holdings though the ruling coalition has halted privatization for now. The government also provides the agricultural sector with subsidies.

Government regulations are transparent and effective. Competition is fostered by the Competition Act of 1991, which provides the legislative framework for control of anti-competitive practices and dominant market positions.

### Freedom to Participate in the Market Economy 2/2

There are no legal barriers to women or minorities owning property or businesses. Although the Anti-discrimination Act of 1974 and the Employment Equality Act of 1977 provide for protection and redress against gender discrimination, women face inequality in pay and promotion in both the private and public sectors.

Corruption is not a widespread problem and the legal system is effective.

# Italy

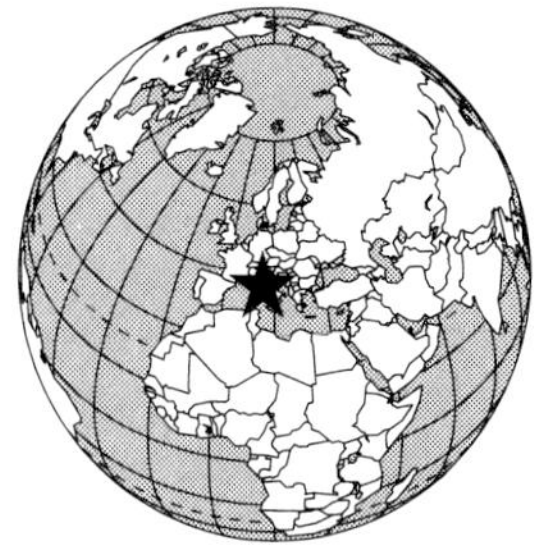

ECONOMIC FREEDOM STATUS: **FREE**
POLITICAL RIGHTS AND CIVIL LIBERTIES STATUS: **FREE**
PRESS FREEDOM STATUS: **FREE**
POPULATION: **57,675,000**
PPP: **$18,090**

## Background

Modern Italian history dates from nineteenth-century unification as a parliamentary monarchy under the House of Savoy. After a twenty-one-year period under fascist dictator Benito Mussolini beginning in 1922, the monarchy was abolished by popular referendum and a provisional government was established to oversee the transformation to a republic under a new constitution effective January 1948. The ensuing four decades saw over fifty governments, most dominated by the Christian Democratic Party.

As the traditional postwar political system collapsed under the weight of rampant corruption, billionaire media tycoon Silvio Berlusconi launched his Forza Italia movement, forged a rightist coalition with the Northern League and the fascist-oriented MSI/National Alliance party, and captured a parliamentary majority in March 1994. The Northern League withdrew its support less than a year later, however, and Berlusconi's government fell. In spite of persistent center-right efforts to topple his government and force early elections, new Prime Minister Lamberto Dini survived 1995 while methodically holding to his self-declared mandate.

Economic growth slowed in the last quarter of 1995 to below the anticipated 3 percent. Unemployment remains at around 11 percent. Political instability has hindered efforts at deregulation and economic reform though privatization is making progress. Italy's 200,000 laws hinder rather than promote the rule of law, fostering corruption and neglect. A massive anticorruption campaign over the last four years has led to the arrest of thousands of high-level politicians and business figures.

## Freedom to Hold Property 2/3

Italians are able to own property and can sell, exchange and structure their property holdings as they choose. Intellectual property protection has been problematic, particularly for computer software and films.

## Freedom to Earn a Living 3/3

Workers in Italy are free to form and join trade unions of their own choosing and enjoy the right to bargain collectively. Unions are free of government controls and have loosened their ties with political parties. Wages are determined through national collective bargaining agreements and workers are free to choose their occupations.

## Freedom to Operate a Business 2/3

Italians are able to open and operate business entities and then dispose of them. However, starting a business means navigating an extensive bureaucracy and dealing with corruption. Smaller businesses are at a distinct disadvantage in the face of huge conglomerates. The banking sector has been described as effectively closed to new entrants due to close ties between the dominant Mediobanca and client industries.

The government operates several monopolies, including the petroleum, railroad, electrical and tobacco industries. Government procurement procedures are highly fragmented and lack transparency, fostering an environment where corruption is rife and local as well as foreign businesses are often shut out of government contracts. To remedy the situation, the Parliament introduced legislation to increase transparency in the process and create monitoring mechanisms. The law will go into effect in 1996. Prices are largely market-determined except for rental property and pharmaceuticals. However, the government has the right to determine other prices under the seldom-invoked Price Control Act.

### Freedom to Invest One's Earnings 3/3

Since 1990, there have been few restrictions on Italians investing domestically or abroad. In preparation for monetary union, the Bank of Italy has gained autonomy in formulating the discount rate and interest rates charged for open market operations. Credit flows are determined by market forces.

### Freedom to Trade Internationally 2/2

With the exception of a few agricultural items, most goods can be imported without constraints from licensing or quantitative limits. An exception includes textiles, which require a license that is generally granted automatically. As a member of the European Union, Italy bases its tariffs on the international harmonized system of product classification. There are few export restrictions and Italy has an extensive array of export promotion programs ranging from export subsidies to assistance in improving competitiveness. There are no restrictions on traveling abroad.

Foreign investment is encouraged, but the multitude of approvals and permits required by the Italian bureaucracy for industrial projects can intimidate the novice investor. While most foreign investment proposals receive close scrutiny, several sectors are closed to foreign investment including the domestic airline, airline manufacturing, banking, insurance, and the state monopolies mentioned above. The last remaining foreign exchange restrictions were removed in 1990.

### Freedom from Unreasonable Government Interference in the Economy

The government has traditionally had a significant presence in the economy, controlling over a third of all industry and over two-thirds of all banking operations before the privatization drive began in 1992. The role of the state is declining but remains formidable, with government expenditures comprising 52 percent of GDP. The state operates several monopolies including the petroleum, railroad, electrical production, and tobacco sectors. Privatization has been delayed frequently by political infighting and bureaucratic snags, but the placement of the state petroleum company ENI on the international market offers hope that the sale of Italy's principal government-owned assets may finally take place.

Competition is inhibited by the prevalence of family empires and dynastic alliances in Italian business. Italy's banking sector is dominated by the giant Mediobanca, which has used its position to prevent the entry of competitors and squelched efforts by other banks to introduce new financial instruments. The Antitrust Authority finally opened an investigation in July 1995. Italy has over 200,000 statutes (compared with 10,000 in most Western industrialized countries) that create a regulatory nightmare for businesses. Many regulations are simply ignored and the possibility of corruption is high.

Government subsidizes small and medium-sized enterprises as well as the steel and shipbuilding industries. Subsidies are also used to foster high technology industries and investment in the economically depressed south.

**Freedom to Participate in the Market Economy 1/2**

Laws intended to protect women from hazardous conditions have in turn restricted their entry into several occupations. For instance, women are prohibited from being employed underground in quarries, mines, or tunnels. There are no restrictions on women in the ownership or transfer of businesses or property. There are no legal barriers to minorities owning or transferring business or property, though there has been a recent increase in the number of racial attacks against immigrants, and Roma (Gypsies) in particular.

Corruption is a serious problem in Italy, ranging from low-level corruption involving local officials to the highest levels of government. Despite recent crackdowns, organized crime continues to control certain sectors and collusion between government officials and Mafia is a problem. Public works contracts had been frozen for over a year because of investigations into corruption. Lack of transparency in government contracting and the arbitrary applications of the huge regulatory regime foster an environment in which corruption thrives.

# Netherlands

ECONOMIC FREEDOM STATUS: **FREE**
POLITICAL RIGHTS AND CIVIL LIBERTIES STATUS: **FREE**
PRESS FREEDOM STATUS: **FREE**
ECONOMY: **Mixed capitalist**
POPULATION: **15,459,000**
PPP: **$17,780**

**Background**

The Dutch won independence from Spain in the sixteenth century, whereupon the governors of the House of Orange assumed rule of the United Provinces of the Netherlands. A constitutional monarchy based on representative government emerged at the close of the Napoleonic period. The present monarch, Queen Beatrix, appoints the arbiters of executive authority, the Council of Ministers, as well as the governor of each province. The bicameral States General (parliament) consists of an indirectly elected First Chamber and a larger and more powerful directly elected Second Chamber.

As postwar prosperity has devolved into economic stagnation, the country has felt pressured by international competition to shed some of the excesses of a social welfare system that favors inactivity over labor. For every hundred workers, there are eighty-five people living on some form of public assistance. Much recent political upheaval stems from the debate over austerity measures and controversial Christian Democratic Appeal (CDA) proposals to freeze pensions and benefits. In the May 1994 general election, the Liberal party relegated the CDA to the opposition for the first time in modern Dutch politics.

**Freedom to Hold Property 3/3**

Property ownership is guaranteed and unrestricted. Dutch citizens are free to sell and transfer their property, and the legal system gives adequate protection to property claims. Intellectual property is also protected by the law. The Netherlands belongs to the World Intellectual Property Organization, is a signatory to the Paris Convention for the Protection of

Industrial Property, and conforms to accepted international practices for the protection of technology and trademarks.

### Freedom to Earn a Living 3/3

Dutch residents are not prohibited from entering any line of work. Workers are free to form and join unions and bargain collectively with employers for wages and working conditions. Unions are free of control by the government and political parties. Forced labor is prohibited and the law is effectively enforced. With the exception of a legally determined minimum wage, wages are determined by market forces.

### Freedom to Operate a Business 3/3

Dutch citizens are free to establish businesses in all sectors except state-sanctioned monopolies. These include the defense, aviation, shipping, electric power, gas, water, television, radio, and railroad industries. Although the Netherlands has a complex business culture where companies, unions, and government agencies often engage in close and constant consultation, the formation of a business enterprise is not difficult.

Government contracts are competitive and there is a strong effort to "buy European." Procurement policies are in line with European Union (EU) guidelines and agricultural prices are controlled. Prices for other goods and services produced by the private sector are determined by market forces.

### Freedom to Invest One's Earnings 3/3

There are few restrictions on investing one's earnings in the Netherlands. Capital flows are unrestricted and the Dutch invest heavily abroad. The Central Bank, De Nederlandsche Bank, has independent control over monetary policy.

### Freedom to Trade Internationally 2/2

Historically a trading state, the Netherlands places few barriers on international trade. Certain strategic or environmentally harmful imports require licenses, but otherwise import tariffs and export taxes are based on EU guidelines. There are no restrictions on traveling abroad and there are no exchange controls.

Foreign investment policies are very liberal and foreigners are free to invest in all parts of the economy except those where public and private monopolies exist.

### Freedom from Unreasonable Government Interference in the Economy

The country's consensus society has led to a corporatist model in which economic decisions are made in consultations among government officials, labor unions, business leaders, and academics. The government has been moving toward a more liberalized economy through the privatization of the telecommunications and transportation sectors, with electricity not far off. Total government expenditures in 1993 represented almost 54 percent of GDP. There is growing public support for a smaller state sector and a less comprehensive social security system.

The state utilizes investment incentives to facilitate economic restructuring and promote social and economic welfare policies. Subsidies are available to both foreign and domestic investors and usually take the form of tax credits. The state also gives investment subsidies for economically depressed regions. However, the subsidy program is well defined and there are no reports of unfair use of subsidies or law enforcement.

### Freedom to Participate in the Market Economy 2/2

There are no restrictions on women's and ethnic minorities' ability to own property and operate businesses. Women are increasingly entering the job market despite traditional constraints and now comprise over 40 percent of the Dutch workforce.

The Dutch legal system is strong and corruption is not a significant problem.

# Norway

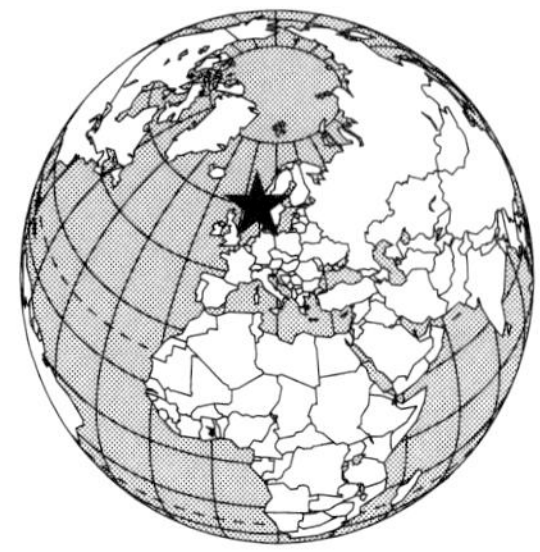

ECONOMIC FREEDOM STATUS: **FREE**
POLITICAL RIGHTS AND CIVIL LIBERTIES STATUS: **FREE**
PRESS FREEDOM STATUS: **FREE**
ECONOMY: **Mixed capitalist**
POPULATION: **4,344,000**
PPP: **$18,580**

### Background

Norway is a constitutional monarchy. The present minority Labor government, led by Prime Minister Gro Harlem Brundtland, was formed following the 1993 general election in which Labor carried only 37 percent of the vote. In 1994, a coalition of environmentalists, leftists, nationalists, and rural and fishing lobbies defeated a proposal backed by the prime minister to join the European Union (EU). Despite fears that a failure to join the EU would dampen economic growth, during 1995 the economy grew by 4.5 percent while Norway enjoyed one of the lowest unemployment rates in Europe.

However, such figures mask Norway's high dependence upon North Sea oil and gas revenues and the relative weakness of the non-petroleum economy. The EU has been receptive to Brundtland's efforts toward a shadow membership, and Norway will be joining the Shengen agreement, which will lower trade barriers among EU countries. The Norwegian government has established the Petroleum Fund, investing surplus oil revenues abroad in anticipation of decreasing oil profits in the decades to come. State participation in the economy is very high, with the government owning half of the businesses in Norway.

### Freedom to Hold Property 3/3

Norway protects the right to property and provides adequate protection of intellectual property rights.

### Freedom to Earn a Living 3/3

Workers can join unions and strike. All workers, including government employees and military personnel, may bargain collectively. The largest trade union is associated with the labor party but all unions are free of government control. The government does not control wages, and does not impose a minimum wage law. Nonetheless, wages normally fall within the wage scale negotiated by labor, employers, and the government.

### Freedom to Operate a Business 3/3

All Norwegian citizens are free to establish and own business enterprises. Investors, however, are barred from investing in industries controlled by state monopolies in postal services, railways, and the production and sale of alcohol. Labor costs are extremely high in Norway and may discourage small entrepreneurs. The tax system is also biased against small and medium-sized enterprises.

Most government procurement contracts are competitively let and the process is transparent. There have been no general price controls since 1990.

### Freedom to Invest One's Earnings 3/3

Norwegians are free to invest abroad and hold foreign shares, bonds and other securities. Norwegians may open accounts abroad and receive loans from overseas, but they must report these transactions to the Bank of Norway.

The Bank of Norway operates independently of the government. Like many of the Scandinavian countries, Norway briefly pegged its currency to the European Currency Unit in 1990 in order to control inflation and stabilize the currency. In the face of rising interest rates, however, Norway quickly unpegged the currency and let it float freely. Currently, Norway maintains a very low inflation rate of approximately 1 percent.

### Freedom to Trade Internationally 1/2

Norwegians recently rejected an opportunity to join the European Union. Nevertheless they are generally strong supporters of open world markets. The Norwegian government does use protectionist procedures to protect some domestic industries, particularly agriculture and retailing. It maintains tight import regulations on agricultural commodities and approval requirements for telecommunications equipment. Norway encourages exports and has an Export Council that helps firms to market their goods abroad more effectively.

Norway welcomes foreign investment but restricts foreign ownership in several areas including financial services, mining, hydropower and acquisition of some property regarded as politically sensitive. The government is in the process of liberalizing its foreign investment legislation.

Since 1990, Norway has abolished virtually all remaining foreign exchange controls.

### Freedom from Unreasonable Government Interference in the Economy

Like most Scandinavian countries, Norway promotes free-market policies but supports an extensive welfare state. The government maintains monopolies over grain, pharmaceuticals, railways and some bus and ship routes. Norway controls or owns most firms in the oil and gas industry, and the telecommunications and commercial banking sectors. Recent banking crises caused the government to nationalize several of the country's largest banks and it is unclear whether this ownership will become permanent. Norway maintains high subsidies for its industry—approximately 7 percent of GDP in 1992, well above the OECD average. In addition, Norwegian farmers have the highest level of government support in the world.

In general, the government has adopted laws to foster competition. The Competition Act of 1993 strengthens Norway's anti-monopoly law and allows the government to break up any business arrangement that might hinder competition.

### Freedom to Participate in the Market Economy 2/2

There are no significant cases of discrimination against women or minorities. Approximately 70 percent of working-age women are employed. Corruption has not been a problem.

# Portugal

ECONOMIC FREEDOM STATUS: **FREE**
POLITICAL RIGHTS AND CIVIL LIBERTIES STATUS: **FREE**
PRESS FREEDOM STATUS: **FREE**
POPULATION: **9,424,000**
PPP: **$9,850**

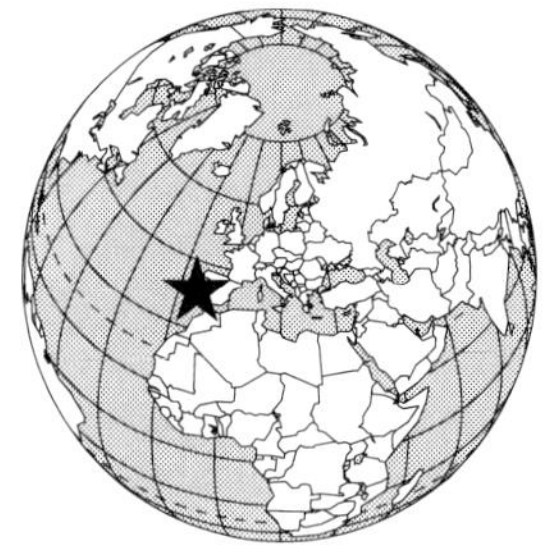

## Background

After leading his Social Democratic Party to two absolute majorities in 1987 and 1991, Prime Minister Anibal Cavaco Silva stepped down as party leader, opting to enter the presidential race rather than face the possibility of heading an unstable minority or coalition government. His successor, former defense minister Fernando Nogueira, was defeated by Antonio Guterres whose Socialist Party won over 43 percent of the vote and fell just short of a parliamentary majority. The new prime minister faces the task of bringing Portugal into closer integration with the European Union (EU) and preparing a 1997 budget that will qualify the small, vulnerable economy for the European single currency by 1999.

Cavaco Silva's ascension to power marked the end of a period of political and economic instability. He oversaw the country's entry into the European Community (EC) in 1986 and a subsequent influx of EC funds largely responsible for an era of modernization and economic stabilization.

With the few exceptions noted below, Portuguese citizens enjoy a full range of economic freedom, and there is now a consensus on the desirability of maintaining such freedoms. The platforms upheld by both Social Democrats and Socialists in the latest parliamentary elections were virtually identical, with the focus mainly on free-market policies and closer integration into the EU.

## Freedom to Hold Property 3/3

There are no legal restrictions on owning property, and property rights are well protected by law. During the 1974 revolution, however, several companies were nationalized and many previous owners complain that they were not adequately compensated. As a member of the EU, Portugal is committed to its privatization programs and it is unlikely that expropriation will be an issue in the future.

Portugal is now a member of several intellectual property conventions and agreements, but in the past it has not adequately protected intellectual property. In 1989 it was placed on an international "watch list" of countries with deficient intellectual property rights protection but was removed from the list in 1990 after taking steps to remedy the problem. Today its enforcement of intellectual property rights is considered quite advanced.

## Freedom to Earn a Living 3/3

All workers are able to join unions and bargain collectively. Unions are independent from the government but are closely connected with political parties. Minimum-wage legislation applies to all full-time workers. There are no restrictions on the ability to change occupations. Forced labor is outlawed and the law is effectively enforced.

**Freedom to Operate a Business 2/3**

There are no significant restrictions to opening a business in Portugal but entry is prohibited into some sectors, including telecommunications, armaments and postal services. Portugal follows the EU directive to the GATT Government Procurement Code and its procedures are transparent. Portugal has eliminated most price controls, but those on electricity, water, and pharmaceuticals remain.

**Freedom to Invest One's Earnings 2/3**

In accordance with EU policy, the Bank of Portugal has liberalized nearly all remaining capital flow restrictions. Credit flows are determined by market forces. Prior approval from the Finance Ministry, however, is still required in order to issue foreign securities in the domestic capital market, issue domestic securities in a foreign capital market, and invest abroad in order to establish branches of credit institutions and financial companies in non-EU countries.

The Bank of Portugal controls interest rates and traditionally maintains a high rate. The Bank recently received greater independence from the government to formulate monetary and exchange rate policies.

**Freedom to Trade Internationally 2/2**

Portugal implements EU import and export regulations and has no exchange-rate controls.

Portugal actively seeks foreign investment and provides a number of incentives to encourage it. Foreign investment is permitted in virtually all sectors open to domestic private investment.

**Freedom from Unreasonable Government Interference in the Economy**

Although the government has implemented an extensive privatization program, public expenditures still account for 52 percent of GDP, higher than the OECD average. Privatization has been initiated in several industries including banking, insurance, cement, petroleum, transport, steel and chemicals. The government subsidizes several industries including tourism and housing rentals.

**Freedom to Participate in the Market Economy 2/2**

There are no significant restrictions on women or minorities, and Portugal's diverse population is well represented in its economy.

The previous administration was marred by corruption scandals.

# Spain

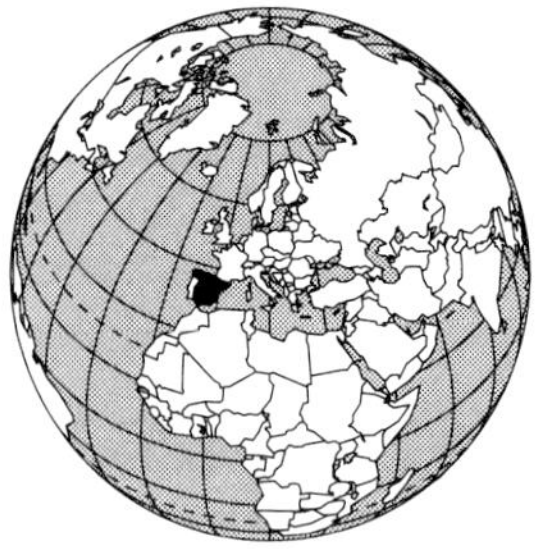

ECONOMIC FREEDOM STATUS: **FREE**
POLITICAL RIGHTS AND CIVIL LIBERTIES STATUS: **FREE**
PRESS FREEDOM STATUS: **FREE**
POPULATION: **37,398,000**
PPP: **$13,400**

## Background

Spain has been a democracy since 1977, and for the most part Spanish citizens now enjoy a full range of economic freedoms. But corruption and unequal application of the laws remain a problem.

Although Spain rotated into the presidency of the European Union (EU) this year, the country has been having difficulty meeting the requirements of the Maastricht Treaty. Necessary steps include reducing government spending and lowering inflation. In March 1995, the government announced that it would create a legal framework for the privatization of state enterprises in an effort to raise revenue and bring economic policy in line with the rest of the EU. Unemployment is estimated to be 23 percent despite labor reforms in 1994.

## Freedom to Hold Property 3/3

The Spanish constitution establishes the right of private ownership. The Spanish legal system protects property rights, but court action may be slow.

Intellectual property rights, however, have traditionally not been well protected. Since 1989, Spain has been on the international "watch list" under the Special 301 provision of the 1988 Trade Act for failing to adequately enforce intellectual property law. Recent legislation and increased enforcement efforts have increased the number of criminal and civil actions taken against violators of intellectual property laws.

## Freedom to Earn a Living 3/3

With the exception of military personnel, judges, magistrates, and prosecutors, all workers are allowed to form unions. Collective bargaining has been allowed since 1980. In 1990 public-sector collective bargaining was broadened to include salaries and employment levels. All unions are independent of the government and political parties. There is a legal minimum wage, which is revised annually. While individuals technically can change jobs freely, strict regulations can limit the geographic and functional mobility of workers. Forced labor is prohibited by law.

## Freedom to Operate a Business 3/3

All citizens are free to establish and own businesses. The process of starting and registering a business is not difficult in Spain. The local regulatory framework compares favorably with those of other major European nations. Bureaucratic procedures have been streamlined and most red tape eliminated. Private firms are not barred from entering any line of commerce.

Spain acceded to the GATT Government Procurement Code when it joined the EU in 1986, but did not implement the code until 1992. The government now follows a relatively transparent policy. Price controls have been eliminated except in those sectors where a monopoly controls supply. As a member of the EU, Spain has guaranteed minimum prices on many agricultural products.

**Freedom to Invest One's Earnings 3/3**

Spanish citizens are now free to invest abroad and hold foreign currency and securities. Remaining foreign exchange and capital controls were eliminated in 1992. The Spanish government encourages investment abroad in order to diversify the country's industrial base. The Bank of Spain has gradually gained complete independence from the government and now has the autonomy to adjust interest rates to ensure price stability.

**Freedom to Trade Internationally 2/2**

Since 1993, Spain has harmonized its tariff and export policies with those of the EU. Spain encourages foreign investment and allows 100 percent foreign ownership except in a small number of strategic sectors. Prior authorization is required for foreign investment in munitions companies and telecommunications services. All exchange controls were lifted in February 1992.

**Freedom from Unreasonable Government Interference in the Economy**

The government maintains extensive influence in the economy but has committed itself to a privatization program. Currently the government exercises monopoly control over postal services and major railways. In 1991 most government-owned banks were gathered into one corporation, Argentaria. Since 1993, Spain has sold most of the capital in this corporation. It has conducted similar partial privatizations in the oil, electricity, telephone, and airline industries.

The government continues to subsidize the production of steel, shipbuilding, textiles, and household appliances. In addition, the government recently offered a subsidy to help citizens purchase new cars when they traded in their ten-year-old cars. Although the government has made moves to end this subsidy, car producers have lobbied for it to continue.

**Freedom to Participate in the Market Economy 1/2**

Minorities and women are generally free to pursue economic opportunities and there are no reports of significant discrimination.

Several corruption scandals have surfaced in Spain since 1990. The scandals have touched members of the government and the former governor of the Bank of Spain. Government officials have been accused of forcing state-owned companies to make contributions to the ruling Socialist party, among other allegations. It is unclear how significantly these events have affected the functioning of the market economy.

# Sweden

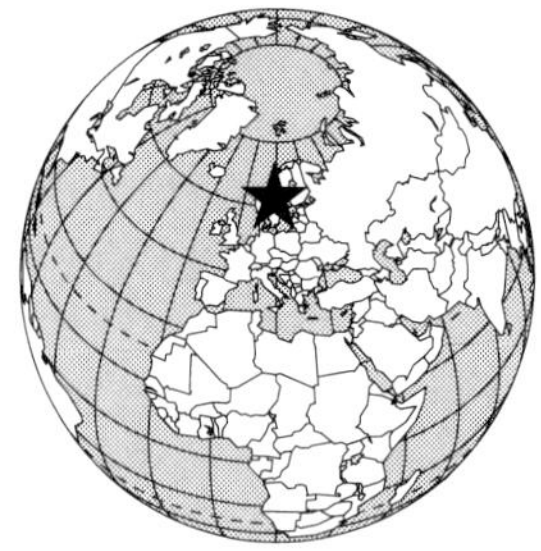

ECONOMIC FREEDOM STATUS: **FREE**
POLITICAL RIGHTS AND CIVIL LIBERTIES STATUS: **FREE**
PRESS FREEDOM STATUS: **FREE**
POPULATION: **8,857,000**
PPP: **$18,320**

## Background

Sweden's minority Social Democrats spent much of 1995 introducing austerity measures to curb a huge budget deficit inherited from their center-right predecessors. After ushering the party back into power following three years in opposition and persuading a reluctant electorate to vote for European Union (EU) membership, Prime Minister Ingvar Carlsson announced he would resign as both premier and party head in March 1996.

Sweden's long history of neutrality has allowed the government to concentrate on industrial development and create an extensive system of social welfare. For a century prior to 1970, Sweden enjoyed a growth rate unrivaled by any other industrialized nation and channeled its wealth into the generous benefit system. The early 1990s saw the worst economic recession in sixty years, with unemployment shooting up from virtually nothing in 1991 to 13 percent four years later. Amid plummeting popularity, the Social Democrats introduced four austerity packages that included welfare cuts and higher taxes.

Despite these proposed reductions, Sweden's expenditures on education, health, and other government social programs as a percentage of the economy's total output of goods and services remain among the highest in the world. Swedes are free to hold property, earn a living as they choose, open new businesses easily, trade internationally, and invest their earnings as they wish. Women and minorities participate fully in the market economy.

## Freedom to Hold Property 3/3

Swedish law does not explicitly acknowledge the right to private ownership but the legal system effectively protects private property.

Sweden is a member of a number of intellectual property conventions and associations. It effectively protects intellectual property.

## Freedom to Earn a Living 3/3

Unions in Sweden have traditionally been an influential force in the Swedish economy. All workers have the freedom to form unions, strike, and bargain collectively. Unions are independent of the government but some are allied with political parties.

Wages are set by centralized collective bargaining contracts.

## Freedom to Operate a Business 3/3

The rules governing the formation of business enterprises are relatively transparent and there are no significant restrictions to entering any line of commerce. However, Sweden's tax structure, which taxes capital heavily and retained earnings relatively lightly, has encouraged the growth of large corporations at the expense of small- and medium-sized businesses. Only 6 percent of Swedes employed in manufacturing work at firms with fewer than twenty people, a percentage much lower than those of other OECD countries.

Sweden's government procurement process is transparent. Government-owned companies are not subject to government purchasing requirements and are free to establish their own procurement policies, which are usually based solely on commercial considerations. Sweden joined the EU in January 1995 and so will have to harmonize its policies with EU competitive procurement policy.

Sweden has no significant price controls but does set minimum prices for many agricultural goods. Acceding to the prices set by the Common Agricultural Policy of the EU will actually decrease the price levels for most of these products.

## Freedom to Invest One's Earnings 3/3

Swedish citizens have access to domestic and foreign financial instruments. Capital flows have been fully liberalized and the government does not allocate credit to specific sectors of the economy or particular businesses.

The autonomous *Riksbank*, Sweden's central bank, regulates the interest rate to control inflation. The bank briefly pegged the currency to the European Currency Unit in 1990 in order to ensure currency stability and lower inflation. The result, however, was a sharp rise in interest rates that dampened demand and helped spark a recession. The bank has since unpegged the currency.

## Freedom to Trade Internationally 2/2

Sweden will have to harmonize its import and export policies with those of the EU. Sweden has generally had some of the lowest tariff levels in the world, averaging less than 5 percent *ad valorem* on finished goods. Most goods and services for domestic consumption are, however, subject to a value-added tax of 25 percent. Sweden does not have any significant export restraints. All foreign exchange transactions have been decontrolled.

Sweden welcomes foreign investment and restricts it in only a few strategic areas of the economy.

## Freedom from Unreasonable Government Interference in the Economy

The Swedish government supports the principles of a free market but maintains an extensive social welfare state and, in the past, has implemented massive spending programs to expand the economy. The government plays a strong role in providing social services such as medical, family, old age, disability and unemployment benefits. State-owned companies and cooperatives account for only 20 percent of business-sector employment and state-run industries tend to be run as effectively as private ones. Nonetheless public spending accounts for more than 60 percent of GNP. Most government subsidies support regional development, particularly in the north of Sweden.

Government regulations in the past have been intrusive. Recent deregulation, combined with a banking crisis, has introduced more competition into the system.

In 1993, Sweden implemented the Competition Act, which consolidated previous legislation and was drafted to harmonize Sweden's competition rules with those of the EU. Sweden, however, has been criticized for not doing enough to encourage competition in some industry sectors. A recent study highlighted the low level of internal competition in the food processing sector generated by the dominance of cooperatives, which control up to 100 percent of the markets.

## Freedom to Participate in the Market Economy 2/2

There is no significant discrimination against women or minorities.

Sweden has a well-developed legal system that facilitates economic exchange among its citizens. The system is free of corruption.

# Switzerland

ECONOMIC FREEDOM STATUS: **FREE**
POLITICAL RIGHTS AND CIVIL LIBERTIES STATUS: **FREE**
PRESS FREEDOM STATUS: **FREE**
POPULATION: **7,045,000**
PPP: **$22,580**

## Background

With the exception of a brief period of centralized power under Napoleonic rule, Switzerland has remained a confederation of local communities as established in the Pact of 1291. The 1815 Congress of Vienna formalized the country's borders and recognized the state as one of perpetual neutrality. Despite the adoption in 1874 of a new constitution increasing the power of the central government, a noncentralist tradition continues. An enormous degree of responsibility rests at the local and cantonal levels, and with the electorate itself.

Switzerland is often cited as a rare example of peaceful coexistence in a multi-ethnic state. Encompassing German, French, Romansch and Italian groups, the republic is divided into twenty cantons and six half cantons, with individual political systems, dominant ethnic or linguistic groups and distinct customs. Stable language borders clearly delineate the regions inhabited by linguistic groups, and adjustments are generally expected of migrants. Growing concern over immigration played a large role in the 1992 referendum rejecting European Economic Area membership. With over 20 percent of the population currently comprised of foreigners, Swiss nationals feared a mass influx of European Union (EU) immigrants.

Switzerland eschews free and open competition among firms in favor of a system of cartelization unlike that found in any other industrialized state. It also maintains a number of restrictions on its citizens' freedom to trade internationally. Despite these exceptions, however, Switzerland's citizens enjoy a high degree of economic freedom.

## Freedom to Hold Property 3/3

Property rights are very well protected by the constitution and the legal system. Switzerland has one of the best regimes for intellectual property protection in the world. Land ownership by foreigners is restricted and subject to local government approval. Voters rejected any easing of this restriction in a 1995 referendum.

## Freedom to Earn a Living 3/3

Union activity is protected by law in Switzerland and workers have the right to form and join unions of their choosing. Unions are independent of government and political parties and may engage in collective bargaining. Wages are market-determined and individuals are free to change occupations, although certain regions require a work permit. There are no legal prohibitions against forced labor, but it does not occur.

## Freedom to Operate a Business 2/3

Registering a business entity in Switzerland is easy and straightforward. However, planning regulations, local building codes, equipment standards, approval procedures, and the need to prove "public need," which can vary from canton to canton, can inhibit investment. The greatest barrier to private enterprise lies in the dominance of cartels in several sectors, particularly domestic farm products. Producers, wholesalers, processors and retailers form collusive organizations which, although not barriers to entry, afford protections and mutual benefits that make it difficult for nonmember competitors to enter the market. Consumer groups have complained about the cartels, and the government recently established a Cartel Commission to review and draft further legislation promoting competition.

The approximately 500 cartels that exist have a strong say in what comes into the country, its packaging, where and by whom it may be sold, and how much it will cost. Prices for consumer goods tend to be 40 percent higher than in other OECD countries and price fixing or exclusive supply contracts exist in 90 percent of seventy-two industrial activities ranging from building products to health insurance. Government contracts are competitive.

**Freedom to Invest One's Earnings 3/3**

Switzerland has been associated with private banking for centuries and Swiss citizens face very few restrictions in capital transfers and investment. The independent central bank has kept inflation low, and credit flows are determined by market forces.

**Freedom to Trade Internationally 1/2**

Switzerland, with high tariffs and non-tariff barriers, has one of the most protected agricultural sectors in the world. Movement toward conformity with the GATT has led to reductions in export subsidies and the phasing out of non-tariff barriers such as quantitative restrictions, licensing requirements, and decreases in price supports in most sectors of the economy. There are no export restrictions. Controls have therefore been lax in the export of sensitive materials and technologies to countries seeking weapons of mass destruction.

Foreign investment is largely unhindered and exchange controls exist only for countries without a convertible currency.

**Freedom from Unreasonable Government Interference in the Economy**

The government is largely concerned with creating a favorable environment for business and investment rather than interfering in the market, and state enterprises are confined to defense and public services. However, the state imposes its will through an extensive range of regulations including labor laws, administered prices, regulated hours, and environmental controls.

Competition policy is lenient, and as described above, cartels control significant segments of the economy. Although the state does not subsidize industry, Alpine agricultural producers receive subsidies in the form of price supports and are protected from import competition by a complex system. The goal of 65 percent self-sufficiency in food production was the primary motivation for agricultural protection.

**Freedom to Participate in the Market Economy 2/2**

Women are currently prohibited from working at night and on Sundays, though the labor law is being revised. There are no restrictions on women's ability to own property or businesses but women do not enjoy suffrage in some cantons and cannot participate in the local political system. Noncitizens are subject to local approval before purchasing real estate.

The legal system is highly effective. Corruption is rare.

# Turkey

ECONOMIC FREEDOM STATUS: **PARTLY FREE**
POLITICAL RIGHTS AND CIVIL LIBERTIES STATUS: **PARTLY FREE**
PRESS FREEDOM STATUS: **NOT FREE**
POPULATION: **61,380,000**
PPP: **$5,230**

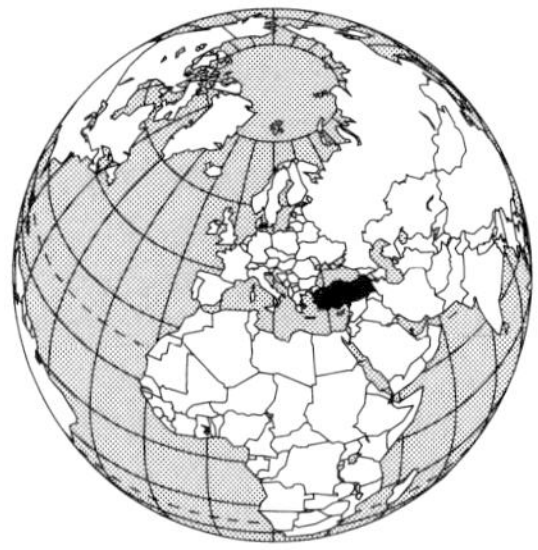

## Background

Mustafa Kemal Ataturk proclaimed Turkey a republic in 1923. Ataturk's secular, nationalistic legacy remains a powerful influence. The military used the doctrine of "Kemalism" to justify three coups between 1960 and 1980. The country returned to civilian rule in 1983. Turgut Ozal of the conservative Motherland Party served as president from 1989 to 1993. After Ozal's death in 1993, parliament elected Demirel president, and the True Path Party's (DYP) Tansu Ciller became Turkey's first woman prime minister. Turkey's westward orientation is embodied in active membership within NATO and the OECD. However, efforts to join the European Union (EU) customs union in 1995 were hindered by Turkey's human rights record.

Building on the economic reforms of predecessors, Prime Minister Ciller's government has struggled to bring Turkey's economic policies in line with EU requirements. However, years of statist and protectionist policies as well as entrenched vested interests have hindered reform.

## Freedom to Hold Property 2/3

Turkish citizens are able to own property and there are no restrictions on selling, transferring or structuring private property. Expropriation is prohibited unless the government can demonstrate public interest and proper compensation is made. However, in the provinces where the government is fighting Kurdish insurgents, many families have been forced off their lands and homes have been razed by government troops.

There are problems in the protection of intellectual property although the government is striving to implement legal frameworks and mechanisms in line with EU requirements. Pirated copyrighted material, especially recorded music, comprises an estimated 20 percent of all recorded music sales. With successful legal action carrying just a U.S. $150 fine for the infraction itself and a U.S. $2 fine for each impounded copy, piracy has increased in the last two years with pirates often working openly.

## Freedom to Earn a Living 2/3

Turkish citizens are free to enter whatever occupation they are qualified for. Wages are set by market conditions. There is no forced labor, though child labor is a problem.

Workers are able to associate freely, form unions and bargain collectively, except for teachers, civil servants, police, and military personnel. The right to strike is guaranteed in the constitution, but workers in the petroleum, security, and sanitation industries as well as teachers are prohibited from striking. Unions are independent from the state and from political parties. To hold a meeting or a rally, a union must have the government's permission and must allow the police to attend all functions.

## Freedom to Operate a Business 2/3

Establishing a business is not difficult for either domestic or foreign entities, and virtually all areas of the economy are open to private investment. Competing for government contracts can often be confusing and inconsistent, but is generally a nondiscriminatory process. Occasionally, bidders are faced with tenders being opened, closed, revised, and opened again over a period of years without a selection being made, causing many complaints of bid-rigging. Prices of goods and services produced by the private sector are not controlled by the government.

### Freedom to Invest One's Earnings 2/3

Turkey is rapidly establishing itself as a major international finance center in the Middle East, although recent financial crises have somewhat tempered enthusiasm. Various credit and financial instruments are available to investors and companies. Credit flows are determined by market forces. Interest rates are no longer set by the government, and the Central Bank Law has been amended to give greater autonomy to the Bank. However inflation has hovered around 60 percent, fueled by high public-sector deficits. The government has continued to borrow heavily from the Central Bank, and a 12 percent of GDP public-sector borrowing requirement has squeezed credit available to the private sector.

Turkish citizens are able to invest freely abroad and hold foreign currency and securities. Turkish citizens' savings accounts are currently higher in foreign denominations than in lira, the national currency.

### Freedom to Trade Internationally 2/2

Although stalled temporarily, when implemented the customs union agreement with the EU will eliminate import and export duties and charges on EU goods as well as the Mass Housing Levy, a non-tariff tax levied on all imported goods. There are currently import licensing requirements for a few items, and tariffs for non-EU goods remain relatively high. Importers must register with their local chambers of commerce and obtain an import certificate from the Undersecretariat for Treasury and Foreign Trade, though both procedures are described as straightforward. There are no export taxes or quotas.

Foreign investment laws are liberal and investors receive national treatment. However, all incoming foreign investments require prior authorization and licensing. This process can sometimes be ill-defined and confusing, but is otherwise routine and nondiscriminatory. There are few restrictions on where foreigners may invest.

Turkey has few capital controls and foreign exchange is easily obtained. Travel abroad is unrestricted.

### Freedom from Unreasonable Government Interference in the Economy

Turkey is moving toward full participation in the EU. Until the 1980s, state economic enterprises (SEEs) played a dominant role in the Turkish economy. However privatization has been a political hot-potato in both the Ozal and Ciller administrations and privatization has progressed slowly. Thirty-one enterprises were privatized in 1992 and seventeen in 1993. Currently, there are forty-one major SEEs involved in everything from shoemaking and tea to mining and airlines.

The Turkish bureaucracy remains powerful and state influence is pervasive. State subsidies to agriculture and industry persist. At present, monopolies and cartels are not prohibited, though the new Companies Law makes such arrangements illegal. During the rapid changes in the 1980s there were cases of arbitrary application of regulations and laws to punish or foster certain firms or industries.

### Freedom to Participate in the Market Economy 1/2

In general, there are no legal barriers to women or minorities entering any occupation, running a business, or owning property. Women hold many upper-level positions in government and business.

Although Kurds who assimilate and do not agitate for a separate cultural or linguistic identity generally face little discrimination, the 1991 Anti-Terror Law has provided the government with the means to jail, harass, or shut down businesses owned by anyone who supports the Kurdish separatist movement. The continuing human rights violations committed by the Turkish government in the Southeast have threatened Turkey's inclusion into the EU customs agreement.

The legal system is functioning and contractual agreements are secure. However, obtaining and enforcing court orders in commercial matters can take a long time. The Ciller government has been rocked with several corruption scandals, and corrupt practices within the bureaucracy are pervasive.

# United Kingdom

ECONOMIC FREEDOM STATUS: **FREE**
POLITICAL RIGHTS AND CIVIL LIBERTIES STATUS: **FREE**
PRESS FREEDOM STATUS: **FREE**
POPULATION: **58,560,000**
PPP: **$17,620**

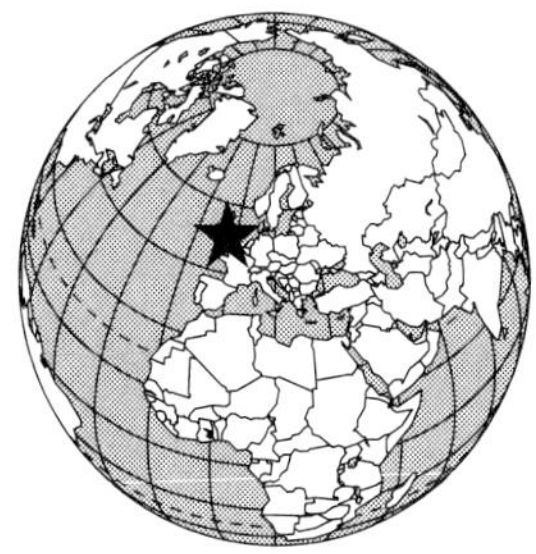

## Background

The Conservative Party has held power since 1979, when Margaret Thatcher became prime minister. After taking over in 1990, John Major abandoned Thatcher's unpopular poll tax, continued to privatize state industries, and attempted to balance pro-Europe forces against specific national interests. However, by 1992 several major policy reversals and scandals, coupled with gaping divides over Britain's role in the European Community, had begun to erode the Conservatives' support. Under the leadership of Tony Blair, the Labour Party has abandoned its longstanding commitment to a nationalized industry policy in favor of a more centrist endorsement of a dynamic market economy where "markets work in the public interest." In June, nationwide polls showed Blair was the most popular opposition leader since records began fifty years ago.

Many of the principles of economic freedom find their ideological roots in the United Kingdom and remain strong today. Despite some difficulties with competition policy and the regulatory environment, the fundamental institutions necessary to protect economic freedom are strong.

## Freedom to Hold Property 3/3

Britain has strong private property protection. Intellectual property rights in particular are strictly and comprehensively enforced.

## Freedom to Earn a Living 3/3

Workers are able to form and join unions. Although the right to collective bargaining is not explicitly granted in law, it is a common practice and collective bargaining agreements cover about 40 percent of the workforce. Unions are free of government control but most support the Labour Party. Forced labor is outlawed and the ban is effectively enforced.

## Freedom to Operate a Business 3/3

Anyone may form a business enterprise and establishing one is a relatively straightforward and transparent process. The regulations governing the operation of a business, however, can be confusing. Many business owners have complained specifically about the application of fair-trading regulations. Although the regulations are meant to promote competition, they tend to be applied to businesses haphazardly. The government restricts competition in telecommunications, gas and electricity, even though these industries are now privately owned.

The government adheres to a competitive public procurement process. In general, British prices are freely determined by the market. However, the government regulates prices charged by public utilities and can set prices on matches, milk, and London taxi fares. Book prices were freed of government control in 1995.

### Freedom to Invest One's Earnings 3/3

United Kingdom citizens are able to invest without restriction both domestically and abroad, and capital flows are fully liberalized. Credit flows are determined by market forces.

Since the exchange crisis of September 1992, the British pound has floated outside the restrictions of the European Exchange Rate Mechanism so the Treasury has been free to adjust interest rates more independently than its fellow European Union (EU) members. Inflation has plagued the country since World War II but recent tight monetary policies seem to have reined in inflation despite economic growth. Interest rates are not directly controlled by the government and the Bank of England is independent.

### Freedom to Trade Internationally 2/2

The United Kingdom has implemented EU policy regarding imports and exports. The Department of Trade and Industry was established to aid exporting firms, but some businesses complain that the department aids primarily large United Kingdom businesses and has not done enough to help small- and medium-sized firms.

The country encourages foreign investment and has not implemented any significant foreign investment restrictions. There are no controls on foreign exchange.

### Freedom from Unreasonable Government Interference in the Economy

Since 1979, the government has implemented an extensive privatization program that has significantly reduced the government's role in the economy. The government has privatized the telephone, water, gas, and electric utilities. It has also sold its majority interests in major automobile and aerospace companies and in its national airline. In addition to privatization, the government has taken many steps to increase the competitiveness of the economy, including tax reform, abolition of capital controls, deregulation of financial services, and labor law reforms. The government is also reducing its industry-specific subsidies but many still exist, particularly for industries being privatized.

Although one of the priorities of government policy is to promote competition, some complain that regulations, particularly governing monopolies, are burdensome and randomly applied. Business owners complain that the Monopolies and Mergers Commission, which is supposed to prevent monopoly practices, restricts the integration of firms in some industries while allowing the integration of others. Banking overregulation is also coming under sharp criticism in the wake of the Barings collapse.

### Freedom to Participate in the Market Economy 2/2

The law provides for equal opportunity for minorities and women. They are not discriminated against in operating businesses, pursuing careers, or owning or holding property.

Corruption has not been a significant problem in the United Kingdom.

**Political Freedom v. Economic Freedom for Central-East Europe and NIS**

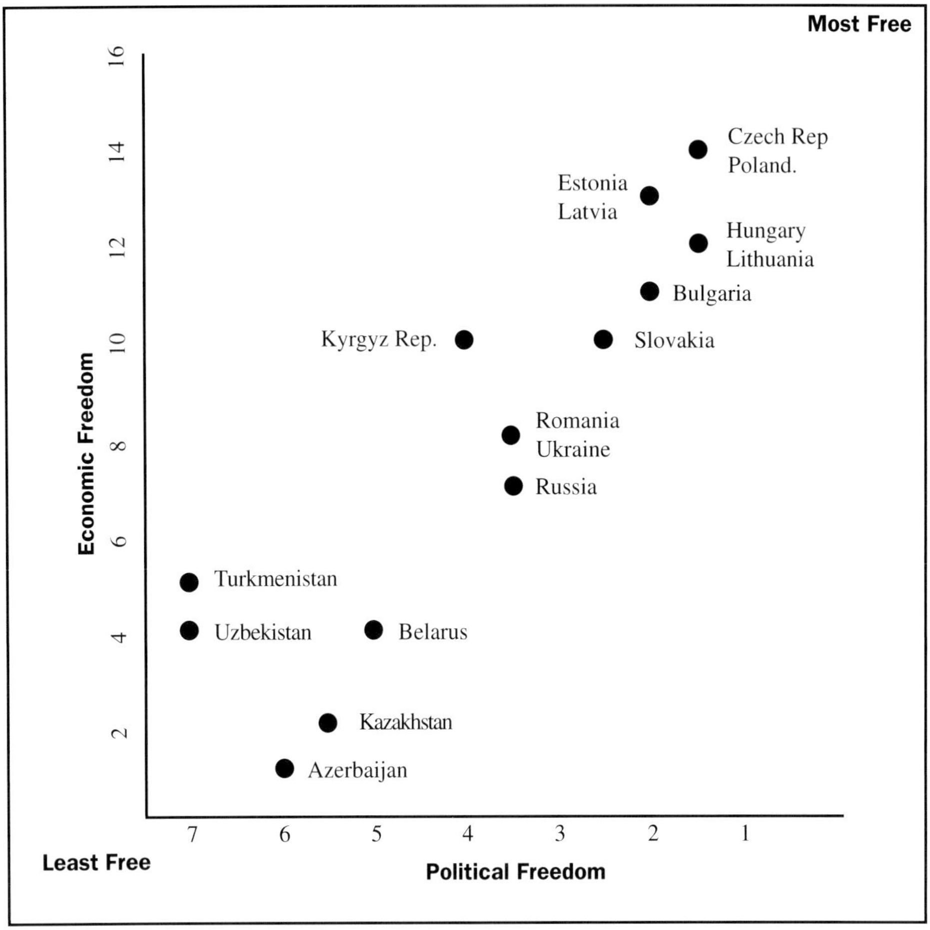


## POLITICAL FREEDOM VERSUS ECONOMIC FREEDOM

The graph above shows the relationship between the level of political freedom and economic freedom for countries in Central-East Europe and NIS. The ratings for political freedom were derived by averaging Freedom House's political rights and civil liberties ratings from the *Freedom in the World: The Annual Survey of Political Rights and Civil Liberties, 1995-1996*. A score of "1" represents the most free and "7" the least free.

Economic freedom is graphed on the vertical scale with "0" representing "Not Free" and "16" representing "Free."

# Central East Europe and NIS

## Azerbaijan

ECONOMIC FREEDOM STATUS: **NOT FREE**
POLITICAL RIGHTS AND CIVIL LIBERTIES STATUS: **NOT FREE**
PRESS FREEDOM STATUS: **NOT FREE**
POPULATION: **7,275,000**
PPP: **$2,550**

### Background

Azerbaijan is ruled by Gaidar Aliyev, a Soviet-era politburo member who has built a personality cult since assuming power amid civil strife in 1993. Faud Guliyev, acting prime minister since early 1994, was confirmed by parliament on 5 May 1995.

The Nagorno-Karabakh War has drained the treasury and ordinary Azeris have not benefited from new-found oil wealth. Aliyev maintains that political stability and economic improvement necessitates stronger control. For the average Azeri this has translated into an almost complete absence of economic freedom. Land cannot be privately owned, wages are set by government fiat, and most goods are either produced by state-owned enterprises or subject to price controls.

### Freedom to Hold Property 0/3

Azeris and foreigners may lease land, but not own it outright. The exception is the tiny fraction, less than 1 percent, of land owned by private farmers. The 1995 privatization law envisions the ownership of land, but the mechanism has not been determined. If passed in its entirety and implemented, the new privatization law would allow for private ownership, transfer and sale of land.

Legal protection of intellectual property rights is inadequate and enforcement does not exist. There is no copyright law, and Azerbaijan has not adhered to any international agreements in this area. There is widespread use of pirated films and music recordings. A presidential decree offers some protection on patents.

### Freedom to Earn a Living 0/3

The largest labor organization is the post-Communist Azerbaijan Labor Federation, which is largely dependent on the government. An independent oil workers' union represents 85,000 workers, 80 percent of the employees in that industry.

Wages are set by the various government ministries in this predominantly command economy, and unions do not participate in determining wage levels. While workers can theoretically change jobs, hiring and firing for government-controlled positions and state enterprises are linked to fealty to the ruling regime. Laws bar forced labor and the labor code restricts child labor.

## Freedom to Operate a Business 1/3

As of June 1995, only a few small businesses had been privatized, although a substantial number of government-owned businesses are reported to have de facto owners. A streamlined process of registering and legalizing new businesses was introduced with initial legislation privatizing state enterprises. A new privatization plan envisions turning at least 50 percent of all medium and large enterprises into open joint-stock companies by the end of 1996. At least 51 percent of shares in 300 medium and large enterprises will be offered publicly through the end of 1996, with a goal of putting 70 percent of the companies' assets in private hands. Most of the economy will be open to private investment except the military, oil and gas sectors.

Key commodities such as bread, natural gas, and gasoline remain under price controls. Since nearly all goods are produced by state-owned enterprises or monopolies, the government continues to set prices it will pay to enterprises. Government contracting lacks transparency and is subject to cronyism and corruption, though the state order system has been gradually phased out.

## Freedom to Invest One's Earnings 0/3

Credit markets have not developed and an annual credit plan, subject to approval by the parliament, directs available credit. Interest rates are not regulated. Individuals cannot invest abroad or hold foreign currency and securities, though these restrictions are flouted by the quasi-legal "shadow economy." The central bank, the Azerbaijan National Bank, is not independent of political control. In the past, the government has fueled inflation by printing more money to pay off the government debt and raising prices of goods and commodities. Although about 180 banks are registered in the capital, Baku, corruption and the war in Nagorno-Karabakh rendered them ineffective for the purposes of investment.

## Freedom to Trade Internationally 0/2

There are no import restrictions. The government regulates the export of strategic commodities, among them refined oil products, cotton and wine. The 18,000 or so Armenians believed to remain in Azerbaijan have been deprived of internal and external passports. All foreign travel requires exit visas from the government. Entry and exit regulations change frequently and without warning.

The 1992 Foreign Investment Law dictates that all foreign investment must be pre-approved. There are restrictions on the number of foreign personnel an enterprise may hire. In 1994, the government signed an $8 billion deal with a consortium of eleven Western oil companies to explore three oil fields in the Caspian Sea.

The currency, the manat, has been allowed to float freely against major currencies, and foreign exchange markets have been introduced to help make the manat convertible. There are several controls on foreign exchange such as a surrender requirement and a limit on the amount of foreign currency that can be taken out of the country. Only a few banks have access to foreign exchange.

## Freedom from Unreasonable Government Interference in the Economy

The economy is dominated by large state enterprises and cooperative farms, all of whose production is based on state orders prepared by state ministries. Privatization laws of 1994 and 1995 have yet to be implemented. Until they are, opportunity is limited mostly to the state sector, which is rife with corruption. Misguided economic policies and the war with Armenia over Nagorno-Karabakh have virtually depleted the national treasury, and few Azeris have the means to advance economically. In the absence of accurate statistics and the large informal economy, the World Bank estimates that a figure of less than 20 percent of GDP generated by private ownership is as accurate as any other approximation.

**Freedom to Participate in the Market Economy 0/2**

The government continues to subsidize production at state enterprises to maintain production levels and employment, both hindered by faltering deliveries of raw materials from former Soviet states which led to a dramatic drop in industrial output.

The constitution includes anti-discrimination provisions and provides for the protection of ethnic and minority rights. But the few remaining Armenians and Kurds are subject to discrimination and intimidation. Women nominally enjoy equal rights in employment, but cultural norms have led to discrimination.

The country is in the formative stages of adopting some requisites for a market economy, such as privatization and fiscal and monetary reforms. However, there are no bankruptcy or commercial transaction laws, much trade is unregulated, and a "gray zone" private economy operates outside the laws that exist.

# Belarus

ECONOMIC FREEDOM STATUS: **NOT FREE**
POLITICAL RIGHTS AND CIVIL LIBERTIES STATUS: **PARTLY FREE**
PRESS FREEDOM STATUS: **NOT FREE**
POPULATION: **10,340,000**
PPP: **$6,850**

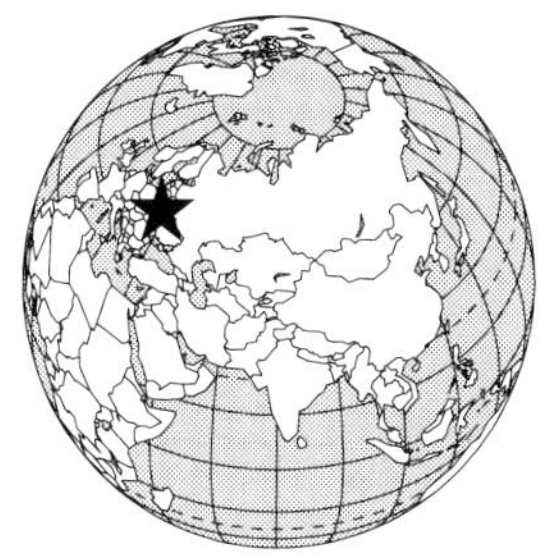

**Background**

A predominantly industrial country, Belarus has the highest standard of living among the twelve Newly Independent States. The agricultural sector accounts for 40 percent of the economy and employs 21 percent of the workforce. The economy has been contracting since 1993 as the country adjusts to President Alyaksandr Lukashenka's "market-socialism." Russia remains the country's primary trading partner and Germany is the largest non-NIS trading partner. In a May 1995 referendum, over 80 percent of voters backed a presidential proposal to tighten economic ties with Russia and restore Russian as the official language.

Present-day Belarus was part of the tenth-century Kievan realm. After a lengthy period of Lithuanian rule, it merged with Poland in the sixteenth century and became part of the Russian Empire after Poland was partitioned in the eighteenth century. It became a constituent republic of the USSR in 1922. Belarus declared its independence from the USSR in 1991 and nonparty populist Lukashenka was elected as its first president in 1994. Lukashenka strengthened his grip on power in 1995 by reintroducing censorship, banning independent trade unions, reimposing the use of Soviet-era textbooks, ignoring the Supreme Court when it overturned his decrees and limiting the rights of candidates for the year's parliamentary elections.

Although Lukashenka has advocated a gradual liberalization of the economy to avoid widespread social unrest, little has been accomplished. Privatization of the predominantly state-owned economy has been slow, land ownership is still prohibited, it is extremely difficult to open a new business, and interest rates and the prices of many goods and services are controlled.

### Freedom to Hold Property 1/3

Article 13 of the constitution provides that the state guarantees "equal protection and equal conditions for the development of all forms of property." Land cannot be owned by Belarus citizens except for small tracts for gardening, housing and farming. Although 10 percent of arable land was reportedly leased or privately owned in 1994, most of this consisted of individual plots dating from Soviet times. Agricultural and industrial land can be leased for up to ninety-nine years. The 1993 Law on the Right of Land Ownership states that private owners have the rights of "alienating land plots, pledging and leasing them and assigning in inheritance in accordance with the law." On this land construction is permitted of houses or other structures "for horticultural and country construction."

Intellectual property rights are inadequate in Belarus, though the country has joined the World Intellectual Property Organization.

Although a 1992 law provides for allocation of vouchers for purchasing housing, only several thousand units, mostly in the major urban areas, have been privatized. There are restrictions on the purchase and sale of land and property, which has hampered privatization and economic reform. Private housing and property have changed hands, though often outside the law.

### Freedom to Earn a Living 1/3

The 1992 Trade Union Law allows workers to form and join independent unions. The principle of collective bargaining, though codified, is frequently violated. In August 1995, the government suspended the largest independent union, the Free Trade Union of Belarus (SPB) and detained several labor leaders following a series of transport strikes. The Federation of Trade Unions of Belarus (FPSB), the largest union and successor of the Soviet-era central federation, controls social functions such as pensions. It has supported strikes and wrangled with the government over wages and economic policy.

The government sets state-sector wages. The FPSB has won wage concessions from the government in certain sectors such as education and health care. Under several privatization laws and edicts in the 1990s, enterprises are technically free to determine wages, though they often follow scales comparable to those used by the government in the public sector.

### Freedom to Operate a Business 0/3

Bureaucratic obstacles, licensing and registration requirements and the absence of a clear-cut legal framework have stymied the growth of truly private entrepreneurs; most are vendors and small tradespeople.

About one-third of state enterprises are ineligible for privatization and these sectors, mainly defense-related and energy, are closed to private investment. Government contracts are not competitively let. Industries filling state orders get preferential credit, tax breaks and guaranteed materials and payment. Most wholesale prices have been freed, but there are limits on enterprise profit margins. Prices are subject to the whim of presidential decrees. In mid-1995, the president determined prices for basic foodstuffs were too high, and ordered they be rolled back at state expense.

### Freedom to Invest One's Earnings 0/3

Interest rates are still under the direct control of the government. Central planning authorities allocate longterm, directed credits. Profit limits apply to about one-third of industrial output, and distribution margins are imposed on all products at the wholesale and retail levels.

Individuals cannot invest abroad. There are restrictions and fees on foreign currency exchange and the conversion of deposit balances into cash.

The National Bank of Belarus (NBB) has limited legal authority in monetary policy and is subject to controls by the government and parliament. The president exercises arbitrary powers over economic activity including banking.

## Freedom to Trade Internationally 1/2

Import restrictions exist on some products such as medicines, industrial waste and movies. Belarusians must obtain a license for foreign trading activities. In 1992, formal licensing requirements were placed on the export of an extensive list of "vital goods." Export quotas are distributed by the governmental Center for Foreign Economic Relations with priority given to producer enterprises. Most trade is handled by the official Central Foreign Trading Organizations, though 15 percent is handled by private organizations. A complex system of export taxes was introduced in 1992 for trade outside the former USSR, with rates rising to 30 percent.

The Law on Foreign Investment allows for profit repatriation, 100 percent foreign ownership, and tax breaks. A "unified" exchange rate is fixed once a week by the NBB. The application process for foreign travel is cumbersome, but there are no reports of unfair or arbitrary refusals.

## Freedom from Unreasonable Government Interference in the Economy

The state's share of the economy is some 90 percent of GDP. Officially, private-sector activity accounted for 8 percent of total output. (Just over 1 percent of agricultural output was produced by private farmers.) Government expenditure in 1994 was 51 percent of GDP.

There are about 9,400 state-owned enterprises at all levels. About 7,000 companies were scheduled to be converted to joint-stock companies by the end of 1995, though the actual number was closer to 600; some 250 large-scale enterprises have been cooperatized as a prelude to privatization. Under a government plan, the non-state sector would represent 50 percent of the national economy by the year 2000, but only 4 percent of state property has been privatized since 1991. There are 5,000 small businesses (most purchased through auction) and an equal number of cooperatives, and an estimated 22,000 workers (out of nearly 5 million ) are employees of private enterprises.

Despite laws and decrees, the government remains ambivalent about far-reaching privatization and genuine market reforms. Almost 80 percent of enterprises are monopolies. Direct price controls and regulation of gross profits, as well as a tax system that decimates sales income, have retarded competition and individual opportunity. Commercial laws are inconsistently implemented.

The government continues primarily to subsidize large state enterprises and agriculture, though energy subsidies to state firms were eliminated in 1994.

## Freedom to Participate in the Market Economy 1/2

Women and ethnic minorities are not legally prevented from participating in the economy, though opportunities for all Belarusians are circumscribed given the lack of meaningful economic reforms. Women have faced discrimination in the allocation and sale of housing.

Laws on privatization and other aspects of market reform are in place, but are subject to changes by presidential decree or, as in the case of the Bankruptcy Law, not enforced; there is little confidence in the judiciary or the Supreme Court, whose attempts to overturn presidential decrees have been ignored. Corruption is a problem, particularly in the privatization of businesses and housing.

# Bulgaria

ECONOMIC FREEDOM STATUS: **PARTLY FREE**
POLITICAL RIGHTS AND CIVIL LIBERTIES STATUS: **FREE**
PRESS FREEDOM STATUS: **PARTLY FREE**
POPULATION: **8,454,000**
PPP: **$4,250**

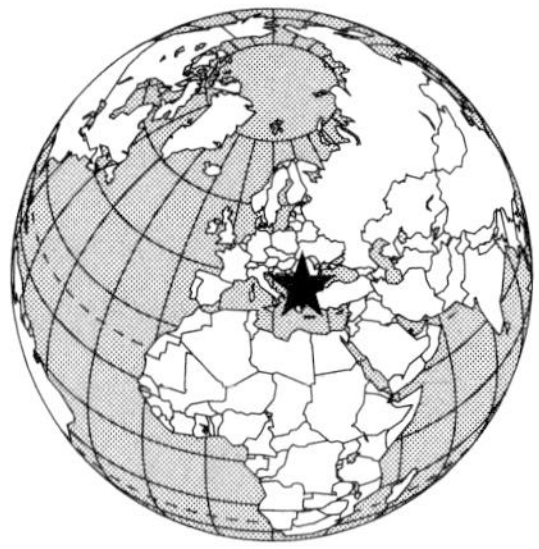

## Background

Occupied by Ottoman Turks from 1396 to 1878, Bulgaria only achieved complete independence in 1908. Communists seized power after Bulgaria's 1944 "liberation" by the Soviet Army. Communist party strongman Todor Zhivkov, whose rule began in 1954, was forced to resign one day after the fall of the Berlin Wall in November 1989.

Parliamentary elections were called in December 1994 after Prime Minister Lyuben Berov's nonparty government, in power since 1992, collapsed amid widespread criticism of the slowness of economic reform and unpopular price and tax increases. The vote saw the former-Communist Bulgarian Socialist Party (BSP) win a clear majority with 125 of 240 seats.

In 1995, the key issue facing the BSP government of Prime Minister Zhan Videnov—the country's sixth since 1990—was improving the economy, which trailed others in East-Central Europe. The BSP, elected by pensioners and the poor, had promised to ease the pain of reform (including 20 percent unemployment, triple-digit inflation and lagging productivity) without abandoning the goals of a market economy and integration with Europe.

Obstacles included the old Communist elite's entrenchment in private business, weak or nonexistent business laws that allowed these elites to abuse their new power, and slow privatization (only thirty-four medium- or large-sized enterprises had been privatized by early 1995). In August, the government launched a plan including cash and mass privatization, in which citizens could buy vouchers to be exchanged for shares in 1,300 state enterprises. President Zhelev and oppositionists criticized the plan because it did not allow foreign ownership of land and provided favorable state credits for Bulgarian business, thereby favoring former Communists who have disproportionate control over the private economy—all of Bulgaria's 1,000 millionaires and five billionaires are BSP members.

## Freedom to Hold Property 2/3

The constitution guarantees the right to private property. In general, the legal system protects the acquisition and disposition of property rights, but processes are cumbersome. Intellectual property rights laws conform with international standards, but enforcement is problematic, leading to a black market of pirated products.

Land reform mandated the return of nationalized land to former owners whenever possible. Although many farmers received "protocol" designating their rights to land, few received actual legal rights. Bulgaria's president estimated that only about 10 percent of agricultural land has been fully privatized through restitution or sale. Over 90 percent of housing is in private hands (though much housing was private prior to the fall of the Soviet-era regime.)

The commercial code addresses the transfer of property rights, incorporation, and liquidation procedures. The law recognizes secured interest in real property and has a well-established system of mortgage financing. However, the law is weak in transactions, and secured interests in chattel property is not recognized. Banks and creditors cannot seize property, and must rely on proceeds from sales or auctions by court. There are about one hundred unlinked registers throughout the country which makes it impossible to verify if a piece of property is being used as collateral for several loans at the same time. For individuals, there are no significant restrictions on selling or exchanging property.

## Freedom to Earn a Living 2/3

Under the 1991 constitution and Article 4 of the Labor Code, workers can organize and join independent trade unions. The largest are the Confederation of Trade Unions of Bulgaria, a successor to the Communist-era federation, and *Podkrepa*, one of the first post-Communist unions. Article 3 of the Labor Code establishes the right to collective bargaining.

Wages are negotiated at the enterprise level, even as many large- and medium-scale enterprises are controlled by the government. Individuals are free to change jobs, although, as in many post-Communist countries, there are practical hindrances to relocation and changing residencies that affect employment opportunities.

Though forced labor is prohibited by the constitution, some ethnic minorities and draft-evaders have been shunted into work units. Child labor is illegal but goes on in the emerging informal and private sectors and in agriculture.

## Freedom to Operate a Business 3/3

There are nearly 412,000 registered, private firms. Most are small single-proprietor or family businesses. Some 60 percent are engaged in trade and services, while 15 percent are in industry.

The process of registering new businesses has been streamlined with sole proprietorships taking about a week at a registration cost of about thirteen U.S. dollars. The establishment of titles to existing property is still slow. A bill to allow private notaries is currently being considered. No special permission is required to start a business, with exceptions for defense, banking and insurance.

There is no legal discrimination in procurement. Government procurement mostly works through competitive international tenders, though procedural difficulties have been reported. Prices are largely free though energy prices are still controlled.

## Freedom to Invest One's Earnings 2/3

Credit ceilings are set by the central bank, but commercial banks are free to set their own credit and deposit rates. There are no controls on rates of return on investment.

Individuals and companies can hold foreign currency and securities. Capital outflows are controlled; local individuals and legal entities may transfer earnings abroad with Ministry of Finance permission, but there is no restriction on the repatriation of profits on foreign investment, though procedural barriers to such investment have been reported.

An autonomous central bank, the Bulgarian National Bank, was established in 1991 and has adhered to restrictive fiscal and monetary policies. The inflation rate in 1995 was 35 percent.

## Freedom to Trade Internationally 1/2

All quantitative import restrictions have been eliminated and the granting of import licenses was made automatic except for a small group of items. Export licensing bans were retained for twenty-one items. Export licenses for goods subject to quantitative restrictions by trading partners are allocated to the domestic producers who can obtain the highest export price from foreign customers. Foreign trading rights have been granted to firms applying for them. There are no arbitrary or restrictive travel provisions for entering or leaving the country.

The Foreign Investment law is liberal, allowing for full profit and capital repatriation, access to land through long-term leasing, and the registration process is free from restrictive screening procedures. Licenses are required in the military production, natural resources, and banking sectors. Foreign investors have complained of a lack of transparency, particularly through arbitrary and capricious tax practices.

Importers have free access to foreign exchange on presentation of order papers. Exporters have to repatriate earnings within a month, but can keep the receipts in foreign exchange accounts. The lev has been allowed to float under a system of internal convertibility.

## Freedom from Unreasonable Government Interference in the Economy

It is estimated that 43 percent of GDP is generated by private economic activity. Government expenditures are 46 percent of GDP. There are some 3,700 state enterprises. The law allows state-owned enterprises to be privatized through creation of joint-stock companies, sale to foreign investors, and worker/management buyouts. In 1995, only about one-third of the state-owned enterprises were in the process of being privatized. Privatization has been slow due to a lack of political will and complicated procedures. Delays also stemmed from obstruction by the Ministry of Industry and other agencies, extreme caution by the Privatization Agency, and the question of ownership stemming from a restitution program.

While the Competition Law safeguards against collusion, cartels, and other practices that impede competition, procedural and enforcement mechanisms have created ambiguities and abuses.

The few private firms engaged in production (as opposed to services) have been the beneficiaries of subsidized credits. Most state subsidizes have been removed though hidden subsidies via energy prices remain. Taxation policies lack transparency and can be considered arbitrary and venal, but lax enforcement and other obstacles have allowed most Bulgarian enterprises to evade taxes. Many Western investors have noted that massive tax evasion by Bulgarian enterprises (public and private) puts them at a competitive disadvantage.

## Freedom to Participate in the Market Economy 1/2

Informal discrimination against Roma (Gypsies) in employment and social benefits exists. The so-called Panev Act bars former high-ranking Communists from many educational and editorial positions. Some 1,700 people have been affected.

Women are guaranteed equal rights under law, and women have held prominent government offices, including caretaker prime minister. Women face *de facto* discrimination in employment. Rural Roma have been discouraged from claiming land to which they are entitled under the law dividing cooperatives.

Privatization laws, commercial codes, and related measures provide a comprehensive framework for the establishment of a market economy. Yet, Bulgaria has lagged in privatization, implementing agricultural reforms and improvements in infrastructures such as communications.

Reports of corruption are widespread, particularly in illegal privatizations and the banking sector.

# Czech Republic

ECONOMIC FREEDOM STATUS: **FREE**
POLITICAL RIGHTS AND CIVIL LIBERTIES STATUS: **FREE**
PRESS FREEDOM STATUS: **FREE**
POPULATION: **10,357,000**
PPP: **$7,690**

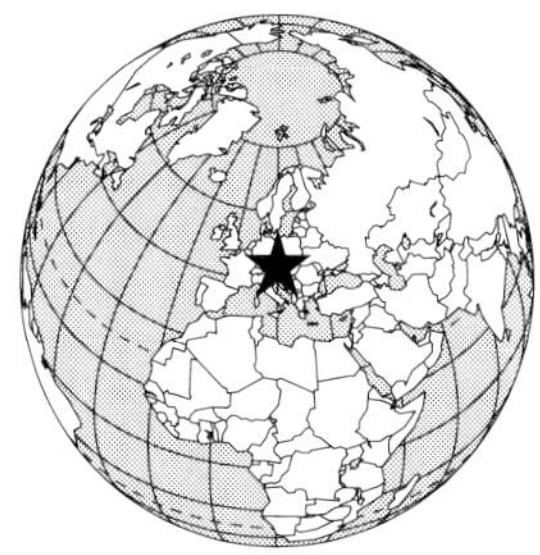

## Background

The Czech Republic emerged in 1993 after the peaceful dissolution of Czechoslovakia. Former dissident playwright and Czechoslovak President Vaclav Havel was elected Czech President in January 1993, and Premier Vaclav Klaus and his aggressively pro-market Civic Democratic Party (ODS) led a four-party coalition that had won control of the Czechoslovak parliament in 1992.

In 1995, Premier Klaus's government continued fine-tuning the market reforms that have given the Czech Republic the strongest economy in East-Central Europe. In November, it became the first post-Communist country to be admitted to the Organization for Economic Cooperation and Development.

Economic measures taken in 1995 included abolishing wage regulations, making the currency, the koruna, fully convertible, changing bankruptcy laws to expedite liquidation proceedings, and tightening conflict-of-interest laws. Low inflation, little foreign debt, a 3 percent growth in output, 3 percent unemployment, and record hard currency reserves contributed to political stability and relative prosperity.

## Freedom to Hold Property 3/3

The constitution guarantees the right to hold property. As part of property reforms, the government passed legislation shortly after the fall of the Communist regime giving housing and land to the municipality in which it was located. Those living in these units could then apply to buy them from the municipal government at a discounted price. Between 40 and 60 percent of all housing units have been privatized. Land restitution has been completed and land registries and other mechanisms are fully in place. There are no significant restrictions on selling or exchanging property, and individuals can structure their property holdings as they choose.

The government has signed several international agreements dealing with protecting intellectual property rights. However, enforcement has been spotty and difficult. The commercial courts are overwhelmed with cases involving trademarks.

## Freedom to Earn a Living 3/3

Workers have the right to form and join independent labor unions, the largest being the umbrella Czech and Moravian Trade Union Confederation. The Law on Collective Bargaining is observed.

Wage regulations were abolished in 1995.

The growth of private business provides the opportunity for citizens to change jobs, though some large-scale manufacturing industries remain in government hands. Coercive labor does not exist, and child labor laws protect minors.

## Freedom to Operate a Business 3/3

Businesses need to be registered with district offices of the Entrepreneurship Bureau. Certain standard information must be provided, including articles of incorporation and bank account numbers.

Foreign investors have complained about the lack of transparency in the bidding process for government contracts, though the government has been working to adopt European Union and OECD procurement procedures.

The government has broad powers to regulate prices. The Ministry of Finance can fix prices directly, set minimum or maximum prices for any commercial transaction and establish periods when prices may not be changed. However, the government generally favors a laissez-faire pricing policy on most products. Prices are still controlled on energy, some raw materials, domestic rents, and rail and bus transport. Imports are not subject to price controls.

## Freedom to Invest One's Earnings 3/3

Due to the heavy influx of foreign currency—the government estimates 30-40 percent to be speculative—the central bank has been controlling interest rates to reduce inflationary pressure. Generally, interest rates are market-determined.

Credit is allocated by the market, and there are no controls on rates of return on investments. There are no barriers to capital outflow except a 25 percent tax on repatriated earnings. Individuals can hold foreign currency and securities, and invest abroad.

The central bank is independent and the inflation rate for 1995 averaged 9-10 percent.

## Freedom to Trade Internationally 2/2

Non-tariff restrictions on imports have been greatly liberalized. Official permission is still necessary to import crude oil, pharmaceuticals, natural gas, firearms or explosives. Licensing requirements apply to imports of clothing, black coal, certain raw materials and agricultural products from sources other than the European Union.

There are no special taxes or restrictions on exports of normal goods and services. There are no arbitrary restrictions on the right to enter or leave the country.

On paper, regulation of foreign investment does not differ from that of most other European states. There is growing popular opposition to foreign ownership of remaining Czech assets slated for privatization, among them the lucrative telecommunications and energy sectors.

There are few exchange controls. The Czech National Bank still holds control over the convertibility of the koruna, though it seldom exercises these controls and the koruna is generally fully convertible. Late in 1995, parliament ratified a new foreign exchange law that will make the koruna fully convertible for current-account transactions and partially convertible for capital-account transactions.

## Freedom from Unreasonable Government Interference in the Economy

It is estimated that over 90 percent of GDP will come from private ownership. Government expenditures are 45 percent of GDP, but the government is trying to reduce that amount.

Privatization laws allow for direct auction of small-scale enterprises, joint ventures with foreign companies, and a two-phase sale of voucher shares to citizens. A restitution process has returned industrial, agricultural, and housing or business structures to former owners or heirs. Under these provisions, 90 percent of agricultural operations have been privatized.

There are some 700 state-owned enterprises. Most large Czech enterprises are still subject to direct state control through large, though not majority, blocks of shares purchased by the National Property Fund operated by the government. The state still controls the mining, steel, telecommunications and petroleum-refining sectors. But state subsidies to unprofitable enterprises and other sectors are being cut.

The government is particularly vigilant about maintaining competitive markets. Laws forbid cartel agreements, price-fixing, collusion and trust practices, and abuse of dominant market position. There have been several well-publicized scandals involving fraudulent securities, tax evasion, extortion and other schemes, which highlighted weak domestic controls and inexperience in the international capital markets.

### Freedom to Participate in the Market Economy 1/2

De facto discrimination against the Roma (Gypsies) is widespread in housing, education, and business. There are no significant barriers to women in housing, property rights, business, or employment.

Commercial codes, privatization legislation, and codification of business practices have laid the foundation for a vibrant free-market system moving into line with European Community norms. There have been several cases of corruption in privatization and other economic crimes, but the problems are not indicative or pervasive, nor are these practices tolerated when discovered.

# Estonia

ECONOMIC FREEDOM STATUS: **FREE**
POLITICAL RIGHTS AND CIVIL LIBERTIES STATUS: **FREE**
PRESS FREEDOM STATUS: **FREE**
POPULATION: **1,477,000**
PPP: **$6,690**

### Background

Few nations have transformed their economies as rapidly as Estonia. Incorporated by force into the Soviet Union and its command economy on the eve of World War II, in the short period since the collapse of the Soviet empire, Estonia has dismantled controls on prices, wages, and trade, created a stable currency, and established a set of laws and institutions to facilitate its citizens' exercise of their economic freedoms. Some minor restraints on economic freedom still remain.

### Freedom to Hold Property 2/3

The government is committed to restore property to or compensate with vouchers all owners of property prior to the Soviet takeover in 1940. As of January 1995, the validity of claims covering 70 percent of those properties had been resolved (210,300 claims on 159,100 properties). However, only 10 percent of these properties have been returned due to delays caused by remaining disagreements on value and related factors.

Land ownership and the dividing line between state and private property remain contentious issues. In 1995, collective farms successfully sued to hold up housing privatization in cases where the collective organizations had contributed to housing construction. At least 93 percent of approximately 350 collective and state farms have been corporatized into over 7,000 units

(5,000 of which are individual farms). But the process is moving slowly, and only about 14 percent of agricultural land in Estonia is privately farmed. Individuals can structure their property holdings as they choose.

Intellectual property rights are up to international standards, though enforcement has been difficult.

## Freedom to Earn a Living 3/3

Trade unions operate independently of the state and political parties. The Central Organization of Estonian Trade Unions (EAKL) replaced the official Soviet-era confederation. The right to strike is legal, legal safeguards protect strikers from retribution, and a collective bargaining law was adopted in 1993.

The minimum wage is set monthly by the government in consultation with the EAKL and the Central Producers Union. The Law on Labor Contracts provides for severance pay for full-time employees upon termination of employment. Wages are determined by market forces.

Workers can change jobs freely. There are laws forbidding forced labor and the exploitation of children.

## Freedom to Operate a Business 2/3

Private businesses, particularly in services, have grown under privatization and related legislation since 1991. The proportion of domestic private ownership is estimated at close to 80 percent of wholesale trade, and 65 percent of retail and catering. Other forms of ownership include cooperatives and foreign ownership. There are virtually no restrictions on the type of commerce undertaken by citizens, and government contracts are competitively let.

Price liberalization was enacted in 1989-92. The only prices controlled are electricity, precious stones and metals, and energy inputs. Some services such as telecommunications and passenger transport are subject to price regulations.

## Freedom to Invest One's Earnings 2/3

Interest rates are pegged to German rates. Directed credits to state enterprises have dropped significantly, and there are no controls on investment returns. There are no restrictions on international capital transactions and citizens are free to hold foreign currency and securities.

The Bank of Estonia is independent and does not lend to local or central governments. Lending to commercial banks is restricted to emergency situations and limited by the need to maintain full cover for currency board liabilities.

## Freedom to Trade Internationally 2/2

After independence, Estonia dismantled the restrictive Soviet-era trade policies and now has one of the most liberal trading regimes in the world. Virtually all import tariffs were eliminated by 1992. There are no import quotas, and licensing requirements are standard and non-restrictive. Quantitative restrictions on exports have been removed and export tariffs apply only to items of cultural value. Export duties are levied only on the following items: rapeseed oil, items of cultural value, and metals. Any legal entity in Estonia can apply for a commercial operational license. There are no exchange restrictions.

There are no domestic or internal travel restrictions. The Foreign Investment Law grants foreign investors the same rights and obligations as domestic individuals and companies. Foreign investors require licenses in mining, power engineering, telecommunications, gas and water supply, transport, and banking.

### Freedom from Unreasonable Government Interference in the Economy

Over 60 percent of GDP is in private hands, and the percentage is much higher in retail trade. Government expenditure accounts for 34 percent of GDP. Several privatization measures passed in the 1990s allow for compensation vouchers, cash sales, compensation instead of return of property in cases affecting enterprises, and a choice for citizens to sell vouchers for cash. By the end of 1994, almost all small enterprises—mainly shops and service enterprises numbering some 1,500—were privatized through auctions. From 1993 to mid-1995, 337 purchase agreements were concluded for sale of large enterprises, whether for total assets or shares. Following original estimates of the total number of large enterprises to be privatized immediately (400), roughly 80 percent have now been sold.

In taking dramatic steps toward market reforms, the government has sought to promote competition and individual opportunity. There are no export subsidies. Subsidies to enterprises have been virtually eliminated and are limited to covering a small proportion of the operating costs of public transport, mainly urban and inter-urban bus services, accounting for only .5 percent of GDP.

### Freedom to Participate in the Market Economy 2/2

Although there are allegations by the Russian community regarding discrimination in employment, housing, and education due to Estonian-language requirements, there are no legal restrictions on business ownership due to ethnicity. Only Estonian citizens may own land, though all residents may participate in housing privatization. Women possess the same legal guarantees as men and are legally entitled to equal pay for equal work.

Privatization laws, bankruptcy statutes, and commercial and banking regulations form the framework for a market economy. Corruption usually takes the form of bribing officials to expedite business transactions or bureaucratic obstacles.

# Hungary

ECONOMIC FREEDOM STATUS: **PARTLY FREE**
POLITICAL RIGHTS AND CIVIL LIBERTIES STATUS: **FREE**
PRESS FREEDOM STATUS: **PARTLY FREE**
POPULATION: **10,238,000**
PPP: **$6,580**

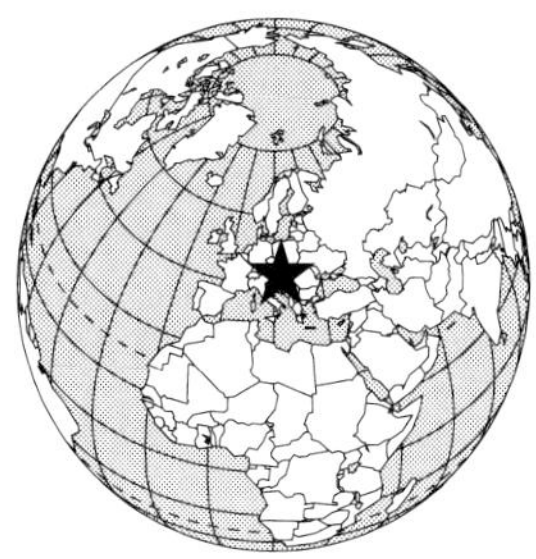

### Background

From 1956 until 1988, the regime of Janos Kadar followed a policy of political repression and pseudo-market economics, or "goulash communism." In 1988, Kadar was ousted and multiparty democracy was introduced in 1989. The conservative Hungarian Democratic Forum and the "reform Communists" who succeeded them in 1994 have dismantled most Communist-era restraints on private economic activity. Building on a pre-Communist foundation of respect for the rule of law, many of the legal and institutional prerequisites for a market economy have been put into place.

Citizens are free to earn a living, and reasonably free to open businesses, trade internationally, hold property, and invest their earnings as they see fit. In March 1995, Socialist Prime Minister Gyula Horn sought to restore confidence in market reforms by naming pro-reform candidates to the posts of Finance Minister and Central Bank Governor, initiating an unpopular austerity program, and stepping up the privatization process. A poll found two-thirds of Hungarians "outraged" at the reforms, but by the year's end, the economy had begun to pick up again.

## Freedom to Hold Property 2/3

The constitution gives legal protection to common and private property. It also protects investors from expropriation without due process and proper compensation. The 1994 Land Law restricts the purchase of land by foreigners and prohibits businesses from purchasing arable land, though they may lease specified amounts.

Hungary has comprehensive intellectual property rights protection which has been updated to incorporate trade secrets and high technology. Hungary is a member of the World Intellectual Property Organization and a signatory of several conventions.

The courts have proved to be an effective vehicle for enforcing property and contractual rights. There are no restrictions on selling or exchanging property, and individuals can structure their holdings as they choose.

## Freedom to Earn a Living 3/3

The two largest independent unions are the Democratic Confederation of Free Trade Unions (LIGA) and the Hungarians Workers Council. Hungary's former-Communist organization of trade unions, the National Federation of Hungarian Trade Unions (MSzOSz), which represents the majority of Hungary's workers, is controlled by the Socialist Party, and is thus not free and independent. Workers are guaranteed the right to collective bargaining and the right to strike.

Individual unions and management negotiate wage levels above the nationally mandated minimum wage.

In an increasingly market-oriented economy, workers may freely change jobs. Coerced labor and child exploitation are legally prohibited and do not exist in practice.

## Freedom to Operate a Business 2/3

Both foreign and domestic private entities may establish and own business enterprises and engage in various forms of remunerative activity. Article 9 of the constitution states that: "the economy of Hungary is a market economy, where public and private ownership shall be equally respected and enjoy equal protection."

Excessive and time-consuming bureaucracy often encumbers business, and this extends to the registration of businesses and the privatization process. Courts have been overwhelmed by business applications and unclear lines of authority can make it difficult to determine who, in which ministry, can make the necessary decisions and approvals.

Only security-related industries and service utilities are restricted. The state reserves the right to grant partial monopolies in some areas traditionally reserved for regional or local governments, including road construction, railways and airports, power utilities, mining, and gambling.

Hungary has yet to sign the GATT Agreement on Government Procurement. There is increasing criticism regarding the tendering process because of non-transparency and irregularities. However, a new procurement law should introduce greater transparency.

Prices are set by government decree and apply to a small number of goods and services. The Agriculture Ministry has the power to establish minimum prices for wheat, pork, corn and beef. Maximum prices are mandated for all energy supplies, mail and telecommunications, rail and bus transport, pharmaceuticals, and public water services.

## Freedom to Invest One's Earnings 2/3

Interest rates are free-floating. The banking law restricts large credits, internal credits, and credits for securities transactions, real estate investments, and durable investments. However, credit is generally granted on market terms, and there are no controls on the rates of return on investment. Local entrepreneurs are having difficulty affording credit, which currently carries interest rates of 40 percent.

Individuals can invest abroad, though capital outflow and foreign investment require prior permission of the government. Individuals can hold foreign currency and securities. The Central Bank is independent and inflation averaged 28-30 percent in 1995.

## Freedom to Trade Internationally 1/2

Hungary imposes a $750 million global quota on imports of consumer goods and there are quota allotments for imports from the European Union. New trade regulations are often introduced without advance notice. Only 19 percent of imported products now require import licensing. Import licenses are required for some consumer goods. There are no unreasonable or arbitrary restrictions on foreign or domestic travel.

Foreign investments are not screened, the exceptions being financial institutions and insurance. The current environment encourages foreign investment in almost all aspects of the economy. Foreign investors are allowed to repatriate earnings and capital and are protected from expropriation.

The currency, the forint, is not fully convertible, though for business purposes it approaches full convertibility. All companies are required to sell foreign exchange receipts from exports to the Hungarian National Bank within eight days of receipt unless an exemption has been granted. All companies are also required to receive permission from the National Bank before taking out hard currency loans. The forint's value is determined by a currency basket consisting of 30 percent of the U.S. dollar and 70 percent of the European Currency Unit.

## Freedom from Unreasonable Government Interference in the Economy

The private sector has grown significantly since the fall of communism, and now produces almost 60 percent of GDP. However, government expenditures are still above 55 percent, much of it comprised of cash social benefits. Since the collapse of Communism, the state has privatized 30 percent of its holdings and liquidated 20 percent, but privatization stalled in 1995. Under the June 1995 Privatization Law, the state will retain partial ownership in 156 companies.

Competitive equality is the standard applied to private enterprises in competition with public entities with respect to access to markets, credit, licenses and supplies. However, state enterprises sometimes enjoy superior access. A 1990 law on the Prohibition of Unfair Market Practices is intended to foster the establishment and maintenance of a competitive market, prohibit consumer fraud, and eliminate abuses of dominant market position and unfair competition.

The government still provides approximately 12 percent in subsidies to various sectors of the economy and transfers about 23 percent of the national budget to local governments. Fifteen sectors have been designated "activities of special importance" and are eligible for tax exemptions and special benefits.

## Freedom to Participate in the Market Economy 2/2

Women and ethnic minorities are not foreclosed from any occupations or businesses, and face no legal hurdles to property ownership and transfer. The constitution, laws and commercial codes provide a framework for a market economy. The commercial code has been expanded both in scope and coverage and the law on bankruptcy procedures, liquidation, and final settlement is on a par with Western standards. The legal system has proved fair and effective in enforcing these laws.

Corruption is not a significant problem, particularly when compared to other post-Soviet transition economies.

# Kazakhstan

ECONOMIC FREEDOM STATUS: **NOT FREE**
POLITICAL RIGHTS AND CIVIL LIBERTIES STATUS: **NOT FREE**
PRESS FREEDOM STATUS: **NOT FREE**
POPULATION: **16,876,000**
PPP: **$4,270**

## Background

When Nursultan Nazarbayev was elected president of the newly independent state of Kazakhstan in 1991, he put economic reform at the top of his agenda. But while Nazarbayev has succeeded in attracting some foreign investment into the oil and mineral sectors, his government has not made reform of the command economy inherited from the Soviet era a priority. Laws creating rights to land and other forms of property have yet to be enacted, and much of the economy remains under the control of state-owned enterprises. Furthermore, Nazarbayev, the former first-secretary of Kazakhstan's Communist Party, eschews parliamentary consent in favor of over seventy presidential decrees.

What little private enterprise exists must contend with corrupt government officials and a powerful network of organized crime. As a result, citizens of Kazakhstan enjoy virtually no economic freedom.

## Freedom to Hold Property 0/3

The right to property is not recognized by law, and a minuscule percentage of land is under private use. Land and other natural resources are considered state property and cannot be privately owned, though they can be leased for ninety-nine years. In general, leases are transferable and inheritable, but cannot be used as collateral. Individuals cannot structure their property holdings as they choose. Enforcement of intellectual property rights is lax.

## Freedom to Earn a Living 0/3

The largest union remains the successor to the Soviet-era General Council of Trade Unions and is practically a government organ. Among independent unions, the largest is the Independent Trade Union Center. Registering a legal independent union is lengthy, difficult and expensive, and the decision process is arbitrary, lacking published criteria. There are significant limits on the rights to organize and bargain collectively. Workers who join independent unions often face harassment, dismissal, and transfer to lower-paying jobs.

Many enterprises continue to pay in scrip, which is often not accepted at local stores or, if it is, at devalued levels. While workers are free to change jobs, the government still controls most housing, and residency permits make it difficult to move.

Forced labor is prohibited by law, but in some cases compulsory labor occurs. Child labor is generally not a problem except during harvest time in the southern part of the country.

## Freedom to Operate a Business 1/3

While individuals can freely pursue mutual economic interests, bureaucratic obstacles and crime inhibit sound business practices. A locally financed manufacturing sector is growing rapidly. Family businesses are thriving in the ready-made garment industry. Crime syndicates have put pressure on entrepreneurs to sell part of their enterprises or pay protection.

There are price controls and subsidies for certain consumer commodities; however, most consumer goods prices are determined by the market. An elaborate system of controls prevails in the distribution of intermediate and final goods among enterprises.

**Freedom to Invest One's Earnings 0/3**

Interest rates are largely regulated. Average annual inflation was over 200 percent but the National Bank of Kazakhstan (NBK) has been relatively successful in reducing inflation in recent months. The NBK receives the bulk of its loanable funds from the Central Bank of Russia and allocates them according to parliamentary or government directives. Refinance quotas have been used by the NBK as an instrument of selective credit allocation. Rates on investment returns are not controlled.

Currency operations connected with capital transactions between residents and nonresidents are subject to licensing by the NBK. Residents can hold foreign currency.

**Freedom to Trade Internationally 1/2**

There are no significant barriers to imports. The government has adopted a liberal trade policy to encourage international exports. There is no import licensing. Imports of nonessential goods have been restricted through tariffs, duties and quotas. Customs procedures remain cumbersome and confusing. Domestic enterprises are permitted to export goods directly and are required to channel exports of eighteen critical products through approximately ten state trading organizations controlled by the government. These include oil and gas, coal and coke, ore and concentrates, metals, precious metals and stones, chemical products, radioactive materials, grain, cotton, and caviar. These goods are also subject to export quotas. There is an export tax that varies according to the product and can range up to 30 percent. An exit visa is still required to travel abroad but refusals are rare. However, officials will occasionally demand bribes.

Foreign firms cannot purchase land though they may obtain lease rights for ninety-nine years through a domestic partner. In addition, government and local authorities have, on occasion, insisted that foreign firms support and invest in social programs for local communities.

The government does not seem to enforce foreign exchange controls except that enterprises earning foreign exchange are required to sell 50 percent of the total earnings on the local market. The market rate of currency exchange is the rate of the ruble against the U.S. dollar. There are two other exchange rates stemming from a foreign exchange auction at the Almaty Center of Interbank Foreign Exchange, transactions through the National Bank, and a third rate that emerges from the approved foreign exchange operation of authorized banks with resident enterprises and individuals, which is market-determined.

**Freedom from Unreasonable Government Interference in the Economy**

About 20 percent of GDP comes from private ownership. Some 60 percent of industrial production is state-owned. In 1992, 6,000 small enterprises were privatized out of a total of roughly 31,000 enterprises. Most were sold to worker collectives. Agricultural production is organized around 1,500-2,000 state and cooperative farms. The private sector contributes 15-20 percent of agricultural production.

Privatization and anti-monopoly legislation are aimed at promoting competition and individual opportunity. Consumer subsidies have been reduced. Subsidies to state-run enterprises are expected to cover some 20 percent of Kazakh output. Government regulatory polices are extensive. Implementation remains capricious and a major source of corruption.

## Freedom to Participate in the Market Economy 0/2

There is increasing discrimination reported against non-Kazakhs (mainly Russians) in employment, education and housing. Women may participate in and operate businesses. Despite some efforts at privatization, Kazakhstan remains largely a command economy, with the state participating in virtually every aspect of business, agriculture and finance. Corruption is pervasive, as is organized criminal activity, both of which are major impediments to freely participating in the market economy.

# Kyrgyz Republic

ECONOMIC FREEDOM STATUS: **PARTLY FREE**
POLITICAL RIGHTS AND CIVIL LIBERTIES STATUS: **PARTLY FREE**
PRESS FREEDOM STATUS: **PARTLY FREE**
POPULATION: **4,405,000**
PPP: **$2,850**

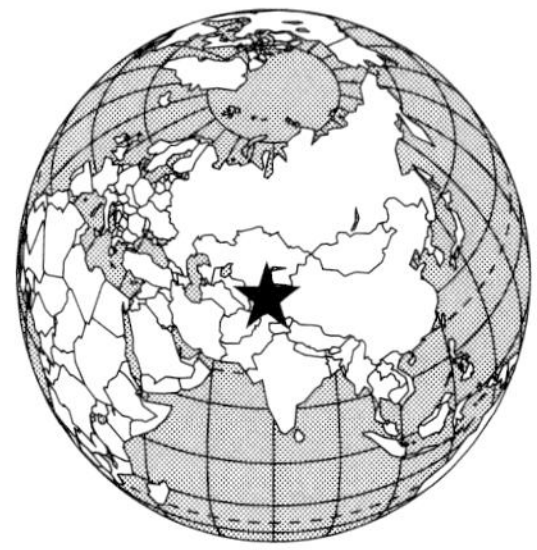

## Background

This small, impoverished Central Asian country declared independence from the Soviet Union in 1991. President Askar Akayev, a respected physicist, committed the country to democratic and market reforms in what was called the "Silk Revolution." Prices have been freed, an independent central bank established, and many financial restrictions lifted. But legal protection of contracts and property rights is still inadequate and corruption is pervasive.

## Freedom to Hold Property 1/3

Individuals may use land through forty-nine-year leases, rather than owning it outright. Ownership of land as well as mineral and other natural resources is restricted to the government. Private plots are permitted for growing crops for personal consumption. The protection of intellectual property rights has not been codified.

The privatization of land has proceeded slowly in 1994-95. Land can be exchanged, leased or used as collateral for obtaining bank credits.

## Freedom to Earn a Living 1/3

The labor law provides for the right of all workers to form and join unions. However, the Federation of Trade Unions of the Kyrgyz Republic, successor to the official Soviet-era union, remains the sole union federation. The union has criticized government policies regarding privatization and declining standards of living for workers.

Wages are set freely in the private sector, but are still set by the government in the largely state-dominated economy.

Under a Soviet-era law, citizens need official government permission to work and settle in particular areas of the country. Home and apartment owners are legally restricted from selling their property to buyers without official sanction. In reality, people do relocate within the country and have sold their homes or businesses without interference. Forced labor is used in prisons, but is not practiced in the general economy. Child labor is not a problem.

## Freedom to Operate a Business 2/3

There are no excessive restrictions on business formation. In urban areas, small private businesses are registered, but many businesses are estimated to operate "unofficially" in a gray-zone economy to avoid excessive and often capricious taxes.

Entry into strategic sectors is restricted, but other parts of the economy are open to investment. Private investment has been hindered less by legal and regulatory barriers than by lack of infrastructure and the continued dominance of unwieldy state enterprises.

Prices are set competitively, except for nine natural monopolies including gas and electricity, which are regulated through control of profit margins. Energy prices are still controlled, though domestic sale prices of imported fuels have been gradually liberalized and increased. Transportation and communications are also subsidized.

## Freedom to Invest One's Earnings 3/3

Interest rates are determined by the market. Since October 1993, the government has vigorously pursued restrictive credit policies that have reduced inflation to single digits. Monetary policy has been conducted through market-based instruments, with the National Bank of the Kyrgyz Republic refinance credit channeled through weekly credit auctions. Profit taxes apply to all legal entities engaged in business. A 30 percent profit tax applies to most enterprises, but banks are taxed at 45 percent, sporting and show events at 50 percent, and agriculture at 25 percent. Individuals are allowed to invest abroad, and to hold foreign currency or securities.

The 1992 Central Bank Law established a high degree of independence for the National Bank and since the 1993 introduction of the national currency, the som, the bank has conducted monetary policy with increasing autonomy.

## Freedom to Trade Internationally 2/2

Unrecorded imports, some from chartered flights by private importers, totaled an estimated $64 million in 1994. All persons must pay duty on imports over a certain threshold. Most import and export licensing requirements were abolished in early 1994. A common customs zone with Kazakhstan and Uzbekistan was created in 1994. The number of export taxes has been reduced significantly in the last two years and only four remain. Citizens who apply for an international passport must present a letter of invitation from the country they intend to go to. There are no other significant restrictions on travel.

Under law, foreign investors and companies are assured the same rights as citizens. Investment incentives are offered to foreign investors. The Overseas Private Investment Corporation signed a deal committing more than $250 million of U.S. government support to an American-Kyrgyz joint venture to extract and process gold.

The som was introduced in 1993 under a freely floating exchange system. Informal controls on interbank foreign exchange auctions were relaxed in late 1993. All existing exchange restrictions on account as well as capital account transactions have been eliminated.

## Freedom from Unreasonable Government Interference in the Economy

Some 20-30 percent of GDP is estimated to be in private hands. Government expenditure was 49 percent of GDP in 1994. By December 1994, 5,000 enterprises had been privatized, representing about 50 percent of state enterprises. About 99 percent of the service sector has been privatized, 93 percent of trade and public catering, and 46 percent of industry. Government monopolies have been reduced to only nine natural resources. With the exception of grain, some 45 percent of total production of major agricultural products and livestock was contributed by small-scale private farms or household plots.

## Freedom to Participate in the Market Economy 1/2

Women are well represented in the workforce, professions, and institutions of higher education, though in rural areas traditions limit women's progress. Non-Kyrgyz have alleged discrimination in hiring, promotion, and housing, though the constitution protects the rights and freedoms of ethnic groups and prohibits discrimination. Women can hold and transfer property.

The legal system and judiciary remain weak in the area of providing mechanisms, procedures and laws related to business rights and practices.

Organized crime and corruption are serious problems. Foreign businessmen have been intimidated or murdered. The president has acknowledged that corruption and bribe-taking have hampered greater foreign investment.

# Latvia

ECONOMIC FREEDOM STATUS: **FREE**
POLITICAL RIGHTS AND CIVIL LIBERTIES STATUS: **FREE**
PRESS FREEDOM STATUS: **FREE**
POPULATION: **2,527,000**
PPP: **$6,060**

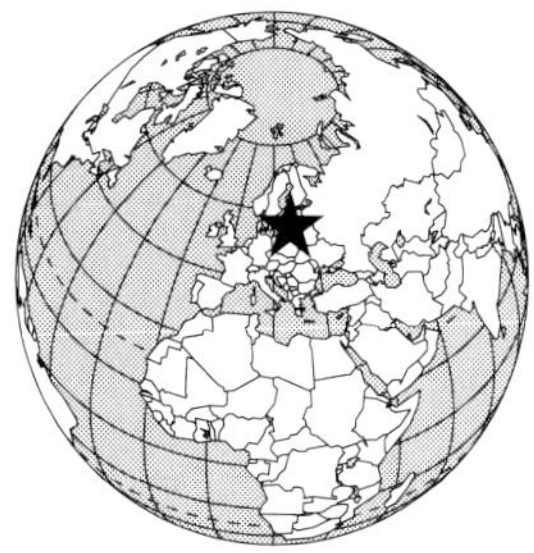

## Background

Following independence from the Soviet Union in 1991, the small Baltic state of Latvia has rapidly dismantled the Soviet-era command economy and established a market economy. Virtually all sectors of the economy have been opened up to private enterprise, property rights and contracts are protected and enforced, trade barriers have been reduced, financial restrictions lifted, and prices freed.

## Freedom to Hold Property 2/3

The right to own property is recognized for Latvian citizens. In February 1995, amendments were made to the land law that would allow companies registered in Latvia or in a country with an investment agreement with Latvia to become landowners. Control of housing and land has been restored to previous owners. Yet legal mechanisms for title registration, sale and mortgaging of real property are not yet fully developed and a land market does not yet exist. Legally transferable rights to private property are slowly being re-established as are the rights of individuals to structure their property holdings as they choose.

The government is committed to protect intellectual property rights in conformity with international conventions. However, implementation can be lax, and penalties for violations have not been defined.

## Freedom to Earn a Living 3/3

The Free Trade Union of Latvia, established after the breakup of the Soviet Union, is independent of government influence. Workers in most sectors can strike and collective bargaining is provided for in the Collective Agreements Law. Unions must have at least thirty founding members in large enterprises and include one-fifth of employees in small enterprises in order to be recognized.

Wage decisions are increasingly being made at the enterprise level, although government ministries still retain control of wages in large, state-owned enterprises. Workers are free to change jobs. Forced labor is not permitted, and child labor is regulated to protect minors from exploitation.

## Freedom to Operate a Business 3/3

Procedures for forming and registering a business are not restrictive or complex. However, bureaucracy, corruption and organized crime affect trade and investment. Private investment is allowed in most areas of the economy, while areas such as defense and energy are regulated. Government procurement is competitive, and procedures conform to European Union standards.

Almost all farm procurement and retail food prices have been decontrolled, and restrictions on industrial goods pricing have been removed. Fewer than 8 percent of goods and services remain subject to price controls, among them energy, telecommunications, rents, and other public services such as transport and utilities.

## Freedom to Invest One's Earnings 2/3

Interest rates are not regulated and with the exception of certain considerations given the remaining state-owned enterprises, the flow of credit is determined by market forces. There are no restrictions on rates of return and citizens are free to invest abroad and hold foreign currencies.

The autonomous Central Bank pursues a very conservative policy aimed at price and currency stability.

## Freedom to Trade Internationally 2/2

The import tariff regime is still evolving. However, tariffs are generally low for manufactured products and high for agriculture. Import documentation and classifications are modeled on Western standards. Export taxes exist for lumber and metals but exports are otherwise unrestricted. Movement within and outside the country is free from undue or arbitrary restrictions.

The government is actively encouraging direct foreign investment. Under the 1991 Foreign Investment Law, foreign investors are allowed to repatriate profits. However, acquisition of controlling shares in a Latvian enterprise with assets exceeding $1 million must be approved by the cabinet of ministers. Foreign companies (though not individuals) registered in Latvia may lease and own land.

The currency, the Lat, floats freely and there are no controls on foreign exchange.

## Freedom from Unreasonable Government Interference in the Economy

The private sector accounts for about 50 percent of GDP. Government expenditures represented about 11 percent of GDP in 1994. The government expected as much as 75 percent of medium- and small-scale state-owned enterprises to be privatized by the end of 1995. Only about a dozen of the largest state-owned enterprises have been privatized. Agriculture has been largely privatized with over 58,000 private farms established and the remaining collective farms transformed into private joint-stock companies.

The Latvia Anti-Monopoly Control Committee oversees the implementation of laws prohibiting monopolies, the manipulation of prices and the creation of artificial shortages to boost prices. Mergers resulting in market shares exceeding 25 percent must be approved by the committee.

Private and public enterprises have competitive equality with respect to access to markets and business operations. State enterprises may have preferential access to credits that are backed by the Latvian government and not available to private companies. The only export subsidies are in agriculture—for butter, cheese and rye.

The Latvian judiciary is independent of government influence. Latvia is in the process of updating and implementing pre-1940 commercial and bankruptcy laws.

### Freedom to Participate in the Market Economy 1/2

Only Latvian citizens are allowed to hold state positions and own property, and the Latvian language is required by law for use in private enterprise. A substantial percentage of mainly Slavic residents is excluded from citizenship and voting rights, and their opportunities to own businesses and land are limited. Noncitizens were given fewer privatization certificates to be used for purchasing stocks and apartments. But many non-Latvians have been naturalized and are fully eligible for property rights.

While privatization, fiscal and monetary reforms, and legal restructuring have provide a framework for a free-market system, regulatory and tax structures are not fully functioning. Corruption is recognized as a problem, but does not unduly interfere with normal market forces.

# Lithuania

ECONOMIC FREEDOM STATUS: **PARTLY FREE**
POLITICAL RIGHTS AND CIVIL LIBERTIES STATUS: **FREE**
PRESS FREEDOM STATUS: **FREE**
POPULATION: **3,705,000**
PPP: **$3,700**

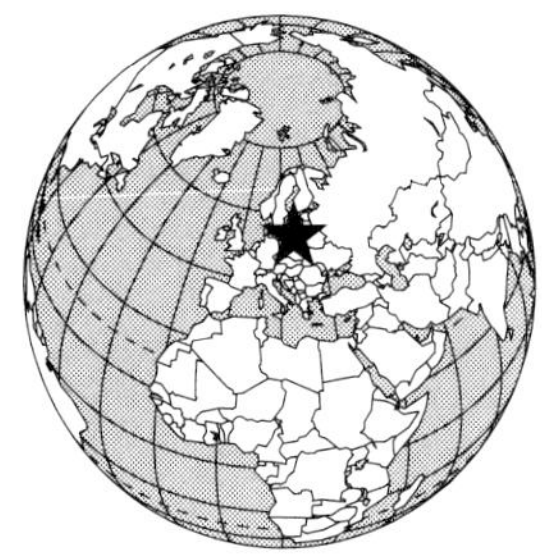

### Background

The Baltic state of Lithuania declared independence from the Soviet Union in 1991. Since then, Lithuania has undertaken a series of reforms to transform its economy. Under an International Monetary Fund-guided structural reform program, prices have been freed, state enterprises have been privatized and private property ownership has been legalized. In 1995, economic reforms sparked demonstrations by pensioners as well as bank depositors angry at the collapse of several banks. As a result, the government of Prime Minister Adolfas Slezevicius planned to increase government expenditures for social programs in 1996.

### Freedom to Hold Property 2/3

Private citizens are allowed to own land. Lithuania has upgraded intellectual property rights protection codes to meet Western standards. However, enforcement mechanisms as well as copyright law and amendments to criminal and civil codes are lacking. While land cannot be sold to foreigners, it can be leased for up to ninety-nine years. In order to become a member of the European Union, Lithuania would have to rescind prohibitions on foreign private land ownership. Individuals can structure their property holdings as they choose.

### Freedom to Earn a Living 2/3

Both the 1991 Law on Trade Unions and the constitution recognize the rights of workers and employees, including even police and members of the armed forces, to form unions. The Lithuanian Trade Union Center is made up of the former Communist-era union and other groups. Two other large independent unions are the Lithuanian Workers Union and the Unification of Trade Unions. Workers can strike. A 1994 law eliminated provisions protecting union officials from dismissals by employers.

Wages are freely set, subject to a minimum wage since 1993. Individuals are free to change occupations. The constitution forbids forced labor, and the exploitation of minors is prohibited.

## Freedom to Operate a Business 3/3

Laws and regulations governing the establishment of business do not foreclose large sectors of the population from participating in business if they have they means and inclination to do so. Commercial entry into strategic sectors such as energy, defense and telecommunications is regulated by the government.

The government has initiated reforms to create competitive markets through the removal of barriers to starting new businesses, elimination of restrictive licensing requirements for production and distribution, lifting geographical restrictions on trade, and splitting up conglomerates and large state enterprises. Government contracts are competitively let, conforming to Western standards. While most prices were liberalized in 1992, energy prices are still indirectly subsidized.

## Freedom to Invest One's Earnings 3/3

Interest rates are not regulated. While the three large state-controlled banks have generally operated on a commercial basis, the Agricultural Bank, the nation's largest, has extended credit partly under the direction of the government and parliament, sometimes to secure financing for the cash-strapped energy sector.

Much of the lending by private banks is directed toward profitable trading and industrial sectors. Private banks are unwilling to lend to state-owned companies because they do not have the legal right to use property as collateral. Returns on investments are not regulated, and individuals can invest abroad. Citizens may open foreign exchange accounts at authorized banks and may be credited or debited without restrictions.

The Bank of Lithuania is independent. However, since 1994, Lithuania has operated under a currency board arrangement where full foreign exchange backing is provided for by reserve money and other litas-dominated (the litas is the national currency) liabilities of the central bank. Growth in the money base is limited by foreign exchange reserves. Exchange rates are fixed and central bank credit to commercial banks is limited to the amount of forex reserves in excess of that needed to back base money requirements.

## Freedom to Trade Internationally 1/2

Almost all import controls have been removed. Average import tariffs are low by international standards. The agricultural lobby has called for non-tariff barriers, including the fixing of minimum prices at which agricultural goods can be imported. Import tariff quotas apply to some agricultural goods, alcohol, strategic technology, and those items deemed vital to Lithuania's cultural heritage. Most export restrictions have been eliminated. There are export bans on five products that will expire in May 1996. Regulation of trade in strategic goods and technology, cultural objects, nonferrous scrap and waste apply to exports as well as imports.

There are no restrictive requirements for domestic or foreign travel. A series of laws dealing with foreign investments guarantees repatriation of after-tax profits and capital. From 1990 to 1994, 3,274 joint-ventures and 1,077 wholly owned foreign companies were registered. Moves are under way to allow for foreign companies to own property.

The exchange rate is fixed by the government in consultation with the Bank of Lithuania.

There are no restrictions on making transfers and payments for imports of goods and services. Proceeds from exports of goods and services are not required to be repatriated to Lithuania.

## Freedom from Unreasonable Government Interference in the Economy

Approximately 25-35 percent of GDP is generated by the private sector. Government expenditure was 29 percent of GDP in 1994. State-sector employment has decreased from 77 percent in 1990 to 39 percent in 1994. Self-employment rose from .5 percent in 1990 to 19.2 percent and private employment rose from 3.2 percent to 41.5 percent.

The Ministry of Economics originally prepared a list of 3,800 enterprises to be sold in the initial phase of privatization. As a result of the divisions into smaller units of several enterprises contained in the original list, the number of enterprises to be privatized rose to 6,500. Privatization of agriculture was preceded by a break-up of 1,100 collective and cooperative farms into 12,300 units designated for privatization. By mid-April 1995, about 80 percent of the targeted enterprises had been privatized. In February 1995, parliament approved a list of companies that would remain in government hands until the year 2000. Most were already on a 1991 List of Enterprises of Specific Designation and included enterprises in strategic sectors such as energy, transportation and telecommunications.

While considerable headway has been made in removing external and domestic controls that hinder competition, hard budget constraints have not been fully enforced. Progress has been uneven in other structural policy areas, notably the financial sector and legal reforms, and enterprises have been allowed to accumulate arrears in taxes and payments to energy companies. Little progress has been made in breaking up large state-owned enterprises. State subsidies decreased from 14 percent of GDP in 1990 to 1.3 percent in 1994. Indirect subsidies are given to the energy sector to maintain artificially low energy prices for consumers.

The 1992 Competition Law monitors unfair competition and monopoly practices. The State Price and Competition Office monitors market developments and handles complaints about abuses of market power.

## Freedom to Participate in the Market Economy 1/2

Women and ethnic minorities are not foreclosed from occupations or certain types of businesses. There are no limits on minorities or women holding or transferring property.

The Bank of Lithuania Law and the Commercial Banking Law, both passed in December 1994, established the legal basis of the banking system and brought regulatory standards closer to European Union requirements. But while the legal framework for a market economy is in place, financial and legal structures and the judicial system have yet to fully catch up with the exigencies of a free enterprise system in such areas as bankruptcy, tax policy, regulatory enforcement, and procedural mechanisms.

Corruption is widespread and organized crime engages in activities from money laundering to smuggling narcotics, oil and arms. As in other post-Soviet countries, Lithuania's private businessmen complain of arbitrary high taxes, import restrictions and corrupt bureaucrats.

# Poland

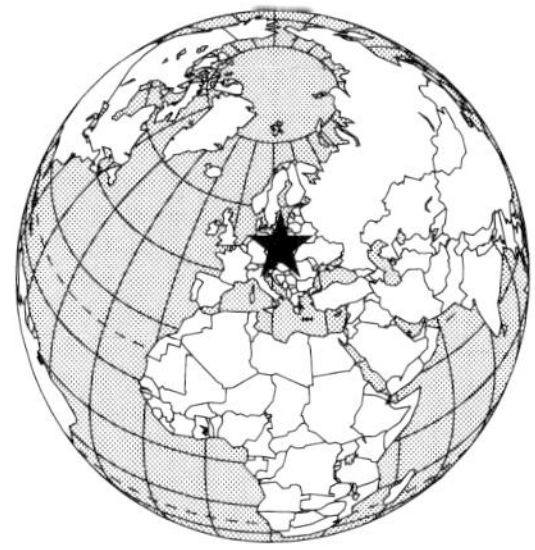

ECONOMIC FREEDOM STATUS: **FREE**
POLITICAL RIGHTS AND CIVIL LIBERTIES STATUS: **FREE**
PRESS FREEDOM STATUS: **FREE**
POPULATION: **38,613,000**
PPP: **$4,380**

## Background

Forty years of Communist dominance ended in 1989 with a peaceful transition to democracy following nine years of martial law. Lech Walesa, founder of the Solidarity trade union movement, became president. Radical economic reform initiated by Finance Minister Leszek Balcerowicz lifted most restrictions on private economic activity. Institutions protecting property rights, enforcing commercial laws, fostering competition and executing independent monetary policy have been established. Privatization of state enterprises began in 1995 after a delay of almost two years. Frequent changes in government and political infighting have strained the reform process. In November 1995, Alexander Kwasniewski of the post-Communist Democratic Left Alliance (SLD) defeated Walesa in the presidential elections and has vowed to continue market reforms.

## Freedom to Hold Property 1/3

Secured interests in property are recognized and enforced, but there are some idiosyncrasies to the Polish system that need to be resolved before the process of securing property is satisfactory.

Despite attempts to enforce international standards protecting intellectual property rights, piracy remains a significant problem.

## Freedom to Earn a Living 3/3

Workers are free to establish and join trade unions. There are four national interbranch industrial unions registered, along with seventeen other major independent industrial branch unions and three agricultural unions. The rights to strike and to bargain collectively are legal.

Wages are freely set in ad hoc negotiations at the local enterprise level. Workers can change jobs freely, and forced labor and child labor are prohibited.

## Freedom to Operate a Business 3/3

After the 1989 Law on Economic Activity was adopted, over 800,000 people set up sole proprietorships and 16,000 new companies were registered by the end of that year. In a survey conducted in mid-1994, 70 percent of respondents emphasized that the current commercial environment allowed them opportunities to show individual business initiative, and nearly 90 percent appreciated the fact that they lived in a country with political and economic freedom. The process of registering a new business is not difficult.

Except for security-related areas, the economy is open to domestic investment. Government contracts are competitively let and the process is transparent. Most prices were liberalized in 1990 under the "shock therapy" of the Balcerowicz plan.

## Freedom to Invest One's Earnings 3/3

Poland's banking system has been restructured and banks now set their own lending and deposit rates. Credit is largely market-determined though some credit restrictions exist. Rates of return on investment are not controlled, and Poles are allowed to invest abroad. Citizens can hold foreign currency and securities.

## Freedom to Trade Internationally 2/2

Tariff rates fluctuate frequently. There is a 6 percent import tax. There is a value-added tax of 22 percent. Tariffs currently average between 8 and 12 percent. A few imports such as gasoline and used cars are subject to quotas. The review process of approving imports has been described as "costly, lengthy and confusing." There are no significant barriers to exports.

Foreign and domestic travel are relatively unrestricted. Restrictions on profit repatriation have been eliminated. Legislation seeks to open the Polish economy to foreign investment and create a level playing field between foreign and domestic investors. Up to 100 percent foreign ownership is allowed. There is no screening of foreign investments. Permits are required to acquire property and to invest in a number of enterprises. Polish privatization programs are open to foreign investors. The currency, the zloty, is not expected to become fully convertible until 1996. However, foreign exchange is freely available.

## Freedom from Unreasonable Government Interference in the Economy

More than 50 percent of GDP is produced by the private sector, which accounts for 60 percent of total employment. Political considerations have slowed the process of privatization of over 413 state-owned enterprises. Over 4,400 enterprises remain in the public sector.

An anti-monopoly office exists to oversee fair competition. However, the large state sector and the dominance of industrial state-owned enterprises have undercut private attempts to compete. State-owned enterprises continue to have access to credits, indirect subsidies, and bureaucrats, many of whom are members of the Communist-era nomenklatura.

Direct government subsidies to large state-owned enterprises have been eliminated. There have been no accounts of law enforcement being used arbitrarily to favor or punish certain sectors or firms.

## Freedom to Participate in the Market Economy 2/2

Polish law does not specifically address equality in hiring practices. Women are not restricted in opening a business. There are no restrictions on women or minority citizens owning property.

Laws on privatization, customs, taxes, and foreign investment are in place in Poland, and follow-up amendments have, in theory, reduced bureaucracy and government interference. Poland's economy continues to make impressive gains. With the advent of the neo-Communists in 1993, members of the former nomenklatura, some openly nostalgic for central planning, are back in government, though this is unlikely to derail Poland's transition to a full market economy. Corruption in the privatization process and other sectors is a problem.

# Romania

ECONOMIC FREEDOM STATUS: **MOSTLY NOT FREE**
POLITICAL RIGHTS AND CIVIL LIBERTIES STATUS: **PARTLY FREE**
PRESS FREEDOM STATUS: **PARTLY FREE**
POPULATION: **22,687,000**
PPP: **$2,840**

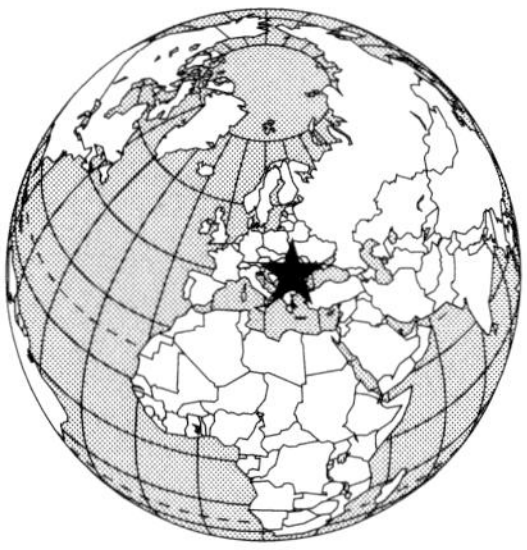

## Background

For twenty-four years, Nicole Ceausescu's autarkic economics impoverished Romania. In 1989, a popular uprising and palace coup by disgruntled Communists toppled Ceausescu, who was tried and executed. A provisional National Salvation Front (NSF) government under President Ion Iliescu, a high-ranking Communist, was established.

Despite political turmoil, some economic reforms have been enacted since 1989. Institutions and a legal framework for a market economy have been established and the private sector is being encouraged through privatization, the lifting of price controls, an end to central planning, tariff reductions, and the liberalization of financial markets. A bourse was created in 1995. However, many problems remain with property rights, corruption, discrimination against ethnic minorities, and a dominant state sector.

## Freedom to Hold Property 1/3

The 1991 constitution guarantees the right to ownership of private property, excluding mineral resources, air rights, and a few other entities. Only 20 percent of farmers have gained title to land, though millions of provisional licenses have been issued. Only 15 percent of arable land is currently covered by land title. A law on the restitution of nationalized housing was passed in June 1995 after fierce debate. Residential housing units built with state funds can be sold to their occupants. There are no legal restrictions on selling or exchanging property, and individuals can structure their property holdings as they choose, though without titles new owners cannot easily sell their land or use it as collateral for bank loans.

Romania is a signatory to international conventions concerning intellectual property rights and has enacted domestic legislation to protect these rights. But implementation and enforcement have been difficult and uneven.

## Freedom to Earn a Living 2/3

Except for public employees, police and military personnel, workers are able to establish and join unions and engage in collective bargaining. Unions are organized in some twenty labor federations, the largest being the independent Fratia National Trade Union Confederation. The 1991 labor law stipulates that unions should be free from government interference and political party control.

Wage rates are established through collective bargaining in the state sector and are set by market forces in the private sector. Individuals are free to change jobs. Forced labor and child labor are not problems.

## Freedom to Operate a Business 2/3

Both private and state-owned enterprises are free to make their own business decisions and to import or export directly. The constitution establishes a market economy in principle, but accompanying provisions and subsequent statutes leave significant room for parliament and the government to influence business practices and activities.

A survey of entrepreneurs outlined two basic barriers to private-sector entry: lack of access to raw materials, business supplies and equipment because state-owned suppliers do not honor contracts; and widespread corruption in obtaining materials and premises. Security-related sectors are restricted, but all other sectors are open to private investment.

There is strong evidence that contracts favor state-owned firms, and old-line members of the bureaucracy distrust the private sector. Price-setting has been largely liberalized. Government policy aims to ensure the supply of materials to industry and of essential goods to the population, and to prevent gouging by monopolies. Remaining price controls on basic goods are updated to reflect world market levels.

## Freedom to Invest One's Earnings 0/3

Interest rates on all liabilities were liberalized, though all interest rates are subject to regulation. Credit is not directed by the government, but banks are still incapable of allocating credit along market guidelines. There are no controls of rates of return on investments, and residents can invest abroad and hold foreign currency and securities. The Central Bank is subject to parliamentary control.

## Freedom to Trade Internationally 2/2

Import licenses have been eliminated. Commercial companies can import and export directly, and no export license is needed for most goods. There are no intrusive proscriptions on domestic or international travel. The exchange rate for the currency, the lei, is set by the market.

## Freedom from Unreasonable Government Interference in the Economy

The government asserts private share of GDP to be 30-35 percent based on its claim, contested by independent observers, that 80-85 percent of agricultural land is private. The Romanian economy is still largely socialized. The government owns virtually all major industry, and state farms still contribute a significant amount of agricultural output. As of mid-1995, some 600 small enterprises had been privatized. The State Ownership Fund holds a 70 percent stake in over 6,000 state-run companies slated for privatization over the next six to fifteen years. At the end of 1994, only 1 percent of capital stock of state-owned enterprises had been divested. There are an estimated 525,000 private businesses, 60 percent registered as commercial companies and the rest as individual or family businesses, engaged primarily in services and import-export. Most direct subsidies have been eliminated. However, 494 public corporations in sectors considered of special economic importance continue to receive government subsidies.

Romania has taken a gradualist approach to economic liberalization and market reforms. And while privatization laws, regulations and procedural structures are in place, an underdeveloped and weak judiciary, hazy commercial provisions and unclear enforcement responsibilities have hindered the establishment of a market system under the rule of law.

The state is capable of hampering private economic activity should it see fit to do so, as indicated by government control of large sectors of industrial and raw materials; ministerial-level instructions limiting access of materials to private companies, or barring government-owned units from dealing with private enterprises; and remaining "profiteering" laws and bureaucratic practices.

**Freedom to Participate in the Market Economy 1/2**

Ethnic Roma (Gypsies) face discrimination in housing, employment and education. Women are able to start and operate businesses, and there are no specific restrictions against women or minorities regarding the ownership of property.

Since 1989, the Romanian parliament has passed a large volume of legislation establishing new institutions and the fundamental statutory framework needed to govern public and private activities in a free-market setting. However, polices and regulations are characterized by insufficient coherence and a lack of credibility and transparency. Corruption, nepotism and cronyism are problems in privatization.

# Russia

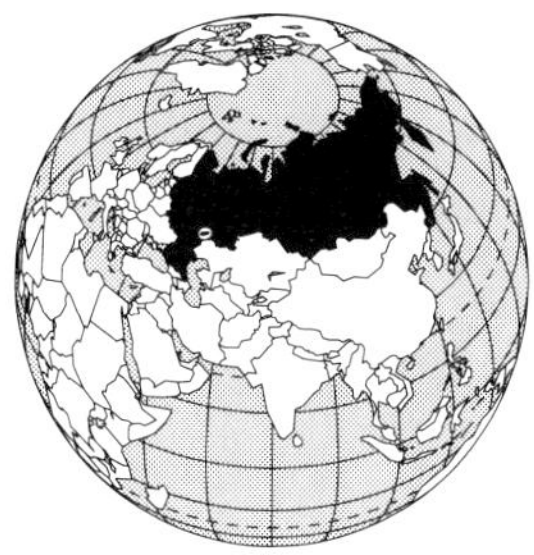

ECONOMIC FREEDOM STATUS: **MOSTLY NOT FREE**
POLITICAL RIGHTS AND CIVIL LIBERTIES STATUS: **PARTLY FREE**
PRESS FREEDOM STATUS: **PARTLY FREE**
POPULATION: **147,480,000**
PPP: **$6,140**

**Background**

Russia gained de facto independence in 1991 under President Boris Yeltsin. Since then, Yeltsin has faced considerable pressure from an increasingly conservative parliament over foreign policy and the pace of economic reforms. Throughout much of 1994, Yeltsin sent mixed signals on the future of reforms. When Deputy Prime Minister Yegor Gaidar, in charge of the economy, and Finance Minister Boris Fyodorov resigned in protest against irresponsible economic policies, Prime Minister Viktor Chernomyrdin declared the era of "shock reforms" over. Yet in June of 1994, Yeltsin reasserted his role in economic policymaking, announcing a series of decrees to loosen government export controls, reduce taxes, and define procedures for liquidating bankrupt state industries.

In 1995, widening disparities between the small economic elite and those left out of the process, growing poverty, and a dramatic rise in organized crime and corruption eroded popular support for economic reform. With presidential elections looming amid the rising political popularity of nationalists and Communists, reforms have slowed significantly and could very well be reversed.

The rules for opening a business make it difficult for small entrepreneurs to get started, the central bank is not independent, less than 5 percent of all farmers own their land, and only a handful of collective farms have been privatized. Furthermore, recent changes in personnel in President Yeltsin's government suggest there will be no progress on economic reform at least until after the 1996 presidential elections.

**Freedom to Hold Property 1/3**

The right to own real property is still being legislated, and a lack of legal protection of property has been of significant concern to investors. Urban residents are allowed to purchase their residences for nominal fees. Foreigners cannot own land but can lease it for up to ninety-nine years. Russian companies may own the land on which their facilities stand. State and collective farms have been reorganized. About 47 percent became closed joint-stock farms, and 11 percent formed cooperative agricultural enterprises. Although there are almost 200,000 private peasant farms, by the fourth quarter of 1993, for every 100 farms created, 52 had stopped operating.

There is a labyrinth of restrictions on selling and exchanging property, and the concepts of private property rights and outright land ownership have yet to be codified in a cogent, comprehensive form. This limits the way individuals can structure their holdings.

Laws have strengthened the protection of intellectual property rights, trademarks, computer programs, audio/visual tapes and recordings. However, enforcement remains lax and pirating is widespread.

## Freedom to Earn a Living 1/3

Workers are able to establish and join trade unions. Labor unions must register with local authorities, who in the past have obstructed the formation of new bodies. The Federation of Independent Trade Unions of Russia (FNPR), the successor to the Soviet-era All-Union Central Council of Trade Unions, has largely retained the privileges and control mechanisms of the old official structure. Membership in smaller independent unions—including formerly official unions that have disaffiliated themselves from the FNPR—and associations does not exceed 3 million out of a workforce of 72 million. The two largest non-FNPR unions are the Metalworkers and the NPG miners.

Labor courts do not exist, and the overburdened legal system has neither the experience nor the will to enforce existing legislation. As a result, local governments and enterprises pressure and intimidate union activists. Collective bargaining is protected by law but not widely practiced, and many enterprise directors reject it.

Wages are set through negotiations, but the state still controls large sections of the economy, including heavy industry. Individuals are technically free to change jobs, but the dominance of the state in the economy and residency limits mobility.

Although labor codes prohibit compulsory labor, there are persistent allegations that some military conscripts were forced to work or, in some cases, sold into servitude. North Korea pays Russia to operate logging camps in Siberia that use prison labor, including North Korean prisoners of conscience.

## Freedom to Operate a Business 2/3

Foreign and domestic legal entities may establish, purchase and dispose of businesses in Russia, but the process is complicated and far from transparent. Nevertheless, a significant proportion of the population has entered into business. Lack of regulation, licensing, and clear procedures have led to the formation of shady banks, investment funds, and financial companies that have defrauded the public.

Private commerce is barred from areas related to national security. Private and state enterprises are entitled to equal treatment, but private firms operate at a competitive disadvantage. The government has introduced auction tenders for official procurements. An established and transparent set of regulations regarding bidding is lacking.

Roughly 85 percent of wholesale and retail prices had been liberalized as of 1992. However, energy prices continue to be controlled at the wholesale level.

## Freedom to Invest One's Earnings 1/3

Interest rates are regulated. The allocation of Central Bank gross credit to banks is determined by the Central Policy Commission, an interagency body with representatives from the ministries of finance, economy and agriculture, as well as from the Central Bank. Directed credit determined by government decisions declined from 20 percent of GDP to 7 percent in 1993. These credits were channeled primarily to agriculture and areas classified as having urgent needs.

Without special permission, it is illegal for Russian companies to maintain bank accounts outside Russia for purposes other than operating expenses. Licenses are required for offshore accounts and can be difficult to obtain. A June 1994 decree reversed a two-year moratorium on foreign bank operations by Russian citizens, but only for banks from countries that had an investment agreement with Russia. Russian enterprises are required to convert 50 percent of foreign currency earnings into rubles by selling such currency either on the currency market or to the Central Bank.

The banking sector in Russia is unstable. There are over 2,000 banks in Russia, many of which are very small and lack adequate capitalization. Dozens of bankers have been murdered, banks have collapsed without protection for small investors, and there have been charges of collusion against a consortium of banks in Moscow. In mid-November, the Central Bank revoked the licenses of thirty commercial banks, bringing the total of closures in 1995 to 150.

## Freedom to Trade Internationally 1/2

By mid-1994, Russia had liberalized domestic trade and dismantled virtually all non-tariff restrictions on foreign trade. However, tariff rates have increased several times. The mean tariff of 13-15 percent is several times higher than that levied by most Western countries. In addition to the tariffs, there are excise taxes and a value-added tax of 23 percent. Import licenses are required for such items as chemicals, arms, and radioactive materials. Most export quota requirements have been removed.

There are no significant restrictions on domestic or foreign travel. There are no significant legal barriers for foreign companies doing business in Russia. The absence of sufficiently developed civil, commercial and regulatory law is the key impediment to foreign investment. Prior approval is required for investment in many enterprises.

To stem capital flight, exporters are required to exchange 50 percent of hard currency earnings for rubles. The exchange rate floats based on the daily Moscow interbank currency auction, where the Central Bank intervenes to smooth fluctuations. In practice, the Central Bank exerts considerable influence on the rate, as it collects and resells most of Russia's export earnings.

## Freedom from Unreasonable Government Interference in the Economy

The state sector dominates the economy. International institutions estimate that the private sector accounts for some 40 percent of GDP. Massive privatization began in 1992; in small-scale privatization, by mid-1995, 95 percent of Russia's shops had been privatized. By mid-1994, over 100,000 enterprises had been privatized through vouchers or auctions, representing about two-thirds of formerly state-owned enterprises. Many private entrepreneurs have joined the informal, "shadow" economy to avoid federal restrictions, gangsters and high taxes. Estimates of the size of the gray economy range from 25 to 40 percent of the officially recorded economy.

Although the government has repeatedly emphasized its commitment to reform, a conservative, often obstructionist parliament has forced the government to maintain some statist policies such as price controls, slowdowns in property rights, subsidies, controlled credits, and bottlenecks in privatization. Direct credits and subsides have declined, but agriculture and some large, state-owned industries, both of which have substantial influence in parliament, continue to receive state subsidies.

## Freedom to Participate in the Market Economy 1/2

Many jobs in the private sector are reserved specifically and legally for men. Women are usually the first to be laid off from atrophying state enterprises, and 65 percent of Russia's unemployed are women. Discrimination against people from the Caucasus is prevalent in work and housing. There are no legal restrictions on women and minorities in terms of business activity, but cultural factors and ethnic discrimination are serious barriers.

Russia has the rudiments of a market system, but there are serious problems with establishing the rule of law. Bankruptcy laws are not applied. Taxation is unpredictable and capricious. Many government decisions affecting business are taken by executive fiat. The judicial system is poorly developed and corrupt. Authority and jurisdiction among various government levels and agencies are too often unclear or duplicated.

Corruption is prevalent and much crime is tied to commercial activity. Bankers and other business leaders have been assassinated, and 8,000 gangs involved in racketeering, kickbacks and protection are known to operate in Russia.

# Slovakia

ECONOMIC FREEDOM STATUS: **PARTLY FREE**
POLITICAL RIGHTS AND CIVIL LIBERTIES STATUS: **PARTLY FREE**
PRESS FREEDOM STATUS: **PARTLY FREE**
POPULATION: **5,370,000**
PPP: **$6,690**

## Background

Slovakia became independent on 1 January 1993, with the breakup of Czechoslovakia. By the time of the dissolution, Czechoslovakia had made significant progress in dismantling Communist-era economic controls and restoring economic freedom, and while Slovakia has continued to make some advances since, it has lagged somewhat behind the Czech Republic. Slovakia's citizens are not yet free to open new businesses and invest their earnings as they please, and rights to both tangible and intellectual property are not yet fully protected by law. Intellectual property rights were not always enforced, some businesses were still subject to price controls during 1995, and citizens still encountered restrictions on their ability to invest abroad.

## Freedom to Hold Property 2/3

The right to property is recognized by law. Slovak laws on intellectual property rights are compatible with western European legislation but enforcement and prosecution are problematic. A new law on trademarks was passed in 1995.

Under a property restitution law passed by Czechoslovakia, 156,702 hectares of land were returned to 24,000 claimants, and an additional 32,379 hectares representing joint claims were returned to communities. Restrictions on land usage by existing owners have been lifted for 461,810 hectares of arable and wooded land. Individuals can structure their property holdings as they choose.

## Freedom to Earn a Living 2/3

All unions are associated with the Confederation of Labor Unions-Slovak Republic (KOZ-SR), the Slovak remnant of the Communist-era union that existed in Czechoslovakia. Workers enjoy the right to strike and collective bargaining is protected by law and freely practiced. Unions are independent from government and political parties.

In July 1994, selective wage controls were implemented in loss-making enterprises, as well as the energy and finance sectors. However, most private-sector wages are exempt from these controls, and are set by free negotiation.

Workers are free to change jobs, though in a transition economy hidden unemployment and state control of key industries are factors. Forced labor and the exploitation of minors are prohibited.

## Freedom to Operate a Business 2/3

The Slovak government has streamlined the process of organizing and registering businesses, and there are no excessive registration requirements. Government-granted monopolies no longer exist, and few areas are off-limits to private commerce.

The national and regional governments abide by a procurement law that outlines a set of procedures establishing competitive bidding. Nearly all price controls have been removed. Controls on food, fuel and energy were scheduled to be phased out by the end of 1995.

## Freedom to Invest One's Earnings 2/3

Interest rates are not regulated and credit flows are determined by market forces. There are no controls over the rates of return on investments. Individuals may not yet invest abroad, but a new law is pending. Citizens may maintain hard-currency accounts and are entitled to purchase 9,000 korunas worth of hard currency a year.

The National Bank of Slovakia is independent of the government and has maintained a tight monetary policy to keep inflation down to 14.2 percent per year.

## Freedom to Trade Internationally 1/2

Import licenses are governed by a 1991 decree of the former Czechoslovak Ministry of Foreign Trade. For most of the 100 categories, licensing is a mere formality; however, permission from the Ministry of Finance is required for products with environmental or military significance. Customs procedures are not overly burdensome or complicated. There are no export subsidies and no significant barriers to exports. Domestic and international travel are generally unrestricted.

Foreign investment has been encouraged by the government. While foreigners cannot own land, there are no significant barriers to hiring foreign personnel, and no restrictions on repatriation of profits or capital. The Slovak koruna is internally convertible and is slated to become fully convertible by the year 2000.

## Freedom from Unreasonable Government Interference in the Economy

The World Bank put the private sector's share of GDP at 58 percent in mid-1995. Privatization began in 1991-92 with direct auctions and joint ventures. In June 1995, the government announced that the new "privatization" would be accomplished through issuing bonds not representing shares in any particular industry. Most small-scale privatization of retail and services has been completed, encompassing 9,500 enterprises. Large-scale privatization has repeatedly been held up by political factors, conceptual changes, and bureaucratic bottlenecks. The privatization minister is a fierce opponent of selling off state companies to outsiders. The government has no immediate plans to privatize telecommunications, energy or other strategic infrastructures.

The government has sought to ensure competition by adopting laws banning monopolistic and unfair business practices. Direct subsidies to enterprises have fallen to about 8 percent of GDP.

**Freedom to Participate in the Market Economy 1/2**

Ethnic minorities and women are not foreclosed from any occupation or from running any type of business, though periodic political and cultural tensions have arisen between the government and the 560,000-strong Hungarian minority.

While privatization legislation, tax laws and commercial codes provide a legal framework for a market economy, inefficient state companies continue to receive government subsidies, mass privatization has stalled, and there have been persistent allegations of corruption. Corruption was particularly evident in the early phases of the privatization process, when government officials used their positions to advance "spontaneous privatization" schemes involving friends and associates.

# Turkmenistan

ECONOMIC FREEDOM STATUS: **NOT FREE**
POLITICAL RIGHTS AND CIVIL LIBERTIES STATUS: **NOT FREE**
PRESS FREEDOM STATUS: **NOT FREE**
POPULATION: **4,471,000**
PPP: **$3,400**

**Background**

For the people of Turkmenistan, the collapse of the Soviet Union has meant little in the way of an increase in either political or economic freedom. President Saparmurad Niyazov, former first secretary of the Turkmen Communist Party, has fostered a cult of personality around himself. Niyazov has actively sought foreign investment to exploit vast energy reserves. However, Soviet-era restrictions on the rights to earn a living and to operate a business remain, the laws establishing private property rights and otherwise creating the conditions for a market economy have yet to be enacted, and some 80 percent of all economic activity is government-controlled.

**Freedom to Hold Property 1/3**

There is no property ownership allowed in rural areas. Outright ownership in urban areas is granted where a well defined property is associated with an enterprise. Where a property is shared with another enterprise, a longterm lease is granted.

Land reform has taken the form of leaseholds. Only 2 percent of the land is arable. Undeveloped plots of land were distributed among those intending to grow agricultural products in exchange for forfeiting the right to sell or give away such products. Farmers must sell their products to the state at fixed rates and do not own their own land. Less than 10 percent of the land has been privatized, most of it desert. Less than 10 percent of the agricultural sector has been privatized. The state can reclaim land it deems is not being used judiciously. Land may be inherited, but not sold or subdivided.

**Freedom to Earn a Living 0/3**

The Soviet-era Federation of Trade Unions is the only labor union. The law does not protect the right to collective bargaining. Although there are no specific prohibitions against forming an independent union, the overall repressive political atmosphere is a serious impediment.

State-sponsored unions control key social benefits, and deductions from payrolls covering these benefits are transferred directly to the Federation.

Salaries are regulated by the Unified Tariff Schedule, which determines minimum wages for state enterprises, the private sector and joint-ventures. Annual discussions between the government trade union and management determine specific wages and benefits for each factory or enterprise. Technically, workers can freely change jobs, but political factors, arbitrary travel restrictions and an internal passport system can be used to prevent moving or changing residences.

The constitution specifically prohibits forced labor. However, high school students are often forced to work in cotton fields for minimal pay. Child labor is a problem in rural areas.

## Freedom to Operate a Business **1/3**

The process of registering a new business is not difficult, and small businesses are flourishing. The government has created several agencies to help foster small-scale private enterprise.

Businesses employing fewer than 100 workers are set for rapid privatization. So far, less than 25 percent of small businesses have been privatized. The government makes the dubious, unconfirmed claim that there are 12,500 small business enterprises (including manufacturing) employing some 50,000 workers.

The government maintains control over sectors dealing with oil and gas, electricity, rail and air transport, communications, education, science, health and culture.

With power centralized in the president and his office, there are a lack of procedural transparency and frequent complaints of corruption.

Prices are controlled for staples, medicines, rent, public transportation and services. As of 1995, fifty products were subsidized.

## Freedom to Invest One's Earnings **1/3**

Most banks have great leeway in setting deposit and lending rates. Credit is directed to state enterprises based on need. There are no controls on rates of return on investment, but individuals cannot invest abroad.

Currently, individuals are not allowed access to foreign exchange except limited amounts for foreign travel.

A Central Bank Law adopted in 1994 gave the Bank a more prominent role in the conduct of monetary and credit policy and the development of effective monetary control. However, policy developments suggest that the bank continues to be subject to extensive political constraints that undermine its authority over the conduct of monetary policy.

## Freedom to Trade Internationally **1/2**

Imports require licenses, but are largely free of restrictions. Some 60 percent of the country's food is imported. Quantitative and price restrictions are imposed on exports of cotton and other raw materials to protect domestic supplies. Also, all exports outside the former Soviet Union require a special license which, according to authorities, is granted freely. All foreign exchange earnings from exports must be repatriated and connected to the manat, the national currency.

The government uses its power to issue passports and exit visas as a means of restricting international travel to political opponents or anyone out of favor with the government.

Foreign investment is encouraged. Foreigners may gain land-use rights for up to twenty-five years at an appropriate, predetermined rate, but only in connection with joint-venture agreements. The president oversees most major foreign investments, which has led to charges of mismanagement and corruption. The government has signed contracts on exploration and production of the country's substantial oil and gas reserves with several countries, including the U.S.

The exchange rate of the manat, introduced in 1993, is set by the Central Bank. The manat is not freely convertible, and the exchange system has become increasingly restrictive and less transparent. In general, the overvalued exchange rate has severely distorted relative prices and retarded external trade. Since its introduction, the manat has been devalued by 90 percent in stages. Commercial banks are allowed to engage in foreign exchange operations, and six banks are currently licensed to do so.

### Freedom from Unreasonable Government Interference in the Economy

It is estimated that as of mid-1995, no more than 15 percent of GDP was generated by the private sector. In 1994, government expenditure represented almost 10 percent of GDP, down from 20 percent the previous year. The government still controls the overwhelming majority of large- and medium-scale enterprises. While 1995 legislation was to address small-scale business privatization, no action was taken. The goal for large industrial enterprises is to rapidly expand the processing of the country's natural and agricultural resources. Mass privatization is planned for a later stage, but will include no industries connected with energy or other major sources of revenue.

The government provides substantial subsidies to state enterprises, including transportation, communications, and particularly the export-oriented energy sector.

### Freedom to Participate in the Market Economy 1/2

Women face considerable discrimination in Turkmenistan in terms of employment and education opportunities. There is increasing fear among non-Turkic peoples, particularly Russians and Uzbeks, about being shut out of economic and educational opportunities, and many Russians have left Turkmenistan.

The judiciary is not independent of presidential and government control. The rule of law does not exist. The president appoints all judges without legislative review. A Supreme Economic Court hears cases involving disputes between state economic enterprises and ministries. Corruption is pervasive in government and business.

# Ukraine

ECONOMIC FREEDOM STATUS: **MOSTLY NOT FREE**
POLITICAL RIGHTS AND CIVIL LIBERTIES STATUS: **PARTLY FREE**
PRESS FREEDOM STATUS: **PARTLY FREE**
POPULATION: **52,000,000**
PPP: **$5,010**

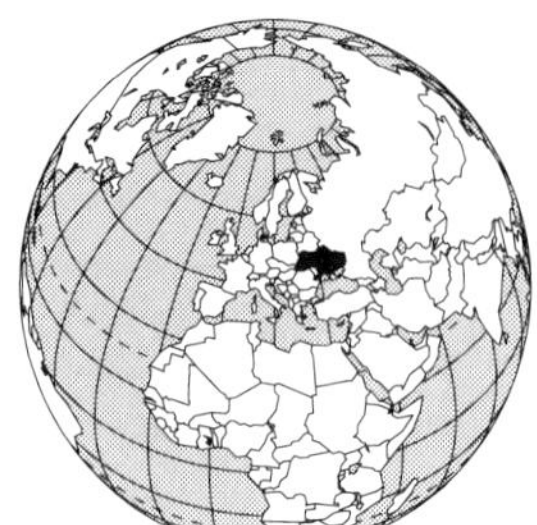

### Background

President Leonid Kuchma's plans to dismantle Soviet-era economic controls have been repeatedly frustrated by a conservative, statist majority in parliament. Once the breadbasket of the Soviet Union and with the potential to be a major exporter of foodstuffs, the Ukrainian agriculture sector is still hobbled by the absence of a legal framework within which privately owned farms can prosper. The nation also lacks a genuinely independent central bank, and restrictions on foreign investment and repatriation of earnings have discouraged needed private capital.

But while economic freedom has still to be realized, some progress has been made since Ukraine declared its independence from the Soviet Union in 1991. The process of registering new businesses has been simplified, and government's control of trade unions has diminished significantly.

### Freedom to Hold Property 1/3

The right to private property is ill-defined in law. Land reform and privatization efforts have lagged. Although collective farm workers are theoretically able to claim their share of land and leave the collective, ambiguous regulations and procedures have discouraged participation. The number of private farms remains negligible. The government allowed ownership of household plots for current tenants, including the right to sell and amalgamate holdings. This land can be used for small-scale cultivation.

Almost 15 percent of apartments in state housing stock have been privatized. Tenants have been allowed to buy, sell and rent apartments, but much of real estate activity occurs in the "gray zone" of the informal economy through hard cash transactions.

Intellectual property rights are not protected, and pirating, particularly of films, video and music, is a problem. Parliament has yet to provide a clear definition of private property, and laws on the transference of property are murky.

### Freedom to Earn a Living 2/3

Workers are able to establish and join trade unions and to affiliate with international labor organizations. The largest federation, the Federation of Trade Unions, is the successor to the Soviet-era body. Five independent unions formed the Consultative (Advisory) Council of Free Trade Unions in 1992; over 80 percent of the workforce is unionized.

The enterprise law states that wages are to be set by joint worker-management commissions. The government, in consultation with trade unions, sets wages in each industrial sector. Wages in the state sector are controlled. The collective bargaining law is slanted against independent unions in favor of officially sanctioned bodies. Individuals can change jobs freely. Forced labor and the exploitation of minors are prohibited.

### Freedom to Operate a Business 2/3

Ukraine has streamlined the process of registering businesses which, along with small-scale privatization, has led to a growing private sector. However, excessive taxes have led many businesses to function in an informal or "shadow" economy which some estimate to account for 30 to 40 percent of business activity.

All sectors of the economy are open to private investment except sensitive sectors such as nuclear energy, weapons production, and some pharmaceuticals. Ukraine does have some price controls in agricultural, but farmers can sell their products freely on the commodity exchange or to trading houses after state quotas are met.

### Freedom to Invest One's Earnings 1/3

There are few restrictions on investments. Interest rates are not regulated, and there are no controls regarding rates of return on investments. However, significant restrictions remain for capital account transfers that affect investing abroad. Individuals can hold foreign currency and securities.

The Central Bank is not truly independent and is accountable to the parliament, making it difficult to refuse credit demands from industrial and agricultural interests whose representatives dominate the legislature.

## Freedom to Trade Internationally 1/2

There are no non-tariff barriers on imports except standard rules for safety and the environment. International lending institutions have pressured Ukraine to reduce many export controls, which are abused by corrupt officials. However, exports remain below 10 percent of GDP. Ukrainian officials fear that liberalizing exports could lead to domestic shortages of food and agricultural products. Firms are allowed to export outside the quota system by paying an export tariff of 5-30 percent. Firms can also export by purchasing export quotas at auctions arranged by the Ministry of Foreign Economic relations and local commodity exchanges. In all, quotas cover 390 products, including raw materials, intermediate goods and agricultural products. Licenses are also required for all exports except manufactured goods.

Domestic and international travel is generally unrestricted; exit visas are no longer required. Foreign travelers must register with local militias, but this rule is arbitrarily enforced.

Foreign investment has been encouraged by the government, though licenses are required for some businesses. Foreign exchange was liberalized in 1993. Firms must still repatriate all foreign earnings to domestic commercial bank accounts, but they need to surrender only half the proceeds. Residents can easily obtain foreign exchange. There are no limits on the amount firms can purchase for imports, as long as they present a valid import contract, and no restrictions on remittances of profits. Limits exist on the purchase of foreign exchange for business travel or personal use.

## Freedom from Unreasonable Government Interference in the Economy

Although 8,000 large and medium state enterprises and another 22,000 smaller enterprises have recently been privatized, the state sector still dominates the economy. By the end of 1995, the state sector still represented some 55 percent of fixed commercial assets. In June 1995 a decree, "On Measures to Ensure Privatization in 1995," allowed foreigners to participate in the privatization of enterprises on equal terms with Ukrainian citizens.

A thicket of restrictions and high taxes on private businesses has, de facto, favored the state sector and forced much private business activity into the "shadow economy." State subsidies on oil and gas imports, mostly from Russia, have delayed the restructuring of industry, and contributed to a balance of payments deficit of $5.5 billion in 1995.

## Freedom to Participate in the Market Economy 1/2

There are no restrictions on ethnic minorities and women in terms of business opportunities. While privatization legislation and foreign investment laws have opened up the economy, the infrastructure for a market system remains weak. Ill-defined property rights, complex regulations and a seemingly arbitrary system of taxation have hindered economic reforms.

As in most of the former Soviet Union, corruption is widespread and organized criminal activity has impeded legitimate business interests, both foreign and domestic.

# Uzbekistan

ECONOMIC FREEDOM STATUS: **NOT FREE**
POLITICAL RIGHTS AND CIVIL LIBERTIES STATUS: **NOT FREE**
PRESS FREEDOM STATUS: **NOT FREE**
POPULATION: **22,694,000**
PPP: **$2,650**

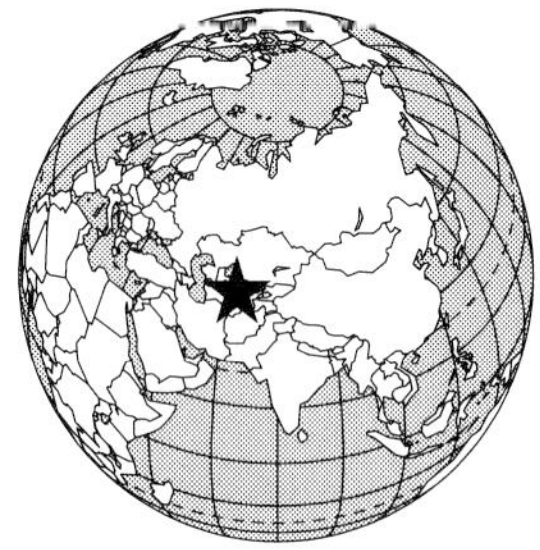

## Background

In the five years since its independence from the Soviet Union, Uzbekistan has made little progress in dismantling Soviet-era controls on the economy. Trade unions are still to all intents and purposes an arm of the government, most land cannot be privately owned, and government-owned or -controlled entities account for a large share of economic activity. The current government denies citizens even the rudimentary elements of economic freedom.

## Freedom to Hold Property 0/3

The government issued a decree legalizing private ownership of land in January 1994. However, the decree refers specifically to land under small business establishments in the trade and service sectors, such that an individual purchasing a small business can also buy the plot of land on which it stands. Agriculture is in the early stages of privatization. Under the plan, collective farms are being reorganized into cooperatives through leasing the land to former collective farm workers, on either an individual or a group basis. Each family unit receives a private plot, the produce from which it may sell at local markets. State farms are being converted to collective farms.

Several laws address property and leaseholding. A presidential decree in March 1994 opened the way for limited private housing construction. In rural areas, many if not most homes have been privately built and are de facto privately owned. Tens of thousands of apartments have been turned over to their occupants. However, property may not be sold or transferred, though leases can be inherited.

Uzbekistan is not party to any international conventions protecting intellectual property rights, and such protection is nonexistent.

## Freedom to Earn a Living 0/3

Trade unions remain structured along Soviet lines, and there are no independent unions. With few exceptions, all workers who are employed in state-owned enterprises belong to the Uzbekistan Federation of Trade Unions, which does not negotiate wages or other issues and acts like a professional association.

Wages in the state sector are set by the government, but the few private businesses can structure their own wages. The constitution promises citizens the right to work where they choose, but most employment is found in the state sector. A few professional groups and associations, representing doctors, lawyers, and entrepreneurs, aim to have a role in licensing and otherwise regulating the economic activity of their members.

While the constitution forbids forced labor, government workers and students are often used in harvesting cotton for nominal wages.

## Freedom to Operate a Business 2/3

The state sector remains dominant. State-owned shops and services can be bought at auction, but with the stipulation that the new owners may not change the production profile of the business purchased. New small private businesses, mostly in the trade, retail and catering sectors, operate on a leasehold basis.

The rules governing the formation of business enterprises have been simplified. The energy sector is the only sector totally closed to private investment.

Noncompetitive bidding is still common practice, with trade deals often based on relationships between government officials and domestic and foreign firms. The government has recently made more use of tenders and competitive bidding. Most prices were liberalized in 1992 though prices for nineteen basic goods are fixed for social welfare stability.

## Freedom to Invest One's Earnings 1/3

Few in this impoverished land have money to invest. Interest rates are not regulated. Individuals can invest abroad. In August 1994, citizens were given the right to purchase $250 (later increased to $1,000) in foreign exchange through the commercial banking system. The currency, the som, is the only legal tender for domestic transactions, though in reality many deals are done with hard cash.

A central bank, created in 1992, is supposedly independent but is in fact under direct government influence. Credit policies accommodate the government, which has extended interest-free credit.

## Freedom to Trade Internationally 1/2

No import licenses are required. According to the U.S. Department of State, customs procedures are "bureaucratic, often arbitrary, and sometimes complicated by corruption." The bulk of exports is handled by the Ministry of Foreign Economic Relations through foreign trade associations. However, an increasing volume of exports has been carried out through production firms themselves. Licenses are required for exporting to countries outside the former Soviet Union and for goods considered to be of strategic importance to the national economy, such as cotton, mineral products, fertilizer and silk worms.

Although the constitution provides for free movement within the country and across borders, foreign travel is still restricted by difficulties in obtaining overseas passports and exit visas.

The 1991 Foreign Investment Law defines property rights of firms, allowing them to export their products, import without licenses, and retain foreign exchange earnings. The process of registering a joint venture and gaining approval is long and cumbersome, requiring review by the highest levels of government.

The som was introduced in 1994 after the country left the ruble zone. There is a two-tiered exchange system—the official rate is set by the central bank based on the outcome of a biweekly auction of dollars to authorized commercial banks by the Republic Currency Exchange. The commercial rate set by the central bank is determined by its own set of unpublished calculations. A parallel exchange market operates openly, albeit outside the law, and in late 1994 its premium was 25-30 percent over official rates. Only four of twenty-one banks are licensed to conduct foreign currency transactions and have some leeway in setting their own exchange rates. There is a requirement that 60 percent of foreign exchange earned be surrendered.

## Freedom from Unreasonable Government Interference in the Economy

The World Bank estimated in mid-1995 that the private share of GDP is no more than 15 to 20 percent.

Goods produced under state-directed planning (*goszakaz*) such as cotton must be sold to the government. Although price controls have technically been abolished, the state planning system still determines quantities, and thus, indirectly, prices for many industrial goods. By July 1993, only 12 percent of mostly small-scale state-owned enterprises were privatized: 13 percent through conversion into joint-stock companies or collectives, 86 percent through direct sale to private individuals or families, and the remainder through leasing.

Government-owned banks continue to support failing state enterprises through heavily subsidized credit. The government has targeted oil and gas, mining, agricultural processing, textiles, and tourism as priority areas for foreign investment.

The commercial laws appear fair and encourage competition. The absence of the rule of law and legal procedures encourage arbitrary application of regulations and rules by the government.

## Freedom to Participate in the Market Economy 0/2

Non-Uzbeks, mostly Slavs and Turks, face discrimination in housing, employment and business. Women are not legally restricted from engaging in business, but face daunting cultural obstacles.

While the legal framework exists for a market economy, a repressive political system and the intrusion of government in virtually all major sectors of the economy have seriously impeded the establishment of all but the rudiments of genuine reform. Graft, bribery and criminal activity form a pervasive part of the business climate.

## Political Freedom v. Economic Freedom for Asia

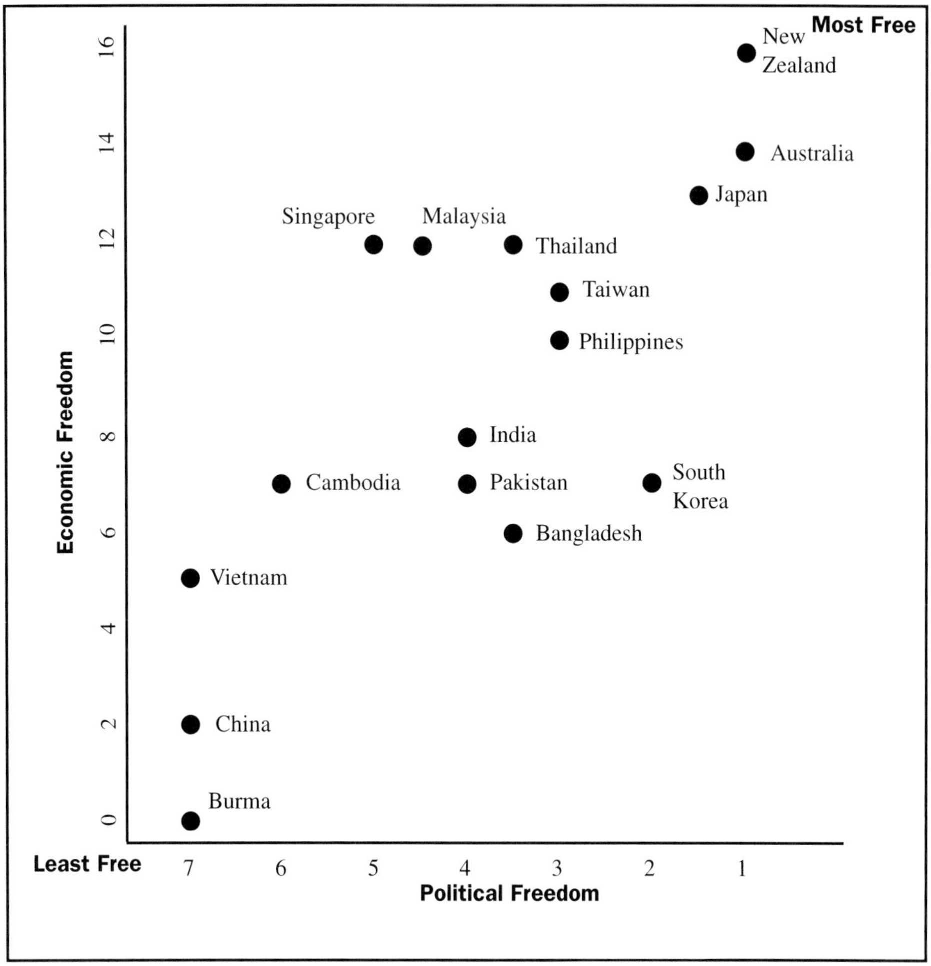


### POLITICAL FREEDOM VERSUS ECONOMIC FREEDOM

The graph above shows the relationship between the level of political freedom and economic freedom for countries in Asia. The ratings for political freedom were derived by averaging Freedom House's political rights and civil liberties ratings from the *Freedom in the World: The Annual Survey of Political Rights and Civil Liberties*, 1995-1996. A score of "1" represents the most free and "7" the least free.

Economic freedom is graphed on the vertical scale with "0" representing "Not Free" and "16" representing "Free."

# ASIA

## Australia

ECONOMIC FREEDOM STATUS: **FREE**
POLITICAL RIGHTS AND CIVIL LIBERTIES STATUS: **FREE**
PRESS FREEDOM STATUS: **FREE**
POPULATION: **18,031,000**
PPP: **$18,220**

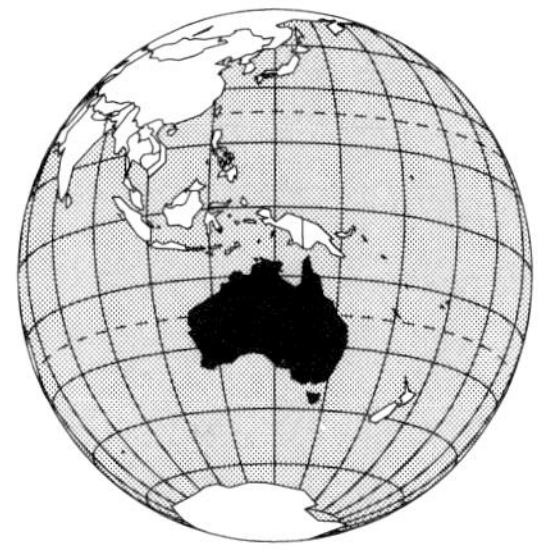

### Background

Although Australia follows some policies at odds with economic freedom, such as the maintenance of high tariffs on selected items and the retention of the power to impose price controls on some goods and services, these restraints are relatively minor.

Australians have not always enjoyed such a high level of economic freedom. It was only in the mid-1980s that Australia reversed a statist economic policy—opening its markets to international competition, liberalizing the exchange rate, privatizing state enterprises, and freeing the financial sector. These policy changes have not been free of controversy. The opposition Liberal/National coalition, which has questioned the wisdom of deregulating certain sectors of the economy, won a key by-election in March 1995 and topped the opinion polls as Australia headed into federal elections due by May 1996.

### Freedom to Hold Property 3/3

The right to property is recognized by law and the legal system effectively enforces these laws. The Native Title Act, passed in 1993, acknowledges the rights of Aborigines to land with which they have traditional links but also confirms the validity of existing lease titles.

Patents, trademarks, and copyrights are all effectively protected by the Australian Intellectual Property Law.

### Freedom to Earn a Living 3/3

Australians are not restricted in choosing their place of residence or occupations.

Australia has freedom of association and freedom to bargain collectively. In the past, minimum wage levels have been determined by centralized fixed wage agreements but the Industrial Relations Reform Act of 1994 allows a more flexible system of bargaining. Unions are free from government control but most belong to local branches of the Australian Labor Party.

Australians are free to change jobs. Although there are no laws specifically prohibiting forced labor, it is not practiced.

Recent legislation by the government has encouraged the amalgamation of unions and, since 1989, has reduced the total number of unions from 143 to 48. This legislation, however, has not inhibited workers' ability to join or participate in unions.

## Freedom to Operate a Business 2/3

Regulations governing the formation of businesses are relatively transparent and do not vary among states. Australians are not forbidden from entering any particular line of commerce. The government does currently control all major utilities and major communications firms but it has taken steps to increase competition and open entry into these sectors.

While establishing a business may be relatively simple, Australia is still a country with strong unions which, some complain, make it difficult to operate an efficient business. Many business owners complain particularly about strict union laws that can make it virtually impossible to fire someone. They argue that recent changes in union law have not alleviated the situation.

Australia has not yet signed the GATT Government Procurement Code and is in the process of revising its procurement guidelines. The revised guidelines will allow the government to use procurement policy to encourage local industry development. The guidelines, however, do not specifically direct government agencies to give preference to local suppliers.

Australian states retain the legislative power to enact price controls, but few price controls currently exist. The Prices Surveillance Authority (PSA) examines prices in certain industries to ensure competitive pricing, and some major industries, such as oil and petrol, must notify the PSA before any price increases.

## Freedom to Invest One's Earnings 3/3

Interest rates are not controlled by the government. The semi-autonomous central bank, the Australian Reserve Bank, has kept inflation at a low 5 percent. The government does not allocate credit, and there are no impediments either to investing abroad or to holding foreign currency and securities. Australians have access to a wide range of investment options and have been establishing a strong presence abroad.

## Freedom to Trade Internationally 1/2

Australia is a signatory of GATT and a member of the World Trade Organization but it still maintains high tariffs on certain items. For example, it currently has a 27.5 percent tariff on imported motor vehicles and their equipment. In addition, Australia applies some restrictive standards requirements that can effectively inhibit the import of certain goods. The only remaining import quotas are on cheese and curd.

A large percentage of Australia's exports are subject to some restriction. Export licenses are issued by various government agencies, and permits are required by the Department of Defense to export certain sensitive items. Australia's exports, however, have grown dramatically in recent years and have become a driving force in its economy.

The Foreign Investment Review Board (FIRB) screens all foreign investment proposals. Foreign investment in some areas such as civil aviation, media, and urban real estate is limited.

The Australian dollar is fully convertible and has floated freely since 1983. The government currently does not maintain currency controls but the Reserve Bank does legally have the power to implement exchange controls.

## Freedom from Unreasonable Government Interference in the Economy

The government does not interfere extensively in the economy and generally promotes a free-market philosophy. While the government does control all major utilities and telecommmunications it has taken steps to introduce competition into these sectors and lift any barriers to entry. The government subsidizes agriculture. Since 1994, the government has implemented a number of microeconomic projects, including tariff reform and financial market deregulation, to further increase competition. The government, however, remains a significant force in the economy. Only two-thirds of the workforce is in the private sector, the lowest share in Western Europe.

**Freedom to Participate in the Market Economy** **2/2**

Australian law does not discriminate against women or minorities. They are free to enter any occupation they choose and to operate any type of business they wish. The Affirmative Action Act of 1986 obliges employers to provide equal opportunities to female employees.

Corruption is not a significant problem in Australia's economic and political system.

# Bangladesh

ECONOMIC FREEDOM STATUS: **NOT FREE**
POLITICAL RIGHTS AND CIVIL LIBERTIES STATUS: **PARTLY FREE**
PRESS FREEDOM STATUS: **PARTLY FREE**
POPULATION: **119,184,000**
PPP: **$1,230**

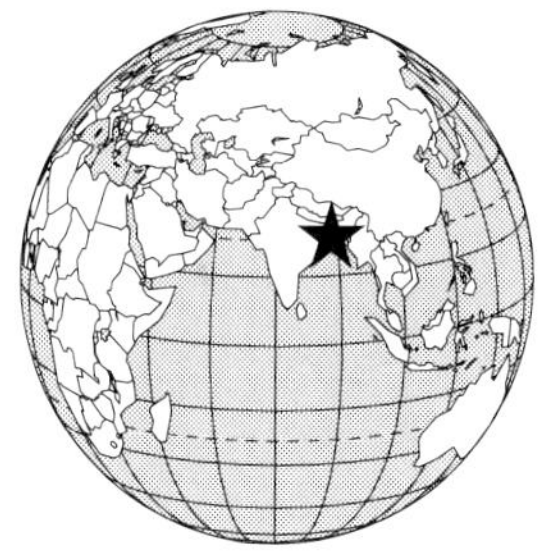

**Background**

Bangladesh became independent in 1971 after India invaded then-East Pakistan. There have been some nineteen coup attempts or successful takeovers since. The last, in March 1982, brought General H.M. Ershad to power. The country's democratic transition began with Ershad's resignation in December 1990 following weeks of pro-democracy demonstrations.

Since 1994, Bangladesh has been torn by violent nationwide strikes called by an opposition Awami League-led coalition against the ruling Bangladesh National Party, led by Prime Minister Khaleda Zia. Widespread strikes frequently paralyze the Bengali economy. In November 1995, Zia dissolved parliament in advance of elections called for January 1996.

Forty-five percent of the country's population lives below the poverty line in the largely agricultural country. Economic reforms necessary to fuel growth have been hindered by an unstable political situation, corruption, entrenched vested interests and a highly statist bureaucracy. Citizens thus enjoy little economic freedom.

**Freedom to Hold Property** **1/3**

In the years following independence in 1971, a nationalization program left over 90 percent of fixed assets in manufacturing, banking and insurance in government hands. The 1980 Foreign Investment Act forbids nationalization or expropriation without adequate compensation, and this has been respected in practice. Intellectual property laws are inadequate and enforcement is rare.

Property laws are archaic and land registration records are unreliable. To avoid stamp duties and other charges, many mortgages and other encumbrances are never registered. Similarly, documents affecting title to real property are often not registered, complicating transfer of ownership.

**Freedom to Earn a Living** **1/3**

Although the constitution guarantees freedom of association and the right to belong to a union, workers wishing to organize face a variety of obstacles. The formation and continuity of unions are hampered by a strict requirement that a union represent at least 30 percent of employees in a workplace. In addition, the 1994 Labor Code gives the government the right to declare certain industries to be a "group of establishments." This requires a potential union to obtain support from 30 percent of all the workers in an entire industry. There are no legal provisions against firing workers for participating in union activities, and anti-union discrimination is prevalent in the garment sector.

Most civil servants are legally barred from joining unions but are permitted to join "associations" that perform some union-related functions.

Unions are independent of the government, but many are politicized and rarely serve as true labor advocates. The law gives the Registrar of Trade Unions broad powers to intervene in the internal operations of a union.

Unions are prohibited in the two export processing zones (EPZ) at Chittagong and Dhaka, although employees have formed worker associations. Strikes are prohibited in EPZs, and all wages are set by the zone authorities. Nationwide strikes are illegal, but are frequently called by opposition parties and are often accompanied by violence. The Essential Services Ordinance permits the government to bar strikes for three months in sectors it deems "essential." Collective bargaining is legal only in the private sector.

Constitutional safeguards against forced or compulsory labor are generally ignored and are inadequately enforced. Blue-collar employees are often required to work longer hours than permitted by law, and without receiving additional compensation. In July 1995 the Bangladesh Garment Manufacturers and Exporters Association signed a memorandum of understanding with international organizations that pledged to end child labor by September 1997. The U.S. Department of Labor estimates that there are between 5 million and 15 million children under the age of fourteen working in Bangladesh, many of whom are in the garment industry where they are often overworked, not paid, and exposed to hazardous conditions.

## Freedom to Operate a Business 1/3

Although individuals are free to form businesses, entrepreneurs face significant bureaucratic barriers to registering a new firm. Private businesses are barred from several key sectors, including airways, railways, and power transmission and distribution. The large state-owned enterprise (SOE) and parastatal presence in many sectors forms a barrier to regulatory and bureaucratic reform. In particular, the banking and insurance industries are heavily regulated and licenses for entry are not readily granted. The process of awarding government contracts is prone to corruption.

The government sets prices for many basic commodities. In the spring of 1995 a severe fertilizer shortage developed because the government price of $93 per ton against the international price of $233 per ton led much of the domestic output to be exported.

## Freedom to Invest One's Earnings 1/3

Government-mandated lending by state banks to money-losing SOEs has caused a shortage of credit for the private sector; however credit quantity targets have been eliminated. Annual inflation is 4.1 percent. The government generally discourages capital outflow, and various government agencies and the Bangladesh Bank must approve investments abroad. The currency, the taka, is largely unconvertible for capital account transactions, except for foreign investors. Interest rates are subject to a government-set floor which has pushed real lending rates to between 10 to 12 percent. The Central Bank is not independent of the government.

## Freedom to Trade Internationally 1/2

The government has taken measures to liberalize what is still one of the most restrictive tariff regimes in Asia. Import licensing involves substantial bureaucratic obstacles. Numerous items are banned from export. The government prohibits some persons considered security risks from traveling abroad.

Foreign investors are allowed 100 percent ownership in most sectors, and the Foreign Investment Act guarantees the right of repatriation of invested capital, profits, capital gains, post-tax dividends and approved royalties and fees. However, repatriation of capital gains, other than from publicly held shares, is limited to 10 percent of the capital gain and is often difficult to carry out.

The taka is fully convertible for current account transactions, and the government plans to make it convertible on the capital account as well. However there are restrictions on foreign exchange transactions.

### Freedom from Unreasonable Government Interference in the Economy

SOEs account for 25 percent of industrial output and exercise a disproportionate and distorting influence on government policy and on the economy as a whole. Most SOEs are money-losers and are propped up by subsidies. Government expenditures represent 20.4 percent of GDP. The World Bank is assisting a $250 million program to restructure and privatize the jute sector, which accounts for 13 percent of exports. Overall, government policies retard competition through bureaucratic hassles, corruption, and a general antagonism to free enterprise.

### Freedom to Participate in the Market Economy 1/2

Women hold a small fraction of wage-earning jobs and fewer than 5 percent of government jobs. The Grameen Bank has received worldwide attention for its microgrant program, which is targeted mainly to rural women. Under the 1961 Muslim Family Ordinance female heirs inherit less than male heirs.

The country's legal system is a disincentive to investment, characterized by antiquated laws, backlogged and corruption-prone courts, and lax enforcement of business contracts. At the Supreme Court level, the judiciary is considered independent of the government. However, Articles 115 and 116 of the constitution allow the head of state to control and discipline judges, even those who sit on the Supreme Court. Economic policy and commercial regulations are often vague and inconsistent, and are not uniformly enforced. Corruption is a serious drain on economic productivity.

## Burma (Myanmar)

ECONOMIC FREEDOM STATUS: **NOT FREE**
POLITICAL RIGHTS AND CIVIL LIBERTIES STATUS: **NOT FREE**
PRESS FREEDOM STATUS: **NOT FREE**
POPULATION: **44,759,000**
PPP: **$751**

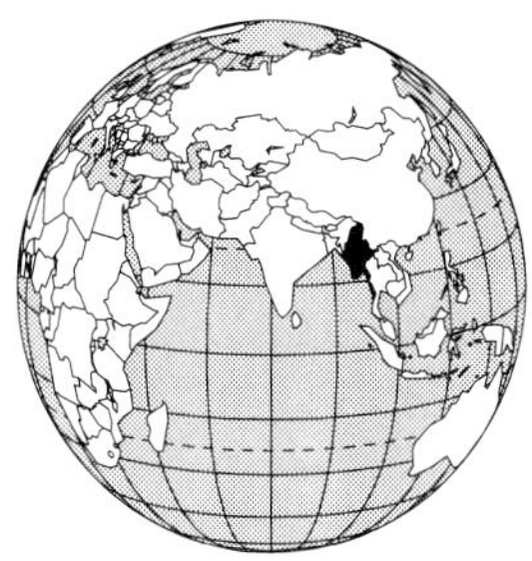

### Background

Citizens of Burma, burdened by over three decades of one-party military rule, enjoy almost no economic freedom. There is no right to own property, earn a living, open a business, trade, or invest.

Since 1962 the country has been run by the military or military-backed governments.

Between 1962 and 1988, General Ne Win's Burmese Socialist Program Party turned one of Southeast Asia's richest countries into one of the world's poorest with its "Burmese Way to Socialism." In 1989, the army placed Aung San Suu Kyi, secretary general of the National League for Democracy and the country's foremost pro-democracy campaigner, under house arrest. After Suu Kyi's NLD party won 392 of the 485 parliamentary seats in elections held in 1990, the junta refused to recognize the results and jailed hundreds of NLD members, including several elected MPs.

The junta has courted foreign investors, particularly in exploiting Burma's rich natural resources. Foreign investment has helped to reverse economic decline and contributed to growth of 6-7 percent in 1995, but Burma remains one of the poorest nations in the world.

## Freedom to Hold Property 0/3

Property rights are nonexistent. A small ruling elite holds most property in the country. The general population has tenuous land-use rights, and land cannot be transferred, traded or sold. However, in some areas local land committees have given families permission to inherit land. In recent years the government has forcibly relocated some 500,000 residents of the capital, Rangoon, to squalid satellite "new towns." The rule of law does not exist in Burma, and commercial statutes composed by the British during the colonial era are ignored. The legal system is controlled by the government, is massively corrupt and barely functions. Intellectual property laws are not enforced.

## Freedom to Earn a Living 0/3

Trade unions and collective bargaining are illegal. The only outlet for workers' grievances, the state-controlled township supervisory boards, have only limited scope for addressing labor concerns. Burma's military government, the State Law and Order Restoration Council (SLORC), sets public-sector wages. Private-sector wages are set by the market.

Throughout the country hundreds of thousands of citizens have been forced to work on the construction of roads, railways and other infrastructure projects, often enduring brutal conditions. The workers generally have to pay for their tools and food, and receive no wages. The government has periodically forced civilians in Mandalay to "donate" three days per month for public works projects associated with the official "Visit Myanmar Year" tourist campaign for 1996. Military families and those who can pay a 200 kyat fee (roughly $1.88 at the black market rate) are exempt. In the south the army has forced tens of thousands of civilians to clear terrain and build embankments for an eighty-mile railway line from Ye to Tavoy. The army routinely conscripts civilians as porters, and thousands have been wounded or have died from beatings, disease or malnutrition.

## Freedom to Operate a Business 0/3

There are no formal regulations governing business formation, and no guaranteed rights to operate a business. There are generally no problems with operating a small stall or other similar entity. However, starting an enterprise that produces industrial goods, particularly for export, requires both a sponsor within the military and numerous bribes. Even then there is no guarantee that a business will not be arbitrarily shut down. Government contracts are not competitively let. Price controls exist for many basic goods. The government forces farmers to sell rice at below market-level prices.

## Freedom to Invest One's Earnings 0/3

The government sets a cap on interest rates. The majority of banks are state-owned, and these banks scarcely operate and do not lend to the public. The government closely regulates the fifteen private banks it has permitted to operate, and constrains their growth by not allowing them to form joint ventures with foreign partner banks. The government sets caps on maximum rates of return on investment. Individuals are not permitted to invest abroad or hold foreign currency and securities. This is in keeping with the government's policy of actively attempting to keep all capital within the country. There is no independent central bank and no protection against an inflation rate that is estimated at about 40 percent.

### Freedom to Trade Internationally 0/2

Nominal tariffs range from 15 to 300 percent, but a complicated system of application results in an effective tariff of about 10 percent. Among the country's largest exports are heroin, jade, teak and gems smuggled across the Thai and Chinese borders. Most Burmese are not permitted to travel abroad.

An investor with a minimum of $100,000 in cash or equipment can go through the official Myanmar Investment Corporation and receive a three-year tax holiday. The government is keen to attract foreign investment and approval is fairly straightforward. Exchange controls are strict. Foreign currency must be converted into Foreign Exchange Currency (FEC) units, with one unit equivalent to $1. These FECs can then be converted into kyats at a rate of about 110 to the dollar, which is close to the black market rate of 106-120 to the dollar.

Foreigners can repatriate earnings only if they buy local products to sell abroad for hard currency. This drives up the price that ordinary citizens pay for these staples. Hotel and transport must be paid for with FECs.

### Freedom from Unreasonable Government Interference in the Economy

The government dominates the economy, although no accurate figures exist on the number of state-owned enterprises or on the government's share of Gross Domestic Product. Most businesses in the formal sector are owned by the government or by military officials. There is no real competition except among traders at the local markets. The state subsidizes the industries it owns.

### Freedom to Participate in the Market Economy 0/2

Since independence in 1948 more than a dozen ethnic groups have been fighting for greater autonomy for their people. Most ethnic minority groups live in border areas, where government investment and expenditure are minimal. In eastern Kayah and Karen states, the army has in recent years forcibly relocated thousands of villagers to government-controlled towns for fear that they might support the rebels. Thousands of Burmese women and girls have been trafficked across the Thai border by criminal gangs to work in brothels.

Corruption is rampant, and the U.S. Internal Revenue Service has classified bribes as a "cost-of-business" in Burma. Every dealing between a business and the government requires a signature, and this in turn requires a bribe.

# Cambodia

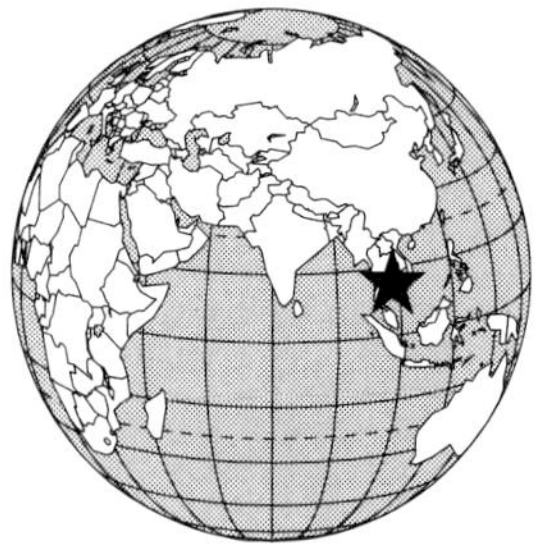

ECONOMIC FREEDOM STATUS: **MOSTLY NOT FREE**
POLITICAL RIGHTS AND CIVIL LIBERTIES STATUS: **NOT FREE**
PRESS FREEDOM STATUS: **PARTLY FREE**
POPULATION: **10,561,000**
PPP: **$1,250**

## Background

Cambodia's two-year-old democratic transition appeared to end in 1995 as an increasingly authoritarian government cracked down on the opposition and independent media.

Cambodia achieved independence from France in 1953 under King Norodom Sihanouk. In 1970 premier Lon Nol ousted Sihanouk in a bloodless coup. In April 1975 the Maoist Khmer Rouge, led by Pol Pot, took power and began a genocidal effort to create a classless agrarian society, in which over one million Cambodians died through torture or starvation. Vietnam invaded in December 1978 and installed the Communist Khmer People's Revolutionary Party (KPRP), led largely by Khmer Rouge defectors. In 1982 Sihanouk, the Khmer Rouge and former premier Son Sann joined their armies against the KPRP. Several rounds of internationally supervised talks yielded a peace accord in Paris in October 1991. In 1993, U.N.-monitored elections for the national assembly were held, with the royalist party gaining the majority and the ruling KPRP coming in second. The Khmer Rouge boycotted the elections and has since resumed fighting in the northwestern provinces.

The newly elected government initiated a series of market reforms and opened the country to badly needed foreign investment. The country's first commercial code was introduced in April 1995. However, initial optimism has diminished rapidly. Heavily dependent on international aid and short-term investment, Cambodia has been wracked by corruption and increased government repression of political opposition. Delays in implementing International Monetary Fund reforms jeopardized loans several times in 1995. Furthermore the rule of law and an adequate institutional infrastructure to safeguard basic economic rights do not yet exist. Economic freedom in Khmer Rouge territory does not exist.

## Freedom to Hold Property 0/3

Laws providing for the recognition of private ownership or the transfer or sale of rights in property are inadequate or nonexistent. Foreigners may not own land but can hold longterm leases. The judiciary is not independent of the government and the legal system is rudimentary. There is a severe shortage of judges, lawyers and other court officials, and low salaries make judges prone to corruption. There are no property rights in Khmer Rouge areas.

## Freedom to Earn a Living 2/3

The constitution permits workers to form independent unions, but due to the rudimentary nature of Cambodian civil society few have formed. The government must approve any collective bargaining agreements, but the lack of union activity precludes collective bargaining. The government does not control wages.

Enforcement of child labor provisions, working hours and conditions, minimum wages and other aspects of the 1992 Labor Law is nonexistent. Forced prostitution is common. In the 15 percent of the country under Khmer Rouge control, workers' rights are nonexistent in practice, and forced labor imposed by the insurgents is routine.

### Freedom to Operate a Business 2/3

Individuals are free to form and operate businesses. The Cambodian government is pursuing fairly liberal economic policies, and formal bureaucratic procedures are fairly relaxed. However, entrepreneurs starting and operating businesses must make frequent payoffs to government officials. The process of letting government contracts is also routinely accompanied by bribery. Many government contracts with foreign companies have been negotiated secretly, as short-sighted government officials seek deals that give them the best cut of the profits. It is unlikely that any large-scale private investment or industry will soon be permitted or possible in Khmer Rouge territory.

### Freedom to Invest One's Earnings 1/3

The central bank is not independent of the government. The banking system, and indeed capital markets as a whole, are in a very early stage of development. Banks are not well regulated, but in any case they have few customers, deposits or loan portfolios. Interest rates are not fixed, although the National Bank sets a floor for deposit rates. There are no developed capital markets. According to the *Far Eastern Economic Review*, 98 percent of all business conducted by the banks is in Thai baht and U.S. dollars, the bulk of which are transferred offshore.

### Freedom to Trade Internationally 2/2

There is a 100 percent tariff exemption on foreign imports used to build the country's physical infrastructure. Most non-tariff barriers and import licenses have been eliminated. The export of whole logs is prohibited, although control over logging has been handed over to the military and logs are illegally exported on a large scale. The 1994 Investment Law permits repatriation of profits, prohibits the government from nationalizing industries and prohibits price controls. Investors can purchase foreign currency and remit abroad as payment.

### Freedom from Unreasonable Government Interference in the Economy

Most state-owned firms have been privatized or leased out. The military controls the logging industry and practices extortion and banditry in the countryside. The Khmer Rouge controls an illicit multimillion-dollar trade in gems and logging across the Thai border in the areas under its control. Given the uncertainties of traveling outside major cities, most private investment is concentrated in Phnom Penh and the provincial capital of Siem Reap.

### Freedom to Participate in the Market Economy 0/2

There are an estimated 200,000-500,000 ethnic Vietnamese in Cambodia. Many have roots going back several generations, although perhaps half entered following Vietnam's 1978 invasion of Cambodia. The September 1993 constitution specifically guarantees the human rights of ethnic Khmers, leaving the Vietnamese minority in a legal void regarding human rights and economic affairs. A September 1994 immigration law allows the government to summarily expel undocumented refugees and, in the absence of a nationality law defining citizenship, observers fear this law will be used to arbitrarily expel ethnic Vietnamese. Women comprise at least half the workforce.

The legal environment for business and investment is characterized by a lack of most necessary commercial laws relating to property, transfer of assets, contracts, bankruptcy and other areas. Therefore, most private business is not conducted according to the rule of law. Corruption is a severe and pervasive feature of the Cambodian economy, and has a distorting effect on the market. There is no formal market economy in Khmer Rouge areas.

# China

ECONOMIC FREEDOM STATUS: **NOT FREE**
POLITICAL RIGHTS AND CIVIL LIBERTIES STATUS: **NOT FREE**
PRESS FREEDOM STATUS: **NOT FREE**
POPULATION: **1,214,233,000**
PPP: **$1,950**

## Background

Established in 1949, the People's Republic of China suffered through a series of disastrous mass campaigns organized by Chinese Communist Party (CCP) Chairman Mao Zedong. Mao's effort to accelerate industrialization and agricultural collectivization through the disastrous Great Leap Forward created a rural famine that killed over 30 million peasants. In 1966 Mao encouraged an infamous mass movement, the Cultural Revolution, in a bid to regain control of a fractious CCP. By 1976 up to one million had died and millions more had been disgraced, including party secretary Deng Xiaoping. Following Mao's death in September 1976, Deng assumed several top-level posts, and in December 1978 began introducing market reforms while suppressing all political dissent.

In 1992 Deng initiated his strongest effort to root economic reforms deeply enough to make them irreversible after his death. In January he made a highly symbolic visit to the booming Shenzhen Special Economic Zone in southern Guangdong Province, and later that year, at its Fourteenth Party Congress, the CCP formally adopted the goal of a "socialist market economy," a seemingly innocuous phrase that in fact all but buried the 1949 revolution's orthodox Marxist ideology.

But the death of Marxism has not meant the birth of economic freedom in China. There is still no freedom to earn a living or operate a business, to invest one's earnings or participate equally in the market economy. Engaging in economic activity in China today is still considered a privilege, not a right, and a privilege that can usually only be obtained through bribery and high level connections. In short, despite Deng's efforts, China's economy remains unfree.

## Freedom to Hold Property 1/3

The right to hold property is not recognized in practice. The government routinely arbitrarily relocates businesses and families to clear land for commercial interests. Even large multinational corporations have been targets, as was seen in 1994 when municipal officials evicted McDonalds from its downtown Beijing location to make room for a real estate venture, despite McDonalds' twenty year lease. Arbitrary land seizures by local governments for use in commercial development have been a factor in peasant riots in the countryside. Although in theory most land is still collectively held, in April 1995 the government approved a thirty-year extension of leased-land contracts. These contracts allow households to use plots of land on a longterm basis in return for meeting production quotas. Families can then sell any output in excess of the quotas at the market. Farmers will also be able to subcontract land.

Local officials frequently seize property from couples for failing to adhere to China's one-child family planning policy. In February 1995, China signed an agreement with the United States pledging to crack down on piracy of intellectual property and a number of high profile crackdowns by the government have taken place. In October a Beijing court found one of

China's largest software distributors guilty of selling pirated material. However, piracy of intellectual property remains widespread.

**Freedom to Earn a Living 0/3**

All unions must belong to the All-China Federation of Trade Unions, which is controlled by the Communist Party. Independent trade unions are illegal. The 1994 National Labor Law permits collective bargaining in all labor sectors, although it is practiced infrequently. The majority of the organized labor force still works in state-owned enterprises (SOEs), where the Ministry of Labor sets a ceiling on total wages for each establishment. Workers then generally sign individual contractual agreements.

The success of both the Special Economic Zones at Shenzhen and Zhuhai and the small-scale Township and Village Enterprises (TVEs) have removed millions of Chinese from dependence on the *danwei*, or state work unit. However for some 100 million state employees the danwei still controls where one lives or works. In order to meet increased labor demand in the southern provinces, the system of *hakou*, or residence permits, has been relaxed to give workers more flexibility in filling jobs. According to the official Chinese press, the hiring and in some cases kidnapping of small children to work at odd jobs or in prostitution is relatively common. The abduction of women for prostitution is often abetted by local officials. Forced labor is practiced in prisons, in the *laogai* ("reform through labor"), and in the *laojiao* ("reeducation through labor") facilities.

**Freedom to Operate a Business 0/3**

The semi-private TVEs now account for one-quarter of China's industrial output, giving millions of citizens a stake in the market economy. The process of establishing and running a business is subject to a substantial and often arbitrary bureaucratic process, particularly for foreign investors. Once in process, projects are often subject to arbitrary and retroactive changes. Government contracts are generally not competitively let and many procurement projects are not open to foreign investors. Prices for fuel and many other raw materials are still controlled by the state. In the spring of 1995 the government placed restrictions on commodities futures trading.

**Freedom to Invest One's Earnings 0/3**

Cooperative banks offer slightly higher interest rates than state banks. The government has floated the idea of capping rates of return on equity investments at 12-15 percent, although it now appears to have backed away from this position. The government has ordered pension plans to place 80 percent of their investment in treasury bonds, with the remainder held in bank deposits, rather than invest in the stock market. Similarly, insurance and health funds must be invested in government securities.

The State Planning Commission periodically places restrictions on credit when it feels the economy is overheating. The government also dictates how credit is allocated. State banks are required to extend loans to money-losing SOEs, squeezing some small private customers out of the formal credit market. In early 1995 the Commission said that for the year 10 percent of bank loans would go to the agricultural sector in order to help farmers cope with higher production costs. The July 1995 national banking law, which aims to put the country's state-run banking system on a par with international standards by the year 2000, encourages urban credit cooperatives to reorganize as small banks in order to meet the needs of small entrepreneurs.

The central bank is not independent of the government, and monetary policy is often subject to political whim. In recent years inflation has reached over 20 percent in the major cities, in part due to reckless lending by local state banks.

## Freedom to Trade Internationally 1/2

There are restrictive tariffs in many sectors, and export manufacturers often receive indirect subsidies. Local officials have detained or seized the passports of foreigners to exert pressure in commercial disputes, with ethnic-Chinese businessmen at greatest risk. Kidnappings and other forms of violence are sometimes used by Chinese businesses to settle debts and enforce agreements. Western creditors have had trouble getting paid by Chinese businesses. In 1994 Lehman Brothers announced it would sue several big state enterprises for nonpayment of debts accrued through foreign exchange trading. Foreign travel is sometimes denied on political grounds.

Exchange rates are allowed to fluctuate within a narrow band set by the central bank, and currency is convertible for certain current account transactions. Joint ventures are now required to convert hard currency into the national currency, the rembini. Although the government says that this rule has existed for years foreigners claim it is a new requirement.

## Freedom from Unreasonable Government Interference in the Economy

SOEs consume a disproportionate amount of capital relative to their output. According to official figures the state share of industrial output was 40 percent in 1994, half of what it was when the economic reforms began in late 1978. Some 1,000 state enterprises out of 14,000 large and medium size units are targeted for privatization, although this process will depend on political exigency. The government fears that privatization will lead to mass layoffs and social unrest. The People's Liberation Army has business interests in many sectors.

## Freedom to Participate in the Market Economy 0/2

China's first commercial laws were not put in place until the 1980s, and they play little role in most transactions. The judiciary in China is not independent of the government and the rule of law is virtually nonexistent. Foreign businessmen, particularly ethnic Chinese, often have little recourse from occasional strongarm tactics by their local counterparts or by the Chinese government. Enforcement of 1992 legislation protecting women's rights is inadequate.

Corruption is pervasive, epitomized by the term *guanxi*, or connections. At the highest levels, corruption purges are generally politically motivated.

# India

ECONOMIC FREEDOM STATUS: **MOSTLY NOT FREE**
POLITICAL RIGHTS AND CIVIL LIBERTIES STATUS: **PARTLY FREE**
PRESS FREEDOM STATUS: **PARTLY FREE**
POPULATION: **922,312,000**
PPP: **$1,230**

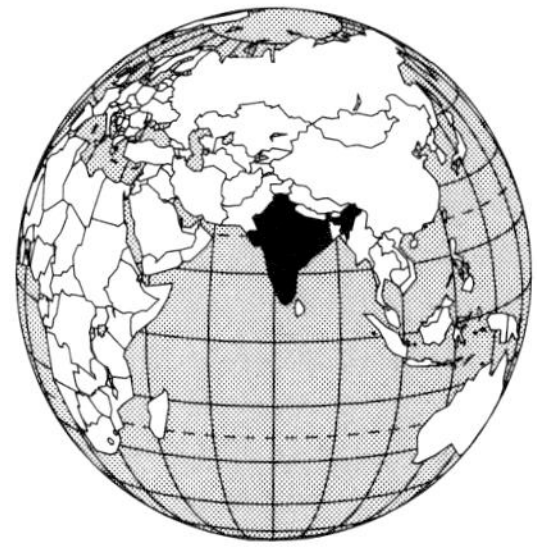

## Background

In 1989 V.P. Singh and the centrist National Front Coalition put the Congress Party out of power for only the second time since independence in 1947. Singh's proposal to increase the reservation of university slots and government jobs for members of the lower castes caused widespread rioting across northern India. P.V. Narasimha Rao led the Congress Party back to power in 1991.

Since 1991, the Congress Party government has introduced sweeping economic reforms, under the direction of Finance Minister Manmohan Singh, reversing forty years of state dominance and autarkic policies through deregulation and liberalization. As a result, economic and political power has been shifting to the states and the economy has grown by 6 percent while inflation has remained around 8 percent. Despite such reforms, constraints remain on economic freedom. Significant restrictions on trade remain, and entrepreneurs still must overcome a daunting number of bureaucratic obstacles. Entrenched vested interests, a *dirigiste* mentality and pervasive corruption also present formidable barriers to economic freedom. In addition, far deeper issues including religious and caste-based discrimination prevent a significant proportion of the population from being able to participate fully in the market economy.

## Freedom to Hold Property 2/3

The right to property is protected by law, but outdated and complex land regulations in urban areas inhibit the freedom to structure and transfer land. For example, the Urban Land (Ceiling and Regulation) Act distorts property prices by barring individuals or businesses from holding more than 500 square meters of land in any city. Consequently, property prices in Bombay and other cities are highly overvalued.

The U.S. Department of State reports that tribal groups have been displaced by development projects. Recognition and enforcement of intellectual property rights are weak and inadequate. The judiciary is independent of the government, although at lower levels it is prone to corruption, and overall is severely backlogged and largely inaccessible to poor people.

## Freedom to Earn a Living 1/3

Workers can exercise their constitutional right to join independent unions. Although the five major trade federations are linked to political parties, they do serve as advocates for workers' rights. Collective bargaining is freely practiced in the industrial sector, but informal sector workers are generally unable to organize. State governments set minimum wages, but otherwise wages move freely. For industries covered by the Essential Services Maintenance Act, arbitration is required before a strike takes place and the central government can ban strikes outright.

Bonded labor exists in some rural areas, and forced prostitution is widespread. The International Labor Organization estimates there are up to 44 million child laborers in India, many working in conditions of servitude.

### Freedom to Operate a Business 1/3

The government of Prime Minister Rao has undertaken substantial economic reforms that have largely reversed more than four decades of socialist-oriented policies. This has spurred the growth of small firms, which have benefited from reduced regulation and increased access to the stock market to raise capital. There are still considerable bureaucratic obstacles to forming and operating a business, but the government has been trimming away the "license raj," which had required businessmen to seek approval for even minor decisions.

The insurance industry is still a government monopoly, although other industries, such as electricity generation, air transport, and parts of the telecommunications industry, have been opened up. However, more than 800 items, including many consumer goods, are still reserved for companies with an investment of less than 6 million rupees ($193,000). This 1950s-era stipulation is designed to keep such industries small and therefore labor-intensive.

Government procurement practices occasionally discriminate against foreign suppliers. The process of letting government contracts has become more transparent but is still subject to favoritism and corruption. The central and state governments still regulate the prices of many basic foodstuffs and other essential goods, including sugar, edible oils, and basic medicines, as well as energy prices and industrial inputs. Poverty and politics make price liberalization difficult; for example, an opposition party took power in Andhra Pradesh state in November 1994 in part by promising heavy subsidies on rice.

### Freedom to Invest One's Earnings 2/3

In October 1994 the government floated interest rates, although the Central Bank maintains a ceiling on short-term rates. Under a September 1994 agreement the Central Bank sells treasury bonds on the open market whenever the government's cumulative borrowing exceeds 90 billion rupees. Previously the Bank gave the government unlimited credit, inflating the money supply. The twenty-eight state banks are saddled with bad loans to the state sector. The Companies Act places restrictions on the transfer or acquisition of shares. Foreigners cannot invest directly in Indian stock markets, but instead must invest through approved institutions.

### Freedom to Trade Internationally 1/2

There is a ban on the import of most consumer goods, and some staples such as sugar and edible oils are subject to import controls. The government hopes to replace all quotas and import bans with tariffs by April 1997. Most direct export subsidies have been phased out, but numerous indirect subsidies remain, including exemptions from income and trade taxes. Although the maximum tariff is down from 400 percent to 65 percent, customs duties remain high, with a weighted average tariff of 40 percent. In general citizens may exit the country without restriction, although the government sometimes uses the 1967 Passports Act to prohibit dissidents from traveling abroad.

At the national level, the Rao government has radically transformed policies that were hostile to foreign investment. Nearly all sectors of the economy are now open to foreign investment, with automatic approval for equity stakes of up to 51 percent in most businesses, except for security-related areas such as defense, railways, and atomic energy. Foreign companies can open fully owned subsidiaries. However, the corporate tax rate on foreign entities is 55 percent, versus 40 percent for domestic companies. Since March 1993 the rupee has been fully convertible on the trade account, and since August 1994 on the current account. There are still controls on capital account transactions.

State governments have been actively courting foreign investment, but there have been setbacks. Several foreign ventures approved by the central government are being reviewed by opposition state governments.

### Freedom from Unreasonable Government Interference in the Economy

State enterprises still account for a considerable share of GDP, and the government has made little headway in privatization. Only 49 percent of equity in state enterprises can be sold off, and in practice the figure usually drops to 20 percent or less.

The Industrial Disputes Act's "exit laws" prevent private businesses from laying off more than 100 workers, closing money-losing factories, and selling off assets without permission from the state government, which is rarely granted. The bureaucracy retains broad powers of regulation and retards enterprise and competition.

### Freedom to Participate in the Market Economy 1/2

Caste discrimination is illegal, but in practice occupation choices for Hindus are strongly determined by caste distinctions. So-called untouchables are generally relegated to menial labor. Women do not face legal restrictions in the owning and running of businesses though discrimination does exist. There are some restrictions on the ability of women to own, utilize and transfer land, especially in tribal land systems.

Corruption is widespread to the point of being a routine cost of doing business.

# Indonesia

ECONOMIC FREEDOM STATUS: **NOT FREE**
POLITICAL RIGHTS AND CIVIL LIBERTIES STATUS: **NOT FREE**
PRESS FREEDOM STATUS: **NOT FREE**
POPULATION: **195,924,000**
PPP: **$2,950**

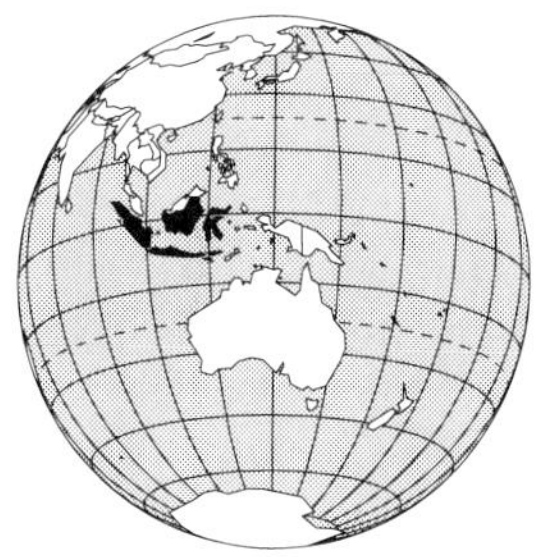

### Background

Following an aborted left-wing coup in 1965, in March 1966 General Suharto assumed key political and military powers, formally becoming president in March 1968. Highly authoritarian and corrupt rule have characterized Suharto's administration. Besides the ruling Golkar Party, the government permits the Indonesian Democratic Party (PDI), which favors some political liberalization, and the United Development Party (PPP), a coalition of Islamic groups. The world's fourth most populous country, Indonesia is made up of hundreds of ethnic groups.

Since the mid-1980s, Suharto's regime has been liberalizing the economy, fostering sectors outside of oil and gas, reducing the level of government regulations, and easing restrictions on trade and investment. Nonetheless, pervasive restrictions on citizens' economic freedom remain. Workers are not free to form unions, entrepreneurs face a number of handicaps, and key areas of commerce are off-limits, controlled by presidential cronies or senior military officials. Corruption is rampant.

### Freedom to Hold Property 1/3

The legal code recognizes the right to private property, but the government has in some cases forcibly expropriated land for development. Private firms may acquire and sell property.

There is adequate legislation to protect intellectual property rights but enforcement is weak. Bankruptcy laws and secured interests in property and mortgages are unenforceable.

## Freedom to Earn a Living 1/3

The Ministry of Manpower maintains strict requirements for trade union registration. The state-controlled All Indonesian Workers Union (SPSI), whose leadership is dominated by members of the ruling Golkar party, is the sole union recognized by the government. Since January 1994 employees have been permitted to form plant-level "associations" in companies with more than twenty-five employees. These associations can bargain and sign agreements on behalf of the employees in the plant.

In August 1994 the government declared the independent Indonesian Workers Welfare Union (SBSI) to be illegal, claiming it had not met the necessary requirements. The government has not disbanded the SBSI, but has attempted to undermine it. Evidence suggests that the government instigated a series of workers' riots in the city of Medan in April 1994 to discredit the independent labor movement.

Since May 1993 at least three labor activists have died under suspicious circumstances. Union activists frequently lose their jobs, and while some have been awarded money through administrative tribunals, they are rarely rehired.

Indonesian nongovernmental organizations say SPSI-affiliated unions often serve as weak advocates for labor during collective bargaining procedures. Although the government does not set wage rates, it does fix a minimum wage by region. However, factory owners often fail to pay the minimum wage without sanction. In the disputed province of Irian Jaya, logging companies have induced some local residents into bonded labor through debts allegedly run up at company stores.

## Freedom to Operate a Business 1/3

The bureaucracy still exerts considerable influence over economic decision-making, although in general the government encourages private enterprise. Many businessmen and economists feel that the government's deregulation measures have not gone far enough. President Suharto's family members and close associates enjoy monopolies granted by the government in several key agricultural and industrial sectors. For example, the giant conglomerate Bimantara Group, which has holdings in cars, telecommunications, televisions, and petrochemicals, is run by Suharto's second son. Analysts note that much of the group's success is owed to the family relationship.

Price are controlled for numerous goods. Among other things, controls have produced a shortage of cement, which, in turn, has hindered infrastructure development.

The bidding process for government contracts is not transparent and favors politically connected businessmen. The judiciary is not independent of the government, and many investors say the legal system is not strong enough to resolve commercial disputes. In late 1995, a Jakarta court reversed the suspension of three newspapers' licenses in an unusual show of independence.

## Freedom to Invest One's Earnings 2/3

Interest rates and the flow of credit are determined by the market. Deregulation of the banking system has been underway since 1988, and in 1994 local private banks outpaced state banks in lending volume for the first time. The government has moved to tighten supervisory procedures after some private banks became awash in bad debts in the early 1990s. Individuals are free to invest abroad and there are no restrictions on rates of return. The central bank is not independent of the government. It maintains policies to keep the rate of inflation low.

**Freedom to Trade Internationally** **1/2**

The government has eliminated or reduced most tariff and non-tariff barriers. A tariff schedule issued in May 1995 outlined reductions for the next eight years and made across-the-board cuts on some 6,000 products. Import duties range from 5-200 percent, with an average of 37 percent, while import surcharges range from 5-100 percent. Non-tariff barriers include four types of import licenses. The May 1995 regulations also added eight sectors to the "negative investment list," areas partially or completely closed to foreign capital, including electricity production and distribution and telecommunications. Most export taxes are levied on forestry products.

In June 1994 the government introduced a deregulation package that eliminated barriers to 100 percent foreign ownership in most sectors by dropping a requirement that foreign companies divest their shares to Indonesians. The package also ended rules on minimum investment and location. The currency, the rupiah, is convertible and floats within a band set by the government. Capital may flow freely in and out of the country.

**Freedom from Unreasonable Government Interference in the Economy**

The public sector accounts for an estimated 15 percent of GDP. The government is increasing its efforts to privatize some 184 remaining state enterprises. Among those likely to be privatized soon are Telekom, the domestic telephone company, and PLN, the state electricity company. According to the World Bank, there are significant non-tariff barriers in state-affiliated industries. The state-run Agency for Management of Strategic Industries has set up several high-technology companies, which are heavily subsidized by the government.

**Freedom to Participate in the Market Economy** **0/2**

In November 1994 a group of visiting New Zealand MPs said that up to 100,000 people from neighboring islands had arrived in East Timor—occupied by Indonesia since 1976—in recent years. The influx may be due to financial incentives from Jakarta. Trading is now dominated by ethnic Buginese from the neighboring Indonesian island of Sulawesi. The Batara Indra group, a conglomerate with close ties to the military, holds a near monopoly on industry in the territory. In Irian Jaya villagers receive no direct compensation from massive mining operations.

Women face sexual harassment and discrimination in the workplace. Ethnic Chinese, who make up 2 percent of Indonesia's population but dominate private business, are not allowed to form Chinese-based trade associations. The commercial code is outdated and often vague, although it is being revised. Throughout Indonesia, corruption, nepotism, and influence-peddling are widespread.

# Japan

ECONOMIC FREEDOM STATUS: **FREE**
POLITICAL RIGHTS AND CIVIL LIBERTIES STATUS: **FREE**
PRESS FREEDOM STATUS: **FREE**
POPULATION: **125,236,000**
PPP: **$20,520**

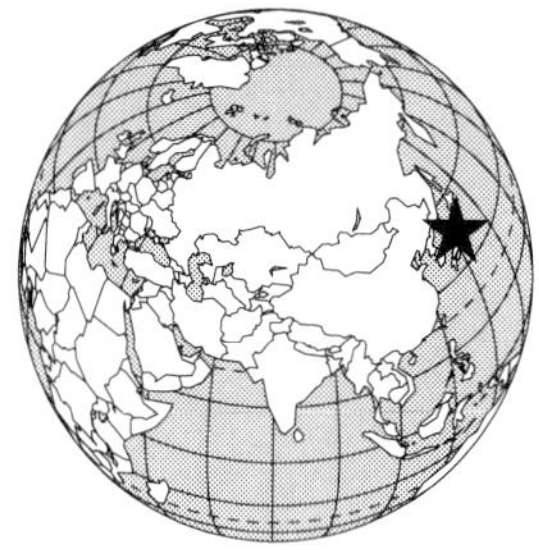

## Background

Japan has the second largest economy in the world, and although the government role in the economy is different than in many other industrialized nations, on the whole Japanese citizens are free to earn a living, open businesses, trade internationally and otherwise participate in the market economy.

The Liberal Democratic Party (LDP) ruled Japan continuously from 1955 until 1993, when a series of corruption scandals brought a coalition led by the Japanese Socialist Party to power. However, the LDP returned to power in 1994 in a coalition with the Social Democratic Party (SDP) and the New Harbinger Party. Muruyama Tomiichi of the SDP became Prime Minister but resigned in January 1996. In his place, Minister of International Trade and Industry Hashimoto Ryutaro became Prime Minister.

A sense of uneasiness took hold in Japan during 1995 thanks to a series of bank failures, a rapidly rising yen, terrorist gas attacks in the nation's capital, and a devastating earthquake. Politically, the promise of clean government has dissolved as the old order of LDP, business and the bureaucracy has reemerged after three weak coalition governments. After four years of economic stagnation, Japanese consumers are calling for an end to the massive regulation that has protected domestic producers at the expense of consumers. Although several deregulation reforms were introduced, they fell far short of domestic and international expectations.

## Freedom to Hold Property 3/3

The right to own property is well established in Japan and property rights are protected. Expropriation is compensated though individual landowners are often helpless against public infrastructure development programs. However, there are many restrictions on private and public plans to modify structures, and rural land prices are regulated. Virtually every major project undertaken by local governments as well as decisions regarding zoning, roads, and the conversion of farmland to urban use are made by unelected bureaucrats in the capital, Tokyo.

Intellectual property protection can be difficult to secure in Japan. The process of obtaining and protecting patent and trademarks can take up to five or six years. Although Intellectual Property Rights laws exist, they are enforced selectively with some sectors benefiting from lax enforcement. As a result of such practices, Japan has remained on the "watch list" for Super 301 provisions of the 1988 Trade Act.

## Freedom to Earn a Living 3/3

The labor union movement in Japan has been vocal. However, national and local government employees as well as employees in public corporations may not strike or engage in collective bargaining. Although forced labor is prohibited and prohibitions are generally enforced, there are disturbing exceptions. Many manual day laborers and sweatshops are under the control of *yakuza* who provide unscrupulous construction companies and manufacturers with workers. Often the victims are guest workers and minorities. Forced prostitution of illegal immigrants, brought to Japan by the lure of legitimate jobs, is growing rapidly.

The Japanese labor market is fierce. The competition for coveted and lucrative lifetime employment with large corporations begins with intense competition to enter elite schools. Once employed with a company, workers suffer high social stigma by changing firms or occupations. Furthermore, although discrimination is illegal many employers conduct comprehensive personal background checks on potential hirees, and items such as a relative who has been convicted of a crime can eliminate one's candidacy.

## Freedom to Operate a Business 2/3

There are over 11,402 types of required licenses, permits, and approvals (over 1,145 more in 1994 than in 1991) that tightly regulate business activity in Japan. Informal, but in practice virtually compulsory, administrative edicts euphemistically termed "administrative guidance" further restrict businesses.

The formation of a business can be very difficult and frustrating. Entry into many fields of business is tightly controlled. For example, as part of a major deregulation program, the Ministry of International Trade and Industry (MITI) exempted stores with floor space under 1,200 square meters from the lengthy application process required of larger stores, leading to a doubling of small stores. The *keidanren*, an association of Japanese big businesses, has demanded an end to restrictions on retailers and barriers to entry into several consumer sectors, but recent MITI reforms have been criticized by domestic businesses as being grossly insufficient.

Bidding for government contracts has been another powerful means by which the government has "managed the economy," often determining by default what firms or sectors will succeed.

Although in principle prices are market-determined, in reality many prices are set by companies according to signals sent by the government bureaucracy as well as by a lack of competition in highly regulated industries. A case in point is the transportation sector, where fares from airline tickets to taxis are set nationwide by the Ministry of Transportation. Consumers end up paying more to fly from one end of Japan to the other than to fly to the United States. Japanese airlines are not allowed to freely discount their fares either. Calls for price deregulation have been growing stronger as cheaper imports have forced domestic producers to slash prices.

## Freedom to Invest One's Earnings 2/3

The recent spate of scandals in the banking and securities industries and the collapse of the stock market in 1992 have brought into scrutiny the tight control held over the financial sector by the Ministry of Finance. Financial institutions are strictly regulated, preventing banks from freely setting interest rates and denying customers many of the conveniences expected elsewhere. Yet despite the heavy hand of the Ministry of Finance, regulators have turned a blind eye to market manipulation and the compensation of favored clients for losses, costing innocent investors billions of yen.

## Freedom to Trade Internationally 1/2

Although the average import tariff in Japan is among the lowest in the world, tariffs on some selected goods are exceptionally high and myriad non-tariff barriers present significant barriers to foreign imports. The imports of some products, such as rice, are fiercely opposed by powerful lobby groups.

Numerous regulatory barriers and discrimination against foreign investment still exist. Several sectors such as the financial, airline, agriculture, fishing and forestry, oil and gas, mining, nuclear power, and military are restricted, and foreign investors require prior authorization. Despite the many obstacles, foreign companies and individuals have successfully invested in Japan.

There are very few export restrictions and foreign exchange transactions have been largely liberalized.

## Freedom from Unreasonable Government Interference in the Economy

Although government consumption comprises only 9 percent of GDP and the proportion of government enterprises relative to the overall economy is very small, government involvement in the economy is pervasive. The near-mystical stature of the bureaucracy's success in managing Japan's economic development has fueled a stubborn arrogance reflecting the belief that chaos would ensue if the people were left to their own devices.

Twelve ministries and ten agencies in the Kasumigaseki section of Tokyo control over 11,000 regulatory powers. The Ministry of Transport alone has 1,966 regulatory powers controlling every aspect of the transportation sector. Former Prime Minister Hosokawa, as a provincial governor, had to wait two years for permission from Tokyo simply to move a bus stop. The Ministry of Finance has 1,915 specific licensing and approval powers, micromanaging the financial sector. The different ministries and agencies jealously guard the areas over which they have jurisdiction.

## Freedom to Participate in the Market Economy 2/2

Japan is largely a homogeneous society. However, several minority groups, some old like the *burakumin*, Ainu and Korean-Japanese, and some recent arrivals including immigrant workers from Vietnam and China and expatriate Japanese-Brazilians face varying degrees of discrimination both in hiring as well as in surviving bureaucratic hurdles.

The status of women has been improving slowly in Japan. Although there are no legal barriers to women gaining access to careers, owning businesses, or owning property, traditional perceptions still present formidable barriers.

Although petty corruption is rare, high-level corruption and collusion between industry leaders and politicians is common. "Gift giving" of considerable cash amounts is an established tradition and often is expected by officials. The lack of strong conflict-of-interest regulation fosters the practice of hiring of high-level bureaucrats by the very businesses the officials were supposed to regulate. Businesses will often give generously to politicians who can assist companies in ensuring that regulatory oversight would be less stringent.

# Korea, North

ECONOMIC FREEDOM STATUS: **NOT FREE**
POLITICAL RIGHTS AND CIVIL LIBERTIES STATUS: **NOT FREE**
PRESS FREEDOM STATUS: **NOT FREE**
POPULATION: **23,487,000**
PPP: **$3,026**

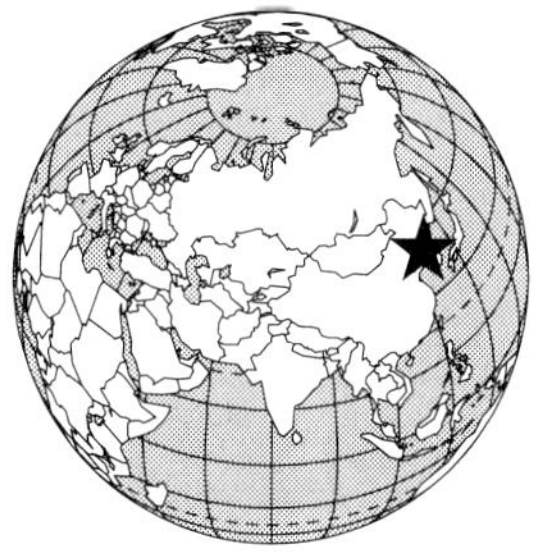

## Background

North Koreans live in the most tightly controlled society in the world. They cannot own property, earn a living, open a business, invest their earnings, or trade.

The Democratic People's Republic of Korea was formally established in September 1948, three years after the partition of the Korean Peninsula. Marshall Kim Il Sung, installed with Soviet backing, created a Stalinist personality cult based largely on his supposed leading role in fighting the Japanese in the 1930s. For decades Kim used an all-encompassing "ideology," *Juche* (I Myself), stressing national self–reliance and independence, to justify the country's isolation from the rest of the world. Meanwhile the government nurtured a slavish devotion to the "Great Leader" Kim and his son, "Dear Leader" Kim Jong Il, by indoctrinating citizens through the media, the workplace, the military, mass spectacles, and cultural events.

In December 1991 the younger Kim replaced his father as Supreme Commander of the armed forces in what appeared to herald the world's first Communist dynastic succession. Kim Il Sung died suddenly of a heart attack on 8 July 1994. The February 1995 death of defense minister Marshall Oh Jin-u left Kim Jong Il as the sole surviving member of the three-man politburo of the ruling Workers' Party. However, by year's end Kim, who is known to be unpopular with the military, had still not assumed the two top positions held by his father—state president and general secretary of the Workers' Party. Nevertheless, South Korean intelligence analysts say Kim is firmly in charge of the country.

The perilous state of the economy, which has contracted since 1990, has forced North Korea to open up somewhat to the outside world. In October 1994 the United States and North Korea signed a complex, three-stage deal under which North Korea agreed to a ten-year timetable for dismantling its clandestine nuclear program. In exchange the U.S., South Korea and Japan are providing emergency oil supplies and will build two light-water reactors. Although the economic situation appears to be marginally improving, in recent years defectors have reported severe food shortages, which were exacerbated by widespread flooding in late 1995. During the year North Korea accepted emergency rice donations from South Korea and Japan.

## Freedom to Hold Property 0/3

The right to hold private property is not recognized. The authorities do not respect the right to privacy, and conduct arbitrary, unannounced checks on homes. The North Korean government has not signed any international conventions regarding intellectual property rights.

## Freedom to Earn a Living 0/3

The General Federation of Trade Unions of Korea is in effect an arm of the government, and its affiliated unions are instruments of state control. Independent unions are illegal. Wages are set by the government, and collective bargaining is not permitted. Individuals are assigned jobs by the government, a process largely determined by loyalty to the state, and they cannot change jobs without permission. Citizens are often forced to provide "voluntary" manual labor. There are reportedly more than 100,000 prisoners, many of them charged with political crimes, in brutal forced labor camps.

### Freedom to Operate a Business 0/3

Private enterprise is not permitted. All economic decisions, including pricing, are made by the state.

### Freedom to Invest One's Earnings 0/3

Private investment is not permitted, there are no capital markets and credit is allocated by government fiat. Individuals may not invest abroad or hold foreign currency or securities. Ethnic Koreans in Japan send millions of dollars in hard currency each year to relatives in North Korea, most of which is seized by the government. There is no independent central bank.

### Freedom to Trade Internationally 0/2

Private citizens are not allowed to import or export goods, so there is no applicable system of tariffs, quotas, or export licenses. State organs, including ministries and provincial governments, are establishing their own foreign trading companies under the nominal supervision of the External Economy Commission of the Administration Council. The government has created a special free trade zone in the Rajin-Sonbong area in the northeast corner of the country. Several foreign-operated factories have been established, including garment joint ventures with Japanese partners. Travel abroad is strictly controlled and is rarely permitted. The currency is not convertible. A few shops in Pyongyang, the capital, cater to foreigners and require hard currency.

### Freedom from Unreasonable Government Interference in the Economy

Although the government controls all formal economic activity, a black market exists, particularly in goods smuggled in from China. There are unconfirmed reports that smugglers have been summarily executed near the Chinese border. In line with the radical self-reliance philosophy of the late Stalinist dictator Kim Il Sung, state enterprises produce 95 percent of manufactured goods, the rest being imported. The economy has been contracting since 1990 following the loss of Soviet subsidies. The government reportedly produces counterfeit cigarettes and other goods for export and is involved in the international ivory-smuggling industry.

### Freedom to Participate in the Market Economy 0/2

Free-market activity is illegal, so commercial codes and other mechanisms of a market economy do not exist. Economic conditions are so poor that the government encourages citizens to cut back to two meals per day. In some areas people have resorted to foraging for twigs and nuts out of desperation. The ruling elite, showing utter disregard for the deprivation it has created, is the world's largest consumer of exotic cognacs.

# Korea, South

ECONOMIC FREEDOM STATUS: **MOSTLY NOT FREE**
POLITICAL RIGHTS AND CIVIL LIBERTIES STATUS: **FREE**
PRESS FREEDOM STATUS: **FREE**
POPULATION: **44,851,000**
PPP: **$9,250**

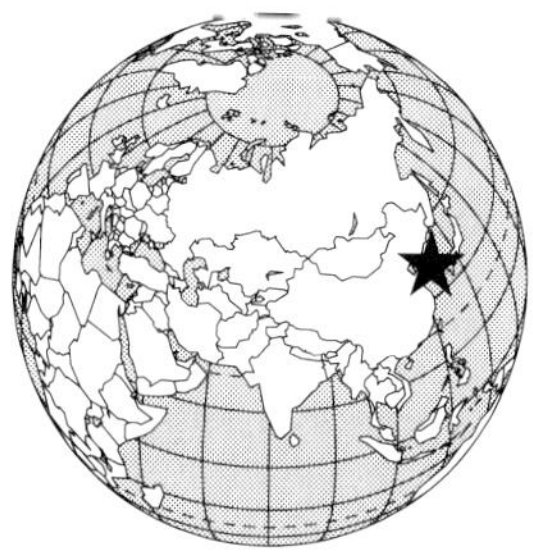

## Background

The Republic of Korea was established in August 1948. General Park Chung Hee led the country under military rule from 1961 until his assassination in 1979. In February 1993, Kim Young Sam became the first civilian president since 1961.

In forty years, South Korea has transformed itself from an impoverished nation to a world leader in automobile, ship and steel production. General Park forged an industrial economy by establishing new industries, using the military to suppress labor activism, and exercising draconian control over the financial system. Since his assassination, Korea has sought to undo much of Park's legacy, but many elements remain. State direction of industry, overregulation of the financial system, the concentration of economic power in the *chaebol* family-owned industrial conglomerates, and high trade barriers are some of the main limits on economic freedom. Kim continues to use the intelligence services and tax inspectors to intimidate political opponents and damage their businesses. The National Security Law, empowering the state to jail anyone for suspected Communist activities or sympathies, is still used though not as frequently.

The Kim government has made progress in economic reform. In 1995, Kim initiated criminal proceedings against two former presidents, Roh Tae Woo and Chun Doo Hwan, for corruption. Several chairmen of chaebol were investigated as well. Over 142 departments in the federal bureaucracy were eliminated in 1995 and the grip of the chaebol has slowly been pried open. However, Kim has been criticized for not taking the reforms far enough.

## Freedom to Hold Property 2/3

Private ownership of property is fully respected in law and practice. Private property can only be expropriated for a public purpose, and this must be done in a fair, nondiscriminatory manner. Industrial construction and land use are stringently regulated through the Agricultural Land Law of 1994.

Intellectual property protection and enforcement are weak though laws and enforcement are being strengthened amid accusations that the patent authorities were passing foreign firms' detailed product information to domestic firms. Foreign investment is protected from expropriation and requisition, and there have been no cases of expropriation of foreign property in recent years.

## Freedom to Earn a Living 1/3

The constitution grants most workers the right of association. Under the Trade Union Law only one union may exist at a workplace. There are two mainstream, legally recognized trade union federations, the Federation of Korean Trade Unions and the Korean Federation of Clerical and Financial Workers. Although the government has begun to recognize some smaller white-collar federations, it has refused to register the dissident Democratic Trade Union Council (DTUC). Civil servants, workers in the defense industry and school teachers cannot bargain collectively.

The two legally registered trade union federations are strongly influenced by the government, and although the government does not control wages directly, it pressures these federations to keep wages low.

Foreign laborers, called "Foreign Vocational Trainees," often lured with promises of high wages and benefits that are not honored, are forced to work long hours and are not allowed to leave factory compounds. Foreign workers are also occasionally physically abused. Former political prisoners are restricted in their movement and activities.

## Freedom to Operate a Business 1/3

Individuals are free form businesses. Registration papers must be filed at a district court, and new firms must apply for business licenses from the district office within thirty days. Licenses must be certified twice a year.

The Korean business environment is highly regulated and subject to administrative guidance from state economic planners. The system of chaebols often prevents the entry of new firms into the economy. No matter how poorly a subsidiary of a chaebol is run, competitors and new entrants simply cannot compete with the subsidiary's guaranteed market and the deep pockets of its parent companies. In this way, if new firms that are associated with a chaebol are introduced into the market non-chaebol small companies in that market will be driven out of business.

The president has the power to control a wide range of prices by emergency decree. The government also regularly pressures large firms to keep prices down to fight inflation.

## Freedom to Invest One's Earnings 1/3

Although the days when the Park regime siphoned off citizens' savings at negative interest rates have passed, elements of authoritarian control over the financial markets and individual's savings still remain. The banking system was partially liberalized in the 1980s when four banks were privatized and five new ones were allowed to open, but restrictions exist on credit allocation and lending. State-mandated "policy loans" force banks to allocate credit largely according to enterprise size, and local banks must assign a large part of their loan portfolios to small- and medium-sized businesses. Banks must also keep 11.5 percent of assets in reserve with the central bank, hampering their lending ability. In this void, hundreds of small "non-bank" lenders have been established, free from these regulations. Interest rates have been partly liberalized.

No individual can own more than 10 percent of a publicly held corporation, and cross-ownership between companies is prohibited. The government frequently intervenes in the stock market. For example, when the state felt that the market was rising too quickly, the government ordered brokers to sell stocks that were gaining too much value. In other cases, the government has banned financial firms from being net sellers on any one day. The government must also approve all stock and bond issuances. There are tight controls on overseas capital transactions.

The use of credit cards is also restricted. Since January 1995, all South Koreans under the age of twenty and all students have been forbidden from using credit cards.

## Freedom to Trade Internationally 1/2

Tariff rates have fallen in recent years to an average of 7.9 percent, and quantitative import restrictions have decreased. However, cars, food and other foreign goods are often subject to rigorous and time-consuming testing procedures. The South Korean press has reported that tax authorities have investigated foreign car buyers in an effort to intimidate other potential buyers. Some 200 Japanese products are banned under "import diversification" legislation. The government has granted eighteen companies permission to visit North Korea to sign joint ventures. There are no export taxes and few barriers to export.

Capital markets were partially opened to foreign investment in 1992, and by July 1995 the ceiling on foreign ownership of quoted firms had been raised to 15 percent. Foreign investment is restricted in 186 sectors, although this is to be reduced to 92 by 1997. Investment in joint ventures will be allowed in all but seven categories. No foreigner can own more than 3 percent of a Korean company, and foreigners can only invest in bonds offered by small- and medium-sized companies. Branch offices of foreign banks cannot borrow from their central offices, thus reducing the scope of their lending capability.

## Freedom from Unreasonable Government Interference in the Economy

Beginning with the authoritarian regime of General Park, the Economic Planning Board has managed the economy's growth by directing firms to build certain types of factories, providing subsidies and tax breaks to strategic firms and sectors, using protective tariffs and controlling access to markets and credit. In 1994 President Kim Young Sam abolished the Board, although the system of tax breaks, subsidies and other incentives continues. However, despite government statements to the contrary, the tradition of strong state intervention and administrative guidance remains. Aircraft, automobile, and communications were just three sectors that received direction by the government in 1995.

The result of these practices is that many sectors are dominated by chaebol, which have benefited from easy access to credit and other forms of government nurturing. Today the thirty largest chaebol control three-quarters of the country's economic output. A handful of founding families still control 60 percent of the equity in the top thirty chaebol. The government has striven to stem the power of the chaebol by restricting their expansion into new businesses and forcing some to break up, but in the process has created new layers of regulation and administrative controls that in the end hurt small businesses.

President Kim has used the state apparatus to intimidate opponents. Notably, opposition politician and billionaire businessman Chung Ju Yung received a suspended three-year prison sentence for infringing campaign finance laws, and his companies were refused permission to raise capital on the international bond markets.

The state sector, including 133 wholly or partially state-owned enterprises, accounts for 10 percent of GNP. The state sector has near monopolies in several strategic industries including electricity, telecommunications, natural gas and steel.

## Freedom to Participate in the Market Economy 1/2

Women face social constraints that limit their participation in the market economy. Many companies strongly encourage women to quit their jobs after they have their first child. Women's wages average just over half those of their male counterparts.

Commercial laws tend to be drafted in a way that gives mid-level bureaucrats considerable latitude over interpretation. This leads to inconsistency, and, at worst, discrimination. Unpublished or unwritten ministerial guidelines are often used to administer laws.

The rule of law is, at present, weak with the result that bribes, reciprocal favors, extralegal payments, and what are delicately called "quasi-taxes" are a regular part of doing business in South Korea. The corruption that underpins much of the economy made headlines around the world in October 1995 when former president Roh Tae Woo admitted to having amassed $650 million in contributions from businessmen during his 1988-1993 term. Roh's arrest has triggered an investigation that may at last force South Korea to confront the massive corruption that stands in the way of genuine economic freedom.

# Malaysia

ECONOMIC FREEDOM STATUS: **PARTLY FREE**
POLITICAL RIGHTS AND CIVIL LIBERTIES STATUS: **PARTLY FREE**
PRESS FREEDOM STATUS: **NOT FREE**
POPULATION: **19,944,000**
PPP: **$7,790**

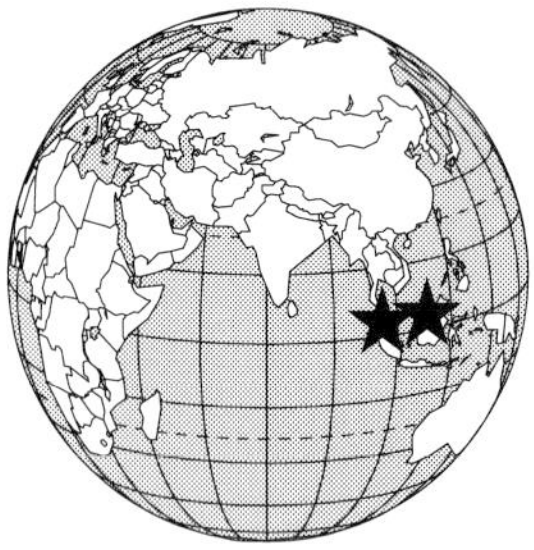

## Background

Malaysia was established in 1963. The fourteen-party, ruling National Front coalition has captured at least a two-thirds majority in the lower house in nine straight general elections since 1957. The coalition is dominated by the United Malays National Organization (UMNO), a secular, conservative, ethnic-Malay-based party. In 1981 Dr. Mahathir Mohamad won the UMNO presidency and became prime minister.

Through close collaboration between the government and business, Malaysia has developed from an economy based on the export of rubber and tin to one where high technology plays a key role. In each of the last seven years, the economy has grown by 8 percent and per capita income has risen to over $3,500 in 1995 as the government has successfully attracted foreign investment and built up the country's infrastructure.

Malays enjoy a considerable degree of economic freedom. But significant restrictions remain on imports, government control of trade unions continues, and women, indigenous people, and ethnic Chinese do not have equal rights to participate in the market economy.

## Freedom to Hold Property 3/3

In 1991 parliament amended the Land Acquisition Act to give state governments the right to expropriate land for any development deemed to be in the national interest, including private development. The amendment also prohibited property owners from challenging land acquisitions in court, permitting only appeals related to the amount of compensation. Opposition parties charge that the government often sells expropriated land to businessmen with close links to the ruling party.

Malaysia has Southeast Asia's strongest legal regime and enforcement procedures for intellectual property rights. The judiciary is generally efficient and effective in ordinary property rights cases, although its independence is questionable in politically sensitive cases.

## Freedom to Earn a Living 2/3

Malaysian unions are independent of the government and are free from interference from political parties. Workers can exercise their legal right to bargain collectively, and wages are set by the market.

However, the government exercises significant control over trade unions. Under the Trade Unions Act, each union can represent only one particular type of establishment, trade or industry. The Director General of Trade Unions must approve, and can dissolve, all unions. The government permits only enterprise level, "in-house" unions in the 120,000-worker electronics industry. Numerous laws, including the Internal Security Act and the Official Secrets Act, can be invoked to restrict trade union activities.

Strikes are legal but are subject to restrictions. Under the 1967 Industrial Relations Act, unions must provide advance notice in several "essential services," some of which are not considered essential by the International Labor Organization. The Ministry of Human Resources can order mediation and eventually send a dispute to the Industrial Court, during which time strikes are prohibited.

Individuals are free to change jobs as they wish, and there are no reports of forced or compulsory labor.

## Freedom to Operate a Business 2/3

The Malaysian government encourages private enterprise, and the regulations for setting up a manufacturing enterprise or running a business are not complex. The process of awarding government contracts allegedly favors businessmen close to the ruling United Malays National Organization. Most prices are determined by the market, although the government controls prices of some key goods and services, including fuel, public utilities, rice, flour and sugar.

## Freedom to Invest One's Earnings 3/3

Interest rates and credit flows are determined by the market. In June the government announced that it would permit full foreign ownership of fund management companies in order to further liberalize capital markets. Foreign brokerage firms are still not allowed to trade on the Kuala Lumpur exchange.

Rates of return on investment are not controlled and citizens may hold foreign currencies and invest abroad. The Bank Negara Malaysia is independent, but following a 1992 financial crisis the government has been monitoring the bank's activities. Inflation averaged around 4.3 percent in 1995.

## Freedom to Trade Internationally 1/2

Import duties range as high as 30 percent, although the average is 10 percent. Import quotas remain on several goods in order to protect specific domestic industries. Special permission is required for rubber exports.

The government generally reviews foreign investment proposals in a nondiscriminatory manner, although foreign and domestic financing are required. In foreign ventures 30 percent of the local equity must be held by *bumiputras* (ethnic Malays, literally "sons of the soil"). Certain sectors of the economy are closed to foreign investors, including financial services and the oil and gas industry; ownership of agricultural land is restricted to Malaysian citizens; and foreign firms are restricted to 30 percent interest in Malaysian firms. Repatriation of capital and profits is freely permitted. Malaysians are not permitted to borrow funds on the domestic capital market for investment abroad.

## Freedom from Unreasonable Government Interference in the Economy

The government's share of GDP is a modest 0.3 percent. The government has raised $4.2 billion since 1983 by partially or fully privatizing 120 state enterprises, although critics say many of the shares ended up in the hands of pro-government businessmen.

Reaction to the economic success of the country's ethnic-Chinese minority led to race riots in 1969. At the time ethnic Malays made up half the population but owned only 2 percent of the wealth. The 1971 New Economic Policy discriminated in favor of bumiputras through racial quotas in business affairs, education and the civil service. The 1991 National Development Policy has less stringent quotas but the same goal of increasing the share of bumiputra wealth. Critics say the policies have largely benefited a core of politically connected businessmen. In 1994 Rafidah Aziz, the Minister of Trade and Industry, admitted that her ministry had allocated

5.7 million shares in various companies to her son-in-law at big discounts. Other blocks of shares went to relatives of high officials.

### Freedom to Participate in the Market Economy 1/2

Muslim women are subject to Islamic law in family and religious matters, and the inheritance law favors male heirs. The Kelantan state government, run by the opposition Pan-Malaysian Islamic Party, restricts the right of female workers to work at night. In peninsular Malaysia, states prevent indigenous people from holding land as individuals. In eastern Malaysia, states recognize "native customary rights" for indigenous people, but indigenous groups in the state of Sarawak say the government and private logging firms encroach on their rights. The government's programs to expand economic opportunities for Malays has made it more difficult for ethnic Chinese to secure necessary business documents and approvals.

Recently doubts have been raised about the legal system's transparency in commercial cases. A notable case in 1995 between Ayer Molek, a rubber company, and Insas, a financial services firm, was one of several instances where lawyers have been accused of exerting influence over trial venues, and in general of manipulating the legal process.

# New Zealand

ECONOMIC FREEDOM STATUS: **FREE**
POLITICAL RIGHTS AND CIVIL LIBERTIES STATUS: **FREE**
PRESS FREEDOM STATUS: **FREE**
POPULATION: **3,546,000**
PPP: **$14,990**

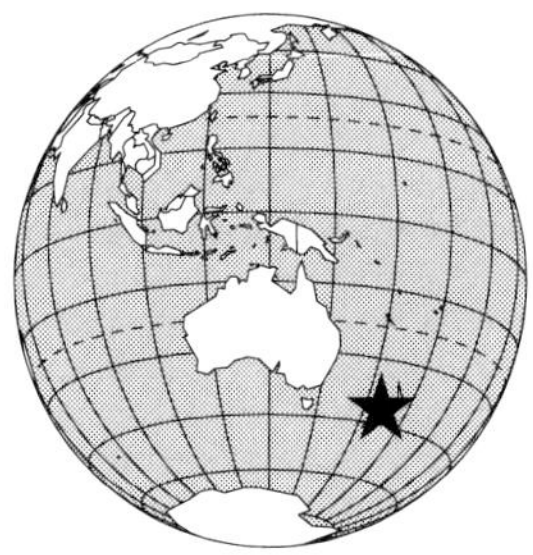

### Background

New Zealand achieved full self-government prior to World War II, and gained formal independence from Great Britain in 1947. Since 1935, political power in this parliamentary democracy has alternated between the mildly conservative National Party and the center-left Labor Party, both of which helped develop one of the world's most progressive welfare states. In response to an increasingly competitive global trade regime, in 1984 the incoming Labor government began an economic deregulation program that included cutting farm subsidies, slashing tariffs and privatizing many industries. The last ten years have transformed New Zealand into one of the most economically free nations in the world.

The harsh effects of the economic reforms and a deep recession contributed to a National Party landslide at the October 1990 parliamentary elections. However, rather than slow the reforms new Prime Minister Jim Bolger's government continued them by cutting back on government spending.

### Freedom to Hold Property 3/3

New Zealand effectively protects private property, including intellectual property. There are no significant restrictions on property owners transferring or structuring their holdings as they wish. The government sought to resolve disputes over land rights with the Maori minority but their proposal was rejected as too small.

**Freedom to Earn a Living 3/3**

Workers are free to form unions and bargain collectively. Unions are independent of the government but do support political parties whose policies they favor. Some unions are affiliated with the Labor Party. The government mandates a minimum wage. A law prohibiting forced or compulsory labor is effectively enforced.

**Freedom to Operate a Business 3/3**

There are no restrictions on the right to establish, own or operate a business in New Zealand. Regulations are relatively transparent and free from bureaucratic red tape. Entry into certain lines of business is not restricted.

New Zealand has not yet signed the GATT Government Procurement Code. Procurement purchasing decisions, however, are decentralized and the process is transparent. The New Zealand government encourages its agencies to buy New Zealand products when all other factors are equal. Prices for goods and services produced by the private sector are no longer controlled in New Zealand, and prices for public services have been adjusted to realistic levels.

**Freedom to Invest One's Earnings 3/3**

New Zealand citizens are free to invest their earnings in a variety of domestic and foreign financial instruments. Credit flows are determined by market forces, and capital flow restrictions have been lifted. The Bank of New Zealand gained autonomous control over monetary policy in 1989. The financial sector has been deregulated and domestic controls on lending and deposit rates have been lifted.

**Freedom to Trade Internationally 2/2**

New Zealand is a member of GATT but still maintains relatively high tariffs on motor vehicles, tires, textiles, clothing and footwear. There are no significant export restrictions but commodity marketing boards have monopoly marketing rights on the export of dairy products, apples, pears, and kiwifruit. Import licensing was eliminated in 1992. Export controls and tariffs were eliminated by 1987.

New Zealand does not discriminate against foreign investment. Investments over NZD 10 million—or investments of any size in commercial fishing or rural land—must be approved by the Overseas Investment Commission. However, most applications are approved. There are no exchange controls and the currency is fully convertible.

**Freedom from Unreasonable Government Interference in the Economy**

The government of New Zealand seems committed to reducing its role in the economy and to encouraging free-market practices. After decades of high spending, the government has greatly reduced public expenditures and has privatized major economic enterprises such as the railroad and telephone monopolies. The government still controls the production and transmission of electric power, some radio and television broadcasting, and some forests, but is reviewing its role in these industries. The government has significantly reduced subsidies to industry although it does provide incentives to small businesses. The agricultural sector faced an abrupt end to price controls and tax concessions. New Zealand has a liberal competition policy.

**Freedom to Participate in the Market Economy 1/2**

There are no significant barriers to the participation of women or minorities in the economy. Corruption has not been a problem in New Zealand.

A key issue facing the Bolger government is the resolution of land claims by the Maori minority. Under the 1840 Treaty of Waitangi the Maori ceded sovereignty to the British in return for guarantees on land rights. However, by 1890 the Maori had lost all but 4.4 million hectares of the country's 26.8 million total, and that figure has since shrunk to 1.2 million hectares. In late 1994 the government established a $633 million fund to settle all outstanding Maori land claims within ten years. In December the government reached a settlement with the Waikato tribe that included a $41.6 million cash payment and public land valued at $66.5 million. However, many Maori leaders rejected the fund for being too small and refused to negotiate.

In 1995 Maori activists waged a civil disobedience campaign that included symbolic occupations of parks and other tracts they claimed as ancestral lands. In May the Tainui tribe signed a cash and land package worth $112 million, putting pressure on other Maori groups to either negotiate or be left out. However, in a population where intermarriage over 200 years has meant few people can claim pure Maori descent, ethnic distinctions will be increasingly difficult to make.

# Pakistan

ECONOMIC FREEDOM STATUS: **MOSTLY NOT FREE**
POLITICAL RIGHTS AND CIVIL LIBERTIES STATUS: **PARTLY FREE**
PRESS FREEDOM STATUS: **PARTLY FREE**
POPULATION: **129,700,000**
PPP: **$2,890**

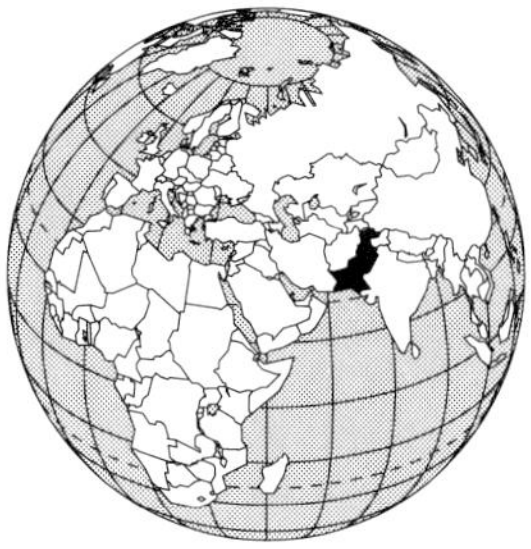

## Background

Pakistan was formed in 1947 through the partition of India. In 1971 the eastern portion of the country separated to form Bangladesh. The 1973 constitution provides for a National Assembly, which currently has 207 directly elected seats and ten reserved for non-Muslims, and an eighty-seven-seat Senate appointed by the four provincial assemblies. The president is chosen for a five-year term by an electoral college consisting of the national and provincial assemblies and the Senate.

In 1977 General Zia ul-Haq overthrew populist premier Ali Bhutto. In 1985, with the country still under martial law, parliament approved the Eighth Amendment, which allows the president to dismiss the prime minister and dissolve parliament. Zia and his successor, Ghulam Ishaq Khan, used the Eighth Amendment to sack three successive elected governments, most recently those headed by Bhutto's daughter, Benazir Bhutto, in 1990, and Nawaz Sharif in 1993. In May 1993 the Supreme Court ruled the latter move unconstitutional as Khan had made no effort at mediation. A deal brokered in July called for fresh elections in October which returned Bhutto's Pakistan People's Party to power.

Pakistan initiated a series of macroeconomic structural reforms in the late 1980s which have been bolstered by Prime Minister Bhutto. In 1994, the government signed a structural adjustment agreement with the International Monetary Fund that has reduced barriers to the private sector, brought about privatization of state enterprises, and reduced trade barriers.

However, high inflation, crop failures, and budget shortfalls pose serious problems for

Pakistan's economic reforms. Bhutto, who is also the finance minister, imposed an unpopular sales tax in June 1995 in an effort to raise revenue. Tariff collection has fallen due to rampant smuggling over the Afghan border. The exemption of feudal landowners from paying taxes on their income is one example of the tremendous inequities in economic policy.

Due to a weak judiciary and an ineffective land registry system, rights to both land and intellectual property are poorly protected. Entrepreneurs face many hurdles in registering new businesses, and once registered find it difficult to raise capital unless they are well connected. The practice of bonded labor is widespread in several industries, and importers face both tariff and non-tariff barriers.

### Freedom to Hold Property 1/3

The legal system recognizes the right to acquire and dispose of property, but as a whole the judiciary is severely backlogged and prone to corruption. Land records are notoriously unreliable, making transfers and securing mortgages difficult. Enforcement of intellectual property rights is inadequate, and pirated goods are sold blatantly.

Between 1972 and 1975, the populist government of Ali Bhutto nationalized a number of businesses, mostly domestic. However, expropriations have been limited since then. The Foreign Private Investment (Promotion and Protection) Act of 1976 specifically protects foreign concerns.

### Freedom to Earn a Living 1/3

There are significant restrictions on workers' rights. The 1969 Industrial Relations Ordinance denies workers in export processing zones the right of association, and does not explicitly provide this right to agricultural workers. The 1952 Essential Services Maintenance Act (ESA) restricts union activity in education, transportation and other sectors, including prohibitions on the right to strike. The ESA also prevents workers in some fields from quitting jobs. Where strikes are permitted, workers must observe legally mandated cooling-off periods and the government may still ban a strike it does not consider to be in the public interest.

Trade unions are independent of the government, and the largest are affiliated with political parties. The ESA allows the government to restrict collective bargaining in the industries it covers. In these cases, special boards set wages. Overall, effective collective bargaining is not possible for most Pakistani workers.

Illegal bonded labor is widespread in fishing, construction, agriculture, and other industries. Although parliament passed the Bonded Labor System (Abolition) Act in 1992, enforcement at the provincial level is nonexistent. At least one landlord has been caught operating a private jail and forcing detainees to do agricultural work, and it is likely that other private jails exist. The use of child labor, particularly in the carpet industry, is widespread.

### Freedom to Operate a Business 2/3

Private enterprise is permitted in nearly all fields, with the exception of certain sensitive sectors. The formation of a business enterprise requires substantial paperwork and there are several approval steps depending on the type and complexity of the business. Prices are not controlled except in the pharmaceuticals sector.

The process of letting government contracts often favors politically connected businessmen. Civil unrest in Karachi, the country's commercial capital, pitting rival factions of the Mohajir Quami Movement (MQM) against each other and the government, and Shiites against Sunnis, has made investors wary. By one estimate up to 30 percent of workers in Karachi are absent on any given day due to fears of violence. Extortion is reportedly widespread in the city as well. A disproportionate share of the economic wealth in Pakistan is held by a tiny, politically connected, land-owning elite consisting of perhaps 500 families.

### Freedom to Invest One's Earnings 1/3

The State Bank of Pakistan caps interest rates by setting maximum mark-up rates for banks. Credit is allocated largely through cronyism to the benefit of big landowners and industrialists. There are few restrictions on holding foreign exchange or moving foreign capital in and out of the country. There are no limits on remittances of profits, capital gains, or returns on intellectual property. The central State Bank of Pakistan is increasingly independent and has made keeping a tight grip on monetary policy a priority.

### Freedom to Trade Internationally 1/2

Tariffs are high, and importers also face numerous surcharges, excise taxes and a sales tax with a higher rate for foreign goods. Import quotas apply to a small number of goods. The government encourages exports through fiscal incentives and export financing, although export taxes exist. There are no restrictions on travel abroad.

The government seeks to attract foreign investment and generally treats foreign concerns in an evenhanded manner. The rupee has been floating within managed bounds since 1982. In 1993 and 1994 the government removed several foreign exchange restrictions and made the rupee fully convertible on the current account.

### Freedom from Unreasonable Government Interference in the Economy

In the late 1980s state enterprises dominated numerous industries, and the government had monopolies in telecommunications, power, and rail and air transportation. Since then, successive governments have favored deregulation and reduced the public-sector role in the economy. Government expenditures for 1995 were 13 percent of GDP. The government seeks to privatize the entire industrial goods sector, and several such factories have been sold off. Sugar and several other industries are subsidized.

Benazir Bhutto's government, like its predecessor, the Islamic Democratic Alliance government of Nawaz Shariff, uses the state's enforcement powers against political rivals, notably in selective investigations of business corruption cases.

### Freedom to Participate in the Market Economy 1/2

Hindus claim discrimination in education and social services. Both Christians and Ahmadis, who under the 1974 constitution are not recognized as Muslims because they do not accept Muhammad as the last prophet of Islam, face frequent harassment. Both groups are often marginalized economically, in part due to discrimination in educational opportunities. Women face significant social discrimination, making full participation in the commercial and public sectors difficult. Although legally a woman's right to an inheritance is protected, in practice women are often denied their share. Corruption is a regular part of doing business and a drain on the economy.

# Philippines

ECONOMIC FREEDOM STATUS: **PARTLY FREE**
POLITICAL RIGHTS AND CIVIL LIBERTIES STATUS: **PARTLY FREE**
PRESS FREEDOM STATUS: **PARTLY FREE**
POPULATION: **68,424,000**
PPP: **$2,550**

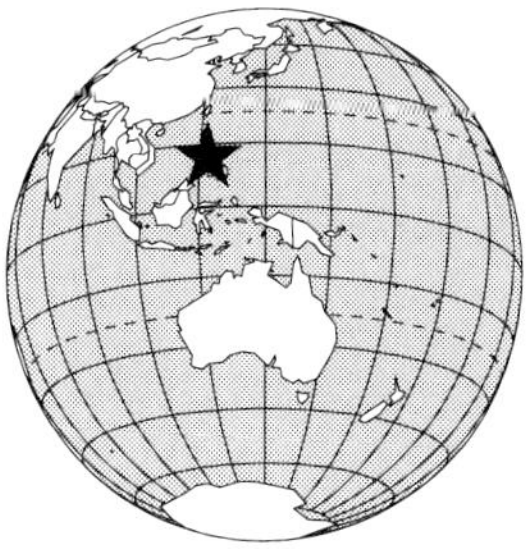

## Background

The Philippines, a 7,100-island archipelago in Southeast Asia, achieved independence in 1946 after forty-three years of United States rule and subsequent occupation by the Japanese during World War II. Strongman Ferdinand Marcos ruled for twenty-one years until he was deposed in the February 1986 "People Power" Revolution and replaced by Corazon Aquino. In 1992, in the first peaceful transfer of power since 1965, Fidel Ramos became president.

President Ramos has been a vocal defender of the viability of democracy amid rhetoric of "Asian Values" and the incompatibility of democracy and economic growth. Midway through his term Ramos successfully pushed through an economic deregulation program, although few of the benefits of the country's recent GDP growth have filtered down to the masses. Restrictions on investment and trade barriers have been removed and almost all state assets have been privatized, creating one of the most liberalized economies in Asia.

Citizens are now free to earn a living and reasonably free to trade internationally and invest their earnings. The most significant remaining restraints on economic freedom are the difficulties entrepreneurs face in registering new businesses and the risk that the goods and services they provide may be subject to price controls. Women, ethnic Chinese, and indigenous peoples also face economic discrimination.

## Freedom to Hold Property 2/3

The right to hold property is recognized by law. Philippine law guarantees investors freedom from expropriation without just compensation, and this is honored in practice. The government is a party to conventions on intellectual property rights, but enforcement tends to be weak due to lack of resources.

On the other hand, many urban residents do not have formal title to their property. Furthermore, land ownership is constitutionally limited to Filipinos or to corporations with at least 60 percent Filipino ownership.

## Freedom to Earn a Living 3/3

The right of association is protected by the constitution and freely exercised in practice. Unions are independent of the government and free of party control. An exception is the Rosario Free Trade Zone eighteen miles south of Manila, where the provincial governor has cracked down on union activity, and where at least three activists have been killed in the past two years and four others are missing.

Strikes are legal, although all means of mediation must first be exhausted and the strike issue has to be relevant to the labor contract. The Secretary of Labor can prohibit strikes on account of an overriding national interest. Seventy instances of police and military harassment of strikers involving 900 workers were documented in 1994. Collective bargaining is permitted in the private sector but limited in the public sector.

The government does not control wage rates. Forced labor is prohibited, and the government enforcement of this ban is effective.

**Freedom to Operate a Business** **1/3**

The government encourages private enterprise. However, doing business involves dealing with substantial bureaucratic hassles. The Board of Investment has set up a "one-stop shop" to centralize the registration of businesses it places on the preferred list. Individuals and businesses can freely acquire and dispose of assets and business interests. Only a few areas are closed to private enterprise, such as the importation of rice. The procurement guidelines for government contracts generally favor domestic firms. The large informal sector is also, in part, indicative of remaining barriers to establishing legal businesses.

Economic power in the Philippines is disproportionately held by oligarchs and wealthy landowners (many of whom maintain private armies). In 1994 the government opened up to competition the telephone industry that had previously been dominated by the powerful Cojuangco family. The government's oil price stabilization fund keeps prices below market levels. Three companies hold an oligopoly on the industry, but the government plans a full liberalization by the end of 1996.

The government controls the price of automobiles and petroleum products as well as services provided by public utilities. It has emergency powers to set ceilings on the prices of milk, sugar, pork, chicken, cooking oil, and flour. The president may also impose controls to check inflation or ease social tension.

**Freedom to Invest One's Earnings** **2/3**

Capital investments outside the country no longer require prior approval by the *Bangko Sentral*, provided the investments are funded by withdrawals from foreign currency deposit units and that the funds are not sourced from the domestic banking system or are less than $1 million per year. Banks must assign 25 percent of their lending to small enterprises and agricultural concerns. The Bangko Sentral is independent of the government. Interest rates are not controlled, and with the exception of the favorable treatment lenders must accord small business, and agricultural concerns, credit is market-allocated. Returns on investments are not controlled.

**Freedom to Trade Internationally** **1/2**

Until recently the Philippines was one of the most protectionist nations in Asia. The government is in the process of reducing, restructuring and simplifying the tariff regime with the objective of achieving a uniform levy of 5 percent on all goods by 2004. Quantitative import restrictions remain on more than 100 industrial products and on more than 100 agricultural and industrial commodities.

The mutual-fund sector is closed to foreign ownership. In early 1995 the government allowed ten new foreign banks to operate in the country. Most sectors, with the notable exception of media and broadcasting, are open to foreign investment. Foreign equity is limited to 40 percent in sectors covered under the preferential 1987 Omnibus Investments Code, although 100 percent foreign ownership is permitted in many areas.

The government has liberalized foreign exchange regulations and has lifted mandatory forex surrender requirements on export earnings.

**Freedom from Unreasonable Government Interference in the Economy**

The government's share of GDP is 18 percent, although state-owned enterprises account for just 0.3 percent of GDP. The administration of President Fidel Ramos has privatized nearly all state assets since 1992. The national power corporation is slated for privatization in early 1996, and the government plans to shed some of its 57 percent stake in the Philippine National Bank.

Enforcement of labor, health, and environmental regulations is weak, piecemeal and often selective. The Ramos administration has made reform of the tax system a priority; currently only 1.6 million people out of a workforce of 27 million pay taxes due to a complex tax regime, weak enforcement and corruption. Critics charge that opponents of the government have been targets of a revenue collection campaign.

## Freedom to Participate in the Market Economy 1/2

Women face discrimination in employment opportunities, and sexual harassment in the workplace is reportedly widespread. Trafficking of Filipino women abroad for prostitution is a serious problem, and domestic prostitution is rampant. Ethnic-Chinese businessmen, who play a significant role in the economy, have been subjected to extortion schemes by bureaucrats, while their children have been targets of kidnappings for ransom.

Indigenous land rights are protected by the constitution, but no legislation has been passed to protect these rights against impingement by developers.

The judiciary is inadequate for an efficiently functioning market economy. The courts are heavily backlogged and are prone to pressure by local officials and wealthy interests. The country loses an estimated $3.6 billion per year due to official corruption.

# Singapore

ECONOMIC FREEDOM STATUS: **PARTLY FREE**
POLITICAL RIGHTS AND CIVIL LIBERTIES STATUS: **PARTLY FREE**
PRESS FREEDOM STATUS: **NOT FREE**
POPULATION: **2,988,000**
PPP: **$18,330**

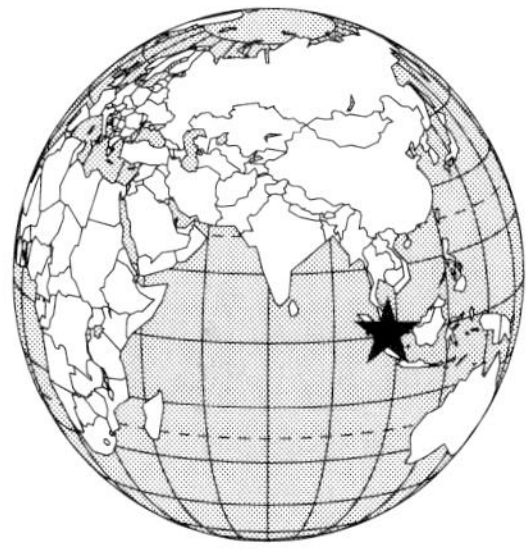

## Background

Singapore came under British control in 1867. The colony became self-governing in 1959, entered the Malaysian Federation in 1963 and in 1965 became fully independent under Prime Minister Lee Kuan Yew. The authoritarian People's Action Party (PAP) swept all elections from 1968 to 1980 before losing a by-election in 1981.

In October 1990 Lee stepped down in favor of his hand-picked successor, Goh Chok Tong, although the former premier still exerts considerable influence as senior minister.

Although Singapore covers only 240 square miles and has no natural resources, it has one of the most dynamic economies in the world, bolstered by an excellent infrastructure and well-educated labor force. Singapore has been engineered by its leadership to be a magnet for foreign capital and investment. State control over a large percentage of the economy, suppression of organized labor, and a big-brother mentality restrict economic freedom of Singaporeans in a way seldom observed by foreign investors. Economic freedom comes at the price of political acquiescence to the ruling PAP.

## Freedom to Hold Property 3/3

The right to private property is respected in law and practice. Singapore is committed to the protection of intellectual property rights and enforcement is strong. The judiciary is an effective and impartial arbiter of most commercial matters, except in politically sensitive cases. However, a legacy of forced relocation and arbitrary expropriation for political motivations remains. The Land Acquisition Act of 1967 allows the government to expropriate private land for public housing and other development programs. This law has enabled the government to replace squatter camps and slums with modern public housing units constructed by the Housing and Development Board (HDB). Between 1967 and 1985, the government acquired over 75 percent of the land available in Singapore and continues to expropriate land for government use. This policy has created a virtual government monopoly on property and housing. Rates are very high, and one's political and social views may result in denial of housing. HDB home ownership, another perceived achievement of the PAP regime, is in reality a leasehold that subjects the "owner" to stringent controls regarding use or alteration of the property. PAP leaseholders may be evicted for offending the morality of the state, and often are not compensated for their lost investment.

## Freedom to Earn a Living 1/3

The right of association is recognized in the constitution. The National Trades Union Congress (NTUC) is an umbrella for seventy-four of Singapore's eighty-three unions, representing 99 percent of unionized workers. The NTUC is closely affiliated with the ruling PAP, even though the Societies Act restricts all political activity to political parties. The NTUC prohibits opposition supporters from holding union office. Wages are set through collective bargaining. Strikes are legal but rarely occur, partly because the government discourages them but also due to a labor shortage resulting from high economic growth rates. Each year scores of foreign workers are flogged for overstaying visas. The Central Provident Fund (CPF) was established in 1955 as a form of forced savings through which 23 percent of an employee's wages are withheld and employers match 17 percent of the wage. The purpose of the fund is to compel citizens to save money to support themselves in retirement. However, individuals have limited access to their savings, and also find it in their interest not to risk their savings by engaging in political or labor agitation.

## Freedom to Operate a Business 2/3

On the surface Singapore has a free-market economy, and the government encourages private enterprise. Foreign and domestic entities may freely establish business entities. The government has striven to maintain an environment conducive to businesses, and red tape is minimal. Government contracts are let competitively and there are no price controls.

However, stability and efficiency are due to highly authoritarian controls imposed by the government over the economic and personal lives of citizens. Many domestic industries—in the services, mass media, and real estate—are dominated by so-called government-linked companies that are in actuality owned by the government. Coupled with market regulation by the state, government control limits entry into these areas by private entrepreneurs.

## Freedom to Invest One's Earnings 3/3

The government does not allocate credit. There are no caps on rates of return on investment. Individuals can freely invest abroad and can hold foreign currency and securities. The central bank is independent of the government and has managed to keep inflation under control despite consistently strong economic growth.

**Freedom to Trade Internationally 2/2**

Singapore has few barriers to foreign trade. Many goods are free of import duties, including electronic equipment, computers, software, medical equipment and most other consumer and industrial products. There are no taxes on capital gains and no local partner requirements or other restrictions on foreign ownership of businesses. Investment regulations are straightforward and the bureaucracy is efficient. There are no foreign exchange controls.

**Freedom from Unreasonable Government Interference in the Economy**

The government has a 6 percent share of GDP. The government plays a key role in economic decision-making through the Economic Development Board. The Board identifies sectors with high potential, which are subsidized through tax and fiscal incentives.

The broadly drawn Official Secrets Act bars the unauthorized release of government data to the media. In June 1992 the *Business Times* published "flash" estimates of quarterly GDP growth several days before the actual figures were officially announced. In March 1994 a court found the editor of the *Business Times*, a journalist and three economists guilty of "endangering state security" and fined them.

The Newspaper and Printing Presses Act (NPPA) allows the government to "gazette," or cap, the circulation of any foreign publication it feels has interfered with domestic politics. In recent years limits have been placed on the *Economist*, *Far Eastern Economic Review*, *Asiaweek*, and the *Asian Wall Street Journal*. The government has harassed several leading opposition figures through dismissal from public-sector jobs, libel suits and the threat of such suits.

**Freedom to Participate in the Market Economy 1/2**

Singapore's commercial codes and regulatory procedures are transparent and foster fair competition. Tax codes and business regulations are not unduly burdensome. However, regulatory bodies often have wide discretion to modify regulations and impose new conditions without informing the public. The government is vigilant in guarding against corruption, and the country is among the freest of corruption in Asia.

Those who oppose government policy face harassment and inquiries by tax authorities. Their businesses are investigated for possible wrongdoing, and they soon find their access to credit and other services cut off as their bankers and clients face harassment as well.

Key "management shares" in the Singapore Press Holdings, which publishes all major newspapers, must be held by government-approved individuals. The NPPA prohibits any person or group from holding more than 3 percent of any newspaper company unless exempted. Citizens are banned from owning satellite dishes.

# Taiwan

ECONOMIC FREEDOM STATUS: **PARTLY FREE**
POLITICAL RIGHTS AND CIVIL LIBERTIES STATUS: **PARTLY FREE**
PRESS FREEDOM STATUS: **FREE**
POPULATION: **21,235,000**
PPP: **GDP (1994) U.S. $b243**

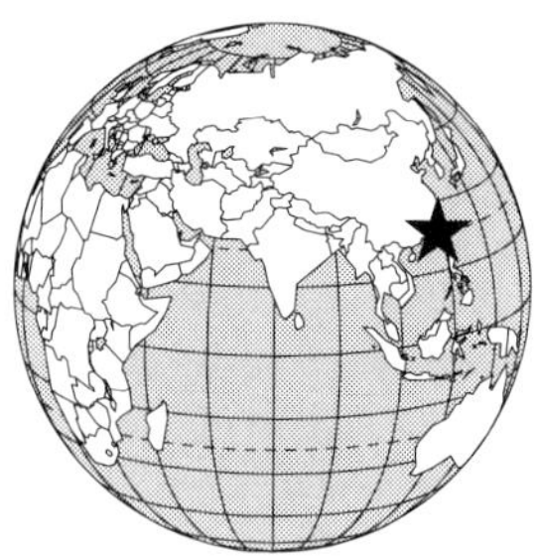

## Background

Located 100 miles off the Chinese coast, Taiwan came under the control of China's Nationalist government after World War II. Following the Communist victory on the mainland in 1949, Nationalist leader Chiang Kai-shek established a government-in-exile on Taiwan. For the next four decades the Koumintang Party (KMT) ruled Taiwan in an authoritarian manner. Both Taiwan and China still officially consider Taiwan to be a province of China. Today native Taiwanese make up 85 percent of the population, while aging mainlanders and their descendants comprise the minority. The country's democratic transition began with the lifting of martial law in 1987. In 1988 Lee Teng-hui became the first native-born Taiwanese president, and a year later the government formally legalized opposition parties.

The Taiwanese economy is based upon export of manufactured goods. Taiwan imports most raw materials and energy inputs. Building on an industrial base left by Japanese occupiers, Taiwan developed light industry through cheap labor and imports substitution policies. Since the late 1980s, Taiwan has moved rapidly into the high-technology and scientific research and manufacturing fields. Democratization has facilitated the liberalization of the economy. In 1995, some sectors of the economy previously closed to private investment were opened, restrictions on the financial sector were relaxed, and market regulations were reduced. Corruption among business leaders and government officials is abundant.

## Freedom to Hold Property 2/3

The right to hold property is respected in practice. By law no joint venture with 45 percent or more foreign interest can be nationalized during the first twenty years of its existence. Expropriation is legally permitted on national security grounds, but adequate compensation must be paid and this is respected in practice. Private entities can freely acquire and dispose of property. Due to weak enforcement, intellectual property protection is below international standards.

## Freedom to Earn a Living 2/3

The government must approve the rules and constitutions of labor unions, and can dissolve a union for disturbing the public order. In some instances the government has refused to certify a new union on the grounds that a union already exists in the given area. Civil servants, defense industry workers and teachers cannot form unions and cannot bargain collectively. No administrative district can have competing labor federations, and thus the only officially recognized labor federation is the Chinese Federation of Labor, which is closely allied with the ruling KMT.

Wages are set according to the market. Laws against forced and compulsory labor are observed.

**Freedom to Operate a Business 2/3**

The Taiwanese government strongly encourages private enterprise, particularly at the local level. The July 1993 Economic Revitalization Program provides financial and technical assistance to local businessmen. The process of forming and operating businesses is transparent and not unduly burdensome. The government maintains limits on foreign ownership in industries that include shipping, leasing and cable television broadcasting.

Major government tenders are offered through a central purchasing agency, the Central Trust of China, which follows a process described by observers as fair and open. Though other government purchases are usually fair and open, companies employing relatives of bureaucrats or former bureaucrats tend to have an advantage over competitors.

Price controls exist for products and services of state owned enterprises. Regular price monitoring is conducted by the Commodity Price Supervisory Board, comprised of representatives of the Central Bank, the Ministry of Finance, the Ministry of Economic Affairs, the Agricultural Commission and the Ministry of Communications. However, this board does not have the power to set prices. Approval of new products and services is painstakingly slow. Furthermore, legislation such as the Consumer Protection Law and the Fair Trade Laws contains clauses that have the potential to severely restrict market access and competition.

**Freedom to Invest One's Earnings 2/3**

Interest rates are market-driven and credit flows are determined by market forces. There are no restrictions on capital movement abroad arising from trade in merchandise and services. For other purposes, approval is required for capital inflows or outflows of $1 million or more per transaction, or above an annual cumulative limit of $5 million or more.

The central bank is independent and exercises significant control over the banking and financial sectors. Most major banks are state-owned, but since the Banking Law was revised in 1989 seventeen private banks have been established. Banks are only allowed to open a maximum of five branches per year, and this has made it difficult for the new banks to expand their market share. Financial markets are still overregulated, and Finance Ministry approval of new insurance and financial products and services is slow.

**Freedom to Trade Internationally 2/2**

Average tariffs on nonagricultural imports have dropped substantially in recent years, and the number of products requiring import licenses is being reduced. Non-tariff barriers include mandatory testing for industrial products and registration for pharmaceuticals, medical parts and cosmetics. There are few bans on exports, although permits are required for numerous items, particularly in the textile, garment, and national security industries. Citizens can travel abroad freely. Foreigners are now allowed to invest in shares listed on the Taiwan Stock Exchange. Foreign exchange controls have been eased.

**Freedom from Unreasonable Government Interference in the Economy**

The government plans to privatize the twenty-odd state-owned enterprises (SOEs). Only one SOE has been sold thus far. The government is in the process of ending monopolies that parastatal companies enjoy in electricity generation, telecommunications and oil refining. There are frequent jurisdictional disputes over economic matters between the central government and local authorities. The central government has deemed fees levied on business by local governments to be illegal taxes. The ruling KMT listed its total business assets at $36 billion in 1992, and these extensive holdings give the government influence over many sectors of the economy.

### Freedom to Participate in the Market Economy 1/2

Women face discrimination in salary and promotion opportunities. Enforcement of laws against sex discrimination in the workplace is inadequate. The 357,000-strong aboriginal population is marginalized economically and has limited influence in policy decisions regarding land and natural resources. Aborigines cannot hunt or raise crops on the parts of their ancestral lands that are under government control.

Corruption is prevalent in the economy. In the absence of adequate ethics laws, members of the Legislative *Yuan* (branch) often sit on committees overseeing the activities of firms they have interests in. Legislative Yuan members can also be hired by private firms as consultants.

# Thailand

ECONOMIC FREEDOM STATUS: **PARTLY FREE**
POLITICAL RIGHTS AND CIVIL LIBERTIES STATUS: **PARTLY FREE**
PRESS FREEDOM STATUS: **PARTLY FREE**
POPULATION: **60,206,000**
PPP: **$5,950**

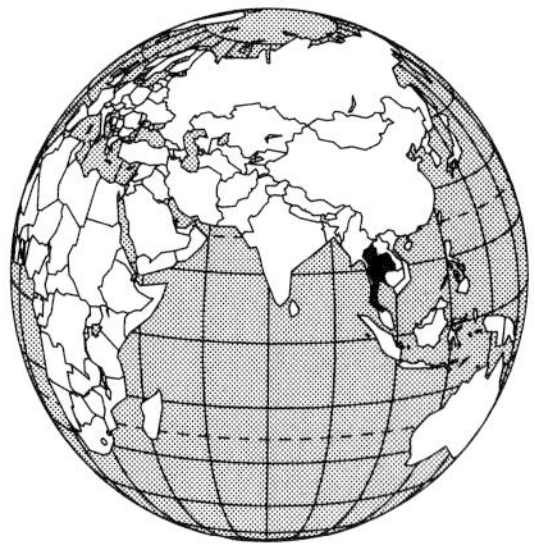

### Background

Thailand is the only Southeast Asian nation never colonized by a European country. In 1932 a bloodless coup, the first of seventeen coups or coup attempts this century, led to a new constitution limiting the power of the monarchy. In September 1992, the Democratic Party took seventy-nine seats and formed a five-party, prodemocracy coalition under party leader Chuan Leekpai. Chuan's coalition collapsed in May 1995 over a land-reform scandal and was succeeded by a seven-party coalition headed by the Thai Nation's Banharn Silpa-archa.

Thailand has enjoyed economic growth of between 8 and 10 percent per year since 1988. Economic liberalization and foreign investment have helped to transform Thailand from a largely agricultural economy to a broad-based, export-oriented, manufacturing economy. Government intervention is minimal but a series of five-year plans since 1961 has shaped general economic goals. The next five-year plan, running from 1997 to 2001, will focus on development issues such as education and health care, and will include, for the first time, input from citizens' groups and non-governmental organizations.

Economic opportunities are expanding rapidly in Thailand. However, coerced labor, a lack of progress in land reforms, remaining barriers to free trade and pervasive corruption remain issues of concern.

### Freedom to Hold Property 2/3

The right to hold property is recognized by law and respected in practice. In October 1995 parliament approved a copyright law protecting intellectual property, particularly computer software. The Microsoft Corporation estimates that currently 98 percent of the software used in

Thailand is pirated, and it is too early to judge the effectiveness of the new law and of the government's enforcement procedures.

The government of ex-Prime Minister Chuan Leekpai introduced a land-titling program that allocated 4.6 million acres to nearly 600,000 people. However, the program did not grant farmers the right to sell the property, so the land cannot be used as collateral for loans. The Chuan government fell in May 1995 amid allegations that ten wealthy Thais had been granted land rights on the southern resort island of Phuket.

## Freedom to Earn a Living 2/3

Private-sector workers' right of association is restricted. Under a 1991 decree each trade union can have only two advisors, both of whom must be licensed by the government. Prior to forming a union, there must be ten "promoters," and these promoters are not protected from anti-union discrimination. Unions are generally independent of the government and are not usually aligned with political parties. State enterprise workers can only form "associations," and only in individual enterprises, if at least 30 percent of the employees in the establishment submit a petition to the Ministry of Labor.

Private-sector workers can bargain collectively. State enterprise workers may not strike. Sweatshops are reportedly fairly common in the garment industry. Non-governmental organizations estimate there are 250,000 prostitutes in Thailand, and some become bonded to brothel owners to pay off debts incurred by their parents. Child labor, particularly child prostitution, is a serious problem.

## Freedom to Operate a Business 3/3

The government encourages private enterprise, and individuals are free to establish businesses in any sector. The process of registering a business is not overly complex. Price controls were established by the 1995 Price Maintenance on Goods and Services Act administered by the Department of Internal Trade. The act allows the state to set prices for twenty-two basic commodities and also to establish minimum prices for agricultural goods.

The 1952 Anti-Communist Act restricts the transportation within the country of oil and other sensitive commodities. Critics charge that the process of letting government contracts is compromised by corruption and favoritism.

## Freedom to Invest One's Earnings 3/3

Interest rates are set by the market, and there are no caps on profits from investment. The banking sector is in the process of being liberalized, and the government does not interfere with the flow of credit. Individuals can invest abroad and can hold foreign currency and securities. The autonomous Bank of Thailand kept inflation at about 3.1 percent in 1995.

## Freedom to Trade Internationally 1/2

High import tariffs, averaging 30 to 60 percent, and arbitrary valuation procedures are disincentives to importers. Many food products face a costly and time-consuming import-licensing process. Firms in export-processing zones are exempt from import duties and from taxes on foreign construction materials and equipment. There are export quotas on textiles and apparel. In an effort to crack down on the trafficking of women and children, travel abroad by single women under age thirty-six and by youths under fourteen must be approved by the Department of Public Welfare.

The 1972 Alien Business Law bans foreigners from owning majority stakes in strategic industries including shipbuilding and petrochemicals. Non-Thais are barred from engaging in many professional services, including accounting, architecture, law and engineering, as well as manual labor. However, many of these and other restrictions are dropped for countries with bilateral investment agreements with Thailand.

Most restrictions on the amount of foreign exchange and Thai currency that can be brought into the country have been lifted. Repatriation of capital and profits is permitted. Commercial banks can process foreign exchange transactions and the ceiling has been raised on transferring money abroad without the need for approval from the Board of Trade. Forex reporting requirements have been simplified, and banks can offer foreign currency accounts to individuals and businesses.

## Freedom from Unreasonable Government Interference in the Economy

The government's share of GDP is 12.4 percent. Some sixty-five state enterprises dominate utilities, communications and transportation. The effort to privatize the transport infrastructure in Bangkok has been largely unsuccessful due to infighting among patronage-oriented politicians.

Government policies promote exports as a means to economic development. The Board of Industry offers fiscal and other incentives for investment in sectors it considers promising or necessary for the country's economic growth. The petrochemical industry, although still largely closed to foreign investment, is being opened to greater domestic private investment. Majority equity stakes in shipping companies must be held by Thais, and critics say this has hindered the growth of a local shipping industry. Military officers hold positions on the boards of many private firms.

According to the *Far Eastern Economic Review*, in recent years officials in northeastern Thailand have encouraged farmers to shift production from staples to more profitable cash crops, often threatening to evict reluctant farmers from national forest reserve areas, where land tenure is not guaranteed. The government then abandoned the farmers when some schemes failed and farmers went heavily into debt. Only recently has the government agreed to consider rescheduling the debt.

## Freedom to Participate in the Market Economy 1/2

Thailand's estimated 500,000 to 700,000 members of hill tribes are marginalized politically and economically. Roughly half do not possess citizenship documentation, preventing them from gaining access to education and from holding property. Many women from hill tribes have been coerced into prostitution, and those without citizenship documents are not entitled to legal counsel if arrested. Some 45,000 Vietnamese who entered Thailand in the 1940s and 1950s and their descendants face similar restrictions. Corruption is rampant to the point of severely undermining citizens' faith in the political system.

# Vietnam

ECONOMIC FREEDOM STATUS: **NOT FREE**
POLITICAL RIGHTS AND CIVIL LIBERTIES STATUS: **NOT FREE**
PRESS FREEDOM STATUS: **NOT FREE**
POPULATION: **75,029,000**
PPP: **$1,010**

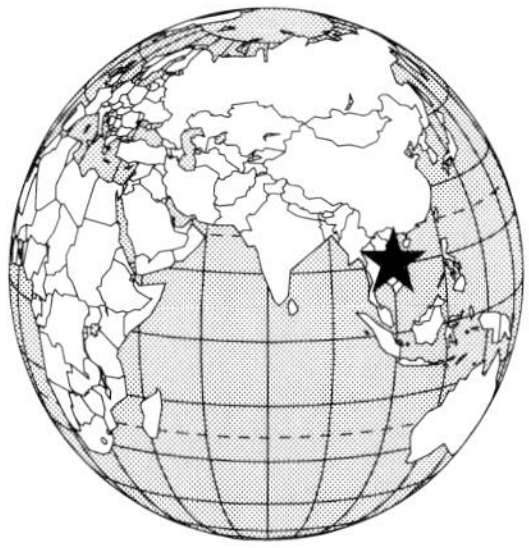

## Background

The French colonized Vietnam between 1862 and 1884. During World War II a resistance movement led by Ho Chi Minh fought the occupying Japanese and later battled the returning French. The country won independence in 1954, and was divided between a Communist government in the North and a French-installed one in the South. Planned elections to reunify the country were never held, and military forces and insurgent groups from the North eventually overtook the South and reunited the country in 1976 as the Socialist Republic of Vietnam.

The Sixth Vietnamese Communist Party (VCP) Congress in 1986 launched a program of *doi moi* (renovation), which has decentralized economic decision-making, encouraged small-scale private enterprises and largely dismantled agricultural collectivization. In April 1992 the National Assembly approved a new constitution that codified many of the economic reforms. However, it formally established the VCP as the sole legal political party and retained the party-controlled "People's Committees," which supervise daily life at the local level. In 1992 elections young technocrats were elected to the National Assembly, which subsequently elected General Le Duc Anh as state president, and re-elected economic reformer Vo Van Kiet as premier.

Nevertheless, the state retains significant control over the economy. The right of citizens to engage in private enterprise is circumscribed by a lack of property rights, corruption, ill-defined and arbitrarily enforced laws, high barriers to trade, restrictions on financial transactions, and a high involvement of the state in the economy.

## Freedom to Hold Property 1/3

Private property ownership is prohibited. Under the 1992 constitution, land is nominally owned by the people and administered by the state. The 1993 Land Law granted individuals and businesses the right to transfer, lease, mortgage and inherit land-use rights. Farmers in particular have benefited from this longterm tenure. Decree CP-18 of January 1995 reaffirms the government's control over all land. Observers see this socialist-capitalist hybrid as an effort by hardliners to slow market reforms and maintain the Communist Party's monopoly on power. On the positive side, Vietnam has gone from being a net importer of rice to being the third largest exporter in the world. In practice, intellectual property rights are not enforceable.

## Freedom to Earn a Living 1/3

All unions must belong to the Vietnam General Confederation of Labor, which is controlled by the government. The June 1994 Labor Law restricts the right to strike. The Law establishes a procedure for arbitration and appeals prior to a strike, but strikes are prohibited in sectors the government considers essential, and the prime minister can suspend any strike. Nevertheless, the government does allow some strikes to occur.

Collective bargaining is now practiced in some private industries and state-owned enterprises, and wages are increasingly set by the market.

**Freedom to Operate a Business 1/3**

The ruling Vietnam Communist Party's Sixth Party Congress in 1986 began a program of *doi moi*, which decentralized economic decision-making, encouraged small-scale private enterprises and largely dismantled collective agriculture. The growing private sector is now dominated by family-owned businesses. Despite the government's stated commitment to private enterprise, the growth of the market economy is still hampered by excessive bureaucracy, punitive taxes and ill-defined rules and regulations. In October 1995 the government announced that the parliament had passed a civil code including commercial laws, although details were not immediately available. Food prices have been largely free from government control since 1988.

**Freedom to Invest One's Earnings 1/3**

The government sets interest rates and plays a major role in allocating credit. In practice the private sector pays a higher interest rate than state enterprises for working capital and for capital investment borrowing. The banking system is rudimentary and dominated by state-owned banks. The central bank is not independent of the government, although it has brought inflation down from triple digits to 10-20 percent.

**Freedom to Trade Internationally 0/2**

Tariffs rates are high, and there is a higher tier for imports made by private factories abroad. Joint ventures are not permitted; instead the government allows "business cooperation contracts," which can be more readily dissolved. These limited ventures are subject to a time-consuming and often bewildering bureaucratic approval process that includes gaining approval from numerous government agencies. The government restricts citizens from traveling abroad. Foreign exchange transactions are strictly controlled by the government, and central bank regulations limit banking options for foreign investors.

**Freedom from Unreasonable Government Interference in the Economy**

State enterprises produced 43 percent of GDP in 1994. The government says that through mergers and closures it has reduced the number of state-owned enterprises (SOEs) from 12,000 in 1990 to 6,000 in 1994. The government has ended Vietnam Post and Telecommunications's monopoly on telecommunication services.

A 1994 bankruptcy law cleared the way for banks to seize assets of insolvent SOEs and shut them down. In April 1995 the rubber-stamp parliament passed a law giving SOEs greater freedom from ministerial oversight, including more latitude in hiring and firing decisions, but also made them more responsible for making a profit. However, the government is resisting further privatization because taxes and profits from SOEs constituted 60 percent of government revenue in 1994.

The government has largely ended direct subsidies to SOEs, but some advantages still exist. In addition to more favorable borrowing requirements, SOEs are granted land and factories by the government, whereas private firms have to rent or buy space.

Police frequently harass shopkeepers and other merchants to secure bribes.

**Freedom to Participate in the Market Economy 1/2**

Women face significant social discrimination that prevents them from fully participating in the market economy. The government's enforcement of anti-discrimination laws in the workplace is lax. The Montagnards and other ethnic minorities living in the highlands are marginalized economically in terms of education and employment opportunities, although the government provides preferential treatment to companies investing in these areas. The judiciary is subservient to the government, and most judges and lawyers have minimal training. As in China, personal connections are an integral part of doing business in a country where the rule of law is weak and ineffectual. Official corruption is widespread, and Communist Party officials use connections to secure loans for businesses and get favorable treatment in the bureaucracy.

## Political Freedom v. Economic Freedom for the Middle East

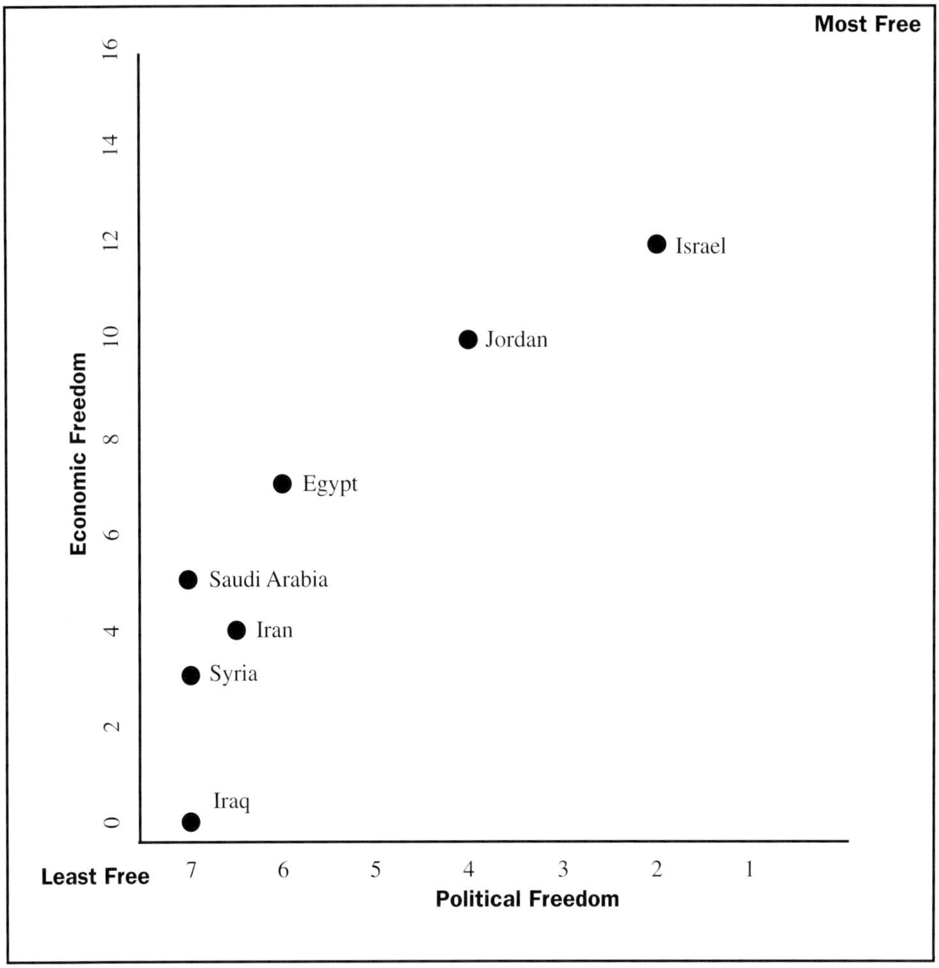


### POLITICAL FREEDOM VERSUS ECONOMIC FREEDOM

The graph above shows the relationship between the level of political freedom and economic freedom for countries in the Middle East. The ratings for political freedom were derived by averaging Freedom House's political rights and civil liberties ratings from the *Freedom in the World: The Annual Survey of Political Rights and Civil Liberties, 1995-1996*. A score of "1" represents the most free and "7" the least free.

Economic freedom is graphed on the vertical scale with "0" representing "Not Free" and "16" representing "Free."

## Egypt

ECONOMIC FREEDOM STATUS: **MOSTLY NOT FREE**
POLITICAL RIGHTS AND CIVIL LIBERTIES STATUS: **NOT FREE**
PRESS FREEDOM STATUS: **NOT FREE**
POPULATION: **61,948,000**
PPP: **$3,540**

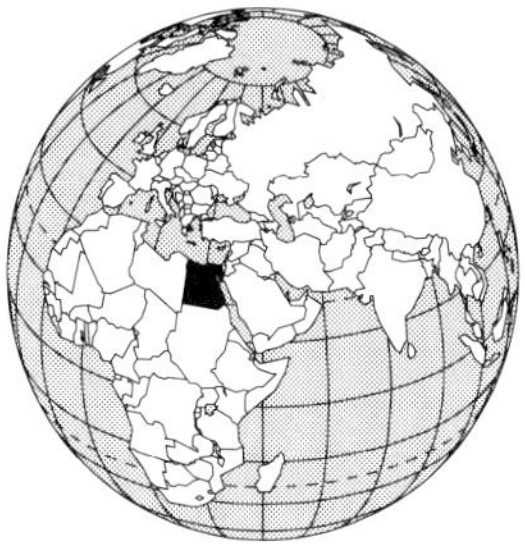

### Background

Egypt became independent in 1922. In July 1952 military leaders overthrew the monarchy, establishing a republic one year later. Coup leader Colonel Gamel Abdel Nasser ruled until his death in 1970. Nasser was succeeded by President Anwar al-Sadat who established the governing National Democratic Party (NDP) in 1978, and subsequently cleared the way for additional parties. In October 1981 Islamic militants, angered by Egypt's recognition of Israeli sovereignty in a peace treaty two years earlier, assassinated Sadat. Under Sadat's successor, Hosni Mubarak, the military-backed NDP continues to dominate politics. In October 1993 Mubarak won a third presidential term with 96.3 percent approval as the sole candidate in a national referendum. However, there is widespread frustration with official corruption, high unemployment and pervasive poverty. Islamic fundamentalist groups, including the nonviolent Muslim Brotherhood and the militant Islamic Group, have built support by tapping into this discontent.

Highly dependent on American financial assistance, Egypt has been moving slowly toward reforming its command economy with help from the International Monetary Fund (IMF). To date, reforms have stabilized the economy, bringing inflation down to 10 percent and reducing the budget deficit. However, privatization and deregulation of the economy remain stalled due to high unemployment and the potential for greater social unrest.

### Freedom to Hold Property 2/3

Individuals and businesses are free to acquire and dispose of property as they wish. Property rights are adequately protected in theory, although Egypt's hopelessly backlogged judicial system means that property and other commercial disputes can take five or more years to adjudicate. Protection and enforcement of intellectual property rights are inadequate.

### Freedom to Earn a Living 1/3

All unions must belong to the state-controlled Egyptian Trade Union Federation, which is the only legal labor federation. Under the current law, state enterprises hold a veto over the right of collective bargaining, but the spring 1995 draft labor law permits collective bargaining. In any case, the government sets wages and benefits in the public sector, which are generally adhered to in the private sector, leaving little room for collective bargaining.

### Freedom to Operate a Business 1/3

New businesses generally must gain approval from several ministries, and this often entails illicit payoffs. There are substantial bureaucratic obstacles to operating a business, evidenced not only by Byzantine procedures but also by the sheer length of time it takes for applications, licenses and other business documents to be processed. Large, loss-making state enterprises enjoy de facto monopolies in many sectors, making entry by private firms difficult. The government is encouraging private businesses to bid on infrastructure projects, and bidding for government contracts in this area has become more competitive. However, the bidding process in other areas is compromised by corruption and cronyism. Prices have been deregulated in recent years, although prices for some basic foodstuffs such as sugar and cooking oil are still controlled.

### Freedom to Invest One's Earnings 1/3

Interest rates are largely market-driven. The four big public banks assign much of their lending portfolios to large public and private enterprises. This forces small businesses to depend on micro-banks that charge usurious interest rates sometimes exceeding 120 percent. A program backed by the World Bank and several nongovernmental organizations is extending micro loans to small enterprises at market rates. The government is complying with IMF and World Bank requirements that it reduce credit to the public sector and increase private-sector lending. Egyptians are free to invest and transfer capital abroad and remit any capital and earnings. The central bank is not independent of the government, although adherence to IMF and World Bank guidelines has brought inflation close to single digits.

### Freedom to Trade Internationally 1/2

Although Egypt has made significant progress in liberalizing its trade regime, tariff rates are still relatively high. Maximum tariff rates were reduced from 100 percent in 1993 to 70 percent in 1994. The government hopes to have all import bans lifted and non-tariff barriers eliminated by 1996. Customs procedures are complex and the authorities have wide latitude in their decisions, and there is no appeals process. Several items are subject to export duties. Investment Law 230 of 1989 allows for 100 percent foreign ownership, guarantees foreign investors the right to remit income and repatriate capital, prohibits confiscation and nationalization without compensation, and assures equal treatment with domestic entities. Exchange rates float freely, and the forex market is open to non-bank dealers.

### Freedom from Unreasonable Government Interference in the Economy

Egypt's economy is dominated by state-owned enterprises (SOE), which account for up to 70 percent of GDP. Many ostensibly private-sector firms are facades for public-sector ownership. The government has been slow to implement the second phase of a World Bank and IMF reform program initiated in 1991 that focuses on privatizing 314 SOEs. However, the government fears losing patronage and inducing layoffs in an economy where unemployment tops 20 percent, and underemployment is far higher. Many subsidies to SOEs have been eliminated. However, the dominant role of the SOEs and the negative effects of an entrenched, 5.3 million-strong bureaucracy are severe disincentives to private investment.

### Freedom to Participate in the Market Economy 1/2

Under Islamic Law Muslim women receive half the amount of an inheritance received by male heirs. Women need permission from their husbands or close male relatives to travel abroad, and face discrimination in employment opportunities. Coptic Christians face significant and often violent discrimination in Egypt, and in economic matters face discrimination in the workplace.

The 1883 Commercial Code and the 1948 Civil Code are the basic laws governing commercial transactions. The 1971 Constitution, as amended in 1980, makes Islamic Law the basis of all law, and any laws promulgated after 1980 must comply with Islamic Law. In an attempt to resolve most commercial disputes out of court, Law 27 of 1994 provides a comprehensive framework for resolution through arbitration, with limited opportunities to challenge these awards in court. Corruption is a routine part of doing business in Egypt.

# Iran

ECONOMIC FREEDOM STATUS: **NOT FREE**
POLITICAL RIGHTS AND CIVIL LIBERTIES STATUS: **NOT FREE**
PRESS FREEDOM STATUS: **NOT FREE**
POPULATION: **61,280,000**
PPP: **$4,420**

## Background

British and Soviet forces occupied Iran during World War II, installing Mohammad Reza Pahlavi as hereditary monarch in 1941. Except for a brief period out of power following a left-wing coup in 1953, the Shah ruled in a corrupt, authoritarian manner until fleeing Iran in January 1979 amid widespread unrest. In February fundamentalists led by Ayatollah Ruhollah Khomeini established the world's only Islamic republic.

The 1980-88 war with Iraq devastated the economy. Following Khomeini's June 1989 death, Ayatollah Ali Khamenei assumed the role of supreme religious leader. In July a constitutional referendum approved a stronger presidency, and in August Ali Akbar Hashemi Rafsanjani, a cleric, took office after winning 94.5 percent of votes. During his first term Rafsanjani introduced limited free-market reforms, overcoming opposition from more radical clerics favoring statist economic policies. Since then, Rafsanjani's power has steadily decreased as his economic reforms have been blamed for low living standards.

On 4 April 1995 riots broke out in the Teheran suburb of Akbar Abad and in a nearby town, Islamshar, after food prices doubled and the value of the currency, the rial, dropped sharply. Security forces responded by shooting at least ten people to death.

## Freedom to Hold Property 1/3

The wholesale expropriations of the immediate post-revolutionary years have largely ended. Today expropriation generally occurs at the local level, ostensibly due to violations of business laws. Because property laws are inadequate and ill-defined, and bribery in the judiciary is common, enforcement through the courts is difficult. Intellectual property protection is lacking. The government has arbitrarily confiscated considerable property holdings from the minority Bahai community and from individual Bahais.

## Freedom to Earn a Living 1/3

Iranian workers have the legal right to join independent unions, but in practice such unions are not permitted. The government has sanctioned only one national labor organization, the state-controlled Worker's House, which is the umbrella organization for local Islamic labor councils.

Iran also has a network of regional guild unions that issue vocational licenses, fund financial cooperatives and help workers find jobs. In the private sector, actual job qualifications are now generally given the same weight in hiring decisions as adherence to Islamic ideology. However, Islamic knowledge is still the key requirement for civil service employment. Under the Penal Code the government can force individuals to find work. Wages are freely set above a government-established minimum wage, although workers are not permitted to bargain collectively.

## Freedom to Operate a Business 1/3

The government generally encourages local entrepreneurs, and the process of forming a business is fairly straightforward. However, reference checks with neighborhood committees are carried out, and certain types of businesses such as bars, clubs and gambling houses are illegal on the grounds they violate Islamic norms. Advertising is strictly regulated by government censors. The process of letting government contracts is heavily influenced by favoritism and corruption. Price controls remain on bread and other staple items, and there have been riots in recent years over price increases. The government says it spent $15 billion on subsidies on food and other basic goods in 1994.

## Freedom to Invest One's Earnings 1/3

The government allows interest rates to float between 6 and 19 percent. Interest rates are technically not considered to be pre-set, thus making them permissible under Islamic law. Although the banking system was nationalized after the 1979 Islamic revolution, the government is encouraging the growth of "non-bank credit institutions" in the private sector to compete fully with state banks. Credit flows are determined by market forces. Restrictions on capital outflow have been eased and Iranians may invest abroad. The central bank is nominally controlled by the government but exercises a fairly high degree of independence.

## Freedom to Trade Internationally 0/2

Import restrictions have gradually been eased, and the list of restricted items has been reduced. There are no export barriers, but exporters are often required to place foreign exchange earnings into state-controlled accounts to ensure that capital is fully repatriated. Foreign travel is tightly controlled, and Jewish families are not allowed to travel abroad together. A woman must have permission from a close male relative to obtain a passport.

The government has been courting foreign investment and 100 percent foreign ownership is permitted. The rial trades in state banks at fixed rates, but independent speculators are generally tolerated. However in May 1995, after the currency plunged to 7,100 rials to the dollar following the imposition of an American trade embargo on Iran, the government banned foreign currency transactions outside the state banking system and imposed an official fixed rate of 3,000 rials to the dollar until March 1996, and police briefly cracked down on black market traders. The rial is not fully convertible.

## Freedom from Unreasonable Government Interference in the Economy

The government nationalized many industries and services following the 1979 revolution, and key sectors, including banking, petroleum, transportation, utilities and mining, are still controlled by the state. Many of the assets of the former elite were transferred to the *bunyads*, or large religious foundations, with the expectation that the wealth would be distributed to the poorer classes. The Mostafazan Foundation alone took control of more than 800 private companies. However, the bunyads kept many of the assets under their control, and these foundations now have virtual monopolies in many businesses, employ hundreds of thousands of workers, and control perhaps one-third of the country's wealth.

The government has been opening *rafah* (welfare) cooperative stores that will sell goods to poor citizens at prices 5-10 percent below market prices. In an effort to gain admission into the World Trade Organization, the government is trying to streamline commercial regulations. State subsidies to some loss-making firms have been reduced or ended, although government subsidies support low prices for bread and other items.

### Freedom to Participate in the Market Economy 0/2

Traditional attitudes often preclude full participation for women in business. The legal code discriminates against women on property rights. The government has tried to enforce parity in pay scales and has set up a special banking system to make small loans to women living in the countryside. The Bahai and Kurdish communities, and to a somewhat lesser extent the Jewish and Christian communities, face discrimination in education, employment and property matters. Commercial laws are based on Islamic codes and are often vague. Corruption is a factor in nearly all economic dealings with the government, including obtaining business documents, customs and visas.

## Iraq

ECONOMIC FREEDOM STATUS: **NOT FREE**
POLITICAL RIGHTS AND CIVIL LIBERTIES STATUS: **NOT FREE**
PRESS FREEDOM STATUS: **NOT FREE**
POPULATION: **16,664,000**
PPP: **$3,413**

### Background

A 1968 coup brought the Arab *Ba'ath* (Renaissance) Socialist Party to power. The frequently amended 1968 provisional constitution establishes a Revolutionary Command Council (RCC) with virtually unlimited and unchecked authority. In 1979 Saddam Hussein, considered the strongman of the regime since 1973, formally assumed the titles of state president and RCC chairman.

Iraqis enjoy no economic freedom whatsoever, a situation exacerbated by a U.N.-imposed embargo. Major sectors of the economy are dominated by members of Hussein's family, and those with property or a business are always at risk that it will be confiscated to enrich a relative of Hussein. Basic commodities are rationed by the government and inflation is rampant.

### Freedom to Hold Property 0/3

Considerable property has been confiscated from the Shammar, Obeid and Dulaimi tribes. Since the Gulf War the army has been carrying out a ruthless campaign against Shiite rebels and villagers in the southern marshlands, burning homes and draining dwelling areas in the Amara and Hammar marshes. There is no legal protection of property rights and no protection of intellectual property.

**Freedom to Earn a Living** **0/3**

Iraqis are not permitted to form independent unions. Workers in private enterprises can join local union committees, but these must belong to the government-controlled Iraqi General Federation of Trade Unions. Strikes do not occur. Collective bargaining is not permitted, and wages in the public sector are set by the government. Government officials are not allowed to resign without permission.

**Freedom to Operate a Business** **0/3**

The private sector has been decimated by the economy's collapse, the consequence of the trade embargo imposed by the United Nations following Iraq's invasion of Kuwait in August 1990. There are no longer any formal procedures for setting up a business, and much private enterprise consists of black market operations, profiteering and smuggling. Nevertheless, some restaurants and shops still exist. The production and marketing of consumer goods are largely controlled by members of President Saddam Hussein's family. Although these sectors are not formally closed to other investors, in 1994 the regime executed forty-two merchants on charges of "sabotaging the national economy." It is widely believed they were executed for trying to compete with the Hussein family's businesses.

There is no competitive procedure for letting government contracts. Due to the U.N. trade embargo, food and other basic necessities are rationed. Prices are controlled for most goods.

**Freedom to Invest One's Earnings** **0/3**

The government controls all aspects of banking, including setting interest rates and allocating credit. The central bank is not independent of the government. Individuals may hold neither foreign currency nor securities, and in 1994 the government executed at least fifteen currency traders.

**Freedom to Trade Internationally** **0/2**

United Nations Security Council Resolution 687 bans oil exports, except for 75,000 barrels a day to Jordan to cover purchases of medicine and food, until the U.N. determines that the regime's ballistic missile, biological and chemical weapons programs have been dismantled. Other trade is also forbidden under additional resolutions. Illegal barter trade in oil and other goods does occur with Jordan, Turkey, Iran and Syria. The U.N. has repeatedly offered Iraq the opportunity to export a limited amount of oil, with some of the profits earmarked to compensate Kuwaiti victims of the Gulf War and cover U.N. costs in Iraq, but the authorities refuse, ostensibly on the grounds that the sanctions are a violation of Iraq's sovereignty. In reality, the government hopes to use its people's continued suffering as leverage to get the embargo fully lifted. High costs for passports and exit visas make it prohibitively difficult for most Iraqis to leave the country. The currency, the dinar, is not convertible.

**Freedom from Unreasonable Government Interference in the Economy**

Despite the ban on oil exports, oil production continues to be the mainstay of the economy. All production facilities are owned by the government. Current output is estimated at 600,000-750,000 barrels per day, compared with 3.5 million barrels prior to the Gulf War. Despite the severe hardship the sanctions have imposed on the Iraqi people, Saddam Hussein has reportedly built thirty-nine new palaces and elite facilities since the war, and renovated several of the nineteen palaces that had existed before the war, all at an estimated cost of $1.2 billion.

Government policies are anti-competitive, as evidenced by the executions of businessmen who have dared to compete with the Hussein family. Prior to his defection in August 1995,

Hussein's son-in-law Hussein Kamal Hassan extracted fees from his control over the distribution of import licenses and skimmed money from government commodity purchases. The government subsidizes the agricultural sector.

**Freedom to Participate in the Market Economy 0/2**

The Shiite and Kurdish communities have suffered from brutal discrimination during Hussein's reign, including the Anfal Campaign against the Kurds in 1988. The Shiite communities in the south and the Kurdish communities in the north receive fewer rations than other citizens. The regime is dominated by members of Saddam Hussein's inner circle of relatives and associates from his birthplace, Tikrit, and the minority Sunni Muslims dominate the economy. The rule of law does not exist. Crime and corruption are pervasive despite draconian measures taken against criminals, including amputation and branding.

# Israel

ECONOMIC FREEDOM STATUS: **PARTLY FREE**
POLITICAL RIGHTS AND CIVIL LIBERTIES STATUS: **FREE**
PRESS FREEDOM STATUS: **FREE**
POPULATION: **5,530,000**
PPP: **$14,700**

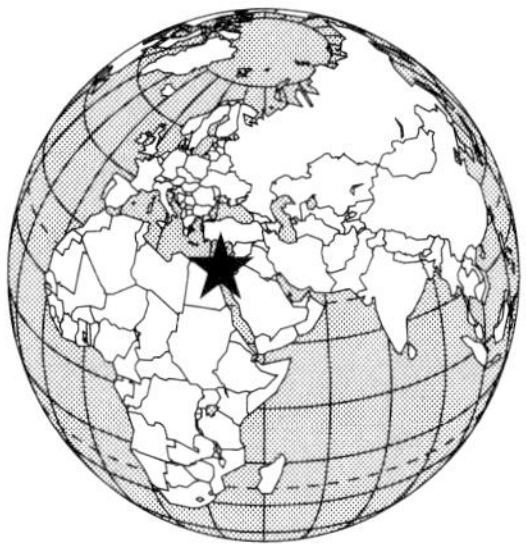

**Background**

Israel has been a parliamentary democracy since independence. Arabs and other minorities freely elect representatives to the 120-seat *Knesset* (parliament). The two major parties are the conservative Likud and the center-left Labor. Former Prime Minister Yitzhak Rabin and the Labor Party returned to power in 1992 in a coalition with the leftist Meretz and ultrareligious Shas parties.

A series of secret negotiations between Israel and the Palestinian Liberation Organization (PLO) reached a breakthrough agreement providing for gradual Palestinian autonomy in the Occupied Territories. A peace accord with Jordan signed in 1994 has raised hope on both sides for greater economic cooperation and trade. However, the November 1995 assassination of Prime Minister Rabin by a Jewish extremist underscored the deep divisions among Israelis over the ongoing transfer of much of the West Bank to Palestinian administration.

With the signing of the peace accords and the transition to an elected Palestinian authority in the occupied West Bank and Gaza Strip, the level of economic freedom in the Occupied Territories may rise despite problems regarding property rights. However, continuing terrorist attacks have strained public patience with the peace process. Within Israel proper, a legacy of democratic socialism remains a barrier to further deregulation and economic liberalization.

**Freedom to Hold Property 2/3**

Property rights are generally respected in practice in Israel proper. However, in the occupied territories since capturing East Jerusalem in the 1967 war, the government has expropriated considerable amounts of the privately held land in the city—33 percent according to *Irshalem*, a nongovernmental organization—of which the majority had been owned by Arabs. Some 33,000 housing units have been built on the land with government subsidies, and most have been occupied by Israeli Jews. Nearly all the Arabs affected have refused to take compensation for fear of legitimizing the expropriations. Another 52 percent of the land has been designated "green land," on which Arabs cannot build. The government also restricts the size of buildings in Arab neighborhoods.

Israel has an adequate legal framework to protect intellectual property rights, although enforcement tends to be weak. The courts are capable of resolving property disputes in an efficient and fair manner.

### Freedom to Earn a Living 3/3

Workers can join independent unions, although Israeli Arabs generally have not chosen to exercise this right. Palestinian nonresident workers in Israel may not form their own unions, and Palestinian unions from the West Bank and Gaza Strip are not allowed to operate in Israel.

Labor unions are independent of the government. Most unions belong to *Histadrut* (General Federation of Labor), which has been linked to the Labor Party since its founding in 1920. However in 1994 the Histradrut membership elected an independent to the top position, and the union's investment arm, once the country's largest industrial and agricultural conglomerate, has sold off most of its assets. Collective bargaining is freely practiced. Nonresident Palestinian workers in the organized sector pay a mandatory 1 percent union fee and are covered under Histadrut work contracts.

Employers must obtain government permits to hire nonresident workers from the West Bank and Gaza Strip. These workers must be paid daily wages and are generally not permitted to stay overnight in Israel. According to the *Far Eastern Economic Review*, an Israeli company, Global Manpower, has been bringing Chinese laborers to the country with promises of high salaries that have not been honored.

### Freedom to Operate a Business 2/3

Israelis of all religious faiths can freely open and operate businesses and acquire and dispose of assets. However, red tape, the nontransparent application of regulations, and the interventionist nature of the regulatory environment hinder private economic activity. The government must approve entry into several sectors, including utilities and insurance. The process of letting government contracts is transparent and fair. The government regulates prices in sectors where a monopoly exits.

### Freedom to Invest One's Earnings 2/3

Interest rates are set by the market. Credit flows are determined by market forces, and foreign investors can receive credit on local markets. However, individual Israelis are not allowed to lend money to foreign investors. There are no caps on return on investments. On 31 January 1995 the government scrapped an unpopular 10 percent capital gains tax that had been imposed at the beginning of the year. Israelis are not permitted to invest abroad in over-the-counter stocks. The government owns a majority stake in the country's leading banks but is moving toward privatization. Three large banks control 80 percent of the country's holdings. The central Bank of Israel is independent of the government.

### Freedom to Trade Internationally 1/2

Import licensing requirements on consumer and industrial goods have largely been eliminated, although licensing requirements and quotas remain on many agricultural products. By law imported food must be inspected on religious grounds. For security reasons Israel has periodically barred all nonresident Palestinian workers from the West Bank and Gaza from entering the country following terrorist attacks. Foreign residents can maintain freely transferable accounts, called *Patah* accounts, at Israeli commercial banks.

**Freedom from Unreasonable Government Interference in the Economy**

The government has sold $3.4 billion worth of state assets since a privatization program began in 1986. However, the sales of Bank Leumi and of a 51 percent stake in El Al Airlines have stalled due to slack demand, raising doubts that the government will be able to complete the program by its target of 1998. The government has cut back on its support for the *Kibbutz* collective movements. The bureaucracy generally grants investors equal treatment but at times can be cumbersome. Recently, the Finance Ministry ignored the legislature's deadline to implement a law establishing a "free processing zone." Instead, the Ministry introduced thirty-three "corrections" a year later, gutting the legislation.

**Freedom to Participate in the Market Economy 2/2**

Israeli Arabs are generally able to participate fully in the market economy. However, since they are exempt (although not prohibited) from military service, they are isolated from the informal networks of veterans in the private sector, as well as denied some social benefits linked to army service. Despite government initiatives, Arab communities are still disadvantaged in terms of education opportunities, public works and civil service positions. Israeli Arabs are not allowed to work in companies with defense contracts. Corruption is not a factor in the economy.

# Jordan

ECONOMIC FREEDOM STATUS: **PARTLY FREE**
POLITICAL RIGHTS AND CIVIL LIBERTIES STATUS: **PARTLY FREE**
PRESS FREEDOM STATUS: **PARTLY FREE**
POPULATION: **4,101,000**
PPP: **$4,270**

**Background**

King Hussein has ruled Jordan since 1952. In April 1989 restrictions on freedom of expression were eased and political parties permitted to organize. The country held nonparty elections in November 1989, the first elections in thirty-three years, and in 1993 the first multiparty elections since 1956 were conducted.

In the five years since Jordan was ostracized for supporting Saddam Hussein during the Gulf War, Jordan has reestablished regional influence and close ties with the West. King Hussein has gradually introduced structural reforms to the economy that have fostered a growth rate of 6 percent while keeping inflation down. In 1995, Jordan introduced sweeping tax and investment laws aimed at attracting foreign investment and reducing bureaucracy, and in October hosted an economic summit where 1,700 business and government officials discussed ways to integrate the regional economy.

**Freedom to Hold Property 2/3**

The right to own property is respected in law and practice. However, the 1992 Copyrights Law protects only foreign intellectual property that is made and registered in Jordan, or that is subject to an international agreement to which Jordan is a party. The Jordanian legal system adequately enforces and protects property rights.

**Freedom to Earn a Living 2/3**

Workers in the private sector and in some state-owned enterprises (SOEs) can join unions, which must be registered with the government. The International Confederation of Free Trade Unions says that the government has fired public-sector employees on political grounds.

The Jordan Federation of Trade Unions is the sole labor federation and receives government subsidies, although it does serve as an advocate of workers' rights. While membership is not required, all unions belong to it. Unions can and do bargain collectively, and wages are set by the market. The Ministry of Labor can refer job disputes to the Council of Ministers and then to Parliament or, by mutual consent of the parties involved, to an industrial tribunal whose decisions are legally binding. Strikes are not permitted while a dispute is in mediation or arbitration, and in practice strikes occur infrequently.

**Freedom to Operate a Business 2/3**

Individuals and entities can establish and operate private businesses. However, the bureaucratic process tends to be cumbersome despite government efforts at reform. De facto monopolies exist in numerous sectors of the economy. The procedures for letting government contracts are competitive on paper, and in practice appear to be administered relatively fairly. The government subsidizes price controls on water, electricity, wheat, sugar, oil and other basic commodities.

**Freedom to Invest One's Earnings 1/3**

Interest rates are determined by the market. There are no caps on rates of return from investments. Citizens are permitted to hold foreign currency and securities. The Central Bank of Jordan (CBJ) influences the allocation of credit and is not independent of the government. Nevertheless, the CBJ has been implementing an International Monetary Fund-backed stabilization program and has kept inflation under control.

**Freedom to Trade Internationally 1/2**

Import licensing requirements have been streamlined and reduced. Export licenses have been fully eliminated, and the government has exempted capital equipment and spare parts from customs duties. Citizens are free to travel abroad, although a married woman needs her husband's approval to obtain a passport. Jordanian law requires a minimum 51 percent local ownership of business entities, with the exception of the industrial sector, and this has been a disincentive to foreign investment. Non-Arab foreigners need government approval to invest in industry, tourism, health, agriculture and housing. A new investment law provides for free repatriation of foreign capital and profits. There are few exchange controls.

**Freedom from Unreasonable Government Interference in the Economy**

The government's share of GDP is estimated at 62 percent. The latest available figures, from 1992, indicate there are only twenty-five SOEs, but the government holds stakes in some eighty listed industries. Official policies generally promote free enterprise, and the government recently created an independent Investment Promotion Corporation with "one-stop" approval for licensing new projects. However, the bureaucracy is still a hindrance to investment. The

CBJ has been offering incentives for the country's banks to consolidate, including low-interest loans and higher interest rates on the deposits banks must keep at the CBJ.

The government occasionally pumps equity into public enterprises, and Royal Jordanian Airlines is the largest single beneficiary of parastatal subsidies. Agricultural credit is also subsidized. The government has a lower corporate tax rate for companies in mining, industry, hotels, hospitals and other priority sectors, as well as lower rates for projects in less developed parts of the country.

### Freedom to Participate in the Market Economy 2/2

Palestinians form a 65-70 percent majority and are well established in business and commerce, while the Hashemites and other non-Palestinians dominate the army, government and civil service. Palestinians complain of discrimination and of background checks, sometimes going back four generations, to ascertain Palestinian ethnicity. The court system adjudicates commercial disputes fairly.

Under Islamic law, women receive half the inheritance that male heirs receive, and a sole female heir receives only half of her parent's estate. Women must retire five years earlier than men and thus receive lower pensions. Women also face social discrimination that inhibits them from participating fully in the economy. Corruption is fairly routine but not to the extent of being a drain on the economy.

# Saudi Arabia

ECONOMIC FREEDOM STATUS: **NOT FREE**
POLITICAL RIGHTS AND CIVIL LIBERTIES STATUS: **NOT FREE**
PRESS FREEDOM STATUS: **NOT FREE**
POPULATION: **18,486,000**
PPP: **$9,880**

### Background

With one-quarter of the world's proven oil reserves, the Saudi Arabian economy continues to be dominated by the petroleum industry. However, low oil prices have forced the government to adopt a fiscal austerity program, which is shredding a social compact in which citizens had largely accepted the regime's corrupt and autocratic rule in return for lavish social spending.

The Saudi royal family, an extended clan with several hundred princes, virtually runs the country as a private fiefdom. Labor rights are severely restricted and foreign-born domestic workers are frequently abused. The rule of law is weak, commercial codes are vague and frequently ignored, and the judiciary is not independent. The economic rights of women, members of the Shiite minority and foreign guest workers are particularly circumscribed. The huge oil and gas sectors operate as state monopolies, and privatization in other areas has been limited.

### Freedom to Hold Property 1/3

Saudi citizens can freely acquire and exchange property. The copyright law does not extend to foreign works published outside the country. In April 1994 Saudi Arabia joined the Universal

Copyright Convention, but enforcement has been weak. American businesses have complained of excessive procedures for trademark registration. Many Saudi judges are trained only in religious law and are indifferent to cases involving trademark and other commercial claims, particularly those brought by foreigners.

**Freedom to Earn a Living** **0/3**

Trade unions and strikes are prohibited by government decree. Collective bargaining is not permitted. Wages are largely determined by the market, although the wages of the estimated 5 million foreign workers often vary according to nationality.

Foreign workers must obtain a residence permit, called an *igama*, within three days of arrival in the country. The Saudi employer or sponsor holds the foreign worker's passport for the duration of his or her employment. This gives Saudi businessmen leverage in resolving business disputes with foreign corporate employees. Saudi employers occasionally withhold the pay of blue-collar workers or coerce them into providing more work at little or no pay. Foreign domestic workers are not covered under the labor laws and receive the worst treatment. Many are subjected to rape and other physical abuse and are often not paid their full wages.

**Freedom to Operate a Business** **1/3**

Individuals can freely engage in private enterprise. However, the rigid bureaucracy complicates the process of setting up and operating a business. Commercial codes are ambiguous and many aspects of doing business depend on personal agreements, rather than contracts and the rule of law.

In general only Saudi citizens are allowed to engage in trading, although non-Saudis can own industrial enterprises and can trade in goods they manufacture. The process of letting government contracts is neither transparent nor competitive. Contracts are often awarded to politically connected businessmen, although the government makes some attempt to see that struggling domestic entities get an occasional share of the state's business. Prices for most basic commodities are controlled.

**Freedom to Invest One's Earnings** **2/3**

Interest rates are set largely by the market. Credit is also allocated by the market. There are no caps on rates of return on investment. Saudi citizens are permitted to invest abroad and hold foreign currency. The Saudi Arabian Monetary Agency acts as the central bank and regulates the banking sector. It is not independent of the government, but pressure from the International Monetary Fund (IMF) and some Western countries has forced the government as a whole to exercise increasingly responsible policies.

**Freedom to Trade Internationally** **1/2**

The government grants several "infant industries" protection through 20 percent tariff barriers. Non-tariff barriers include preferences for domestic and Gulf Cooperation Council (GCC) products in government procurement; a 30 percent set-aside for local contractors on major government projects; and a requirement that foreign contractors import goods exclusively through Saudi agents. Prohibited imports include any products from Israel, alcohol, pork, and pornography. Another category of goods, including books, periodicals, chemicals, pharmaceuticals and wireless equipment, requires special permission to be imported.

Foreign investment is not permitted in several fields, including power generation, transportation, cleaning and maintenance, and businesses that affect national security. Foreign investors are not explicitly required to have a Saudi partner, but in practice a Foreign Capital Investment Committee license is difficult to obtain without at least 25-50 percent local participation.

Individual foreigners are not permitted to own land, although foreign companies may own land in some circumstances. There are no significant exchange controls.

### Freedom from Unreasonable Government Interference in the Economy

The government holds a 28 percent share of GDP, and state-owned enterprises play a leading role in the economy. In general, the ruling family and the state sector are practically indistinguishable.

Faced with declining oil revenues, the government introduced a budget in January 1995 that reduced or eliminated subsidies on water, electricity, telephone service, gasoline and domestic airfares. King Fahd has endorsed privatization, but little progress has been made in this area. Oil and gas companies, the mainstay of the economy, are fully state-owned and are closed to the private sector. All mineral rights belong to the government but concessions are granted to private companies.

The government favors private enterprise but generally does not foster a competitive atmosphere, as evidenced by its large role in the economy. In addition, commercial laws favor citizens of Saudi Arabia and the GCC states in the areas of taxation, credit, investment, procurement, trade, and intellectual property. The commercial code is often applied arbitrarily against non-Saudis.

### Freedom to Participate in the Market Economy 0/2

Women face severe discrimination that restricts their participation in the economy. Women are legally prohibited from traveling unescorted within the country and abroad; must obtain the written permission of their husbands or fathers before traveling; must work separately from men; and are not allowed to drive cars or ride bicycles. Under Islamic law women receive half the share of an inheritance that male heirs receive.

The Shiite minority faces severe restrictions on religious practice as well as in employment opportunities, including a ban on working in the oil industry. The IMF states that Saudi Arabia's commercial laws need to be reworked. Corruption is widespread among the ruling elite.

## Syria

ECONOMIC FREEDOM STATUS: **NOT FREE**
POLITICAL RIGHTS AND CIVIL LIBERTIES STATUS: **NOT FREE**
PRESS FREEDOM STATUS: **NOT FREE**
POPULATION: **14,661,000**
PPP: **$4,960**

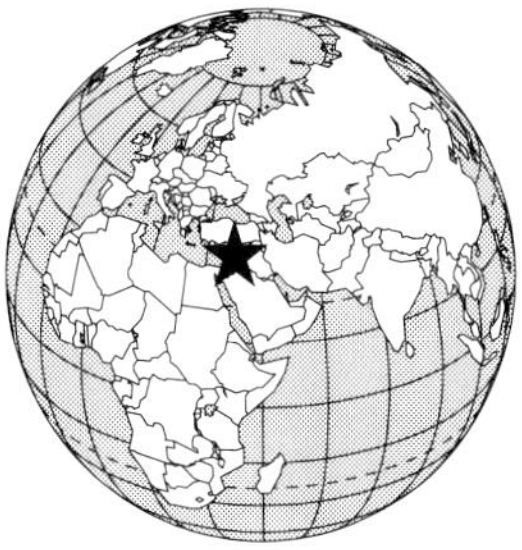

### Background

A 1963 military coup brought the pan-Arab, socialist Ba'ath Party to power. Leadership struggles within the Ba'ath Party continued until 1970 when the military wing, led by then-Lieut.-Gen. Hafez al-Assad, took power in a bloodless coup. Assad formally became president of this secular authoritarian regime in 1971 and has served as head of government, commander-in-chief of the armed forces and secretary general of the Ba'ath Party since. Members of his Alawite minority hold most key military and intelligence positions.

During the 1960s, all large industries were nationalized and the public sector expanded rapidly. The collapse of the Soviet Union and the Eastern Bloc forced Syria to foster private enterprise and foreign investment. Investment Law Number Ten, passed in 1991, and Syria's participation in the coalition against Iraq helped to lay the groundwork for economic reforms. Private enterprise has grown significantly in anticipation of a possible peace accord with Israel and increased trading opportunities. But despite this progress, most Syrians enjoy little or no economic freedom. State control of the economy, financial sector restrictions, and the absence of the rule of law remain serious barriers to economic freedom. The use of basic business tools such as fax machines and computer modems is closely monitored or banned outright.

### Freedom to Hold Property 1/3

Expropriation of private property for public use appears to be infrequent. Intellectual property protection is weak, although piracy does not appear to be widespread. Property rights are protected by the constitution and enforceable through the courts. Individuals can freely sell property and structure their holdings as they choose.

### Freedom to Earn a Living 0/3

The government does not allow Syrian workers to exercise their constitutionally guaranteed right to form independent unions. All unions must belong to the government-controlled General Federation of Trade Unions (GFTU). The GFTU president is a senior member of the ruling Ba'ath Party. Strikes are formally prohibited only in the agricultural sector, but in reality do not occur in any sector due to the security apparatus's tight control over the country.

By law private-sector workers can bargain collectively, but the Minister of Labor and Social Affairs must ratify any agreements. In practice this nullifies any real benefits of collective bargaining. In the public sector the government strongly influences wage agreements. Firms in Syria's seven free-trade zones are exempt from government regulations that limit an employer's right to dismiss workers without due cause. Public-sector employees need permission to leave their jobs, and this is not readily granted.

### Freedom to Operate a Business 1/3

All major private investment must be licensed through an often unwieldy bureaucracy. For medium- and large-sized ventures, the process lacks transparency and can be time-consuming. The Higher Council of Investment generally consults state enterprises within the field of a proposed private investment before approval is granted. Since 1986 the government has permitted joint-stock companies in agriculture and tourism, although the government reserves a 25 percent equity stake in such ventures.

Investment Law 10, introduced in May 1991, granted multi-year tax waivers for approved projects, removed some regulatory hurdles, and allowed entrepreneurs to import certain equipment duty-free. Overall, the regulatory regime aims less to foster competition than to prevent withholding and price gouging.

There is a detailed, seemingly comprehensive process for letting government contracts, but some tenders have deadlines of less than forty-five days. This makes competition, especially from overseas, difficult and leads to suspicion of bid-rigging. Most prices, except for some staple crops, are freely set.

### Freedom to Invest One's Earnings 0/3

The central bank controls interest rates. All banks are owned by the state and are under the supervision of the Commercial Bank of Syria. Transferring capital abroad and remitting capital are prohibited unless special permission is granted by the prime minister, or unless the activity is specifically sanctioned by law. The penalty for individuals or companies holding hard currency is twenty-five years' imprisonment. The central bank is not independent of the government.

## Freedom to Trade Internationally 0/2

Although by law any good not produced locally can be imported, the Ministry of Economy and Foreign Trade tends to give favorable consideration to raw materials and equipment that promote industrial and agricultural development, and less favorable treatment to consumer items. Thus, approval for goods on the list of items that can be imported is not always automatic, and the Ministry occasionally denies licenses for goods it does not consider necessary.

The government maintains monopolies on wheat and flour imports. Exporters must provide a bank guarantee that hard currency earnings will be returned to Syria within a limited period of time. Although the government maintains its official boycott on trade with Israel or with foreign companies that operate in Israel, Syrian firms use backdoor methods to trade with such businesses.

All foreign investment applications are vetted by the Higher Council for Investment. The numerous restrictions on foreign investment include requirements that foreign companies use a less favorable official exchange rate for all business transactions within the country, and obtain re-export licenses for every single item imported and re-exported, regardless of value.

Foreign-exchange controls are strict. The export of capital and overseas borrowing require central bank approval. Private exporters can remit 75 percent of foreign exchange from industrial exports and 100 percent from agricultural exports.

## Freedom from Unreasonable Government Interference in the Economy

All large industries were nationalized in the 1960s, and state enterprises still dominate oil, gas, phosphates, electricity, heavy industry, some agricultural goods and the financial sector. The government is slowly moving toward a more market-oriented economy. In 1993 the government accounted for 38 percent of GDP. Although a growing private sector has diluted the absolute share of the state sector in the economy, the government has largely rejected privatization because most enterprises would be nearly impossible to sell, and because the government needs to provide public-sector jobs.

State enterprises have favorable access to credit and exclusive access to official foreign-exchange loans from the State Bank of Syria. Meanwhile, credit to private enterprises is inadequate. State enterprises also reportedly get priority in allocations of commodities and goods produced by other state enterprises, as well as greater access to electricity and other public services.

## Freedom to Participate in the Market Economy 1/2

Jewish citizens face discrimination in employment opportunities and are barred from civil-service jobs and military service, and their religion is stated on their official documents. Many own small shops. The Palestinian population is generally free to operate businesses. Social matters are adjudicated by courts according to religious denomination, and Muslim women face discrimination in inheritance matters where Islamic law grants them a smaller share than male heirs. Commercial laws are adequate, although negotiating settlements is often a lengthy process. Official corruption is a drag on investment.

## Political Freedom v. Economic Freedom for Africa

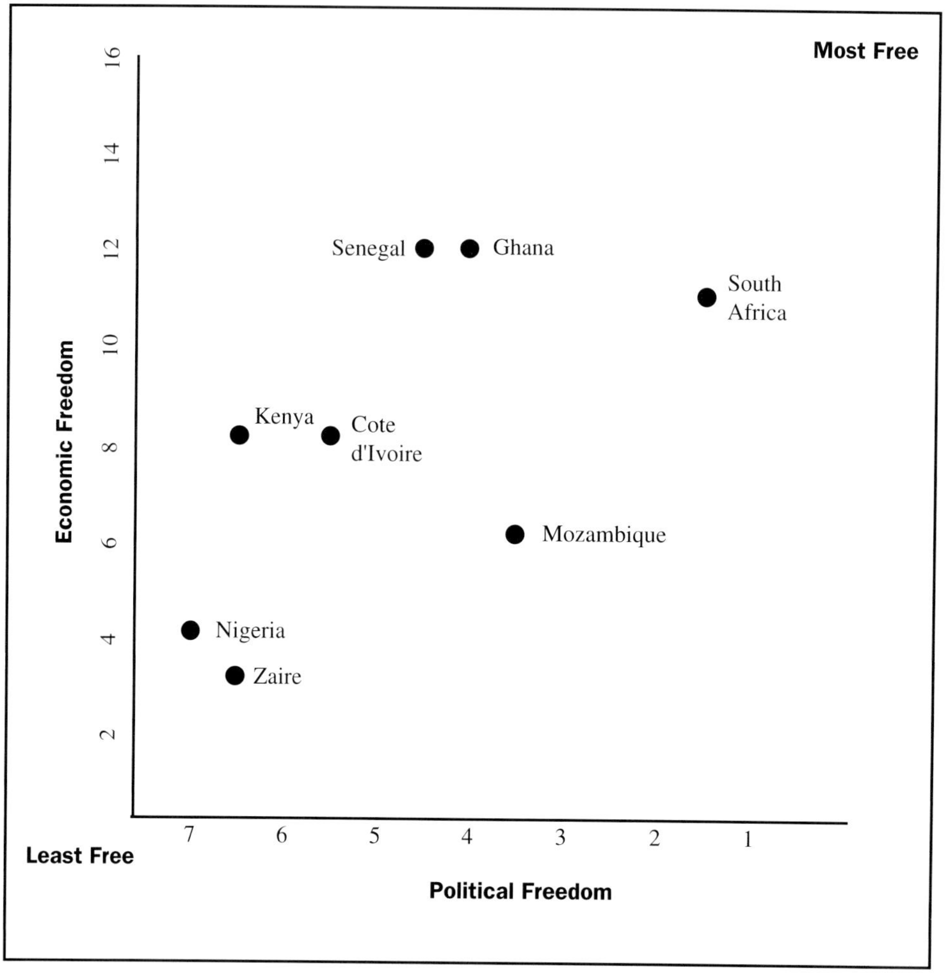


### POLITICAL FREEDOM VERSUS ECONOMIC FREEDOM

The graph above shows the relationship between the level of political freedom and economic freedom for countries in Africa. The ratings for political freedom were derived by averaging Freedom House's political rights and civil liberties ratings from the *Freedom in the World: The Annual Survey of Political Rights and Civil Liberties*, 1995-1996. A score of "1" represents the most free and "7" the least free.

Economic freedom is graphed on the vertical scale with "0" representing "Not Free" and "16" representing "Free."

# Côte d'Ivoire

ECONOMIC FREEDOM STATUS: **MOSTLY NOT FREE**
POLITICAL RIGHTS AND CIVIL LIBERTIES STATUS: **NOT FREE**
PRESS FREEDOM STATUS: **NOT FREE**
POPULATION: **14,253,000**
PPP: **$1,710**

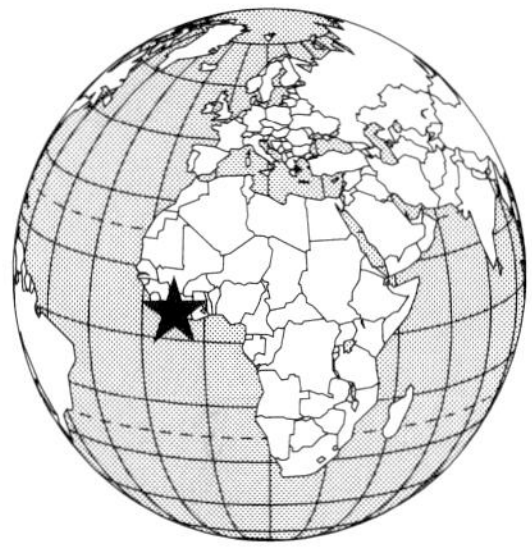

## Background

Although it has the largest industrial base in sub-Saharan Francophone Africa, Côte d'Ivoire's is a largely agricultural economy. Founder Felix Houphouet-Boigny ruled from independence in 1960 until his death in 1993. He was succeeded by Henri Konan Bedie. Bedie's re-election in October 1995 was marred by widespread irregularities and security forces were called upon to quell demonstrations.

Since the devaluation of the CFA franc, Côte d'Ivoire has adopted an International Monetary Fund-drafted structural reform program to reverse a strong *dirigiste* tradition inherited from French colonialism. Although progress has been made, there is much room for improvement in reducing bureaucratic obstacles, improving conflicts in property rights outside of the major cities, reducing corruption at all levels of the government, and reducing barriers to trade.

## Freedom to Hold Property 1/3

Property rights are clearly defined by law and are generally respected, although bureaucratic inefficiency, local corruption and political interference sometimes result in inconsistent application of the law.

Tension also exists between traditional land tenure systems based on village, lineage or group holdings and modern leaseholds or outright land sales. This has usually worked to the disadvantage of rural groups without clear understanding or access to government bureaucracies and regulations. Land-use contracts often involve a welter of obligations including cash payments, crop or other in-kind payments and labor exchange.

New regulations since 1989 have sought to clarify land tenure. No legal restrictions block women or minorities from acquiring or holding property, though women are predominantly engaged in subsistence agriculture or small-scale retail trading.

## Freedom to Earn a Living 2/3

There are no legal restrictions on the type or place of employment Ivorians may choose. The country has the largest industrial base in Francophone sub-Saharan Africa, although most people still work the land. Exports are dominated by agricultural commodities.

Workers can join unions and bargain collectively, although new unions must be registered, a process that takes at least three months. The union movement has long been closely linked to the ruling party through the government-sponsored General Union of Workers of Côte d'Ivoire (UGTCI). In 1992, the general trend toward liberalization allowed formation of the independent Federation of Autonomous Trade Unions of Côte d'Ivoire (FESCACI). For seven job categories, base salaries and wages are set by the Ministry of Employment and Civil Service.

There are no reported cases of forced labor.

## Freedom to Operate a Business 2/3

Although the process of registering a new business is reasonably transparent and unbiased, there is an enormous amount of paperwork involved. Registration is handled by a bureaucracy that is cumbersome but deemed less corrupt than those of many other African countries. A new investment code is under consideration that would simplify the process.

Price controls were temporarily imposed after the devaluation of the CFA franc in December 1993, but were lifted by April 1994.

Large-scale contracts that involve multinational corporate involvement or financial assistance from multilateral institutions are usually let on a competitive basis. However, smaller local contracts are much more open to patronage, favoritism and other influences that distort the market mechanism. Resolution of contract disputes is sometimes capricious.

Access to credit is difficult because of tight monetary policies and because of high public debt. Heavily influenced by France, Côte d'Ivoire's larger industries have for decades been state-dominated, though divestiture is expanding. A lively entrepreneurial sector exists in the retail and trading sectors, but opportunities for growth are limited by tight credit and overall economic stagnation.

## Freedom to Invest One's Earnings 1/3

A small stock exchange is operating, and opportunities for public investment are increasing as the privatization of state enterprises continues. In September 1995, 20 percent of a formerly state-owned rubber firm was sold, with a total of over 432,000 shares offered at 8,500 CFA ($16.66) each.

Export of capital or investment outside the common currency zone of the *Communauté Financière Africaine* (which is backed by France and from which the local currency, the CFA franc, takes its name), is discouraged by currency regulation, and all such investments must receive special approval. Côte d'Ivoire shares a currency with several other Francophone states in West Africa, has no central bank of its own, and cooperates instead in the Central Bank of West African States (BCEAO).

Investment return rates are not controlled, but interest rates are, and fear of further devaluation of the CFA makes many investors wary of CFA-denominated holdings.

## Freedom to Trade Internationally 1/2

The Ivorian Investment Code of 1985 encourages foreign investment through a series of fiscal and tax incentives that favor small and medium-sized businesses that set up manufacturing industries. No significant limitations, such as local content or export performance requirements, restrict foreign investment. France's dominant position as former colonial power, major foreign investor and foreign aid provider, and backer of the CFA franc heavily affects trade and investment patterns.

Ivorians can travel freely. Overseas investment is restricted by regulations that encourage CFA franc investment within the West African CFA zone. The currency is no longer freely convertible.

High tariff and duty levels remain in effect, up to a maximum of 35 percent though there are no export restrictions.

## Freedom from Unreasonable Government Interference in the Economy

A top-heavy web of parastatal companies has dominated Côte d'Ivoire's economic and commercial development. Strong central guidance of the economy was widely deemed a positive force during high growth of the 1960s and 1970s, but increasingly bureaucratic controls and quotas have since turned into a drag on growth. Extensive regulation provides not only fertile ground for corruption, but also incentive for evading and avoiding controls and disincentives to investing at all.

Some 100 state-owned enterprises account for over half of all investment in Côte D'Ivoire. A privatization program is gaining momentum and is reducing the state's direct stake in the economy and increasing private investment opportunities. For example, the government put 20 percent of the rubber firm *Societé des Caoutchoucs de Grand-Bereby* (SOGB) on sale on the local stock market in September 1995, after selling 60 percent of the formerly state-owned company in February 1994.

Political patronage has long been an important factor in awarding official contracts, though this aspect may be moderated, or at least exposed, if Côte d'Ivoire moves toward a more open political system and freer media.

### Freedom to Participate in the Market Economy 1/2

No legal or official impediments obstruct participation by any group in the market economy. The right of a married woman to establish a business without her husband's permission was only recently acknowledged. Women are active in retail trading and operate many small businesses, but remain primarily engaged in subsistence agriculture in the rural areas. There are no reports of systematic or official discrimination on the basis of gender or ethnicity.

Corruption is considered a regular part of life, although it is generally considered to be less severe than in most other West African states.

# Ghana

ECONOMIC FREEDOM STATUS: **PARTLY FREE**
POLITICAL RIGHTS AND CIVIL LIBERTIES STATUS: **PARTLY FREE**
PRESS FREEDOM STATUS: **NOT FREE**
POPULATION: **17,453,000**
PPP: **$2,110**

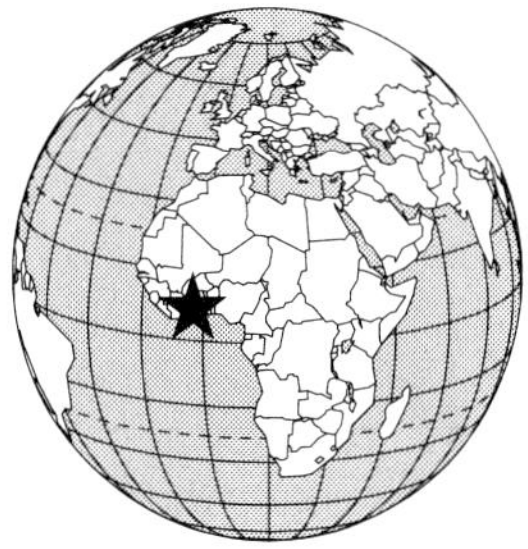

### Background

Long known as the Gold Coast and once a major slaving center, Ghana in 1957 became the first sub-Saharan country to gain independence from Britain. The 1966 overthrow of Ghana's charismatic independence leader, Kwame Nkrumah, led to a fifteen-year series of military coups. Alternating military and civilian governments were nearly interchangeable in terms of incompetence and mendacity. In 1979, then-Flight-Lieutenant Jerry Rawlings led a coup against the ruling military junta, returning power to a civilian government as promised after performing "housecleaning" of corrupt senior army officers. The civilian administration did not live up to Rawlings's expectations, however, and he seized power again in December 1981 and set up the Provisional National Defense Council (PNDC). The PNDC junta, initially radically socialist and populist, brutally suppressed any dissent, banning political parties and free expression. A crumbling economy worsened by severe drought in the early 1980s convinced Rawlings that only massive international aid could help Ghana revive its fortunes. Rejecting socialism,

Rawlings transformed Ghana into an experimental model for structural adjustment programs urged by international lenders.

Since 1991, however, Ghana has not maintained the anticipated strong growth rate due in part to a breakdown in fiscal discipline. The resignation of longtime Finance Minister Dr. Kwesi Botchwey was seen as a setback for economic reforms. Antigovernment opposition heightened during 1995 as inflation eroded living standards and reports of government corruption by the reinvigorated media incensed the public. Human rights abuses and harassment of the business community continued.

Despite these recent setbacks, citizens of Ghana continue to enjoy significant levels of economic freedom. However, heavy government spending in support of President Rawlings's bid for re-election in 1996 could heighten inflation and intensify economic problems.

### Freedom to Hold Property 2/3

The right to property is protected by law. Real property claims can be contentious, partially due to conflicting traditional land claims by different groups, compounded by the absence of a central lands registry and general lack of transparency in public administration. Non-Ghanaians may not own land, but may acquire leases and title to structures.

Intellectual property rights are honored by law. Few infringement cases have been filed in Ghana over the past five years, although pirating of videos and computer software is common. Ghana has adopted British patent law, is a member of the Africa Regional Intellectual Property Organization and World Intellectual Property Organization (WIPO), and officially adheres to the Bern, Paris and Universal Copyright Conventions.

### Freedom to Earn a Living 2/3

There are no legal restrictions on type or place of employment for individuals, nor are there wage or price controls. Ghana's population comprises numerous ethno-linguistic groups, but there are few reports of formal discrimination on this basis. Women participate widely in economic activity, although most are engaged in retail marketing.

The sole labor confederation, the Trade Union Congress, is increasingly critical of governmental policies in an atmosphere of general political liberalization. Restrictions on the right of association remain in the form of the Trades Union Ordinance, and the right to strike is curtailed by compulsory conciliation and arbitration mechanisms. However, these laws are not enforced and are largely ignored as new unions are formed and "illegal" strikes occur regularly. Collective bargaining is used for most labor negotiations.

### Freedom to Operate a Business 2/3

Individuals are free to start businesses, and in 1993, business licensing requirements were eliminated. Now only a tax registration number is required. A vibrant entrepreneurial economy thrives, especially in the small-scale sector, and many businesses are family-run. Price controls were lifted in 1993.

Larger ventures face competition from or market exclusion by about 200 state-owned enterprises (SOEs), though some SOEs have already been privatized and plans to divest others are proceeding.

Further, the entrenched bureaucracy remains an obstacle to systemic change. Allegations of corruption persist, and there are frequent charges that what should be purely administrative decisions in fact hinge on political considerations. In the past, the government has closely monitored whether political opponents have been benefiting from its economic policies. Businessmen associated with the opposition risked tax audits and officially condoned harassment. Although less overt in its actions the government is still intent on preventing political opponents from gaining control over privatized state-owned enterprises or winning government contracts. Commercial disputes are often unresolved for long periods.

### Freedom to Invest One's Earnings 2/3

Ghanaians' investment opportunities are limited both by market forces and by law. Foreign exchange is freely convertible and subject to market rates. Demand for hard currency continues to erode the value of the cedi, the currency. Controls on capital export remain in place, and foreign exchange is not granted to residents to acquire personal real estate or securities holdings abroad. Foreign borrowing by Ghanaian citizens must be approved by the Bank of Ghana.

Domestic investment in financial instruments is problematic because of inflation around 18 percent. The government offers high-yield short-term bonds, though many people prefer to hold dollars or other hard currency as a hedge against both inflation and creeping devaluation of the cedi. The central bank has sought, with limited success, to stabilize the cedi.

There is a small but active stock market, listing fifteen companies. Investment opportunity is expected to increase as a program of privatization of state enterprises progresses.

Although the state does not allocate credit directly, SOEs tend to enjoy greater access to scarce capital than do privately owned firms.

### Freedom to Trade Internationally 2/2

Ghanaians are permitted to travel and trade internationally without significant formal restrictions, but controls on capital export remain. Exchange controls were lifted in 1983, although the cedi's receding value relative to most other world currencies has made it difficult to accumulate local capital to finance imports.

Import controls are few, and tariffs are mostly aimed at luxury goods. An exception is tariffs on imports of used clothing to protect local textile manufacturers. Export policies are also generally liberal, although permits are required for export of agricultural and forest products, most notably cocoa, game and wildlife, and precious minerals.

Both foreign joint ventures and wholly owned foreign ventures are welcomed. All must be approved and the former are encouraged by lower minimum investment requirements. The 1994 Investment Promotion Center Act is intended to streamline investment procedures. Foreign investment is barred from many low-end retail activities such as selling from kiosks, as well as from taxi and car rental operations and the highly popular lottery business. Capital repatriation is unhindered and foreign investment is protected by the 1981 Investment Code. Protection against expropriation is in force and a defined arbitration process exists

### Freedom from Unreasonable Government Interference in the Economy

Significant movement toward privatization of SOEs is reducing the government's direct stake in the economy, although the state remains a significant economic actor. Government expenditures equaled 21 percent of GDP. About one-third of 260 SOEs functioning in 1988 have now been divested. Several large corporations, including the State Housing and State Insurance Corporations and Ghana Oil and Ghana Telecom are still government-held, but continuing privatization is planned in line with agreements with the World Bank and International Monetary Fund.

Some domestic private industries are supported through tax incentives and other measures, though the strong tendency is toward allowing market forces to operate more freely. Corporate profitability has benefited from lowered marginal tax rates. In 1995, new telecommunications licenses were issued, though with financial requirements that could serve to preserve the government's virtual monopoly on electronic media.

**Freedom to Participate in the Market Economy 2/2**

There is little legal interference with Ghanaians' participation in the domestic market economy. Discrimination on the basis of religion, gender, or ethnicity is neither official nor widespread, although ethnic rivalries have led to violent clashes over land tenure in the north of the country.

Corruption remains a contentious political issue, and in 1995 several senior government ministers were under investigation regarding their personal wealth. Some Ghanaians complain that government contracts are steered away from supporters of the political opposition. Advertisements for government tenders that are a prime source of revenue for print media are rarely placed in independent publications.

Despite the overhaul of some regulations, the British common law-based legal system remains cumbersome. Judicial independence seems to be increasing as a multiparty system takes hold, yet both accountability and transparency in governance remain limited.

# Kenya

ECONOMIC FREEDOM STATUS: **MOSTLY NOT FREE**
POLITICAL RIGHTS AND CIVIL LIBERTIES STATUS: **NOT FREE**
PRESS FREEDOM STATUS: **PARTLY FREE**
POPULATION: **28,261,000**
PPP: **$1,400**

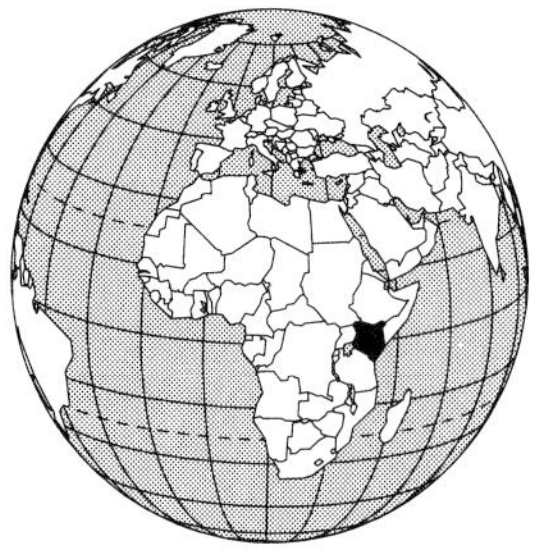

**Background**

Kenya became independent in 1963 under President Jomo Kenyatta's Kenya African National Union (KANU). The accession to power of Vice President Daniel arap Moi in 1978 kept KANU in power but eventually led to a reduction of ethnic-Kikuyu influence. Opposition parties were banned in 1982, and tensions between Moi's Kalenjin ethnic group and others—widely believed to have been provoked by the government—flared by the end of the decade.

Ethnic violence, increased attacks on opposition leaders and rising media repression marked further consolidation of Moi's autocratic rule and Kenya's continued march away from prospects for multiparty democracy and respect for human rights.

In November 1990, western donors led by the World Bank froze most aid to Kenya and made resumption conditional on economic and political reforms. The initial response was positive as trade barriers were lifted, controls on prices and foreign exchange were eliminated, and state enterprises privatized. Politically, opposition parties were legalized, elections were held and reports of corruption were investigated. However, since then, progress has slowed down and even regressed. Human rights violations and harassment of political opponents have increased and the government has not shown a willingness to eliminate the system of patronage upon which the ruling party depends for its survival. President Moi has accused donor countries of racism and attempting to dominate the economy and political system. In 1995, several donor countries withheld portions of their aid to Kenya.

Kenyan's face significant restraints on their freedom to earn a living and invest their earnings. Women and minorities also face significant limits on their economic freedoms.

**Freedom to Hold Property 2/3**

Property rights are generally respected in Kenya in law and practice. Property is widely used as mortgage or loan collateral. There are few restrictions on selling or exchanging property. Intellectual property rights are protected by law under the Kenya Intellectual Property Office, established in 1990, which also screens technology transfer agreements and serves as Kenya's patent office. The office's efficacy is unclear. Human rights monitors have reported that the homes and businesses of relatives of political dissidents have been arbitrarily demolished or damaged by government forces in an effort at intimidation.

Land disputes in the Rift Valley and Western Provinces have escalated into large-scale killings. Under the guise of Majimboism (regionalism), members of parliament have targeted and called for the expulsion of "nonindigenous" groups such as the Kikuyu, Luo and Luhya, who are perceived as supporters of the opposition, from the territories. The government has been sharply criticized by international observers for not stepping in to stop the violence and not protecting property rights.

The 1989 Copyright Act provides audio copyright protection, but enforcement is neither extensive nor efficient. Video copyright infringement, which is rife, is not covered under the 1989 act. Trademarks are protected for a seven-year period from registration.

**Freedom to Earn a Living 1/3**

Kenyans are free to choose the type and place of their employment, and can change jobs as they choose. This freedom is limited in practice for people who speak against government actions or policies. They can be dismissed from official positions or their employers can come under pressure to dismiss them. Over 350,000 Kenyans, roughly one-fifth of the country's industrial work force, are members of unions. Unions are not state controlled.

However, central government civil servants and university academic staff may join only government-designated unions. A 1993 Ministry of Labor decree forbids all strikes. In the country's generally repressive atmosphere, rights provided by law are often ignored by the regime, and there is little hope of judicial redress.

The government has agreed in discussions with the International Monetary Fund to end wage controls, though it is unclear that this policy has had practical effect. Some liberalization in labor laws is noted, although a lack of transparency in the judiciary and administration makes assessment difficult. Collective bargaining agreements are registered with the Industrial Court.

Local chiefs are permitted to demand community service on a local basis, but this right is apparently rarely used. There are no reports of slavery or forced labor, which are forbidden by the constitution.

**Freedom to Operate a Business 2/3**

Corruption and heavy regulation are major obstacles to operating businesses, despite a recent trend toward more liberal government policies. New business registration regulations introduced in June 1994 have simplified the process, and a new Investment Promotion Center is reportedly also easing the licensing procedure. A government commission is currently reviewing the Companies Law with an eye to further reform.

Despite these changes, the informal sector provides most job growth in Kenya, and even a wide-open economy would have great difficulties in absorbing the vast number of new job-seekers—now estimated at 400,000 annually and rising amid Kenya's explosive population growth.

The power and telecommunications sectors, the major sectors long blocked to private investment, are now being opened. The lucrative cellular market is still controlled by the state.

The intention to open it to private investment has been announced, but no timetable has been set.

Preference for government tenders is given to Kenyan-majority-owned businesses, despite procurement regulations that specify there may be no distinction made among bidders for goods or services on the basis of nationality. Foreign firms are excluded entirely from bidding on some government tenders. Bidding on international contracts financed by foreign aid and monitored by external auditors is relatively transparent. Other tenders are often awarded on a non-competitive basis and decided by political influence or other forms of corruption.

Price controls were abolished over the last three years, and regulations restricting the laying off of workers were lifted.

## Freedom to Invest One's Earnings 1/3

Neither interest rates nor rates of return on investments are regulated. Credit is scarce, however, partially due to successful government efforts to bring down triple-digit inflation from 1993 to 1994 by restricting liquidity. Controls on borrowing from domestic or foreign sources were also abolished. The Central Bank of Kenya is firmly under the control of the presidency.

Individuals may hold foreign currency and securities, and the government has announced plans to permit greater foreign investment. Broad state holdings in many sectors are set for divestment, which should increase private investment opportunities. However, corruption, favoritism and patronage remain important avenues to business success.

## Freedom to Trade Internationally 1/2

A number of restrictive practices protect and promote local industries. Import duties and value-added taxes are prohibitive barriers to some imports. Import licenses are no longer required, but all commodity imports are subject to pre-inspection by a government-appointed firm to assess quality and fair pricing, a process described as a safeguard against both dumping and corruption.

Kenyan businesses are given preferences in a number of areas, including construction services and architecture, and foreign companies are totally excluded from receiving some government tenders. The U.S. and European Community have protested a new draft shipping law for its discrimination against non-Kenyan flag shippers.

Direct foreign investment is limited by a ban on external investment in local subsidiaries of foreign corporations. Restrictions on the repatriation of profits are another disincentive, although these regulations are being reviewed and exporters who earn hard currency may now use such earnings for imports or to remit dividends.

Foreign exchange controls are suspended, and the rate for the currency, the shilling, is determined by the market. Although they are still controlled, currency exports in amounts sufficient for business travel are permitted. However, official permission to travel is still required.

## Freedom from Unreasonable Government Interference in the Economy

The state remains an important actor in the economy. The government's share of GDP is approximately 13 percent. The finance minister has pledged to divest at least one-third of 146 state-owned enterprises by the end of 1995 and to institute policies encouraging competition. State subsidies in the agricultural sector are being phased out.

Despite many pledges, the government is only slowly instituting a series of reforms that would reduce patronage for the ruling party. Widespread corruption and political patronage are important forces negatively affecting the economy. This impediment is amplified by the government's strong role as employer and investor—accounting for 45 percent of modern-sector wage employees and 40 percent of total investment. Government contracts and procurement are often steered toward cronies of the ruling party. Even low-level officials are rarely prosecuted for graft. The judiciary is regarded as highly politicized and unwilling to apply the law equally and fairly. Judicial proceedings are often drawn-out and subject to outside influence.

**Freedom to Participate in the Market Economy** **1/2**

Women and ethnic minorities face serious obstacles both in entering the job market and in obtaining credit. Women have long been faced with official restrictions that limit their rights to own property and operate businesses. The government has pledged to eliminate any legal blockages, but traditional societal patterns that disadvantage women in the market economy remain.

Discrimination against ethnic and religious minority groups is unofficial but sometimes serious.

# Mozambique

ECONOMIC FREEDOM STATUS: **NOT FREE**
POLITICAL RIGHTS AND CIVIL LIBERTIES STATUS: **PARTLY FREE**
PRESS FREEDOM STATUS: **PARTLY FREE**
POPULATION: **17,423,000**
PPP: **$380**

**Background**

After over two decades of civil war and repressive rule, Mozambique enjoyed tenuous stability and a slow economic recovery during 1995. Peace prevailed, but rising lawlessness, corruption and lingering rivalry between the ruling National Front for the Liberation of Mozambique (FRELIMO) and its longtime guerrilla foe, the Mozambique National Resistance (RENAMO), threatened even limited progress in what the U.N. classifies as the world's poorest country.

Years of bitter guerrilla war preceded independence from Portugal in 1975 under one-party rule by the then-Marxist FRELIMO. RENAMO rebels were organized and armed first by the white-minority Rhodesian regime, and then by South Africa's secret services. The bush war was among Africa's most deadly. Peace became possible only with the Cold War's end and majority rule in South Africa, which cut the desire of the combatants' supporters to finance a proxy war. Coupled with a general war-weariness, this led to a negotiated peace in the 1992 Rome Accords.

A five-year economic development program was adopted in April 1995 with broad parliamentary backing, but other tensions remained. RENAMO leader Afonso Dhlakama has demanded greater influence in government appointments, particularly in the central provinces that are RENAMO's stronghold, and where it continues to run a parallel administration. Lack of cooperation will hinder chances at even limited small-scale rural development, despite economic liberalization and extensive mine-clearing efforts under U.N. supervision. Nearly all infrastructure, from the educational and judicial systems to roads and port facilities, is badly deteriorated.

Despite this legacy, Mozambique is making some progress toward according its citizens a measure of economic freedom. The most significant steps have been taken in the labor market, where wages have been freed from government control and workers permitted to establish unions that are free of government control.

**Freedom to Hold Property 0/3**

There is no private ownership of land. The state grants up to ninety-year leases on land, but there is confusion even about what official bodies can properly issue leases. It is currently debated whether previous owners or current tenants should have priority in leasing expropriated land. The socialist regime that took power at independence in 1975 nationalized many companies and confiscated large amounts of privately held real estate. There are no plans for compensation or restitution for these seizures, but transition to a multiparty system adhering to open market policies makes future expropriations unlikely.

Intellectual property rights (IPR) are protected by statute, but there is little ability to investigate or prosecute violations. Mozambique is officially the world's poorest country, with a per capita GDP of about $60. Given the scale of the country's problems and level of development of its legal system, pursuit of IPR and copyright violations is unlikely to be an early priority.

**Freedom to Earn a Living 3/3**

Mozambicans are free to choose their type and place of employment. Forced labor is prohibited by law and violations have not been reported recently, nor has official or pervasive discrimination based on gender or ethnicity. Wage levels have been determined by market forces since 1991.

Constitutional provisions provide the right for all workers to join a trade union. Workers' rights to engage in union activities without retribution are guaranteed by the 1991 labor law, and hiring of substitute workers and lockouts by employers are forbidden. The law also protects the right to bargain collectively.

The Organization of Mozambican Workers (OTM) was for many years the sole union body, and was closely aligned to the ruling party during the one-party era. In 1994, OTM leaders were for the first time elected rather than appointed by the government. New OTM by-laws assert the organization's independence from government, political parties, corporate or religious interests. The era of multiparty politics ushered in with the November 1994 election has opened union organizing, and a second labor federation, the Organization of Free and Independent Unions, now competes with the OTM.

**Freedom to Operate a Business 1/3**

A hangover from its socialist period, Mozambique's entrenched bureaucracy remains more of an obstruction than a facilitator to business activity. A string of reforms is aiming at regularizing and streamlining procedures for businesses registration and obtaining operating licenses. Nonetheless, the process remains complex and time-consuming.

A large informal sector is flourishing, especially since the end of the civil war in 1994. However, significant government involvement in the economy through many state-owned enterprises (SOEs) today restricts private growth in many areas. Large contracts appear to be subject to competitive bidding, though it is not clear that smaller local contracts are, and corruption remains pervasive.

Through its ties to the OTM and its SOEs, the government has remained an important actor in labor relations. Voluntary price ceilings on staple foods and a higher minimum wage were agreed in government-brokered negotiations with labor and business groups. Increasing liberalization and divestiture are expected to reduce government influence in the economy.

**Freedom to Invest One's Earnings 0/3**

The state controls about two-thirds of the banking system's assets through the Commercial Bank of Mozambique (BCM). Several private banks are now operating and attract clients from the private sector. Interest rates have been largely liberalized though one or two rates are still controlled. Residents are not allowed to hold foreign currency accounts though companies are.

The long period of civil unrest and economic dislocation from independence until 1994 allowed little domestic capital accumulation. Hard currency is difficult to obtain and few residents hold legally registered investments abroad.

The central bank is under the direct control of the Ministry of Finance.

## Freedom to Trade Internationally 1/2

Mozambique's devastated economy produces a serious negative trade imbalance. High import duties are collected on officially declared imports, documentation requirements are extensive and unevenly applied, and many traders say customs clearance is time-consuming and rife with corruption.

However, corruption and porous frontiers do allow an estimated two-thirds of all imports to enter without official duties. Some foodstuffs are exported, including cashews and prawns, but large-scale commercial development is hindered by lack of credit and poor infrastructure.

New investment regulations were introduced in 1993 in hopes of attracting foreign investment. Investments are screened by the Center for the Promotion of Investment, which can approve investments up to $10 million. Larger investments must be authorized by the Council of Ministers. In either case, inaction after ninety days is considered automatic approval. Foreign entities are permitted to establish and operate businesses in almost every area of the economy. A few industries and services, such as electricity, post and communications, are reserved for the state. Noncitizens are permitted to hold longterm leases on land, but purchase is forbidden.

Portions of profits from investments earning foreign exchange or producing import substitutes may be remitted. Otherwise, hard currency is very hard to obtain through banking channels. A legal secondary exchange market and an active parallel market both offer hard currency at a premium to the official rate.

## Freedom from Unreasonable Government Interference in the Economy

Mozambique has moved from a socialist system since 1987 and has restructured its economy with financial and technical assistance from the World Bank and the International Monetary Fund. Civil war and drought have crippled the transformation, however, which is further hindered by lingering bureaucratic obstruction, corruption and lack of legal and commercial expertise. Government expenditures accounted for an estimated 70 percent of GDP.

Programs to support and develop the private sector are being promoted, including a broad privatization of state-operated enterprises. Nearly 200 small and medium-sized SOEs have been sold, though the state usually retains a significant minority stake, and larger SOEs are set to be divested over the next three years.

## Freedom to Participate in the Market Economy 1/2

Official or societal discrimination is neither sanctioned nor prevalent. However, the rudimentary state of Mozambique's economy, its scant pre-independence development nearly entirely destroyed by nearly two decades of civil war, severely limits opportunity to participate in the market economy for the country's citizens.

An antiquated commercial code, a poorly developed judiciary, and endemic corruption hinder economic development. There is little access to education and training in Mozambique, especially in the rural areas and for women. Little credit is available, since land is held by the state and so cannot be used as collateral.

# Nigeria

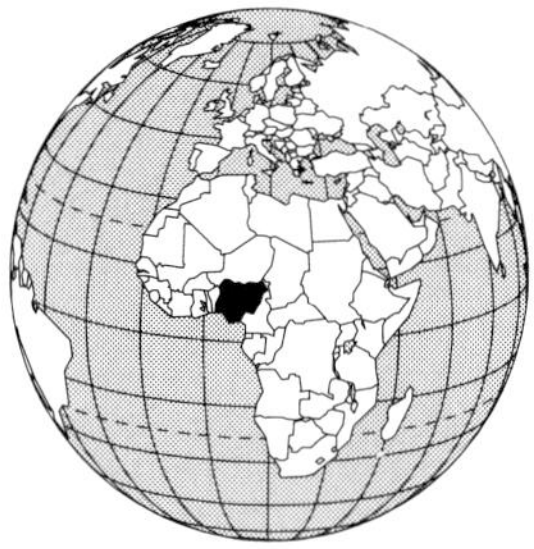

ECONOMIC FREEDOM STATUS: **NOT FREE**
POLITICAL RIGHTS AND CIVIL LIBERTIES STATUS: **NOT FREE**
PRESS FREEDOM STATUS: **NOT FREE**
POPULATION: **101,232,000**
PPP: **$1,560**

## Background

Since independence from British rule in 1960, Nigeria has known only ten years under elected governments. A succession of military dictatorships dominated by officers from the mainly Muslim north of the country has ruled the country for the past eleven years and retained firm control over the far wealthier southern regions. June 1993 presidential polls were meant to mark Nigeria's full and final transition to civilian rule. But the military regime of General Ibrahim Babangida quickly annulled the 1993 elections, won by southerner Chief Moshood K.O. Abiola. The military named an interim government charged with holding new elections, which even the least cynical observers did not expect to see anytime soon.

As strikes against a worsening economic situation wracked the country, the high court returned a surprise ruling declaring the interim government illegal. In November 1993, General Sani Abacha, a principal architect of previous coups, moved this time to take power for himself. All democratic structures were dissolved and political parties banned. A predominantly military Provisional Ruling Council was appointed. In June 1994, Chief Abiola was arrested after declaring himself Nigeria's rightful president.

Political instability also helps explain Nigeria's lack of economic freedom. Rampant corruption and widespread lawlessness undermine the right to own property or operate a business. Further retarding economic freedom is pervasive government involvement in the economy through parastatals and a thicket of regulations burdening the private sector. The steady stream of Western corporations divesting their Nigerian assets despite concerted efforts by the government to attract investment is testimony to the link between economic freedom and development.

Despite nearly global condemnation, General Abacha appears intent on clinging to power. He is bolstered by his army, and also has money. Revenues from oil and gas extracted by European companies such as Shell (Anglo-Dutch), Elf (French) and Agip (Italian), which are expected to begin a $4 billion project soon, and American companies like Chevron, which signed a $320 million investment deal with the Abacha regime in March, help keep the dictatorship solvent.

## Freedom to Hold Property 1/3

Property rights are protected by law and generally respected in Nigeria. Endemic bureaucratic corruption and political interference can make adjudication of disputes unfair, however, and projects supported by senior officials can be undertaken with apparent impunity. In the Ogoni region, oil companies have been criticized for destroying farmlands through pipelines laid across Ogoni farmland and environmental damage from oil spills and flareups. Protests and demonstrations against the arbitrary seizure of land were brutally put down by security forces.

The mix of traditional and modern land tenure systems is another point of difficulty. Land title is often unclear, especially in rural areas, with tenancy likely to be defined by perpetual lease-hold. This system makes use of land as collateral for borrowing very difficult.

Intellectual property rights protection in Nigeria is inadequate. The prevalence of corruption would make enforcement problematic even if such became a priority of the military regime.

**Freedom to Earn a Living 1/3**

Nigerian law stipulates legal protection for people to choose their type and place of employment. However, the International Labor Organization has reported instances of military units forcing civilians to work on various projects.

Labor laws address the rights of workers to organize and to bargain collectively. In practice, workers' rights are severely restricted. Officially, only workers in "nonessential sectors" may unionize. The current military regime has exercised gross interference in union affairs. Union leaders have been dismissed and arrested by government decree, and almost all independent unions have been "deregistered."

Government laws controlling wages were rescinded in 1991.

**Freedom to Operate a Business 1/3**

Business formation is relatively quick and transparent. A "one-stop" agency handles business registration. Beyond registration, however, regulations can be both inconsistent and corrupt. Navigating the often blatantly corrupt bureaucracy to obtain various clearances and approvals can be daunting. Approval to begin doing business can take anywhere from six to eighteen months.

Political influence is often felt as well. The state controls large portions of economic activity through official contracts and other expenditures. People actively opposed to the military dictatorship or merely without good connections inside it may have difficulties in winning contracts or have their business obstructed.

Foreigners are excluded from forty kinds of "essential" enterprises, ranging from candle-making to travel agency ownership, unless they invest sizable sums of hard currency. Many other regulations exist, sometimes imposed on an ad hoc basis, that can make business investment and operation unpredictable and risky. This reflects both the regime's instability and special favors granted to its cronies.

Many price controls remain in effect, and fuel prices are set by the government.

**Freedom to Invest One's Earnings 0/3**

Bank rates are restricted by the government. A strong private banking sector exists, although there are reports that the regime plans to re-nationalize several large private banks. Credit in local currency is usually accessible to qualified borrowers.

The central bank is under the control of the presidency, and its actions are sometimes seen as highly political. Public-sector and parastatal companies often receive loans on concessionary terms, which further limits available private capital. Investment return rates are not restricted. The Central Bank has forced the banking sector to finance part of the government deficit through large, compulsory "purchases" of government securities that have siphoned money out of private banks.

Overseas investment by individuals or corporations is not allowed. Although individuals can hold unrestricted amounts of foreign currency in domestic accounts, bank holdings of foreign assets are restricted.

**Freedom to Trade Internationally 0/2**

Various restrictions prevent Nigerians from traveling freely.

A plethora of import and export regulations and bans is in force. Rice, corn, vegetable oils, meat, poultry, malting barley and an array of both raw materials and finished goods are barred from import. Items are added and dropped from the list with confusing frequency, and ad hoc export bans are occasionally imposed.

The Nigerian Enterprises Promotion Decree of 1962 requires 60 percent Nigerian equity ownership for businesses in the banking, insurance, mining and petroleum industries. Majority Nigerian ownership is also required in forty other categories, unless the foreign partner invests over $400,000. In April 1995, Nigerian junta head General Sani Abacha announced a new decree that would eliminate the 1962 regulations, but legislation to give the changes legal standing has not been promulgated.

Foreign currency exchange, hard currency transfers and import allocations are comprehensively controlled by the government. The exchange rate is pegged by the government. These controls create enormous distortions in the import/export markets and windfall profits for a few businesses. Recent foreign exchange liberalization is improving this situation marginally.

## Freedom from Unreasonable Government Interference in the Economy

The regime is an active player in the economy in areas ranging from financial and monetary policy to import/export quotas, from foreign currency allocations to the awarding of government contracts.

The state owns large power utilities and a number of other enterprises. It is deeply involved in oil industry operations, which provide about 80 percent of the government's revenues and virtually all the country's foreign exchange earnings. The state has ruthlessly cracked down on unions and ecological activists who threaten to disrupt oil production.

Broad privatization has divested many SOEs, increasing opportunities for private investment.

Despite this privatization, government coercion has been directly felt within corporations whose stockholders were denied the ability to replace government-named directors. Large grants to parastatals have allowed unprofitable parastatals to survive. A not-so-benign neglect has also crippled the government's administrative ability and opened the way to widespread corruption, which reaches to the highest levels. In one instance, over $12 billion in oil revenues deposited in official accounts remains unaccounted for. Pervasive corruption is a serious drag on Nigeria's economic prospects.

The government's share of GDP is roughly 40 percent according to official statistics. Corruption in the form of diversion of official revenues, bribery and other graft likely raises the actual figure higher.

## Freedom to Participate in the Market Economy 1/2

Women and minority groups are not legally prevented or officially obstructed from holding land or operating businesses. Traditional societal influences, especially in rural and Islamic areas, can limit opportunities for women's education and access to credit.

Corruption and pervasive political influence are a problem for all citizens. The military regime interferes with both civil and judicial administration, and there is little assurance that adjudication of disputes will be either timely or fair.

# Senegal

ECONOMIC FREEDOM STATUS: **PARTLY FREE**
POLITICAL RIGHTS AND CIVIL LIBERTIES STATUS: **PARTLY FREE**
PRESS FREEDOM STATUS: **PARTLY FREE**
POPULATION: **8,312,000**
PPP: **$1,750**

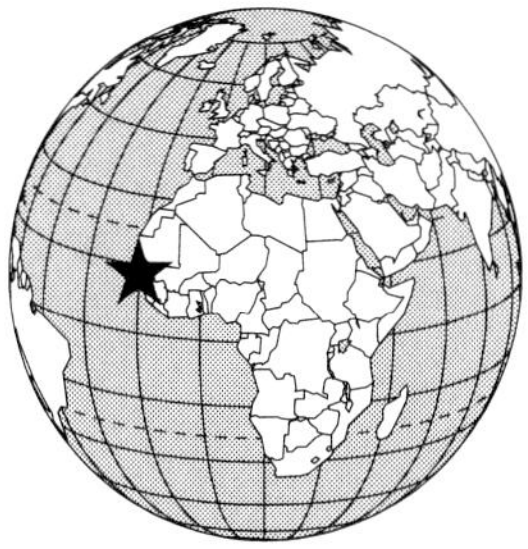

## Background

Since independence from France in 1960, Senegal has escaped the extreme repression experienced by its neighbors. President Abdou Diouf took office in 1981, winning 1988 and 1993 contests marked by confusion and irregularities that oppositionists deemed fraudulent. Diouf has faced strong domestic dissent as he has sought to revive a badly flagging economy by imposing austerity budgets proposed by international lenders. Unemployment and diminished earning power have increased the appeal of both mainstream opposition politicians and Islamist groups.

Largely agrarian Senegal was one of the first countries in Africa to enact structural adjustments in the 1980s. Economic difficulties in the early 1990s and the suspension of further international assistance led to the devaluation of the CFA franc zone in 1994. Following the devaluation, Senegal agreed to implement structural reforms designed to liberalize the economy further. Trade barriers have been reduced, labor markets have been freed, state monopolies have been opened to competition and several state enterprises have been targeted for privatization. But political patronage continues to influence some economic decisions.

## Freedom to Hold Property 2/3

Private property rights are respected by law and in practice. There have been no major expropriations, and the government has encouraged an atmosphere conducive to private investment. Court proceedings are far from transparent, however, and political patronage and other corrupt practices can affect the outcome of cases.

Senegal's intellectual property rights protection regime is adequate. However, seeking redress through the courts is a time-consuming process.

## Freedom to Earn a Living 3/3

Senegalese workers may freely choose their type and place of employment, and may change jobs at their discretion. The government does not control wage rates, although minimum wages and working conditions are regulated by guidelines set in the labor code.

Workers' right of association is respected, and nearly all of Senegal's small industrial sector is unionized. Regulations allow a union to be formed by as few as seven people who have worked within a trade for at least a year. Not all applications to the Ministry of the Interior are recognized, however, and unions can be disbanded by the ministry. The legal right to bargain collectively is respected in practice.

The National Confederation of Senegalese Workers (CNTS) is closely aligned to the ruling party, and leading union members hold high government positions and seats in the national assembly. The National Union of Autonomous Labor Unions of Senegal (UNAS), the other major labor grouping, is not linked to any political party.

Most Senegalese work on the land or in the informal sector without union affiliation. There are no reports of forced labor, which is illegal.

## Freedom to Operate a Business 2/3

Private businesses operated by domestic or foreign private entities require approval by the Ministry of Finance. The authorization process has been streamlined to reduce bureaucratic bottlenecks and possible corruption, and applications not rejected within a one-month period receive automatic approval. Requirements for small business formation are least stringent. The informal sector is estimated to consist of 30,000 small businesses employing over 57,000 persons.

Provisions of the labor code involving wage guidelines and protection of workers from dismissal were eliminated this year. An array of parastatal enterprises also limits business opportunities in some sectors of the economy, although most trading and retail activities are thoroughly entrepreneurial.

Parastatals and other State Owned Enterprises (SOEs) control significant areas of the economy, although privatization is likely to reduce this dominance over the next several years. More serious is a general lack of competitive bidding for government contracts—only 40 percent are let on an international, competitive basis. Senegal has not signed Tokyo-round agreements covering government procurement. Monopolistic agreements in cement, textiles, wheat flour, fertilizer and tomato paste have been eliminated.

Some price controls on basic consumer goods remain in effect. Tight monetary policies and high interest rates make loans problematic for small and medium-sized businesses, and traditional practices make women especially unlikely to be able to meet high collateral requirements.

## Freedom to Invest One's Earnings 2/3

Regulations discourage export of capital or investment outside the common currency zone of the *Communauté Financière Africaine*, which is backed by France and from which the local currency, the CFA franc, takes its name. Senegal shares a currency with several other Francophone states in West Africa, and its central bank functions are undertaken by the Central Bank of West African States (BCEAO). For decades, purchasing power was largely protected by pegging the CFA franc to the French franc. Annual inflation in 1995 was 8 percent.

The size of the parastatal sector has traditionally precluded private investment in much of the formal sector, including agribusiness, railways, telecommunications, transport, mining, and power generation. Over forty parastatals have been privatized over the past decade and more are set to be divested under the terms of loan and finance agreements with the World Bank and International Monetary Fund. These will increase investment opportunities in the formal sector, but most small-scale investments will remain in the informal sector.

Interest rates are not controlled and credit is not directed by the government. However, credit is extremely tight and as a result most private businesses are small and under-financed. There are no restrictions on rates of return for investments, and foreign exchange is readily available. The BCEAO discourages capital investments abroad.

## Freedom to Trade Internationally 2/2

Residents can travel freely, and are allowed foreign exchange for journeys outside the CFA zone. Senegal has eliminated most quantitative import restrictions, and tariffs have been substantially reduced. Export restrictions are few, and an export duty of 20 percent has been suspended, along with export subsidies, as part of government pledges to allow market mechanisms to operate more freely. Goods originating within member countries of the Economic Community of West African States (ECOWAS) receive preference.

Foreign investment is encouraged through a liberal investment code and free-trade-zone legislation. Wholly owned foreign ventures are permitted in almost all industries. Capital and income earned from investments financed by convertible foreign exchange are allowed to be transferred or repatriated freely.

France's dominant position as former colonial power, major foreign investor, and backer of the CFA franc heavily affects trade and investment patterns. Prominent Senegalese businessmen complain that investment by or joint ventures with non-French partners are discouraged through political influence or bureaucratic blockage. Government contracts are often officially let on a restricted basis, and unofficial ties often dictate how others are awarded.

## Freedom from Unreasonable Government Interference in the Economy

Despite an ongoing program of divestment of parastatal holdings, the government remains a significant actor in Senegal's economy. It is the country's largest single employer and consumer. Government expenditures in 1995 represented 29 percent of GDP. Several parastatals still enjoy legal or de facto monopolies, as do some private enterprises. A limited market, and preference given to companies with links to the ruling party, have led to restricted competition and contributed to a stagnating formal sector. Parastatals and private companies retain monopoly control over important industries.

The judicial system is not fully independent, reducing government accountability and opening proceedings to political influence and corruption. The investment code offers incentives to broadly defined "priority" sectors, including agriculture, manufacturing, tourism, banking and finance, mineral exploration and mining.

The ruling party's tight links to one of the country's two major labor organizations create an often ambiguous or conflicting role in governance and economic management.

## Freedom to Participate in the Market Economy 1/2

Constitutional provisions forbid discrimination based on race, religion or gender, and inheritance laws are gender-neutral. However, these legal protections are often far from realized for women, and the enforcement of women's legal rights does not receive high priority. Societal discrimination against women is pervasive. Particularly in rural areas where traditional and Islamic customs prevail, educational and economic opportunities for women are often limited. Only about one-fifth of women engage in paid employment, although those in the formal sector generally receive equal pay for equal work.

Political influence is reported to affect awarding of contracts and government tenders, and corruption is described as common but not crippling. Business disputes are adjudicated through the judicial system.

# South Africa

ECONOMIC FREEDOM STATUS: **FREE**
POLITICAL RIGHTS AND CIVIL LIBERTIES STATUS: **FREE**
PRESS FREEDOM STATUS: **FREE**
POPULATION: **43,474,000**
PPP: **$3,799**

## Background

The scrapping of apartheid and the election of Nelson Mandela as president in 1994 ended minority rule that had been in place in South Africa since 1910. On the economic front, President Mandela has taken great pains to reassure domestic and foreign business that his government of national reconciliation will not destabilize the South African economy, and business confidence increased through 1995.

Although certain sectors of the economy are still dominated by large firms, corruption remains a problem, and certain restrictions continue in the financial sector, South Africans are economically free on balance. Black businesses are growing quickly in number and significance as many black companies partner with established white businesses. Despite the presence of corruption, the judiciary is independent and the tradition of the rule of law remains strong. The institutions that had once ensured that the white minority enjoyed disproportionate economic advantage now benefit all of society. Free international trade has replaced the previous government's policy of economic autarky, and the injection of competition from foreign firms has begun to challenge the dominance some domestic firms once enjoyed in certain lines of business.

## Freedom to Hold Property 3/3

All individuals' rights to hold property are recognized by law and respected in practice. South Africa's economy remains highly regulated, however, and various regulations govern property transactions.

Under the Restitution of Lands Right Act of November 1994, a broad effort is underway to redress land seizures carried out under apartheid laws. A land commission is working to acquire holdings for redistribution to people unfairly deprived of their property. The government has pledged proper compensation for current landholders.

South African intellectual property rights protection is still problematic. New trademark legislation was passed in January 1994.

## Freedom to Earn a Living 3/3

There are no legal or official restrictions on South Africans' right to choose their type and place of employment. Traditional societal values affect the ability of women to gain education, access to credit and business opportunities, particularly in rural areas. The legacy of apartheid remains in real or perceived discrimination against racial or ethnic groups, including recent allegations of "reverse discrimination" in favor of the African majority.

The rights to organize and bargain collectively are protected by law, and wages are not controlled. New labor laws will offer alternative means to resolve labor grievances but will not eliminate the right to strike.

There are no reports of forced labor, though conditions for some farmworkers in remote rural areas remain highly exploitative as a vestige of apartheid-era conditions.

### Freedom to Operate a Business 2/3

Requirements for forming and registering businesses are not onerous, and are applied by a competent, efficient and generally honest civil service. Price controls have been removed from all but a few agricultural products.

Developing a new business can be difficult. Control of most of the country's larger industries by a few interlocking conglomerates severely limits business opportunity. Newcomers are at a particular disadvantage. Monopolistic and other unfair business practices by the leading conglomerates are rarely investigated.

Since the advent of majority rule in May 1994, there are some complaints that awarding of official contracts is influenced by unofficial affirmative action favoring African businesses. Others allege that non-Whites find it difficult to obtain credit, especially since nearly the entire banking community is still controlled by White South Africans.

Aggressive programs to remedy these problems are being formulated. The government is providing training and other incentives to people who present viable plans for micro, small or medium-sized enterprises. Means to tap into traditional African collective savings schemes as a source of collateral for small business loans are being considered. Another source is a $30 million equity fund created by the Commonwealth Development Organization that provides small and medium-sized loans to entrepreneurs from disadvantaged communities.

Foreign exchange is increasingly available, but individuals are barred from transferring sizable assets abroad.

### Freedom to Invest One's Earnings 2/3

Heavy state involvement in a number of key industrial sectors has long limited private-sector investment opportunities. Insider trading and other manipulation of share values are considered common and can hurt small investors. Interest rates are not directly controlled by the government, with the exception of lending rates on small loans, which are subject to the Usury Act. Credit flows are determined by market forces, but access is still difficult for black entrepreneurs though there have been several initiatives by both government and the banking industry to expand access. Rates of return on investment are not controlled; however, individuals are still prohibited from investing abroad and there are restrictions on holding foreign currency. The autonomous central bank has kept inflation at around 8 percent.

### Freedom to Trade Internationally 1/2

South Africans may travel abroad freely, though foreign exchange allocated for overseas travel is limited. Exchange controls remain in place, though the dual-exchange mechanism of the "financial rand," which offered a higher exchange rate for hard-currency investors in South Africa, was abolished in March 1995.

Steep tariffs aimed at protecting domestic industries restrict international trading possibilities. There are no export restrictions. Foreign investment is welcomed in South Africa though subject to Exchange Control approval.

### Freedom from Unreasonable Government Interference in the Economy

The state is deeply and directly involved in the country's economic life. The tendency of the White-minority regime to centralize power was reinforced by international sanctions that pressed South Africa toward greater self-reliance. This goal was largely achieved in many sectors, but at a significant cost in efficiency and competitiveness that is now passed on to the country's consumers. Government expenditures represent 22 percent of GDP. State-owned arms, power, transport and other industries hold market monopolies. Domestic industries were and are protected by high tariffs—for example a 115 percent import tariff on automobiles.

The few conglomerates that dominate South Africa's economic landscape have close ties to top politicians. Many large companies have hired former officials of the ruling African National Congress party to establish closer ties with the new government. The government has taken steps to break the conglomerates' hold over the banking and manufacturing sectors and increase competition. The six largest conglomerates represent 85 percent of the capitalization of the Johannesburg bourse. A draft law on competition is expected by the end of this year.

### Freedom to Participate in the Market Economy 2/2

Women and minorities enjoy specific constitutional protection. There are no limits on the right to own property or open a business. But the legacy of unequal development and racial animosity left by apartheid creates unofficial obstacles to equality of opportunity. Black-owned enterprises comprise less than .5 percent of total market capitalization on the Johannesburg stock market.

Petty corruption is not uncommon, but poses little threat to economic activity. The country has a well developed commercial law that is enforced.

# Zaire

ECONOMIC FREEDOM STATUS: **NOT FREE**
POLITICAL RIGHTS AND CIVIL LIBERTIES STATUS: **NOT FREE**
PRESS FREEDOM STATUS: **NOT FREE**
POPULATION: **44,060,000**
PPP: **$523**

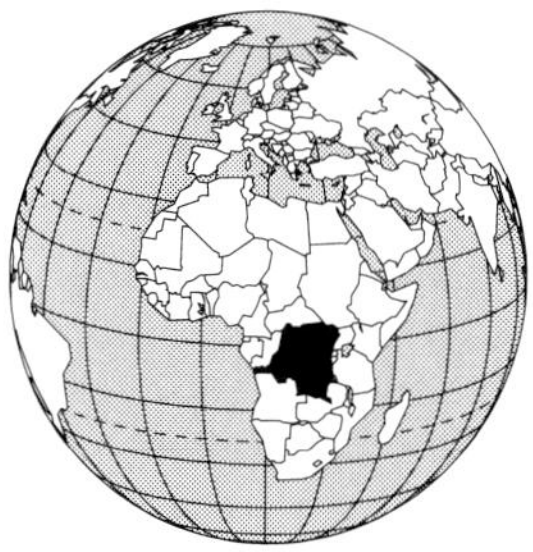

### Background

Colonized as the Belgian Congo in the nineteenth century, this vast area in central Africa was brutally exploited and left ill-prepared for independence in 1960. The country became a focus of Cold War competition until then-Colonel Joseph Mobutu seized power in 1964. A firm ally of the West, Mobutu was long forgiven not only his repressive policies but also his kleptocratic tendencies, which have left him among the world's richest men and Zaire among the world's poorest countries.

The Cold War's end left Mobutu with few friends, and domestic agitation for democratization and good governance forced him to open the political process in 1990. Mobutu's Popular Revolutionary Movement (MPR), the sole legal party since 1965, the Sacred Union of the Radical Opposition and Allied Civil Society (USORAS, a 200-group coalition), and scores of other groups attended a national conference that in December 1992 established a High Council of the Republic to oversee a democratic transition. The conference appointed USORAS leader Etienne Tshisekedi wa Mulumba as Prime Minister, but Mobutu dismissed Tshisekedi in 1993. Current prime minister Kengo wa Dondo has introduced limited economic reforms but holds little real power. Opposition disunity and Mobutu's manipulation have delayed and derailed reforms. A January 1994 agreement called for multiparty elections under a Transition Act by July 1995. Voting has been postponed for at least two years, and the sixty-five-year old Mobutu was reasserting political authority amid continued opposition bickering.

Zaire's economy has essentially come to a standstill as the country's infrastructure has been allowed to disintegrate. Inflation exceeded 6,000 percent in 1994 and corruption is rampant. The financial system has broken down and the rule of law is nonexistent. Although very little is prohibited, the lack of viable institutions to protect property and legal transactions gives Zaire minimal economic freedom.

**Freedom to Hold Property** **0/3**

There is a legal right to property, but few laws enforce this right. In any case, the judicial system is largely broken down and cannot be relied on to administer justice in any real sense. In rural areas, resolution of disputes is often handled by traditional courts operating according to local custom.

There is no enforcement of intellectual property rights or copyright protection.

**Freedom to Earn a Living** **1/3**

People may choose and change their place and type of employment without state interference. Forced labor is forbidden by law, and none is reported. Employment of children under eighteen, while also illegal, is widespread, especially in the informal modern sector and subsistence agriculture. Economic deterioration and virtual administrative anarchy across much of Zaire mean there is neither monitoring of labor conditions nor enforcement of labor laws.

All workers except for magistrates and security personnel are permitted by law to form and join trade unions. The right to strike is also protected, but only after mandatory arbitration procedures, and few legal strikes occur. Collective bargaining is allowed. The government does not control wages.

The National Union of Zairean Workers was long associated with President Mobutu's ruling party, but since 1990 has achieved autonomy and freely elects its leaders. Yet many unions are under the control of various political and economic interests, and do not truly represent their members. Many enterprises have created "tame" unions with the complicity of the Ministry of Labor, and refused to accept genuine trade unions.

Several leading trade union officials have been arrested, and the security forces have violently suppressed marches by trade unionists protesting price hikes and corruption as part of the wider repression of free expression.

**Freedom to Operate a Business** **1/3**

Laws permit business formation, but the associated costs—in terms of both official fees and demands for corrupt payments—can be prohibitive. In practice, legal formulations mean little. All licensing and registration is subject to negotiation, which almost invariably includes demands for bribes and other extralegal payments. The process is highly unpredictable and notably capricious. Businesses are more at the mercy of political than of market forces. Small-scale entrepreneurs can operate in the informal sector with little more than petty graft to concern them. Larger enterprises, however, must face a welter of competing demands from officials, security forces, or simple extortionists operating in a lawless atmosphere.

There are price controls on a few items, but like most other laws, these are flouted with apparent impunity. Government procurement is small. There is now little domestic spending and official imports are minimal. Government payments are often indefinitely delayed, and hyperinflation makes businesses wary of doing any but cash transactions.

**Freedom to Invest One's Earnings** **1/3**

Interest rates are not regulated, and are at times extremely high due to uncontrolled inflation. Credit is very scarce, due to economic uncertainty and illegal capital flight. Rates of return on investments are not regulated, but successful businesses face a serious threat of being taken over by officials. Individuals may hold foreign securities and invest abroad, but there is little compliance with or ability to enforce financial regulations.

The Central Bank has been the subject of a tug-of-war between competing political forces. Monetary policies are affected by excess printing of banknotes without authorization. Efforts to reform the bank's operations are underway, but its operations remain a prime source of political contention.

### Freedom to Trade Internationally 0/2

A tariff and duty schedule exists on paper, but nearly all Zaire's imports are undocumented. The only real "taxes" are those paid as bribes to allow shipments to enter the country and to reach their domestic destinations. Foreigners may do business in Zaire without legal restrictions, but face the same daunting corruption and disorder as do domestic traders.

### Freedom from Unreasonable Government Interference in the Economy

Over seventy parastatal companies are in existence, and some have monopolies over important sectors of the economy—at least on paper. In practice, the parastatals, like the rest of the country's administration, are bankrupt. Their productive contribution to the country's economic life is next to nil. They now receive no state subsidies. The government's share of GDP is officially minimal, although corrupt payments are an important drag on the economy.

Official policies encourage investment and competition. Pervasive corruption and an almost complete absence of the rule of law make these policies meaningless. Businessmen have been kidnapped, tortured and killed by security forces, who sometimes protect only those who will pay the most. Zaire is described by an international banker as having a "privatized government" that is dedicated to working for only a small coterie of officials and their associates, some of whom have become enormously rich.

### Freedom to Participate in the Market Economy 0/2

No legal restrictions affect the rights of women or minorities to participate in the market economy. Traditional societal values, especially in the rural areas, have limited women's ability to obtain credit and buy property.

The breakdown of government administration and the disintegration of the country's economic infrastructure restrict all residents' ability to join the market economy in an organized manner.

# Bibliography

## Sources

We are grateful to the many people and organizations who assisted with this *Survey*.

Many were kind enough to offer their candid assessments of the situations in different nations. Several of those who did, because of their position, asked that their comments remain anonymous. Countless individuals at government offices, trade associations, and NGOs worldwide gave an inordinate amount of their time to answer our numerous queries. We sincerely thank all those who provided us with assistance. Responsibility for all judgments and results rests with the Freedom House staff.

Special thanks to research assistants Laura Klivans, Suzanne Boughner, Anne Champlain, Allison Gamble, Nicole Ormond, Ron Johnson and Amy Maglio of the Washington, D.C. office and Shahrzad Elghanayan and Sarah Gershman of the New York office.

## Organizations


Amnesty International
ASEAN
Asian Development Bank
Business Software Alliance
Caribbean Latin American Action
Catholic Relief Services (El Salvador)
European Bank for Reconstruction and Development
Institute of International Bankers
Inter-American Development Bank
International Center for Research on Women
International Confederation of Free Trade Unions
International Intellectual Property Alliance
International Labor Organization
International Monetary Fund
Organization for Economic Cooperation and Development
Representatives of US and Foreign Embassies around the world
Transparency International
United Nations Development Program
U.S. Agency for International Development
U.S. Department of Commerce
U.S. Department of Labor
U.S. Department of State
U.S. Trade Representative
World Bank


## Periodicals and Reports


*Africa Business*
*Asian Wall Street Journal*
*Brazil Watch*
*Businessweek*
*Christian Science Monitor*
US Department of State. Country Commercial Guides
US Department of State. Country Human Rights Reports.
US Department of State. Economic Policy and Trade Practices.
EIU Country Reports
EIU Investment, Licensing and Trade Report
*Far Eastern Economic Review*
Foreign Broadcast Information Service (FBIS)
*Financial Times*
IMF Economic Reviews
*Japan Echo*
*Jeune Afrique*
*Journal of Commerce*
*Journal of Palestinian Studies*
*Los Angeles Times*
*Mexico Business*
*Middle East Insight*

*Middle East International*
*New York Times*
OECD Economic Assessments
OMRI Economic Digest for EE/NIS
Oxford Business Guides
Price Waterhouse Doing Business In series
Reuters
*Straits Times*
*The Economist*
*The Middle East*
*Wall Street Journal*
*Washington Post*
*Washington Times*
*World Business*

## Other References

Adamson, Peter, ed. *The Progress of Nation: Annual Report.* (New York: UNICEF, 1995)

Agarwal, Bina. *A Field of One's Own: Gender and Land Rights in South Asia.* (Oxford: Oxford University Press, 1994).

Buruma, Ian. "The Singapore Way." *The New York Review of Books.* Oct. 19, 1995. pp. 66-71.

Bhalla, Surjit. *Freedom and Economic Growth: A Virtuous Cycle?* Presented at the Nobel Symposium on "Democracies: Victory and Crisis," Uppsala University, Sweden. August 27-30, 1994.

Block, Walter, ed. *Economic Freedom: Toward a Theory of Measurement.* (Vancouver: The Fraser Institute, 1991).

Bogetic, Zeljko and Arye Hillman. *Financing Government in the Transition: Bulgaria. The Political Economy of Tax Policies, Tax Bases, and Tax Evasion.* (Washington, DC: World Bank, 1995.)

Bolivia: *Structural Reforms, Fiscal Impacts, and Economic Growth.* Report No. 13607-BO. (Washington, DC: World Bank, 1994).

Boza, Beatriz. *Doing Business in Peru: The New Legal Framework.* (New York: 1993).

Brazil: *An Assessment of the Private Sector.* Report No. 11775-BR. Vol. I-II. (Washington, DC: World Bank, 1994).

Brooks, Karen and Zvi Lerman. *Land Reform and Farm Restructuring in Russia.* World Bank Discussion Paper No. 233. (Washington, DC: World Bank, 1994).

*Bureaucrats in Business: The Economics and Politics of Government Ownership.* World Bank Policy Research Report. (Washington, DC: World Bank, 1995.)

*By the Sweat and Toil of Children*: The Use of Child Labor in American Imports. A Report to the Committees on Appropriations—United States Congress. Bureau of International Labor Affairs. U.S. Dept. of Labor. July 15, 1994. (Washington, DC: Dept. of Labor, 1994.)

*Cambodia Rehabilitation Program: Implementation and Outlook.* World Bank Report for the 1995 ICORC Conference. Report No. 13965-KH. (Washington, DC: World Bank, 1995.)

Easton, Stephen T. and Michael A. Walker, eds. *Rating Global Economic Freedom.* (Vancouver: The Fraser Institute, 1992).

*Ecuador Public Expenditure Review: Changing the Role of the State.* Report No. 10541-EC. (Washington, D.C.: World Bank, 1993)

*Exchange Arrangements and Exchange Restrictions: Annual Report.* (Washington, DC: International Monetary Fund, 1995)

Gillespie, John. "Private Commercial Rights in Vietnam: A Comparative Analysis." *Stanford Journal of International Law.* Vol. 30, No. 2, Summer 1994. pp. 325-377.

*Government Finance Statistics Yearbook.* (Washington, DC: IMF, 1995)

Gwartney, James, Robert Lawson, and Walter Block. *Economic Freedom of the World: 1975-1995.* (Vancouver: The Fraser Institute, 1996)

Heath, John. *Land Rights in Cote d'Ivoire: Survey and Prospects for Project Intervention.* Africa Technical Department Series. Technical Paper No. 238. (Washington, DC: World Bank, 1994.)

Holden, Paul and Sarath Rajapatirana. *Unshackling the Private Sector: A Latin American Story.* (Washington, DC: World Bank, 1995)

Hwang, Eui. *The Korean Economies: A Comparison of North and South.* (Oxford: Oxford University Press, 1994)

Iqbal, Zubair. *Islamic Banking.* (Washington, DC: IMF, 1987).

*Kazakhstan: The Transition to a Market Economy.* (Washington, DC: World Bank, 1993).

Kumar, Anjali. *China: Internal Market Development*

*and Regulation*. (Washington, DC: World Bank, 1994).

*Kyrgyzstan: The Transition to a Market Economy*. (Washington, DC: World Bank: 1993)

Lambsdorff, Johann G. *1995 Corruption Index*. (Berlin: Transparency International, 1995).

Mbaku, John Mukum. "Bureaucratic Corruption and Policy Reform in Africa." *Journal of Social, Political and Economic Studies*. Vol. 19, No. 2, Summer 1994. pp. 149-175.

*Mexico Country Economic Memorandum: Fostering Private Sector Development in the 1990's*. Report No. 11823-ME. Vol. I-II. (Washington, DC: World Bank, 1994).

Parker, Ronald, Randall Riopelle, and William Steel. *Small Enterprises Adjusting to Liberalization in Five African Countries*. Discussion Paper # 271. Technical Department Africa Region. (Washington, DC: World Bank, 1995).

*Peru: A Private Sector Assessment*. Report No. 12096-PE. March 31, 1994. (Washington, DC: World Bank, 1994).

*Republic of Estonia: Recent Economic Developments*. Report No. 95/40. (Washington, DC: IMF, May 1995).

Rhoodie, Eschel. *Discrimination Against Women: A Global Survey*.

Scully, Gerald and Daniel Slottje. "Ranking Economic Liberty Across Countries." *Public Choice*. Vol. 69, 1991. pp. 121-152.

Shleifer, Andrei. *Establishing Property Rights*. (Washington, DC: The World Bank, 1995).

Sivard, Ruth. *Women: A World Survey*. (Washington, DC: World Priorities, Inc., 1995).

Thillairajah, Sabapathy. Development of Rural Financial Markets in Sub-Saharan Africa. World Bank Discussion Paper 219. Africa Technical Department Series. (Washington, DC: World Bank, 1995)

Tremewan, Christopher. *The Political Economy of Social Control in Singapore*. (Oxford: St. Martin's Press, 1994).

Webster, Leila and Dan Swanson. *The Emergence of Private Sector Manufacturing in the Former Czech and Slovak Federal Republic: A Survey of Firms*. Technical paper No. 230. (Washington, DC: World Bank. 1993).

Webster, Leila. "Newly Privatized Enterprises: A Survey." In Ira W. Lieberman and John Nells, ed. Russia: *Creating Private Enterprises and Efficient Markets*. (Washington, DC: Private Sector Development, World Bank. 1994).

Webster, Leila. *The Emergence of Private Sector Manufacturing in Poland: A Survey of Firms*. Paper No. 237. (Washington, DC: World Bank. 1993).

Williamson, John, ed. *The Political Economy of Policy Reform*. (Washington, DC: Institute for International Economics, 1994.)

# Freedom House Officers 1995-1996



## Trustees